FRANZ ROSENZWEIG'S CONVERSIONS

FRANZ ROSENZWEIG'S CONVERSIONS

World Denial and World Redemption

BENJAMIN POLLOCK

INDIANA UNIVERSITY PRESS *Bloomington & Indianapolis*

This book is a publication of

INDIANA UNIVERSITY PRESS
Office of Scholarly Publishing
Herman B Wells Library 350
1320 East 10th Street
Bloomington, Indiana 47405 USA

iupress.indiana.edu

Telephone orders 800-842-6796
Fax orders 812-855-7931

∞ The paper used in this publication meets the minimum requirements of the American National Standard for Information Sciences —Permanence of Paper for Printed Library Materials, ANSI Z39.48–1992.

Manufactured in the United States of America

Cataloging information is available from the Library of Congress.

Pollock, Benjamin.
Franz Rosenzweig's conversions : world denial and world redemption / Benjamin Pollock.
pages cm
ISBN 978-0-253-01312-5 (cloth)
— ISBN 978-0-253-01316-3 (ebook)
1. Rosenzweig, Franz, 1886–1929—Religion. 2. Religion—Philosophy. 3. Conversion. 4. Redemption. I. Title.
B3327.R64P665 2014
181'.06—dc23

2014010215

1 2 3 4 5 19 18 17 16 15 14

FOR MY PARENTS,

Scott and Karin Pollock

CONTENTS

PREFACE AND ACKNOWLEDGMENTS

THIS STUDY OFFERS a new account of one of the foundational narratives of modern Jewish thought: the story of Franz Rosenzweig's near-conversion to Christianity in the summer of 1913 and his subsequent decision, at the "baptismal font" three months later, to recommit himself to Judaism. The story that has dominated both scholarly literature and public Jewish discourse for the last sixty years presents Rosenzweig's personal transformation in 1913 as a turn away from a path of academic philosophy to a life of faith, a life which Rosenzweig first believed was possible only for Christians, but subsequently concluded—after experiencing a traditional Yom Kippur prayer service—was likewise eminently available for the committed Jew. I argue here that while this celebrated tale of Rosenzweig's near-conversion and return may well be inspiring and instructive as a myth about modern Jewish identity, there is little evidence to support it. Moreover, this prevailing account of Rosenzweig's conversions has been enormously misleading as an introduction to Rosenzweig's *thought.*

In the pages that follow, I argue that what lay at the heart of Rosenzweig's 1913 crisis was not a struggle between faith and reason, but rather a skepticism about the world and a hope for personal salvation that Rosenzweig came to identify with *Gnosticism.* Understanding the significance of Rosenzweig's struggle with Gnosticism during the summer of 1913 allows us to offer a compelling and coherent account of the series of conversions Rosenzweig underwent during this period; it gives us insight into the severity of the personal crisis that accompanied these conversions; and it enables us to explain—without reliance on dubious claims about faith experiences—just *why* Rosenzweig decided first to convert to Christianity, and then to return to Judaism. Rosenzweig's near-conversion and return are best understood, I argue, as moments in his gradual turn, over the summer and fall of 1913, to a *historical* conception of the realization of the Kingdom of God, in which the individual self and world are reconciled, and hence Gnostic dualism, and the world skepticism at its root, are overcome. Perhaps most importantly, then, this study makes a claim about why the Rosenzweig who underwent the celebrated personal crisis that he did in 1913 would *have* to go on to engage in the philosophical program that he later undertook. In the resolution to the struggle with Gnosticism at which Rosenzweig arrived in the fall of 1913, I show, we find foreshadowed the very vision of redemption that Rosenzweig would later articulate philosophically in *The Star of Redemption*.

The origins of this project lie in a question I asked myself one fall day in 2001, as I sat in the National Library in Jerusalem, reading Rosenzweig's "Paralipomena." I was working on my dissertation at the time and was hunting through these wartime notes from 1916 for hints about the development of Rosenzweig's notion of systematicity. I was struck then and there by a remark Rosenzweig makes in these notes about the 1913 summer night-conversation that precipitated his famous crisis: "What it means that God created the world and [is] *not just* the God of revelation—this I know precisely out of the Leipzig night-conversation of 7.7.13. At that time, I was on the best road to Marcionitism."

There was something all wrong about this remark. The celebrated story of Rosenzweig's near-conversion to Christianity and his return to Judaism—whose veracity I had had no reason to doubt up until then—depicts Rosenzweig's July 7, 1913 night-conversation with Eugen Rosenstock and Rudolf Ehrenberg as that transformative moment in which Rosenzweig discovers revelatory faith as a cogent response to the problem of relativism with which he had been struggling. Rosenzweig's 1916 remark seemed to get the direction of his transformation backwards. In direct opposition to the famous story of his near-conversion, the remark suggested Rosenzweig was already equipped with a sense of "the God of revelation" prior to that night-conversation, and that what he discovered that night had to do with creation, not revelation. Indeed, it suggested that Rosenzweig was on his way to being a *Marcionite* before being transformed through that night-conversation.

I don't think I would have identified Rosenzweig's 1916 comment as so diametrically at odds with the long-accepted scholarly account of Rosenzweig's 1913 summer of crisis, save for the fact that Marcion and Gnosticism were already on my mind in 2001. A graduate course on Weimar that I had the good fortune of taking with Christoph Schmidt at the Hebrew University a few years earlier had introduced me to the rise of theologies of world denial identified with Marcion and the Gnostics during the interwar period. More serendipitously, I came to Rosenzweig's remark about his own flirtation with Marcionism days after I had finished reading Ben Lazier's dissertation on the Weimar heretical theologies of pantheism and Gnosticism (later revised and published as *God Interrupted: Heresy and the European Imagination between the World Wars* [2008]). As a result, Rosenzweig's profession of having been on the road to "Marcionitism" caught my attention. Rosenzweig was evidently identifying the position with which he entered the Leipzig night-conversation with both the "God of revelation" and world denial. How could such a Rosenzweig be converted *to* revelatory faith over the course of the July 7, 1913 night-conversation if he had already been committed to—an admittedly unusual form of—revelatory faith *before* that conversation?

I had no idea how to answer this question in 2001. I tagged Rosenzweig's 1916 remark as in need of future inquiry, and went back to my dissertation. It was not until early 2009, when my *Franz Rosenzweig and the Systematic Task of Philosophy* appeared in print and I was granted a junior research leave from Michigan State University, that I had the chance to follow up on the lead. It was with surprise, but also with increasing excitement, that I soon realized that nearly all of Rosenzweig's later comments about his 1913 crisis were consistent with the 1916 remark that had first caught my eye. A new account of the stakes of Rosenzweig's 1913 transformation came into view. It was very different from the conventional account. But it was supported by the evidence, and I found it to be both internally coherent and unexpectedly illuminative of Rosenzweig's mature philosophy. Further lucky discoveries of writings from Rosenzweig and Ehrenberg, dating back to the years prior to the night-conversation, some through correspondence and some through archival visits, allowed me to fill in gaps that remained, and to develop the account into the form you now have before you.

I want to acknowledge the many colleagues, friends, and institutions that have supported me in the research and writing of this book. At a moment when the last thing I wanted to do was write another book on Rosenzweig, Solomon Goldberg first convinced me that the scope of the project I was pursuing demanded presentation in book form. Michael Morgan read the very first draft of this project back in 2009 and the latest draft in 2013, and he offered copious comments on both. In between, he has contributed immensely through conversations, and through an enthusiasm for the project that has helped me persevere through those doubts that so often arise in academic work. Paul Franks read and commented upon numerous drafts of the manuscript. Conversations and correspondence with Paul have been tremendously helpful for me in clarifying the philosophical stakes of Rosenzweig's night-conversation, and especially in trying to articulate the notion of divine unity which Rosenzweig spells out in the *Star*. Michael Zank has extended thoughtful support for the project over a number of years, reading and offering critical comments on drafts of the manuscript, and inviting me to present my research at Boston University.

I want to thank a number of friends and colleagues who have contributed to this project by reading parts of the manuscript or through conversations over the last few years: Leora Batnitzky, Zachary Braiterman, Amy DeRogatis, Todd Endelman, Christopher Frilingos, Robert Gibbs, Markus Kartheininger, Martin Kavka, Paul Mendes-Flohr, Hindy Najman, Eugene Sheppard, Arthur Versluis, Kenneth Waltzer, Leon Wiener-Dow, and Elliot Wolfson. I thank all the 2012 fellows at the University of Michigan's Frankel Institute for Judaic Studies for reading the introduction to the book and offering an array of helpful comments.

I want to offer special thanks to Michelle Sider who created the work of art you find on the cover of this book.

I have benefited greatly from the feedback I've received when presenting my research in the following contexts: the 2009 AJS Annual Conference; the Boston University Institute for Philosophy and Religion; the University of Toronto Oriental Club; the LeFrak Forum and Symposium on Science, Reason, and Modern Democracy at Michigan State University; and the University of Michigan's Frankel Center for Judaic Studies.

Part of the first chapter of this book appeared as "On the Road to Marcionism: Franz Rosenzweig's Early Theology," *Jewish Quarterly Review* (2012). I thank the journal for permission to reprint here.

I began writing this book in 2009 while on junior research leave from teaching in the Department of Religious Studies at Michigan State University, and I completed the final chapter of the book in December 2012 while on research sabbatical. I thank Michigan State University for its generous financial support. I am likewise grateful for the collegiality and the professional support I have received from both the Department of Religious Studies and the Jewish Studies Program at MSU.

I have benefited greatly from archival visits and from access to original materials generously granted to me throughout the project. I traveled to Kassel in the summer of 2009 to explore the newly accessible Rosenzweig Nachlass at the University of Kassel Library. I went because the Findbuch which Professor Wolfdietrich Schmied-Kowarzik shared with me listed a letter from Rosenzweig to his cousin Rudolf Ehrenberg dated July 15, 1913—one week after the celebrated night-conversation! I was convinced I would strike gold. That letter turned out to include Rosenzweig's impassioned plea that his cousin seek surgical treatment for appendicitis—and little else. But as so often happens in archival research, the gold was there to be found, just not where I expected it. I thank the archivists at the University of Kassel Library for their attention during my visit. I also want to thank the archivists at the Leo Baeck Institute archives at the Center for Jewish History in New York, at the Nahum Glatzer Collection housed at the Divinity Library at Vanderbilt University, and at the Landeskirchliche Archiv der Evangelischen Kirche von Westfalen in Bielefeld, for enabling me to access original sources that greatly informed my research. I want finally to offer my heartfelt gratitude to Professor Maria Ehrenberg, who generously provided me with a draft of her father's (Rudolf's) unpublished play, *Halbhunderttag.*

Turning to more personal debts: I want to thank Allison, Ayelet, Hadas, Asaf, and Zoega for their love and support, and for their patience as I spent countless hours with my imaginary friend, Franz.

I also want to express my thanks here to my parents, Scott and Karin Pollock. It was in their home that I learned to appreciate the value of questioning, the thrill of intellectual debate, and the great fun there was to be had in telling a good story. This one is dedicated to them.

I type these prefatory words on July 7, 2013, the one-hundred-year anniversary of Franz Rosenzweig's transformative night-conversation in Leipzig. For three thinkers as calendrically inclined as were Rosenzweig, Rosenstock, and Ehrenberg, this anniversary would no doubt have been deemed worthy of celebration. I am relieved to mark it as well as the day I send this book out into the world.

Huntington Woods, Michigan
July 7, 2013

FRANZ ROSENZWEIG'S CONVERSIONS

Introduction

Explaining Rosenzweig's Near-Conversion and Return

ON JULY 7, 1913, a twenty-six year-old Franz Rosenzweig engaged in an all-night conversation with two friends, Eugen Rosenstock and Rudolf Ehrenberg, at the home of Ehrenberg's parents in Leipzig.[1] Rosenzweig would look back on this *Leipziger Nachtgespräch* (Leipzig Night-Conversation) as the transformative event of his life. It precipitated a dramatic personal and intellectual breakdown from which it took him several months to recover. Moreover, the terms of this crisis, and the intellectual and spiritual vocabulary Rosenzweig developed on the way to overcoming it, forged, in decisive ways, the direction his thinking would take for the whole course of his intellectual career.

Up to now, there has reigned near unanimity among scholars regarding the stakes involved in the July 7, 1913 conversation, regarding the quasi-conversion Rosenzweig experienced that night, and regarding the path that led him to a resolution of this crisis in October of that year.[2] The story scholars have collectively told about this event runs as follows. Rosenzweig enters the 1913 conversation touting the standard academic or philosophical relativism of his day and encounters there, in Eugen Rosenstock, someone who is his equal in intellect and scholarly prowess, and yet who responds to questions of ultimate meaning with simple faith. This fusion of faith and reason embodied by Rosenstock so impresses Rosenzweig that it leads him to concede the groundlessness and the emptiness of contemporary intellectualism, and to accept the notion that lived faith experience, or more precisely, an experience of faith grounded in revelation, offers a—if not the only—way out of the nihilistic consequences of contemporary relativism. Convinced that Judaism no longer represents an option in his day for those seeking a life of faith, Rosenzweig resolves to convert to Christianity, a move encouraged, if not demanded, by Rosenstock and Ehrenberg, both Christians of Jewish descent. In the course of preparing to convert, however, Rosenzweig changes his mind. This change of mind is the result of—or is at the very least confirmed by—Rosenzweig's participation in a traditional Jewish prayer service in Berlin on Yom Kippur, in October 1913. Enveloped by a community of Jewish believers at prayer, Rosenzweig experiences a vibrant Jewish faith so sincere that he decides to devote the rest of his life to repossessing that Judaism which was his by birth, and to opening up for his peers a path back to Judaism as a cogent contemporary possibility.

As Paul Mendes-Flohr and Jehuda Reinharz noted more than thirty years ago, this account of Rosenzweig's 1913 crisis and conversions "has become the subject of legend."[3] One may well suggest that Rosenzweig's renown among students of twentieth-century religious thought stems no less from this compelling story of his personal existential struggles as it does from an encounter with his published writings.[4] As a thinker whose intellectual integrity not only did not undermine the legitimacy of faith experience but actually demanded such faith experience, and as a modern Jew who took seriously the lure of Christianity but nevertheless wound up affirming the possibility of living a meaningful Jewish life in the modern world, Rosenzweig has come to serve as an exemplar of the sincere modern individual in pursuit of his own religious and existential truth. His "conversion" story has, moreover, become a highlight of undergraduate modern Jewish thought courses and a mainstay of High Holiday sermons.

The problem is that this account of Rosenzweig's crisis and conversions that has dominated the literature and has inspired its fair share of modern seekers, has little basis in the evidence at our disposal. Over the past decades, murmurings regarding the absence of evidence for the definitive role of a "Yom Kippur experience" in Rosenzweig's return to Judaism have indeed been heard among Rosenzweig scholars, and such murmurings found particularly bold written expression in some of the last articles published by Rivka Horwitz before her death.[5] But it turns out that questions surrounding Rosenzweig's Yom Kippur experience are only the tip of the iceberg. The evidence from Rosenzweig's writings overwhelmingly suggests, in fact, that almost *none* of the basic elements of Rosenzweig's 1913 crisis and conversions have yet been properly represented: neither the stakes of the night-conversation of July 7, 1913, nor the position Rosenzweig took up in that conversation, nor the supposed faith position to which he was converted, nor the reasons for his initial decision to become a Christian, nor, finally, his decision some months later to remain a Jew.

The aim of this study is to advance a new account of Rosenzweig's *Leipziger Nachtgespräch,* an account that better conforms to what Rosenzweig himself has to say about it than has hitherto been produced, and one which can likewise better explain—so I will claim—exactly why Rosenzweig's thinking developed, in the years that followed, toward the systematic account of "the All" that he elaborated in *The Star of Redemption.*

I claim, first of all, that Rosenzweig's transformative discussion of 1913 did not center on the possibility of faith in the modern world, nor on the need to opt for faith in the face of contemporary academic relativism. In fact, I will show that Rosenzweig could not have been converted to a position of "faith" through the night-conversation of July 7, 1913, because the position he upheld upon entering the conversation was *already* a position of faith. The position of faith he upheld at that time appears to have been so extreme, in fact, that he later repeatedly refers to his 1913 standpoint as that of *Marcion,* the second-century Christian theologian, later denounced a heretic by the Church fathers, who believed that the salvation brought by Christ so radically freed the faithful from the troubles of the world, that Christ could not possibly have been sent by the God who created it. Rosenzweig had come to adopt this Marcionist position by 1913, I show, as a consequence of his long-standing skepticism about the world itself and about the place of the individual in it—a world skepticism that nevertheless went hand in hand, for Rosenzweig, with a commitment to revelation as a possibility for the individual person. At stake for him in the *Leipziger Nachtgespräch,* we will find, is thus not faith but rather *the moral or spiritual status of the world.* Can one realize one's free selfhood, can one realize the spiritual potential of the soul—Rosenzweig asks himself during the summer of 1913—while constrained within the limits of worldly existence? Or does spiritual or intellectual or moral self-fulfillment demand a radical denial of the world and, inter alia, of one's very existence in the world? The opposing poles at the heart of the Leipzig night-conversation, I will thus show, are not faith and reason, but rather self and world.

Rosenzweig's flirtation with what he understood to be a Gnostic denial of the world does much to explain, I will suggest, the radical character of the personal crisis he underwent over the course of the *Leipziger Nachtgespräch* and in its aftermath, a crisis that led Rosenzweig to contemplate suicide.

Moreover, Rosenzweig's struggle with Marcionism permits us to paint a markedly different picture than we hitherto recognized of what Rosenzweig found so desirable in Christianity in the wake of that night-conversation. Rosenzweig is drawn to Christianity, I claim, not because he is enthralled by the sincerity of Christian faith, but rather because Christianity's vision of a historical realization of the Kingdom of God on earth offers him a credible means for conceiving of the reconciliation of self and world *historically,* and thereby for overcoming the perplexity regarding the relation between self and world that had plagued him since his university years.

Making sense of the struggle with Marcionism that lies at the heart of the *Leipziger Nachtgespräch* also enables us to offer an explanation for Rosenzweig's return to Judaism that does not depend on undocumented claims regarding a "Yom Kippur experience." As we shall see, Rosenzweig comes to understand the Jewish people as serving an essential role in the redemption of the world, whereby Jews ensure that Christians do not forget the redemptive work that is incumbent upon them to perform. Always at risk to celebrate its possession of salvation at the expense of the world yet to be redeemed, Rosenzweig suggests, Christianity needs the Jewish people to ensure that it does not fall into Marcionism. The very existence of the Jewish people, he concludes, serves ever to remind Christians that the God of creation and the God of salvation are indeed one and the same, and hence that the created world—and not merely the individual recipient of revelation—must be considered the object of redemption.

The new account of Rosenzweig's struggle with Marcionism thereby enables us to offer a coherent narrative of his personal development, beginning with his early world skepticism and perplexity regarding the place of the self within the world; extending to his adoption of a position akin to Marcionism in the years leading up to the July 7, 1913 night-conversation; and progressing toward an overcoming of this Marcionist position through the adoption of a historical conception of the realization of the Kingdom of God. It is this historical conception of redemption, then, that first led Rosenzweig to commit himself to convert to Christianity, but then—as the result of conclusions he reached about the vital role the Jewish people must play in the redemptive process as a counterweight to the Christian temptation toward Gnosticism—to return to Judaism. I will claim that the train of thought that leads Rosenzweig from Marcionism, through a near-conversion to Christianity, on to a commitment to Judaism has a coherence to it that is not merely biographical. Indeed, once we understand Rosenzweig's early perplexity about the relation between self and world, and once we understand the factors that led him to turn away from Marcionism over the course of the *Leipziger Nachtgespräch,* we may assert that Rosenzweig *had* to adopt a historical conception of the realization of redemption in the world, and *had* to embark on a series of considerations that would eventually lead him past a serious engagement with Christianity and back to Judaism.

When the story of Rosenzweig's near-conversion to Christianity and his return to Judaism is retold as the story of his struggle with and overcoming of Marcionism, it amounts to a striking tale of personal and metaphysical discovery in its own right. But more importantly, the account of Rosenzweig's struggle with Marcionism makes it possible to offer compelling *explanations* for those transformative struggles and decisions that Rosenzweig underwent during this period. Indeed, I view the explanatory force of this new account of the *Leipziger Nachtgespräch* to be a real advance over the account of Rosenzweig's conversions that has prevailed in the literature for more than half a century. Moreover, it enables us to highlight along the way a striking and particularly problematic feature of the myth of Rosenzweig's conversions in the form in which it has become so foundational for modern Jewish thought: its reliance on claims about Rosenzweig's "faith experiences." Ever since the story was first promulgated in writing by Nahum Glatzer in his essay, "Franz Rosenzweig: The Story of a Conversion" (1952; reprinted as the introduction to *Franz Rosenzweig: Life and Thought*),[6] faith experiences have been posited, in lieu of explanations, as underlying the key moments of Rosenzweig's 1913 transformation, the first of which precipitated this period of crisis and conversion, and the second of which then brought about its resolution. According to this account, Rosenzweig decides to convert to Christianity because Rosenstock's simple faith appears to be the only viable response to contemporary relativism, and because Judaism no longer appears to nurture the same possibility of living faith that Christianity offers. Rosenzweig decides to remain a Jew after participating in a traditional Yom Kippur service that convinces him that such faith is still very much alive within Judaism itself. Glatzer's influential essay may be said to have stamped the story with this two-step structure.[7] Thus, according to Glatzer, "Rosenzweig decided to become a Christian" when, through the night-conversation with Rosenstock, "he came to see, with the clarity of conviction, that an intellectual's attitude toward the world and history can be one of religious faith."[8] And Glatzer concludes that Rosenzweig's letter to Ehrenberg, announcing his decision to remain a Jew, "betrays a certainty that does not come to a man through thinking; it points to a profound, instantaneous event." "The experience of this day [i.e., Yom Kippur] was the origin of his radical return to Judaism." "Had it not been an experience of his own life, all this [i.e., his later account of the Yom Kippur liturgy in the *Star*] could not have been written."[9]

Ever since Glatzer's essay appeared, these two moments of faith experience have been attributed to Rosenzweig as the beginning and end of his process of conversion throughout the literature. To give a sense of the overwhelming authority of this claim about faith and faith experiences within the story as it has been passed down in the scholarship, permit me to cite here roughly one representative voice from the Rosenzweig scholarship for every decade since Glatzer published his influential essay:

- *1950:* In the wake of the night-conversation of July 7, 1913, Rosenzweig "made the standpoint of religious faith his own, but that very fact called his Jewishness into question. . . . And so . . . he decided to become a Christian. Before his conversion could be consummated, however, Rosenzweig went to the Yom Kippur services held in a little Orthodox synagogue in Berlin. There something happened—exactly what has never become known. But when it was over, Rosenzweig was convinced that he could live his religious existence as a Jew and that his place was in the People Israel."[10]

- *1961:* "The fact that a man of science like Rosenstock related to faith with such seriousness, changed Rosenzweig's worldview from its foundations. A tremendous internal revolution occurred within him. . . . Faith conquered Rosenzweig." "Rosenzweig decided to travel to Berlin and spent Yom Kippur in a small synagogue of Eastern European Jews . . . this Yom Kippur prayer service returned him to Judaism. He left the service a different man. For the second time faith had conquered him, and this time the faith of his fathers."[11]

- *1972:* "There are two incidents which are crucial to an understanding of the conception and creation of *The Star of Redemption*. The first was the impassioned discussion that occurred on the night of July 7, 1913, between Rosenzweig and Eugen Rosenstock-Huessy. . . . The first event was defined by the power of the argued word, the word spoken which denies all relativity, beginning as it does from the confession of faith." "The second was his lonely participation in the service of the Day of Atonement in Berlin on October 11, 1913, a service which was intended to mark his departure from Judaism and the Jewish faith and in fact resulted in his reconversion and return as *baal teshuva*. . . . We know nothing about what transpired, but we can guess from certain themes which recur in . . . [his] writings. Rosenzweig discovered the liturgy of Israel as a felt liturgy, a liturgy which actually enabled humble men to be pulled out of time into the rhythm of eternity. . . . Rosenzweig left the service resolved to remain a Jew."[12]

- *1982:* "Rosenzweig's 'real' conversion was to occur in Leipzig in July 1913, at the close of a night of discussion with Eugen Rosenstock in the course of which the latter succeeded in refuting Rosenzweig's relativistic world view of using not so much rational arguments but rather the testimony of his own lived faith. It is faith, looked upon not as a theological notion but as a fact of origin, as a lived experience, that Rosenzweig calls *revelation*. . . . However, before taking the decisive step, Rosenzweig decided to attend the Yom Kippur service in a small synagogue in Berlin. It is there that his real conversion occurred, the conversion that brought him back to Judaism. Rosenzweig does not mention explicitly this experience in any of his writings, but without a doubt, it is the decisive event of his spiritual biography."[13]
- *1982:* "In an all-night discussion (July 7, 1913) with two friends, both Christians of Jewish origin, Rosenzweig found in them a faith so genuine, and in himself a hunger so profound, that he gradually reached the decision that he, too, must convert to Christianity. And during a single day (October 11, 1913, attending Yom Kippur services in a small Orthodox synagogue in Berlin . . .), he made the astounding discovery that 'Religion: Jewish' was not, after all, an empty notation at a registry office, but nothing less than the unique relation between the Jewish people and the God of the world."[14]
- *1988:* "Slowly Rosenstock led his friend to the realization that a votary of culture and reason could with integrity affirm faith in revelation, and that indeed it was the only sensible way of overcoming the philosophical and historical relativism of the day. On the night of 13 July Rosenzweig yielded to Rosenstock's arguments and declared that he would adopt Rosenstock's *Offenbarungsglaube*. . . . In preparation for his conversion, he attended that autumn the Jewish High Holiday services, finding his way for the Day of Atonement to a traditional synagogue in Berlin. . . . Having witnessed, perhaps for the first time, a traditional Day of Atonement service, Rosenzweig concluded that Judaism was not spiritually moribund as he and his friends had assumed. Reversing his decision to enter the Church, he thus affirmed that a meaningful life of faith may be pursued within the precincts, as he put it, of the Synagogue."[15]
- *1995:* "First there is the famous conversation of July 7, 1913. . . . Rosenstock persuades Rosenzweig of the untenability of his or any skeptical relativism . . . in the name of a religious absolute, more specifically, in the name of Christian faith. . . .

The second great event of Rosenzweig's spiritual biography, just three months after the culminating conversation with Rosenstock: the now famous Yom Kippur experience in a small orthodox shul in Berlin, on October 11, 1913. . . . On that Yom Kippur day in Berlin, Rosenzweig discovered that Judaism was neither a relic nor a preparation, but that it was very much alive. . . . These two profound transformations determined the path of Rosenzweig's subsequent life and work."[16]

- *2005:* "Two events, two encounters of 1913, were pivotal in establishing the direction of his life. The first was a conversation with an elder peer [*sic*] Eugen Rosenstock, whose passionate and articulate commitment to Christianity convinced Franz that religion, at least Christianity, could provide a meaningful orientation for modern life. The second was a religious metamorphosis during the holiest day of the Jewish calendar, Yom Kippur. His experience of God's nearness taught him that there was still fire in the smoldering embers of Judaism, despite his having earlier dismissed that religious heritage as moribund."[17]

These accounts of Rosenzweig's near-conversion and return in 1913, offered by some of the most important scholars in Jewish thought of the last sixty years, are merely a representative sample of the myriad retellings of the story in the literature, but they clearly bear out the key role faith experience plays within the dominant scholarly account of Rosenzweig's period of personal transformation. It may come as some surprise, therefore, that Rosenzweig nowhere mentions having undergone any kind of significant experience on Yom Kippur in 1913,[18] and he in fact *explicitly denies* that the transformation he underwent in the wake of the *Leipziger Nachtgespräch* had anything to do with "faith experience."[19] Given this dearth of evidence from Rosenzweig's own pen, it is quite remarkable that the story of Rosenzweig's conversion in its prevailing form has had the astonishing staying power testified to in the above citations. There is no doubt that part of the appeal of this story stems from the way it paints such an inspiring, indeed triumphant picture of possibilities still available for those struggling in the modern world with matters of spiritual identity, in general, and with matters of Jewish identity in particular. The figure of a Rosenzweig who was so evidently drawn to Christian faith but who nevertheless remained a Jew also became an important bridge, after World War II in particular, upon which the possibility of Jewish–Christian interfaith dialogue could be reestablished.[20] But I would suggest that part of the staying power of this foundational myth is wrapped up in the very claims to faith experience around which the story is structured.

Ever since faith experience became a fashionable category of religious discourse in the nineteenth century,[21] it has come to designate that core of religiosity that cannot be explained or understood by scientific discourse, and has thereby served to protect religious discourse from demands for justification in the language of science, and from the reductionism that often ensues from such accounts of religiosity. But precisely in thereby defending the irreducibility and internal legitimacy of religious discourse, the notion of "faith experience" can at once be used for apologetic purposes, implicitly demanding that all thinking and all inquiry come to an end when religious experiences are involved. The construction of the celebrated story of Rosenzweig's near-conversion and return upon the foundation of claims about faith experiences, one might suggest, has protected this story from within against further inquiry in this very way, preserving it as a kind of mythical glimpse into the mystery of Rosenzweig's person, not given to explanation.[22] Glatzer himself, in fact, makes just this apologetic use of his faith claim in accounting for why Rosenzweig never wrote of his Yom Kippur experience: "He never mentioned this event to his friends and never presented it in his writings. He guarded it as the secret ground of his new life. The very communicative Rosenzweig, who was eager to discuss all issues and to share all his problems with people, did not wish to expose the most subtle moment of his intellectual life to analyses and 'interpretations.'"[23]

Beyond the matter of the inaccuracy of such claims about faith experiences as the grounds of Rosenzweig's self-transformation in 1913, viewing his personal and intellectual development through the lens of faith experience has had a deleterious impact on how scholars have come to understand the relationship between Rosenzweig's personal development and his mature thought. Once one has claimed, as Glatzer does, that Rosenzweig's ultimate decision to remain a Jew could not have come from thinking, that such a decision "betrays a certainty that does not come to a man through thinking; it points to a profound, instantaneous event," it becomes too easy to reduce the metaphysical account of redemption that Rosenzweig developed on the way to this decision—in which Judaism and Christianity play complementary roles in the realization of the Kingdom of God on earth through history—to a post facto apology for these particular faith experiences rather than to take it up as a metaphysical position worthy of serious consideration.[24]

The prominence of faith experience within the conventional account of Rosenzweig's 1913 conversions has been deeply problematic for the scholarly understanding of Rosenzweig in another important sense, as well. The story of a young Rosenzweig finding the cure for his intellectualism-induced nihilism in faith alone has been terribly misleading as an introduction to Rosenzweig's *thought,* and it bears some of the responsibility, so it seems to me, for the disorientation that generations of interested students have felt upon picking up Rosenzweig's magnum opus, *The Star of Redemption.* Students inspired by the story of Rosenzweig's realization that it is not traditional philosophy, but rather personally experienced faith that offers life-sustaining answers for existential seekers, rightly expect to find in the *Star* a compelling report on this discovery, or a justification for the spiritual life such faith experience makes possible, or a new form of philosophizing that does away with the dry, systematic, or scholastic characteristics of its academic practice and gets right to the heart of personal experience. The *Star* offers nothing of the sort—or rather, insofar as it offers an account of personal faith experience, it does so as a moment within the very kind of philosophical structure that incoming readers believe Rosenzweig had abandoned in 1913 for a life of faith!

Now, the *Star* is a notoriously difficult book, one that is quite disorienting by itself. But the presentation of Rosenzweig, through the conventional account of his 1913 conversions, as an exemplar of a modern, intellectually tested believer, and the tendency to introduce Rosenzweig's thought through such a presentation, has closed off access to the philosophical program of the *Star* with veritable seven seals. It is no surprise, indeed, that Eliezer Schweid —who still finds meaningful Rosenzweig's response to the question, "How can a modern individual in the Western world, who has been educated on the basis of radical individualism and relativism, reorient himself to religious faith?"—should conclude, after decades of trying to teach the *Star,* that "we would be justified in deciding to exclude the teaching of the systematic parts of the *Star* from our academic curriculum."[25] Simply put: given the premise that Rosenzweig was transformed from academic philosophy to religious faith over the course of his 1913 conversions, the philosophical program of the *Star* is unfathomable.

One of the merits of the new account of the *Leipziger Nachtgespräch* which I present here, I believe, is the way it shows Rosenzweig to have been engaged, during the period of the transformative night-conversation, with a set of metaphysical questions about self and world that in and of themselves demanded a response in the form of metaphysics. These questions were certainly of great personal and spiritual import for Rosenzweig, and they led him to make personal and spiritual decisions of lasting significance. But these personal and spiritual decisions are intertwined from the very beginning for Rosenzweig with a metaphysical one: Gnostic dualism or dialectical monism? Once Rosenzweig abandoned the dualism of Marcion toward which he was drawn in the period of the *Leipziger Nachtgespräch,* and came to view Judaism and Christianity as working in tandem toward the historical realization of the Kingdom of God on earth, one may well argue that he had already taken a leap toward the metaphysical position he would outline in the *Star.*

Grasping the *Leipziger Nachtgespräch* and its aftermath as Rosenzweig's own personal "overcoming" of Gnosticism may thus be most valuable in the light it sheds on that development of Rosenzweig's thought after 1913, which culminated in the writing of *The Star of Redemption.* In the way that it projects the ultimate reconciliation of self and world in the future redemptive end to a historical course begun in creation, and in the way it at once places some of the responsibility for such redemption on the shoulders of free, finite human beings, the *Star* elaborates what may be best understood, I shall claim, as the most compelling metaphysical alternative to Gnostic dualism, a metaphysical doctrine that responds to the same concerns expressed in Gnosticism, but which resolves such concerns through dialectical development rather than static opposition. As we shall see, during the years between the *Leipziger Nachtgespräch* and the writing of the *Star,* Rosenzweig worked out this position of developmental monism precisely through an ongoing engagement with Gnosticism.

In what follows, I begin by presenting the evidence for my claim that the *Leipziger Nachtgespräch* can best be understood as the culmination of Rosenzweig's struggle with his tendency toward Marcionism. Taking its lead from the themes of the Swedish novel that sparked the night-conversation between Rosenzweig, Rosenstock, and Ehrenberg—Selma Lagerlöf's *Antikrists mirakler* (The Miracles of the Antichrist)—and from Rosenzweig's own claims that he was on the "road to Marcionitism" in 1913, the first chapter of this study traces Rosenzweig's personal and intellectual crisis of 1913 back to an early skepticism about the world, and about the place of the human self in it, which Rosenzweig reports on in his diaries of 1906–1907. Although Rosenzweig's hopes for the "Baden-Baden Society" symposia in 1910 reveal his having adopted the historical relativism fashionable in his day, the collapse of Baden-Baden, I claim, resulted in the return of Rosenzweig's skepticism and in an experimental turn toward a theology of radical world-denial. By 1913, I show, Rosenzweig had come to identify with the faith position of Marcion, according to which revelation is understood as the medium through which the individual soul can transcend the world and attain some form of personal redemption. It was precisely as representative of this position, I show, that Rosenzweig was ridiculed by one of his *Nachtgespräch* interlocutors, Rudolf Ehrenberg, in his *Ebr.10, 25. Ein Schicksal in Predigten* (1920).

The night-conversation of July 7, 1913 pulls the rug out from under Rosenzweig's tentative Marcionism and directs him to adopt a different metaphysical position altogether, one that appears to demand his conversion to Christianity. The second chapter of this study tries to fathom how this happens. It begins with an examination of an important parallel Rosenzweig later draws between his own crisis of 1913 and a crisis which he believed Hegel underwent in 1797. Through a careful review of Rosenzweig's most famous statements about the *Leipziger Nachtgespräch,* and through an exploration of Eugen Rosenstock's role in the night-conversation, I then show how Rosenzweig was led to take seriously the Christian commitment to a "world activity" that aims to realize the Kingdom of God on earth through redemptive love. This conception of redemptive love as an active force in the world—and perhaps the experience of such love through his exchange with Rosenstock—offered Rosenzweig a way of thinking about the reconciliation of self and world as a process of historical realization, and thus of overcoming the Gnostic dualism he had been advocating. It is this promise of a reconciliation of self and world, and hence of a resolution to the skeptical perplexity that had troubled him since his early years, I argue, that led Rosenzweig to decide to convert to Christianity. The second chapter concludes by examining the period of severe personal crisis, bordering on the suicidal, which Rosenzweig endured in the months after the *Leipziger Nachtgespräch.* I claim that this crisis, too, bears the imprint of Rosenzweig's earlier Gnostic deliberations.

Rosenzweig does not emerge from this period of personal crisis until he reaches the decision to recommit himself to Judaism in October 1913. The third chapter of this study sets out to show that Rosenzweig understands this decision, as well, to be a consequence of his turn away from Gnosticism over the summer of 1913. Just as the early Church emerged victorious over against Marcionism through its insistence on maintaining a positive—if nevertheless supercessionist—relation to Judaism, its Bible, and its God, Rosenzweig reasons, so the Christian advance toward the realization of the Kingdom of God on earth cannot be fulfilled even today unless the Jewish people continues to carry out its essential role in the course of that realization. By ever reminding Christians that the God of creation and the God of salvation are one and the same, and that salvation has not yet occurred but remains to be realized, the Jewish people ensures that Christians do not themselves fall back into a veritable Marcionism, celebrating their own personal salvation while forgetting the world still in need of their acts of redemptive love.

The elaboration of Rosenzweig's vision of the complementary roles of Jews and Christians toward the realization of redemption on earth, in the third chapter, allows me to make some rather sweeping claims about historical thinking itself. Rosenzweig's turn away from Gnostic dualism toward a historical conception of redemption suggests that such a historical worldview is itself grounded in the thinking together of creation and redemption. As a result, I suggest, in the very moment during the *Leipziger Nachtgespräch* when, according to Rosenzweig's later report, he accepted the biblical account of creation as his guide, the whole course of the personal and intellectual transformation he would undergo in the coming months was already foreshadowed. Rosenzweig's understanding of the significance of the first sentence of the Bible already predetermined, I suggest, his commitment to a historical conception of the Kingdom of God, and—since in his view only the continued existence of Jews as Jews could ensure that Christians remember that the God of creation and the God of salvation are one and the same—his return to Judaism in October of that year. In this very moment of rejecting Gnostic world-denial, Rosenzweig already *had* to become committed to a historical account of the reconciliation of self and world in which Judaism and Christianity play necessary and mutually supportive roles.

The third chapter concludes, finally, with a reflection on the relation between the Marcionism Rosenzweig abandons in the wake of the *Leipziger Nachtgespräch,* and the other-worldly vision of Judaism he wholeheartedly adopts.

The fourth chapter collects what we have learned about Rosenzweig's struggle with Marcionism and his turn to a historical conception of redemption, and tries to show how this background illuminates *The Star of Redemption* itself. Here I take up key moments in the course of Rosenzweig's magnum opus: the book's opening in the fear of death and the philosophical temptation to split soul from body; its account of creation and revelation as both sharply opposed to each other and at once unfolding together toward reconciliation in redemption; the book's account of human freedom and God's dependence on human redemptive action; its depiction of Judaism and Christianity as filling distinct but complementary roles in this redemptive process; and the book's positing of divine unity as a goal to be achieved in redemption alone. Through a pointed examination of these moments, I aim to show how Rosenzweig repeatedly draws on his own personal struggle with and overcoming of Gnosticism in order to articulate the metaphysical course of the *Star* as a whole. Insofar as the *Leipziger Nachtgespräch,* newly and properly elaborated, can now be understood to have directed Rosenzweig toward the metaphysical position he would articulate in the *Star,* the story of what transpired for Rosenzweig during that night and in its aftermath may indeed serve as a proper biographical introduction to Rosenzweig's mature thought.

In the conclusion to this study, we will review the path we've taken from the conversation of July 7, 1913 up through the key ideas of Rosenzweig's magnum opus, and we will return to the question raised here regarding the relationship between Rosenzweig's life and his thought. Can biography truly and responsibly introduce philosophy?

Both Rosenzweig and Rosenstock tell us, in separate reports, that the starting point of their late-night conversation on July 7, 1913, was a novel by Swedish author Selma Lagerlöf, *Antikrists mirakler.*[26] Let us then begin our investigation of what transpired during that conversation, by taking a look at the themes raised in *Antikrists mirakler* itself. A survey of the novel's course will offer us valuable insight into the direction taken in the conversation between Rosenzweig, Rosenstock, and Ehrenberg as the night unfolded.

1

Revelation and World Skepticism

Rosenzweig's Early Marcionism

"NOT JUST THE GOD OF REVELATION"

"On the heights of the Capitol the redeemer of the world shall be worshipped, Christ or Antichrist, but no frail mortal."

So runs the prophecy given to Caesar Augustus by the Sybil, legend has it, atop the hill of the Capitol in Rome on the night of Jesus' birth. Selma Lagerlöf recounts this prophecy in the opening scene of her *Antikrists mirakler* (1897), and tells how, at the very spot of the sibylline prophecy, the Church of Santa Maria in Aracoeli was founded. The monks who maintain Aracoeli, Lagerlöf relates, guard against the dark side of this prophecy: their vocation, as they see it, is to protect the world from the coming of the Antichrist. These warriors of the spirit have in their possession, moreover, a wondrous prize that helps support them in their heavenly work: a two-foot-high statuette of the Christ child, painted all in gold, bedecked in jewels and sporting a magnificent crown. This Christ child icon—*Santo Bambino,* as he is called—works miracles for all who seek it out, and gives the monks of Aracoeli the strength they need to endure in their weighty task.[1]

One day, Lagerlöf's story goes, a wealthy Englishwoman visits the Church at Aracoeli and falls in love with the icon. Determined to possess it, she devises a plan. She has a replica of the Christ child made that *looks* just like the real Bambino, but is crafted of inferior materials and is draped with false jewels. In its crown, moreover, the Englishwoman scratches the inscription "My kingdom is only of this world," in order that she herself be able to distinguish this false icon from the true Christ, who had proclaimed before Pilate, "My kingdom is not of this world" (John 18:36). On a return visit to Aracoeli, the

Englishwoman switches the true Christ child with its false imitation, and the monks unknowingly wind up worshipping this "Antichrist," thereby fulfilling the very sibylline prophecy against which they were on guard to protect.

But then a miracle occurs. The true Christ child finds its own way back to the Church at Aracoeli, and the monks, now inspecting the forgery carefully, realize their error. They return the true Christ child to its proper place, and with the cry, *anathema antikristos,* hurl the false image out of the church and down the mountain.[2]

Unbeknownst to the monks, however, the iconic symbol of the "kingdom of this world" does not meet its end in the fall from Aracoeli. Picked up in a carriage, the icon begins to travel the world. On an early stop, the icon arrives in Paris in the midst of the revolts of 1848. Here the Christ child is examined by an intellectual who has joined the front lines—presumably none other than Marx himself—and the words scratched into its crown, "My kingdom is only of this world," inspire the young man to formulate the tenets of socialism for which he becomes famous. "Your kingdom is only of this world," he proclaims. "Therefore you must care for this life and live like brothers. And you shall divide your property so that no one is rich and no one poor. You shall all work, and the earth shall be owned by all, and you shall all be equal."[3]

As the plot of *Antikrists mirakler* unfolds, upon the backdrop of growing tension between the Church and the socialists in Italy, the false replica of the Christ child finds its way to a small town in the shadow of Mt. Etna in Sicily, called Diamante. Here, the townsfolk fail to notice the inscription scratched into the icon's crown, and as a result they proclaim it to be a genuine miracle-working Christ child. The bulk of the remainder of the novel tells of the miracles that the townspeople actually experience when they bring their most heartfelt prayers to this Antichrist.

Lagerlöf's novel raises weighty theological questions about the ambiguous spiritual condition of the world in which we live and about the meaning of salvation in that world. Does the realization of the kingdom of heaven depend on the elimination of the threat that "worldly" forces—socialism among them—pose to heaven? Is there indeed a force of evil that reigns in the world against which the good must struggle? Does the salvation of one's personal soul depend, then, on denial of the world? If so, does attending even to the most noble of worldly causes, like the cessation of poverty, in fact preclude the possibility of being saved from the world?

In raising such questions, moreover, *Antikrists mirakler* shows that the threat which the world poses to the spiritual life of the soul is not simply a matter of the world's opposition to the spirit. The greater danger lies in the manner in which the world can *deceive* human beings about the difference between the worldly and the spiritual. The worldly, embodied character of the spiritual—the fact that even the true Santo Bambino must take on concrete, worldly form—means that the true Christ is always at risk of being impersonated by the Antichrist and, hence, that precisely the most sincere and pious of believers in the true savior are always at risk of being deceived. This deception, Lagerlöf implies, is part and parcel of *life in the world.*

At the end of the novel—to which we will have opportunity to return—Lagerlöf articulates a vision of the reconciliation of the "kingdom not of this world" and the "kingdom of this world alone." But this very attempt at reconciliation is spurred on by the twofold worry that is evoked in the events of the book as a whole: 1) That spirit and world are irreconcilable, and that one might be forced thus to choose between the salvation of one's soul through faith and the betterment of the world through love; 2) even more troubling, that the human being in the world can never be certain that she is not being deceived in the very moment of this choice. She can never be certain that the path she chooses is that of Christ and not of Antichrist.

Both Rosenzweig and Rosenstock later point to *Antikrists mirakler* as the spark that began the late-night conversation in Leipzig on July 7, 1913. Thus our survey of the themes raised in Lagerlöf's book provides us with important clues regarding the issues at the heart of that conversation. In Rosenstock's recollections years after the *Nachtgespräch,* he concedes that "he has not seen the novel since that night"; he nevertheless recalls that the reading of this book about "the miracle-working effigy of the Madonna [*sic*] in a Sicilian church" prompted a debate among the three over the merits of reason and faith, between the standpoints of "faith based on revelation [*Offenbarungsglaube*] and trust in philosophy [*Philosophiegläubigkeit*]."[4] While *Antikrists mirakler* does touch on questions of faith and credulity, its central concern is the moral and spiritual status of the world. In this chapter, I will argue that when Rosenzweig and his friends began to discuss Lagerlöf's book, it did not prompt a debate over the relative merits of reason and faith.[5] Rosenzweig did not play the "agnostic in matters of religious faith," while Rosenstock, who could "accept religion as his personal answer," stood for the "simplicity of faith."[6] The question which Lagerlöf's *Antikrists mirakler* raised for Rosenzweig, Rosenstock, and Ehrenberg during the *Leipziger Nachtgespräch,* I will argue, was the question of the relation between the personal fulfillment and salvation of the soul, on the one hand, and the conditions of the world, on the other. I will introduce what I take to be overwhelming evidence to suggest that Rosenzweig came to this conversation not at all in the guise of the academic philosopher but, to the contrary, committed to the possibility of a personal revelatory relation to the divine that promised redemption *from* the world.

In later reflections, Rosenzweig identifies the world-denying theological standpoint with which he entered the *Leipziger Nachtgespräch* as the standpoint of Marcion and the Gnostics. *Gnosticism* was the name under which scholars of Rosenzweig's day categorized a cluster of theological positions that shared the view that the individual's spiritual self is trapped in a world of deception, and that his salvation lies solely in a kingdom that "is not of this world." Scholars of Rosenzweig's day understood the myriad forms of ancient Gnosticism to share a commitment to metaphysical dualism, according to which the world was understood to be not the creation of a benevolent God, but rather the work of an inferior, but quasi-independent, divinity, a Demiurge often depicted as evil and deceptive. According to this view, however, beyond our world of illusion and trouble, there is a truly good and merciful God, who awakens those few endowed with "spirit" in the world to the nature of their predicament, and provides them with the knowledge (*gnosis*) necessary to enable their spiritual selves to escape the world's confines.[7]

In the first formative century of Christianity, Marcion of Sinope (85–160 CE) offered an interpretation of the coming of Jesus Christ that shared much with these so-called Gnostic views. Marcion understood the inferior divinity who created the world to be none other than the God of the Hebrew Bible—a God who governs the world with a combination of stern justice and malevolence. Jesus Christ, according to Marcion, was not at all to be understood as the son of this God of creation. To the contrary, Christ made manifest a God and a means of salvation that were wholly foreign to this world and opposed to its creator. This God is a God of love, mercy, and goodness, a God completely unknown before being revealed in Christ, whose inherent goodness led Him to rescue those who suffered in the world under the rule of the creator God. Christ was, according to Marcion, the manifestation of this good God himself, come to earth to show the way to a new, blessed kingdom *not of this world.*

According to the foremost authority on Marcion of Rosenzweig's day, Adolf von Harnack, Marcion's vision of Christianity demanded that Christians sacrifice "the belief that the God of creation is also the God of redemption."[8] In contrast to other Gnostic movements of the day, however, part of what was unique about Marcion's understanding of the redemption Christ brought was that it suggested that redemption from the world was to be achieved not through a special kind of *gnosis*—a form of spiritual knowledge—and thus limited to the few who could possess such knowledge, but rather *through faith.* According to Marcion, Harnack explains, "he who sets his hope in the Crucified can now be sure that he has escaped from the power of the world-creator, and will be translated into the kingdom of the good God."[9]

Interest in the figure of Marcion was on the rise in Rosenzweig's time, in no small part thanks to the work of Harnack. But Marcion's theology appears to have resonated within nineteenth- and early twentieth-century German theology, in general, because of the way it foreshadowed—and at once spelled out the radical consequences of—central notions within Protestant thought. Luther's repudiation of Church institutions and his concomitant affirmation of the authority of Scripture, his Paulinian opposition of gospel to law and his theological insistence on the tension between the hidden and revealed God; Schleiermacher's grounding of Christianity in personal faith experience; Karl Barth's early insistence on the impossibility of speaking of the transcendent God in terms borrowed from the worldly—despite the variations among such diverse Protestant positions and theologumena, Marcion appeared to presage them all.[10]

It is most significant, therefore, that in a number of instances in later years when Rosenzweig recalls the standpoint he brought to the 1913 Leipzig night-conversation, he identifies that standpoint with Marcion.[11] In the 1916 notes he wrote to himself while serving on the Balkan front, collected together as his "Paralipomena," Rosenzweig writes, "What it means that God created the world and [is] *not just* the God of revelation—this I know precisely out of the Leipzig night-conversation of 7.7.13. At that time, I was on the best road to Marcionitism."[12] Likewise, after Rosenstock suggests, in early 1921, that Harnack's monograph on Marcion might have contributed to Rosenzweig's newly published *The Star of Redemption,* Rosenzweig rebuffs Rosenstock's suggestion and writes, "so little could I have written it [i.e., the *Star*] before 1913 when I myself was still a Marcionist."[13] Rosenzweig appears merely to be using different terms to describe the same position he held in 1913, moreover, when he aligns that position with those nineteenth- and twentieth-century Protestant theologians whom Marcion was believed to have foreshadowed. Thus, in a note from November 19, 1916, Rosenzweig describes "7.7.13" as "my de-Schleiermachization."[14] And in a 1923 letter to Buber, Rosenzweig identifies his 1913 position with that of Barth, whose account of the distant God later led Rosenzweig, along with many of his contemporaries, to trace Barth's genealogy back to Marcion:[15] "I myself am a one-time Barthian of many years. It has only been ten years now [i.e., since 1913] since Rosenstock operated my Barthianism away."[16]

In stark contrast to all those accounts that attribute to Rosenzweig an academic intellectualism as he entered the *Leipziger Nachtgespräch,* we thus find that Rosenzweig himself suggests he entered this all-night conversation with a commitment to the soul's faith-relation to the divine and with a skepticism regarding the status of the world. Indeed, his respective commitment and skepticism were so extreme that they most closely resembled the standpoint of Marcion. The evidence suggests, further, that Rosenzweig's transformative discovery over the course of the *Leipziger Nachtgespräch* was not the discovery of "faith grounded in revelation." Before the night-conversation of 1913, Rosenzweig's 1916 description of his early Marcionism implies, Rosenzweig already found God accessible through revelation! The problem was that he found God accessible *only* through revelation. And this left the status of the world—its metaphysical grounding, its value, its relation to the "God of revelation"—in doubt. Was the God of revelation and salvation also the God of creation? Or was revelation the means through which the human being could be freed or redeemed *from* the world, a world *not created* by the God of revelation? Rosenzweig's 1916 note suggests that Rosenzweig learned the unity of the God who creates the world and who reveals Himself to the individual believer at the *Leipziger Nachtgespräch.* Beforehand, this unity remained in doubt. If revelation offers the individual a relation to the God that transcends the world, and thereby grants the individual some modicum of salvation from the imperfections of the world, so Rosenzweig appears to have thought, revelation could not but entail the denial of God's presence in or grounding of that world.[17]

We thus have good reason to think that Rosenzweig brought an anti-worldly theological standpoint to the 1913 night-conversation, which took its starting point from the questions of the moral and spiritual status of the world raised by Lagerlöf's *Antikrists mirakler.* Such an account of Rosenzweig's standpoint receives confirmation, moreover, from an allusive but important comment Rosenzweig makes, in the famous October 31, 1913 letter he wrote to Rudolf Ehrenberg, explaining his decision to remain a Jew. In this letter, Rosenzweig claims that he now rejects the Christianity of Rosenstock and Ehrenberg no longer based on the position he advocated during the *Leipziger Nachtgespräch,* but rather for legitimate reasons. He backs up this claim in the following obscure terms: "I am no longer the heretic of the eighteenth sermon who takes from faith and not from love. I now take other names and teach other statements."[18]

What does Rosenzweig mean by offering such a strange defense of his decision? Who exactly is the heretic of the eighteenth sermon "who takes from faith and not from love"? Rosenzweig's reference here is to a book written by none other than Rudolf Ehrenberg himself, *Ebr.10, 25. Ein Schicksal in Predigten* (1920).[19] Ehrenberg was already at work on this book in 1913, and Rosenzweig's letters show that he read the chapters of Ehrenberg's book as the latter wrote them. The book offers a fictional account of a charismatic young pastor who takes up the ministry at the church of a small German town. Each chapter of the book presents one of this young pastor's sermons, recorded by one of the townspeople, as he struggles to transform the town's churchgoers into a genuine redemptive community, battling local indifference and the onset of war along the way. Each of the pastor's sermons bears a title that reflects the position of the date of the sermon within the Church calendar, and each sermon takes a particular biblical passage as its starting point. The "eighteenth sermon," dated "On the Sunday of Seragesima [the sixtieth day before Easter]," takes as its starting point Jesus' parable of the sower from Luke 8:4–8, in which seeds thrown along the walking path, on rocks, and among thorns come to naught, but those seeds that fall upon good soil yield a crop one-hundredfold greater than what was planted. The sermon then turns to discuss a threat that a particular kind of "heretic" has recently posed to the community, a threat which apparently has led the community to expel that heretic from its midst. This heretic, according to Ehrenberg's pastor, was not one who simply had not yet been reached by the divine "call," and as a consequence "took other names or taught other statements," for the community merely considers such a person as "still before the awakening," as yet to be brought into the Kingdom of God. What makes the heretic of Ehrenberg's eighteenth sermon so threatening to the community, to the contrary, is that he shares in the *faith* of the community, but holds so zealously to his own personal salvation that he "cannot sacrifice the salvation of his soul" for the sake of the "hope of the world."[20]

To use the terms that Rosenzweig himself repeats, this heretic "took of faith and takes not of love"[21]: he celebrated the salvation of his own self through faith so single-mindedly, that he closed himself off from the love of the community, and failed to turn thereby in love toward others in the world. In such a case of a person who "believes with his brothers and does not go into love," Ehrenberg's pastor proclaims, it is as if a plot of the good land mentioned in Jesus' parable were to hold on to the seed it received without producing the fruits of that sowing. Such a person "receives the seed and keeps the fruit," that is, he receives faith but does not turn as a result of that faith to the world in love. "He is the heretic whom we reject," the pastor announces. "We ask God that this man not be as a living soul before Him."[22]

Although an air of mystery surrounds the particular act that the heretic of Ehrenberg's eighteenth sermon commits, the profile of this heretic is already familiar to us. For we are presented here with someone who experiences the salvation of his soul through faith, but who so guards his own personal salvation that he closes himself off to the world. He does not participate in the creation of a community through love. He denies the world its own hopes for redemption. In other words, the heretic of Ehrenberg's eighteenth sermon takes up the same faith position as does the Marcionist with whom Rosenzweig identified in the summer of 1913. When Rosenzweig claims, in October 1913, that he is "no longer the heretic of the eighteenth sermon who takes from faith and not from love," he thus refers back to that same world-denying position of faith with which he entered the *Leipziger Nachtgespräch.*

We have thereby arrived at a new conception of the intellectual and spiritual position Rosenzweig advocated when he began discussing Selma Lagerlöf's *Antikrists mirakler* on July 7, 1913. In stark contrast to the view that has prevailed in the scholarship for more than sixty years, we have found that Rosenzweig did not enter this conversation touting the intellectual standpoint of the academy only to be overwhelmed by Rosenstock's simple faith.

Rosenzweig himself, we have seen, entered the *Leipziger Nachtgespräch* already advocating a position of faith, and already taking seriously the notion of revelation. Indeed, Rosenzweig's commitment to the possibility of the salvation of the individual soul through a revelatory relation to the God who transcends the world is so extreme at this moment in his life, that it is accompanied by a denial of the spiritual status of the world. As the "heretic" of Ehrenberg's eighteenth sermon, Rosenzweig is thereby chided for holding so zealously to his own faith that he denies the world the love which faith is supposed to engender in him.

The array of reports on the world-denying position Rosenzweig advocated as he entered the *Leipziger Nachtgespräch* in July 1913 thus flies in the face of the conventional account of Rosenzweig's intellectual and spiritual profile preceding this critical moment in his life. They suggest that a reexamination of Rosenzweig's development prior to 1913 is in order. How and when did Rosenzweig arrive at a theological position of world denial away from which he would need to be converted in 1913? How far back into Rosenzweig's thinking do we find the roots of such a position?

The remainder of this chapter will seek to answer these questions by reviewing the development of Rosenzweig's thought leading up to 1913. Such a review will show, first of all, the degree to which the very problem of the relation between soul and world which I seek to place at the center of the Leipzig night-conversation was already a source of perplexity for Rosenzweig during his earlier university years. Rosenzweig appears to have seen the 1910 attempt to form a community of intellectuals at Baden-Baden as offering the possibility of reconciling soul and world within the framework of the historical moment. When this community fell apart, however, Rosenzweig evidently returned to a position of world skepticism. Indeed, as we shall see, newly uncovered evidence suggests that in 1910–1911 Rosenzweig began to entertain a theological position that was extreme in its denial of the world.

EARLY WORLD-SKEPTICISM

The extant diaries and correspondences from 1906 through 1910 show Rosenzweig frequently pondering the relation between self and world through a variety of polar formulations: subject–object, spirituality–sensibility, I–world, free will–nature, soul–body. In an early diary entry from January

1906, Rosenzweig suggests that Goethe spent his whole life oscillating between a "subjectivism" in which the self alone is grasped as the standard according to which all else must be measured, and an "objectivism" in which the self is swallowed up by the natural world surrounding it.[23] "Since it went this way with Goethe," Rosenzweig then muses, "so it must indeed go this way with us all, and the tendency to one or the other perspective will only be a matter of mood."[24]

There are entries in these diaries in which Rosenzweig is intent on grasping the human being as the unity of such subjective and objective poles. Thus, on September 4, 1906, he writes that "the 'balance' of outer and inner, the sensible and the spiritual [*geistig*] nature of man, which should mark the complete man, is really less balance than reciprocal penetration of these elements: the spiritual [*geistig*] becomes sensible for him, the sensible becomes spiritualized. Further: the world enters in him, he enters the world."[25] But such a harmonious view of self and world evidently does not hold Rosenzweig's confidence for long. For in December 1907, Rosenzweig has returned to a dualism he now formulates in Kantian terms: "Man as phenomenon (body *and* soul, i.e., 'body' of the physiologists and 'soul' of the psychologists) doesn't die, because it was always already dead. Man as noumenon (personality) doesn't die, because it has never lived (in time)."[26]

Especially noteworthy for our purposes is the appearance, in Rosenzweig's diary entries of 1906–1907, of a series of reflections on skepticism that foreshadow in important ways the kind of world denial that Rosenzweig would come to entertain in the years leading up to the *Leipziger Nachtgespräch*. The skepticism into which Rosenzweig inquires in these entries, moreover, is likewise rooted in worries regarding the gap between subject and object, or between self and world. "Complete skepticism, which thus no longer believes in anything objective or in any 'value', leads necessarily—since yet [something] must be *believed* once—to the proclamation of the subjective as the highest value for the subject, to the proclamation of individualism," Rosenzweig writes, on December 2, 1906. "This way which skepticism goes in *general* is also the only practical . . . way for the individual man who 'struggles' with skepticism. The objective is lost to him. He must create it himself anew, and indeed out of that which skepticism leaves untouched: the subjective. The subjective must be objectivized (i.e., made into objective value)."[27]

It is noteworthy, here, that what Rosenzweig calls "complete skepticism" does not amount to a skepticism about the subject itself. For even if Rosenzweig's skeptic doubts everything, he must at least "believe" his own doubting. Skepticism, that is to say, is *world* skepticism. And thus, Rosenzweig implies, skepticism amounts in fact to subjectivism. When everything objective has come into doubt, the subject can only create "objective value" out of its own subjectivity; the subject alone is fit to serve, as Rosenzweig goes on to write, as the "center" of the human being's worldview. "*But is it capable of being center for itself*?" Rosenzweig proceeds to ask sharply. "That is the question, and if I must deny it, well then—."[28]

Here Rosenzweig breaks off from this more radically skeptical question—what grounds does the subject truly have for trusting her own subjectivity—in order to pursue the more particular and more practical question of whether a given individual is capable of being "center" for herself. To answer the more radically skeptical question, Rosenzweig concedes, one must "believe in an objective truth."[29] And thus Rosenzweig's skeptic finds herself in the vicious loop of skepticism's reciprocal mode: mistrustful of all that is objective in the world, she falls back on her own subjectivity, only to find that in order to estimate the capacity of such subjectivity to serve as highest value, she must be able to evaluate it, once again, by the very objective standard she has dismissed as unworthy of trust.[30] It is perhaps while in the throes of this skeptical circle that Rosenzweig writes, the following day, the briefest of diary entries: "life-center = life-lies??!"[31]

Rosenzweig's early skeptical reflections on the gap between self and world foreshadow his later flirtation with Marcionism in important ways. For the Marcionist dualism of Creator and Redeemer may be said to posit different Gods, or different metaphysical grounds, for world and individual soul respectively; and this dualism presents the salvation of the soul as going hand-in-hand with denial of the world.

Notably, however, it is not always the world that is the source of Rosenzweig's own skeptical experience during his university years. In the wake of some disagreeable personal exchange on New Year's Eve, 1907, Rosenzweig complains to Gertrud Oppenheim that he has so "objectivized" himself that he views his "subjective" side "now as out of grasp, as something unusual—foreign! . . . I am mistrustful toward it. It appears to me like an enemy which I don't know. I dare no longer step out openly toward it as I-myself. The hiding of myself, the concealing in the armor of objectivity."[32]

The cause of the angst Rosenzweig reports on here is unclear, but what is striking in this letter is the way Rosenzweig's self-description points to the very opposite experience to that of the world-skeptic. Here, it is not the foreignness of the world that is the cause of unease, but rather precisely the foreignness of Rosenzweig's *subjectivity*! Rosenzweig suggests he has concealed himself within an "armor of objectivity" and has so identified with this objective armor—perhaps by taking on a certain social identity that served to hide his true self—as to make his true self appear now as an "enemy." In such an experience, it appears, Rosenzweig no longer feels like a subjective self cut off from the objective world, but rather like an objectified self for whom his own subjectivity feels threatening.

Rosenzweig's diaries thus allow us to trace a certain chain of perplexity regarding the relation between self and world from his university years up to the *Leipziger Nachtgespräch*. But his early expressions of uncertainty over the relation between self and world—skepticism regarding the objective world rooted in subjectivism, skepticism regarding the subjective "I" rooted in an experience of objectivity—appear to have subsided for a time by 1909. It was then that Rosenzweig joined his cousin, Hans Ehrenberg, in planning a series of symposia to be held at Baden-Baden, in which some of the brightest young scholars of history and philosophy from southwest Germany were to join together to make "contemporary culture into the object of historical contemplation."[33] The extant letters Rosenzweig wrote leading up to the first—and what was to be the only—meeting of the "Baden-Baden Gesellschaft," show Rosenzweig having adopted the historicism in fashion during those years, and having done so precisely as an answer to his long-standing questions regarding the relation between self and world. He apparently saw as the task of the Baden-Baden group the revival of a philosophical-historical consciousness that would rival what Hegel's "Spirit" had meant for its age. Together, Rosenzweig believed, these up-and-coming intellectuals would reconcile in science their respective subjectivity with the objectivity of their time.[34] They would take seriously the radical individuality of person and specialization of science that typified the age, and would at once forge the "unity" of such "ununifiables" in a holistic vision of knowledge and culture befitting the *Zeitgeist*. The realization of such an "intellectual-historical unity" [*geistes-geschichtliche Einheit*] presumed, Rosenzweig wrote in the weeks leading up to the first scheduled symposium, that each individual coming to Baden-Baden "had the drive, instead of serving himself as private God—this our polemical, anti-subjectivist side—to find himself more or less consciously objectively in his time, to worship in it"—that is, in the time—"the God revealing itself in the here and now."[35]

Such statements betray Rosenzweig's hearty support for the historical relativism fashionable in his day. Suspending the self-worship of individualism, he charged his peers to fuse their respective subjective selves into the objectivity of their historical moment, and thereby to find divinity and truth—that divinity and truth, we might presume, that alone is attainable for human beings—in the historical moment itself.

But if Rosenzweig appears to have had high hopes, prior to the first Baden-Baden symposium, for a historicist reconciliation of subjectivity and objectivity in his time, there are indications that these hopes had already waned by the time the symposium itself took place. Indeed, Rosenzweig concludes the lecture he delivered at Baden-Baden not with a call for a *zeitgeistig* harmonization of self and world comparable to the tone of the letters which preceded the symposium, but rather with the observation that "the abyss between personality and world, which substantive life had covered up, has opened up again for the human being." Today, Rosenzweig suggests at the end of his lecture, the human being lives "purely in the empirical I or in the empirical world"; and if the concept of "life" had once served to bridge this gap between I and world, insofar as it was "life alone" which was seen as the locus in which "personality and world find their actualization," today "life" has become rather a symbol "for personality or world" and not for their synthesis.[36]

The Baden-Baden society failed to realize the kind of *zeitgeistig* synthesis of subjectivity and objectivity that Rosenzweig appears to have envisioned during the weeks leading up to the symposium. In fact, the Baden-Baden society did not even survive until the end of its first meeting. Moreover, the dissolution of the Baden-Baden Gesellschaft appears to have deepened the ambivalence Rosenzweig expressed at the meeting itself over the possibility of a historicist reconciliation of I and world. Thus Rosenzweig wrote to his cousin, Hans Ehrenberg, several months after the failed symposium: "You must draw the consequences of Baden-Baden. . . . You, tempter, led me to believe in the phantom of the 'time': a society [*Verein*] of the un-unifiables [*Unvereinbaren*] on the ground of just this its un-unifiability? . . . But how differently we understand it now than I did at that time."[37]

The rebuke which Rosenzweig aims at his cousin here suggests that mere months after Baden-Baden, Rosenzweig no longer took historicism seriously as a possibility for conceiving of the reconciliation between selfhood and worldliness. He already came to consider his earlier belief in a *zeitgeistig* divine unity worthy of the submission of contemporary individuals to have been belief in a "phantom."

It is noteworthy, moreover, that in rejecting the possibility of a historicist synthesis of subjectivity and objectivity by the end of 1910, Rosenzweig finds himself thrust back once more to his earlier oscillation between world and self. Thus Rosenzweig writes, at the beginning of his letter to Hans Ehrenberg, that despite its failure, "Baden-Baden was a gain for me [because] without Baden-Baden I would not have felt this 'world-desire' and would have always remained a *naïve* Idealist." But only a few lines later, Rosenzweig suggests that the "impossibility" of Baden-Baden lay "in the command lying at the ground of our subjective life-ideal, not to unify our un-unifiability with our unifiability. This consciousness was empowered for me through Baden-Baden."[38]

By the end of 1910, we thus find, Rosenzweig has returned from historical relativism back to the kind of tug-of-war between selfhood and worldliness that he had documented as early as 1906. His rediscovered "world-desire" prevents him from adopting an idealism that would reduce the world to the objective manifestation of the idea; but all at once his endorsement of the unique "un-unifiability" of the individual self, celebrated in his generation's "subjective life-ideal," likewise prevented him from accepting any kind of objective context in which all contemporary subjects could share a common truth.

It is in the wake of the Baden-Baden failure that we also find the earliest evidence that Rosenzweig was beginning to conceive of his world skepticism in theological terms. Indeed, a theology of world denial hinting toward what Rosenzweig would later call Marcionism is already present in a diary entry of Rosenzweig's, which he copied over for Hans Ehrenberg in a letter dated September 26, 1910. Rejecting both the Hegelian "God of history" and the Baden-Baden conception of the divine as the supreme manifestation of one's historical moment, Rosenzweig writes, "Every act becomes sinful if it steps into history. For this reason God must redeem man not through history, but rather . . . as 'God in religion.' . . . For us, religion is the 'single true theodicy.'"[39]

Although not explicitly Marcionist, Rosenzweig's comments here make evident his growing sense of the world as inherently sinful, as a context out of which—rather than through which—the human being must be redeemed. At this moment in Rosenzweig's thinking, "history" represents that sinful worldly context, while "religion" justifies and opens up access to a God capable of redeeming the human being despite the sinful quality her actions take on as part of the historical world. It is only through religious faith, and not through the historical process, Rosenzweig's letter suggests, that the individual can attain a pure relation to God.[40]

As I will show in the following section, newly discovered evidence suggests that in the fall of 1910, Rosenzweig embarked on a period in which he explored the radical theological consequences of his world skepticism in explicit fashion. During this period (1910–1911), he began to exhibit concern for the kinds of threats which the worldly may pose not only to the self, but also to the God with whom the individual soul communes. Rosenzweig appears to have asked himself: Is the personal salvation that the individual soul seeks to attain through a relation to the divine even possible in the worldly context? What is the human soul called upon to do, in order to preserve her self and the God of revelation, from the threats of the world? As the following section will show, the answer to these questions which Rosenzweig and his closest interlocutors appear to have entertained during these years is startling.

DYING FOR GOD

The most striking evidence that Rosenzweig and his closest interlocutors began exploring a theology of world denial in the years after Baden-Baden can be garnered from three unpublished texts from 1910–1911, two of which were written by Rosenzweig and one by Rudolf Ehrenberg. As a way of introducing the themes of these texts as Rosenzweig understood them, I want to cite two later letters, from 1917 and 1919 respectively, in which Rosenzweig refers to and comments upon these texts. In a letter to Rudolf Ehrenberg dated July 9, 1917, Rosenzweig reports on a recent meeting with Hans Ehrenberg. The meeting led him to review the differences between the ways he and the Ehrenbergs, on the one hand, and Eugen Rosenstock, on the other, approached their shared conversations of 1913. Rosenzweig suggests he had shared a "problem" with his cousins during the period of the *Nachtgespräch,* which had not concerned Rosenstock. Rosenzweig reports with surprise that in their recent meeting, Hans Ehrenberg raised the very problem that Rosenzweig recalls having shared with him from years past, as if it were an entirely *new* subject:

> The strangest thing [about the exchange with Hans Ehrenberg] was this: earlier he had not grasped how human love should cause no breach in the love of God. Now he grasps how the two grow together: in love toward Christ. He was somewhat astounded when I reminded him that this indeed was the object of our correspondence of 1913/14. Did you already know that about him? . . . Rosenstock's *Prae* [advantage] over us is perhaps just this: that he didn't know our problem of 1913/14 at all, while you yourself still remained wholly subject to it in the *Half-Hundred Day* (that all-too great human-directed love is the highest danger to love of God) and for this reason you had to save your heroes ultimately in the solitude—empty of human beings—of a mystical being-alone with the "silent God." Rosenstock had just mistrusted the "silent" God from the very beginning, because he believed from the very beginning in the "word."[41]

The letter suggests that in their recent meeting, Hans Ehrenberg engaged Rosenzweig in a conversation about the spiritual dangers of interpersonal human love. He relates that he has had the worry that loving another human being in the world might detract from one's love of God. Ehrenberg apparently finds the solution to this problem in the figure of Christ, which for him mediates worldly and divine love.

Rosenzweig finds his cousin's reflections "strange," it appears, because Hans Ehrenberg doesn't seem to remember that such questions about the possibility of reconciling love for God and love for others in the world were central to the correspondences between Rosenzweig and his cousins during 1913 and—as we shall soon see—earlier. Rosenzweig cites as an example a play that Rudolf Ehrenberg wrote in 1911, the *Halbhunderttag.* According to Rosenzweig's recollection, the play depicts how love directed toward other human beings so threatens the possibility of loving God, that those heroes who seek a connection to the divine must be isolated from the world—and from the possibility of earthly love—in "mystical" solitude with the "silent God." And Rosenzweig suggests that what made Eugen Rosenstock so different from him and from the Ehrenbergs during that period was that Rosenstock was not drawn to such a mystical relation with the divine. Rosenstock did not share the same concern over reconciling human and divine love, apparently because he trusted in the "word" of revelation as the medium through which both divine and human love could be articulated.

Before exploring further the ideas and texts to which Rosenzweig alludes in this letter, I want to juxtapose it to a letter Rosenzweig wrote to Margrit Rosenstock, on June 13, 1919. Here Rosenzweig reports on having read an essay of Eugen Rosenstock's that Rosenzweig calls "The Fruit of Death." I presume this refers to Rosenstock's recently penned "The Suicide of Europe," a lengthy review of Spengler's *Der Untergang des Abendlandes,* which opens with praise for the way Spengler recognizes as "the fruit of death" the respective cultural forms that have emerged over the course of history out of different conceptions of death. Rosenstock ends his essay by suggesting that "in this age God had indeed withdrawn himself from the world," but that the "suicide of Europe" culminating in the World War would result in a renewed awareness of God. As a result, the world would be "created anew, divided into above and below, into heaven and earth."[42] Rosenzweig, clearly perturbed by Rosenstock's proclamation, writes as follows to Margrit Rosenstock:

> Last night in bed I was still reading "The Fruit of Death." I was astounded. It is surely not as important as Eugen thinks. I was astounded because that which is new in it for Eugen ("God wants to have us back"), is really that from which none other than he [Eugen] freed me. This is the theme of the *Half-Hundred Day:* "You great eternal God may live again—a man dies for you." The theme of my letter to Rudi from September 1910 (I once showed you the copy of it, Hedi's). The theme of my Shechina-sonnets to Rudi from 1911.[43]

Rosenzweig's comments here exhibit his surprise, once again, over what he sees as a reversal in the position of one of his close confidants, this time of Eugen Rosenstock. Whereas in Rosenzweig's letter to Rudolf Ehrenberg of July 9, 1917, Rosenzweig points to Rosenstock's distance from the shared penchant for a mystical escape from the world which Rosenzweig had once shared with his cousins, he expresses surprise upon reading "The Suicide of Europe" at finding Rosenstock advocating a form of the very position "from which none other than he [Eugen] freed" Rosenzweig himself ("God wants to have us back").

I will take up the task of delineating Eugen Rosenstock's early theological position, and his role in the *Leipziger Nachtgespräch,* in the following chapter.

Here I will focus on what Rosenzweig's letter to Margrit Rosenstock tells us about the position from which Eugen "freed" Rosenzweig. In recalling this position, Rosenzweig once again makes reference to Rudolf Ehrenberg's play, *Half-Hundred Day,* and once again hints at the way this play exhibits a radical tension between the divine and the worldly. If Rosenzweig's 1917 letter to Rudolf Ehrenberg cited as the play's theme the threat human love for others poses to human love for God, his 1919 letter to Margrit Rosenstock suggests the play makes the more radical suggestion that even human *life* stands in tension with the divine, such that the "great eternal God may live again" when "a man dies for you." Moreover, Rosenzweig suggests two of his own texts share the theme of Rudolf Ehrenberg's play, the "Shechina-Sonnets to Rudi" of 1911 and his "letter to Rudi of September 1910."

It is these three texts that offer us the most direct evidence of the world-denying theology which Rosenzweig entertained in the years between the Baden-Baden symposium in 1910 and the *Leipziger Nachtgespräch.* Indeed, Ehrenberg's *Half-Hundred Day,* Rosenzweig's six-sonnet cycle, "The Shechina," and an undated letter from Rosenzweig to Rudolf Ehrenberg which I will argue is the "letter to Rudi of September 1910," show Rosenzweig and his cousin testing out the limits of world denial, and hence the limits of the tension between the soul beloved of and even united with God, on the one hand, and the worldly, on the other. All three texts build up in different ways, moreover, to the same startling idea: the human being must die for God's sake. The human being must die to the world, first of all, in order to find complete solitary union with the divine. But the human being must die to the world, more radically, for God's own sake. It is first and foremost God who is in need of the self-cancellation of the worldly; God requires that the human being negate his own worldly existence.

The premise of this suicidal theology appears to be the very same inherent tension between the world and the individual soul in relation to the divine which Rosenzweig would later designate as his own "Marcionism." But as we shall see, the three texts offer different accounts of why God requires such worldly sacrifice: because of the tendency of those in the world to identify the divinely inspired human being with God, and hence to worship the human being instead of God; because of a breach *within* the divine linked to worldly time which can only be healed through human death; because the world at a particular historical moment cannot be reconciled to the divine, and hence requires sacrifice in the present, in order to prepare the way for a future reconciliation.

The theological premise of these texts is striking. I should note that I see little evidence in the handful of extant letters written by Rosenzweig during 1910–1912 that Rosenzweig personally contemplated suicide for God during this period, although as we shall see in the following chapter, Rosenzweig did contemplate suicide in the wake of the *Leipziger Nachtgespräch,* and in this later context there is reason to think Rosenzweig was motivated by certain Gnostic notions of world denial. As I understand it, however, Rosenzweig's and Ehrenberg's exploration of the idea of dying for God in 1910–1911 was first and foremost a testing of the limits of that world skepticism which Rosenzweig himself had entertained for some time already. How radical is the opposition between soul and world? How severe of a breach is there between the God whom the individual soul experiences in revelation and the world in which the individual lives? The idea of "dying for God" offered Rosenzweig a limit case through which he could pose these questions for himself.

To bear this claim out, let us now survey the world-denying theology shared by these three texts.[44] Since Rosenzweig himself identifies Ehrenberg's *Half-Hundred Day* as articulating this world-denying theology "from which none other than [Eugen] . . . freed me" in the clearest of terms—"too great a love directed to human being is the highest danger to love of God," "You great eternal God may live again—a man dies for you"—I will first explore how Ehrenberg's play depicts the common theme of these texts, and will then turn to Rosenzweig's "Shechina" and to the letter I believe can be identified as the "letter to Rudi of September 1910."

Half-Hundred Day[45]—perhaps better translated as *Half-Century Day,* because the "hundred" in question designates a number of years—takes place in the "mythic future," shortly after the most recent celebration of a cosmic holiday which occurs once every half-century. During the recent celebration, each individual in the crowd had been called upon to discover the personal God inside him or her; but what ensued was a chaotic proliferation of divinities and turf-wars between townsfolk over which gods belonged to whom.[46] Into this chaotic state of affairs steps the protagonist of the play, Hermann (literally, "Lord-Man"). Hermann reports on his own solitary experience of the One God of all, and he shares his faith in this God with his beloved Hedwig. But when Hermann tries to convince the townsfolk that the God he experienced privately is the God of all, a God whom each can experience through her relation with others, they confuse Hermann's ecstatic preaching about God with Hermann's *own* godliness. Encouraged by the town's "Religious Leader" [*Kultusleiter*]—Hermann's foil in the play—the townsfolk begin to worship Hermann himself as their God. "Is not in truth the prophet himself—God?" asks one of the people.[47] "You must hear us, because we believe in you!" another voice from the crowd exclaims to Hermann. "You men, feel the enormous wonder / God came to us in this man's image / And let us see His Allhood in us, / Now however our young eyes see / The unity of God here in this man, / The whole in one, which we are in All!"[48]

Distraught over the townsfolk's idolatrous misunderstandings, Hermann begs the crowds, "Don't leave me alone again with my God!"[49] but his pleading denial is to no avail. In fact, when he returns to the town incognito after some months of hiding, he finds that the masses, led by the "Religious Leader," have constructed a full "Hermann-Religion," complete with temple and monuments. Hermann resolves to demonstrate his own lack of divinity in the only way he sees left before him. Still unrecognized by the townsfolk, he blasphemes the "Hermann-God" in order to ensure his own public execution, in the last moment of which he plans to reveal his identity to all. He will thereby permit "all to see, that Hermann dies, thus the false Godhead dies."[50]

When the moment of execution arrives, Hermann drinks poison, reveals his identity to the crowds gathered, and proclaims, "Hermann, so you say, is what your God is called! / And Hermann is the one whom you now see die! . . . I am Hermann whom you loved before God, / And who dies to you today in your faith! / Experience then how mortal is your God!"[51]

But Hermann's radical attempt to cure the masses of their false beliefs fails. The "Religious Leader" guides the crowds away from the dying man whom they fail to accept as the real Hermann, and toward the temple in which they will resume their practice of the "Hermann-Religion." As the play comes to an end, Hermann is left to die, alone once again with God, hoping that his death may yet make possible the founding of a community of believers in the true God at some point in the future.

On the whole, *Half-Hundred Day* exhibits the tragic consequences of Hermann's inability to accept the tenet that the spiritual and the worldly simply cannot be bridged. Using Rosenzweig's own disparate comments about the play as my guide, I want to highlight three aspects of the play's exploration of this theme in particular, because they shed great light on the scope of the world-denying theology that Rosenzweig and Ehrenberg were exploring at the time.

1. Is love of God possible for the individual in the world? Hermann speaks the lines that Rosenzweig cites in his 1917 letter to Rudolf Ehrenberg—"That all-too great love directed to man / Is the worst danger to love of God"—just as he decides he must die in order to rid the masses of their mistaken belief in his divinity.[52] In this context, the lines suggest that love of God cannot be shared within a community of human beings in the world, because the masses are too easily inclined to divinize one of their own. While Hermann himself demonstrates that the individual can enter into a loving relationship with God alone, or can at most share that love for God with a beloved other, the masses as a unit in the play symbolize the impossibility of planting that love of God within the worldly context. I will return to this point shortly.

There is an important moment in *Half-Hundred Day* in which Hermann himself exemplifies the danger that human love poses to divine love. After the townsfolk declare Hermann their God, and Hermann fails to convince them they are mistaken, Hermann pursues another means of "proving" to all that he is no God. He attempts to consummate physically the faith-inspired loving relationship he shares with Hedwig. "Lay your arm there! Totally near," he commands Hedwig. "I feel nothing more than this love! A wholly earthly love, you men!—Kiss me dearest! I belong to you, yes, only to you!—Ha, if they could all see how their God loves!" Hedwig rebuffs Hermann's advances, however, and sends him away to redouble his efforts for the true God: "I can no longer love you if you are untrue to Him!—Save me my love, Hermann! Struggle for your God!"[53]

Although Hermann immediately renews his commitment to the one God of all, the frustrated love scene displays the tension between worldly and divine love in both its crisis and its resolution. Hermann's attempt to realize a "wholly earthly love" which would demonstrate that he is not divine, and Hedwig's redirecting of Hermann's love back to the spiritual plane share the same premise: worldly love and spiritual love cannot be reconciled. In order for Hermann and Hedwig to preserve their shared love for the one God, they must suppress their desire for the earthly consummation of their love. There is simply no divinity to be found in earthly love.[54]

2. *Individual spiritual experience (soul) and religious institutions (world).* The second theme of *Half-Hundred Day* is closely related to the first. It is the opposition that Ehrenberg sets out in the play between a personal, solitary experience of God, on the one hand, and the institution of religion, on the other. In a letter to Rudolf Ehrenberg of July 21, 1911, Rosenzweig suggests that the "Hermann-Religion" forces one to ask the question, "How does the Volk come to its religion? How does this historical wonder happen, that a wholly personal experience is felt by the masses?"[55]

There is no doubt that the answer which the play offers to this question is bleak. If the play depicts "personal experience" of God as perhaps the sole possible path to authentic spirituality, it presents institutional religion as little more than mass deception. The moment Hermann attempts to extend the genuine religious experience he has had in isolation into the communal realm, the religiosity of that personal experience is corrupted. The Gnostic premise to which Ehrenberg alludes here is the same as that which we saw introduced in Lagerlöf's *Antikrists mirakler:* in the worldly context, people cannot help but be deceived about true and false gods.

The notion that institutional religion amounts to unavoidable deception is highlighted in surprising fashion by the character of the "Religious Leader" in the play. Although he appears for much of the play as one who manipulates the masses simply for the sake of his own power, the Religious Leader makes it evident toward the play's end that his motives for constructing the "Hermann-Religion" are altogether different. Criticized by the town council for his arrest and sentencing of the real Hermann, the Religious Leader exclaims, "My soul / knows that what I do only serves / The God who brings man peace!"[56] The Religious Leader explains his surprising form of service to the true God in a critical exchange with Hermann in prison before he leads the latter out for public execution. "I believe in God and may not experience it / that the eye of man sees Him!" he tells Hermann. "In order to protect God I make you into God. / In order to save God, you must die today!"[57]

The Religious Leader's statement here suggests a peculiar motive for instituting a false faith. He allows the masses to transform Hermann into a God and to worship him, in order to protect the true God from the kind of misguided worship of which the masses are solely capable. The Religious Leader cannot tolerate "that the eye of man" might observe the true God and thereby corrupt God with his worldly gaze. Thus he permits the deification and then the execution of Hermann—"in order to save God."

Hence, when Hermann decides to face execution before the townsfolk, as an attempt to rid them of their belief that he is God, and when the Religious Leader constructs the very Hermann-Religion that the real Hermann hopes to destroy, both characters seek through their opposing actions to bring about the same goal. Both seek to free the true God from the corrupting worship of the masses.[58]

3. *Live God—A Man dies for you.* This leads us to the final and, for our purposes, the most important theme of *Half-Hundred Day:* Hermann's dying for God. Hermann makes it clear that he does not carry out this act of self-sacrifice in order to save the people of his world; he does not die as expiation for the sins of the world. Thus he tells Hedwig's father, Albertus, "Your error is that [you think] I die for the sake of these people."[59] Rather, *Hermann's death is intended to save God.* Thus, just before he drinks the poison handed him and reveals his identity, Hermann proclaims before the crowds assembled: "One single human life doesn't carry God. / A believing human death eternalizes him!"[60] Hermann's premise here seems to be the same as that of the Religious Leader: when worldly worship of the divine goes astray, it is God, and not only the righteous souls of the world, who suffers the consequences. If the worldly context thwarts the possibility of a genuine relationship between the individual soul and God, this relationship must be consummated in the individual soul's most radical isolation with God—in his sacrificial death—and this both for the sake of the soul and for God.[61]

In his final scene, as he nears his death, Hermann articulates the divine need for human sacrifice in historical terms: "In times the world was full of God, / And early men carried God's life,—/ In others, the sense darkened again, / And in order to hold the eternal eye awake, / Then God must live from the death of his faithful, / Those few alone who still believed." Here Hermann suggests that God's need for sacrifice rests on the "darkening" of the human sense for the divine. In earlier times, when "the world was full of God," no such sacrifice was necessary. But during such epochs in which the world has ceased to be a site God can inhabit, God requires "the death of his faithful" in order to live. Through such periods, it is only as a consequence of the faithful human being's negation of his own worldly existence that "the eternal eye" is held "awake." Hermann sums up this most startling message of the play in his final words: "You great, eternal God may live again! / Here a man dies for you!"[62]

We now return to the letters to Rudolf Ehrenberg and Margrit Rosenstock, of 1917 and 1919 respectively, with which we began this section. When Rosenzweig recalls the way the *Halbhunderttag* presents the threat human love of others poses to human love of God, and the way the play's hero is forced into "mystical aloneness with God"; and when Rosenzweig cites the sacrificial call, "You great eternal God may live again, a man dies for you," he is identifying the two central and connected themes of Ehrenberg's play. "Earthly" love so threatens the individual soul's love of the divine, that the individual must remove herself from the world. She must die for God. It is this startling position, Rosenzweig asserts, from which "none other than" Eugen Rosenstock freed him, in 1913.

A handful of letters exchanged between Rosenzweig and Rudolf Ehrenberg in the summer of 1911 show that while Rosenzweig was reading and commenting upon Ehrenberg's *Half-Hundred Day,* he himself was composing a text that shares central concerns with Ehrenberg's play.[63] Rosenzweig's six-sonnet cycle, "The Shechina,"[64] recasts the Kabbalistic account of the primordial break within the divine that results in the exile of the Shechina, and of the hoped-for reunification of the Shechina with God in redemption. It recounts these cosmic events through six different perspectives: those of three angels, Michael, Gabriel, and Rafael, of God, of the Shechina herself, and of the Heavens. In the opening of the cycle, Michael, guarding the heavens far above the dark, silent earth, is disoriented by what appears to be a "cry from below," and a consequent "tear" [*Riss],* as something "glides like a ray past me into the darkness."[65] Gabriel, with his attention fixed on the "eternal countenance" of God, is the first to grasp the separation that has ensued: "The Godhead of God! The Lordship of the Lord! / You leave the Husband? Innermost bound / Separated! What remained, withered!"[66] Rafael then catches sight of the Shechina having landed far below, "feet sore. Knee weak, worn down from the impact," seeking the path back to the Heavens once again.[67] It is only at this moment that God awakens from the divine slumber, groaning in the pain caused by the separation: "Whose hand crushes my heart? Who turns about therein / And staggers, cries, bellows, and moans? Woe I, unmoved! Pain."[68] But although God senses the Shechina attempting to return—"I hear you companion, wedded as one / . . . you approach and climb upwards, / You knock."[69]—the Shechina herself finds the locked gates of the Heavens barring her return, and fears that she has been exiled by her beloved God intentionally. "I soul knock. Gate unopened. / . . . My blood condensed, seeks your veins' course," she calls out. "The path wandered astray / into the darkness, far into the narrowness unmeasured. / For your sake Lord I gave myself in exchange [*gab ich mich Kauf*]. / In all, I alone am the one obsessed by you. O God, I knock, no one opens for me, / Who left you. And whom you now forget?"[70]

Through the first five sonnets of "The Shechina," Rosenzweig's dramatic poem follows the traditional Kabbalistic account of the break within the divine. For reasons unclear to the angels, and even to God, the Shechina is separated from God, startling the heavenly hosts, and causing pain and anguish to both God, who remains in the Heavens, and the Shechina, who finds herself locked out of them. The "tear" in the divine seems to have been caused by something that occurs "below," and the Shechina herself speaks of wandering into the darkness "for your sake Lord." But Rosenzweig does not make clear what exactly the worldly cause of the breach in the divine might be, or why the Shechina had to be exiled.

The sixth sonnet of "The Shechina" makes it eminently clear, in contrast, how the Shechina is reunited with her God. Here the Heavens report how "a man, dying, raises his hand toward the clouds. / The gate springs open, and turned to you / she enters, salvation for us, who stiffly passed away. . . . O joy, lighting the view! / Raises to us, circled airs quivering / From the step of the stars, in which we are ready to dance / In the wedding rapture, hovering above and below."[71] Locked out of the Heavens, divorced from her God, the Shechina only finds her way back through the heavenly gates to her beloved God when a human being dies on earth, with hands reaching up toward the heavens. In a morbid spin on the Kabbalistic idea that the faithful must perform ascetic acts in order to raise the Shechina up from the worldly confines within which she is trapped, "The Shechina" depicts human death as that act of *tikkun* that opens the gates of heaven and reunites God with the Shechina. Rosenzweig concludes *The Shechina,* moreover, with a direct reference to the sacrificial death with which Ehrenberg's *Half-Hundred Day* ends. Rosenzweig writes: "Time drove a tear into that which is relieved of time. / *You great eternal God may live again.* / Glowing, goes the new span [of] eternity."[72]

We thus possess in "The Shechina" Rosenzweig's attempt to explore the very same idea of "dying for God" that Ehrenberg explored in his *Half Hundred Day*—even making use of Hermann's last dying words!—by testing out this idea within a Kabbalistic framework. Rosenzweig draws on the Kabbalistic view that although the world is far removed from the divine, action in the world can nevertheless impact the divine. Indeed, human action can even serve to redeem divinity. But in Rosenzweig's version, that action in the world that redeems divinity is death. Only the negation of one's worldly existence heals the "tear" that "time drove into that which is relieved of time." Just as Ehrenberg's Hermann concluded, so too Rosenzweig implies that it is only through human death that the "great eternal God may live again."[73]

Let us turn finally to the last of the three texts from 1910–1911 that share an extreme version of the world-denying theology Rosenzweig would later identify with the name of "Marcion." If my estimation is correct, this last text is in fact the first of the three to be written: the "letter to Rudi of September 1910," a copy of which Rosenzweig later reports having shown to Margrit Rosenstock. In the Rosenzweig *Nachlass* held at the library of the University of Kassel,[74] there is an undated letter to Rudolf Ehrenberg in Rosenzweig's handwriting, whose content suggests it be dated, conservatively, between the fall of 1910 and the summer of 1911. The letter shows Rosenzweig deeply immersed in his work on Hegel's early development, citing ideas from *Hegel und der Staat* that Rosenzweig put to paper in July 1911. But it also shares ideas and turns of phrase with the previously cited diary entry that Rosenzweig copied over and included in his September 26, 1910 letter to Hans Ehrenberg—themes such as the relationship between God and history, and human freedom and sin. The undated letter in the *Nachlass* is evidently a copy: it is written in exceptionally clear handwriting that fits evenly on each page, with hardly a word crossed out or replaced. When one notes that there is no letter to Rudolf Ehrenberg from September 1910 in the published *Briefe und Tagebücher*—nor is there one that is extant, if I'm not mistaken, in any of the collections of Rosenzweig's unpublished papers—it becomes probable that the undated letter in question is the very "letter to Rudi from September, 1910" that Rosenzweig saw fit to copy over and to preserve. But the primary reason to suspect that this undated letter is the letter to R. Ehrenberg from September 1910 is that it does indeed share much thematic content with Ehrenberg's *Halbhunderttag* and Rosenzweig's "Shechina," just as Rosenzweig's letter to Margrit Rosenstock of June 1919 would lead us to expect. The letter concludes, moreover, by introducing the very same notion of human dying for God peculiar to these texts we've explored. The letter in question is a marvelous text, worthy of a far-more detailed study than I can provide here.[75] I will limit myself first to a brief overview of the movement of the letter, and then will offer a focused analysis of the letter's conclusion.

In the opening of the letter, Rosenzweig records how the young Hegel has appeared before him in order to communicate a message to his cousin. This message—which spans the whole of the letter—takes the form of a narrative history of divinity from the Enlightenment to Rosenzweig's and Ehrenberg's own time. The God of the Enlightenment, the young Hegel has Rosenzweig report, had indeed been the One most perfect being, but this God's perfection had everything to do with God's remoteness from the world itself. The Enlightenment God was "enthroned in perfection in infinite distance from the world."[76] So distant was the Enlightenment God from the world, in fact, that it became clear even to God Himself that "the world is sufficient to itself." Unable to connect to the "things" of the world, unable to influence the world through human will, this Enlightenment God "died in exile."

As Hegel's report proceeds to tell, however, God underwent a resurrection in Hegel's own time, now as "God in history."[77] Unlike the distant God of the Enlightenment, the God of history could only realize its own infinite nature by consuming all finitude: every individual act and every individual actor, no matter how sinful, fed the historical process, and hence fed the divinity of history's God. But before such a God, no individual act or actor was permitted to stand on its own feet: "You [i.e., the God of history] simply laugh at the will of the one who wills and at the act of the actor; everything finite tumbles ultimately into Your light."[78]

It is in the midst of Hegel's account of the God of history that we meet perhaps the most significant character in the narrative: Empedocles. This philosopher of ancient Greece had been a fascination of Hegel's "poor friend" Hölderlin, because of the way his experience of his own divinity stood in tension with his time. Hölderlin set out, in numerous drafts, to retell the drama of the death of Empedocles. After having been universally cherished by his people as a teacher and visionary, Empedocles comes to view, and even to declare, himself a god. He is consequently banished as one who has blasphemed the gods of the city. Resolving to fuse his own selfhood with the immortal divinity of nature, Empedocles climbs Mt. Etna and takes his life by diving into the mouth of the volcano.

For Hölderlin and his companions, Empedocles represented the infinity of the individual self in tension with the conventions of his world, and this is precisely how Rosenzweig's Hegel presents him in the letter. Hölderlin's Empedocles was "the worst enemy of this God" of history, because he "dared to light the great flame without therein becoming wasted." That is to say, he dared experience and realize divinity, without at once sacrificing his individuality to the course of world history.[79] Rosenzweig's Hegel has God punish Empedocles with loneliness: "Happier not to be an Empedocles. Not only to have to lament the loneliness of one's own life, before the leap into the Etna of All-life became need and act for him. Not to lose oneself indulgently in the feeling of one's own infinity, when God could only take up finitudes as sacrifices."[80] We will return to the figure of Empedocles when we arrive at the end of Rosenzweig's letter.

Just as in the case of the God of the Enlightenment, the very strength of the God of history turns out to betray His weakness. For a God whose fire burns solely from the sacrifices of the finite is ultimately dependent on the very finite actors whom He mocks, "quintessentially dependent on all his quintessential dependents."[81] Thus, according to the narrative Hegel asks Rosenzweig to deliver, the God of history ceased to believe in His own divinity. He "forgot Himself, after he already had lost faith in Himself. So that in the end perhaps no one was less surprised than God Himself when suddenly a voice roused to shrillness called: God is dead."[82]

As Hegel would have Rosenzweig report it, Nietzsche does indeed kill the God of history, but only because he seeks a God he can truly believe in. After the death of God, however, Nietzsche finds no one in whom he can believe, "because all around him lay destroyed nothing but dependencies, since he had shorn away the nail on which they once had hung."[83] It thus awaits the vision of an unnamed "poet" who appears on the scene after Nietzsche—a veiled reference to Rilke—to witness the enlivening and deification of all the particular things of the world through the lifeblood of the dead God.[84] Each of the myriad things of the world now holds up its own divinity. But each at once questions the divinity of others.

It is with this description of an age of myriad weak divinities, of competing individual claims to truth and goodness, that Rosenzweig's Hegel arrives at the relativism of Rosenzweig's own time. In such an age of relativism, Rosenzweig's Hegel declares, even the gods long for true divinity: "You screamed all together, 'Ah, where is the God of our Gods?' But no answer came to you. And where [could the answer have come] from too? Was not all of God divided in yourselves with nothing left over? But you longed for a remainder—a future for all presents. . . . For all believed Gods, there was lacking the pure God of faith."[85]

We thereby arrive at the concluding paragraph of the narrative Rosenzweig's Hegel delivered to Rudolf Ehrenberg. An age of relativism, of competing divinities, longs for the "pure God of faith" beyond "all believed Gods." In order to depict for his reader the path that will lead toward the revival of the true God, Rosenzweig's Hegel revisits the self-sacrifice of Empedocles:

> Once, when I was young, Empedocles died because he didn't believe in himself, but rather in God. He died for himself; dying, he generated himself. He however who dies for God today, to confirm through the murder of the father the faith in the son, through the negation of the believed God the God of faith; dying thus in faith in himself and in the un-belief in God—dying he will give birth to the un-believed God.[86]

These closing words of the message "the young Hegel bid me [i.e., Rosenzweig] to pass along to" Ehrenberg, are opaque and allusive, but I will try to decode them here. Empedocles dove into Mt. Etna in order to reunite with the divinity of nature, as a way of reconciling himself to nature after having had the hubris to declare himself a god. Rosenzweig's Hegel seems to imply that Empedocles had failed to realize that the divinity he experienced in his own selfhood was indeed *his own self*—a selfhood he denied when he performed the ultimate act of submission to the God of nature: self-sacrifice. Rosenzweig's Hegel appears to believe that in performing this very act of self-sacrifice, however, Empedocles "generated himself": precisely by ending his life in an act of self-sacrifice—and not, say, returning to abide by the mores of the community—he preserved himself for posterity as a model of individual selfhood.

Rosenzweig's Hegel now appears to suggest that Rosenzweig's own time calls for a repeat of Empedocles' self-sacrifice for God. But dying for God in Rosenzweig's time would possess a different meaning and different consequences than it did in the time of Empedocles. Rosenzweig articulates these differences in three ways, which I want to consider here in reverse order to that in which they appear. If Empedocles died believing in God, but not in himself, and if his death resulted in the generation of his own selfhood, Rosenzweig suggests, one who dies for God in his own time comes to this act with the complete opposite set of beliefs and doubts. In Rosenzweig's time, when each believes in his own personal god, but at once longs for a God who is beyond the myriad particular gods believed-in respectively by particular individuals, the one who dies for God does so with "faith in himself and . . . un-belief in God," that is to say, with faith in his own personal God but lacking belief—and hence longing for belief—in a God that transcends the relative divinities. Such a human death in Rosenzweig's time, the young Hegel suggests, will generate "the un-believed God"; that is, it will indeed generate this God beyond the worldly realm in which lesser, competing particular deities reign.

Rosenzweig's Hegel appears to formulate this same idea in two further ways: the one who dies "confirms . . . through the negation of the believed God the God of faith." In sacrificing himself, the one who dies negates his own "believed" relative divinity, and thereby confirms that transcendent "God of faith" that can once again be believed in by all. The suggestion of the young Hegel, finally, that the one who dies "confirms through the murder of the father the faith in the son," is most obscure. But in the light of Rosenzweig's later reflections on his pre-1913 Marcionist distinction between the world and revelation, the phrase invites the following interpretation: in negating his own worldly existence, the one who dies kills the God of creation ("the father") in order to affirm that faith relation to the divine symbolized by revelation in Christ ("the son").

Thus in the call to action that ends the letter's history of God's relation to humanity in the world, Empedocles represents both a model and a foil. He is a model for the lonely individual whose experience of his own infinite selfhood stands both in tension with worldly conventions and in intimate relation to the divine. He is, moreover, a model for a relation to divinity—both within and beyond the self—that demands the negation of one's worldly existence. But in multiple ways, the figure of Empedocles also serves as a foil for the kind of dying for God the letter suggests is called for in Rosenzweig's own time. Dying for God in Rosenzweig's time amounts less to a submission to God that immortalizes the self than it does to the reviving of or even the generation of true divinity beyond the world through the self-negation of the world.

The story of divinity that the young Hegel requests Rosenzweig communicate to his cousin thus stretches from the distant, perfect God of the Enlightenment, through the immanent God of History of the nineteenth century, to the relativistic gods of the early twentieth century. The letter's author makes it clear that it is human sacrifice alone which will produce the next epoch in the divine drama.

Let us now take account of the advance we have made through the evidence. We have examined three texts that offer dramatic evidence that in the years prior to the 1913 crisis, Rosenzweig was indeed testing out a theology of world denial that he would later describe as his early "Marcionism," a position "from which none other than [Eugen] freed" him. The texts share the view that this world denial is of *historical* necessity. Each appears to hold out the possibility that the day will come when the soul will be able to realize the fulfillment she attains in her relation to the divine without denying the world. But for so long as the masses fail to differentiate between God and God's prophet; for so long as the Shechina is unable to return through the gates of Heaven; for so long as contemporaries long for a transcendent God beyond the relative divinities of their age—the faithful must negate their worldly existence in order to realize their relation to God.

It is the extremity of the expression of world denial shared by these texts that is most peculiar to them. Our examinations of Rosenzweig's later reflections on his early Marcionism, of Ehrenberg's mockery of Rosenzweig's "taking from faith but not of love," and of Rosenzweig's early world-skepticism, certainly make it evident that Rosenzweig long questioned the possibility of reconciling the soul beloved of God in revelation with the world and all the troubles in it. But Ehrenberg's *Halbhunderttag*, Rosenzweig's "Shechina," and Rosenzweig's "Young Hegel" letter all take this opposition to a startling theological extreme. For all three not only articulate the view that the soul can preserve her selfhood and the purity of her relation to God through death alone, but they share the notion that it is first and foremost God who requires human sacrifice. The view of the human being's death here shares something in common with the traditional view of the death of the martyr, whose murder at the hands of worldly authorities allows him to realize his love for the divine. But unlike the case of the martyr's death, the emphasis here is not on the dying one's realization of love, but rather on what is accomplished for the divine through this act.[87] Likewise, the view of human death in these texts shares something in common with accounts of salvific death, and that of Jesus most explicitly. But the critical difference here is that we are not dealing with a sacrificial death that expiates the world for its sins, but rather with one that secures divine being.

The views of these texts are so extreme, it seems to me, that they exceed the bounds of the world denial Rosenzweig would likely have identified with Marcion himself. Because in the years after the *Leipziger Nachtgespräch* Rosenzweig found the tag of "Marcionism" to be most apt to describe his earlier theological position, I have expressed reservations over how seriously Rosenzweig took the extreme position of dying for God. I have suggested that he utilized this position as a limit case, as the logical but extreme consequence of his world skepticism, in order test out for himself how seriously committed he was to a theology of world denial. But my hunch may be too conservative here—especially given the fact that when Rosenzweig did consider suicide in the wake of the *Leipziger Nachtgespräch,* his considerations recall the very linking of human death and world denial that he articulated in 1910–1911.

—∾—

I have presented a diverse range of evidence in this chapter in order to show that the Rosenzweig who entered the 1913 *Leipziger Nachtgespräch* could not possibly have advocated "a belief in autonomous scholarship and the relativist position of philosophy"[88] as has so often been claimed in the scholarship. Rosenzweig's own later reflections, and Rudolf Ehrenberg's caricature of Rosenzweig the "heretic," together point to Rosenzweig's commitment, prior to 1913, to realizing the soul's faith-relationship to the divine at the expense of the world, a commitment Rosenzweig identified with Marcionism. The diary entries of Rosenzweig's university years suggest that this view of the tension between the soul and the world is rooted in skeptical questions about the world, which Rosenzweig asked himself as early as 1906. Newly discovered texts written by Rosenzweig and Ehrenberg suggest that Rosenzweig explored a world-denying theology in 1910–1911 that was so extreme that it called for the human being's negation of his worldly existence as a means to securing both the individual soul's relation to God and divine being itself.

The evidence is thus overwhelmingly consistent in depicting the Rosenzweig who entered the *Leipziger Nachtgespräch* not as an intellectual in search of faith, but rather as one already committed to faith in the extreme, yet troubled by the question of the moral and spiritual status of the world. The Rosenzweig that the evidence unanimously presents is a Rosenzweig for whom the central questions of Selma Lagerlöf's *Antikrists mirakler* would have resonated loudly.

If Rosenzweig entered the *Leipziger Nachtgespräch* already advocating a faith standpoint, then the standard account claiming that he was converted to a position of faith through his encounter with Rosenstock must be revised. The *Leipziger Nachtgespräch* could not have led Rosenzweig, as Rosenstock later claimed, "to confess as radically as Eugen had to a faith in the revealed, living God," because he already would have endorsed such a confession—perhaps more radically than Eugen himself!—before the all-night conversation. But if Rosenzweig did not undergo a conversion to faith on the night of July 7, 1913, then what kind of conversion did he undergo? In what manner was Rosenzweig transformed through his conversation with Rosenstock and Ehrenberg? What position did he come to advocate as a result of the night-conversation? Why, finally, did the conversation trigger the personal and intellectual crisis that it did for Rosenzweig?

The following chapter will address these questions, taking its lead from a particularly illuminating parallel Rosenzweig draws between the transformation he underwent on the night of July 7, 1913, and in the months that followed it, and what he understands to be the decisive personal and intellectual transformation which Hegel underwent during his years in Frankfurt, 1797–1800. By way of transition, however, I close this chapter by exploring the relationship between Marcionism and the position that scholars have up until now attributed to the Rosenzweig of 1913, namely, relativism.

MARCIONISM AND RELATIVISM

The notion that Rosenzweig upheld a Marcionist standpoint prior to the *Leipziger Nachtgespräch* may well be disorienting for scholars, and I concede that this is not merely because such a view opposes the account of Rosenzweig's standpoint that has dominated the literature. More basically, the evidence we have garnered in support of Rosenzweig's claims about his own early Marcionism appears to contradict Rosenzweig's own earliest and most famous reflection on that Leipzig night-conversation, his October 31, 1913 letter to Rudolf Ehrenberg, in which he reviews the events of the night of July 7, 1913, on the way to explaining his decision to remain a Jew. Here Rosenzweig describes how, over the course of the night-conversation, "Rosenstock forced me step by step out of the last relativistic positions which I still held," and how after that conversation "every relativism of *Weltanschauung* is now forbidden for me."[89] It is precisely this report of Rosenzweig's to Ehrenberg that has led scholars to claim that during his exchange with Rosenstock, Rosenzweig "defended the relativism sponsored by the regnant philosophical and historical perspectives, while Rosenstock affirmed the absolute grounding of human existence provided by religious faith";[90] or that "at the close of [the] night of discussion . . . Rosenstock . . . succeeded in refuting Rosenzweig's relativistic world view by using not so much rational arguments but rather the testimony of his own lived faith."[91] And indeed, if Rosenzweig's own account of his relativistic standpoint were not evidence enough for these scholarly views, Rosenzweig's partner in conversation, Rosenstock, confirms it in his own reflections on 1913, when he likewise claims that "Franz, a student of philosophy and history for eight years by that time, defended the prevailing philosophical relativism of the day, whereas Eugen bore witness to prayer and worship as his prime guides to action."[92]

Such apparently straightforward descriptions of Rosenzweig's 1913 relativism must now be juxtaposed to his self-proclaimed Marcionism. This juxtaposition is in fact demanded not only by the array of evidence for Rosenzweig's Marcionism we've examined over the course of this chapter. In the very lines that follow Rosenzweig's account of his own "relativism of *Weltanschauung*" in his October 31, 1913 letter to Rudolf Ehrenberg, he likewise identifies his position in the following dualistic terms: "Had I been able at that time to bolster my dualism of revelation and world with a metaphysical dualism of God and devil, so I would have been unassailable."[93]

How, then, are we to reconcile Rosenzweig's claims that he was a relativist heading into the *Leipziger Nachtgespräch* with his claims—supported by considerable evidence—to have been a Marcionist? Can anyone be a historical relativist claiming that every world-historical epoch reveals its own truth, and at once hold that truth is found *nowhere* in the world, but only in a relation to the divine that wholly transcends the world and its history?

The review we have conducted through the development of Rosenzweig's thinking from 1906 to 1911 permits us to offer answers to these questions. Although there is no doubt that during the Baden-Baden exercise Rosenzweig was inclined to accept a form of historical relativism, the evidence certainly suggests that in the wake of the failure of Baden-Baden, Rosenzweig abandoned this position in favor of a world-denying theology that depicted the world and its history as "sinful." More importantly, however, our survey of the development of Rosenzweig's thinking from 1906 to 1911 suggests that the root problem with which Rosenzweig struggled throughout this period—and the impetus for his temporary embrace of historicism—remained constant: the tension he discerned between the realization of selfhood, on the one hand, and the realities of the "objective" world, on the other. As we have seen, moreover, Rosenzweig was inclined to respond to this tension between self and world, between subjectivity and objectivity, if not exclusively, then predominantly through different forms of philosophical and theological subjectivism. Recall that in his 1906 diary entries Rosenzweig presents subjectivism—the view that the subject alone could serve as "center" of his own life once trust in objective values had been lost—as the most reasonable response to "classical skepticism," even though he had to concede that without a "belief" in the very "objective truth" that the subject came to displace, there was no standard according to which one subjective position could be measured against another. In other words, Rosenzweig understood subjectivism, while secure against mild skepticism, nevertheless to be a relativistic position. One might well argue, furthermore, that in the years after 1910 when he entertained theological notions of world denial, both his romantic notions of the lonely soul's isolation with God at the moment of death, and his "taking of faith but not of love" amounted to a theological subjectivism that likewise presented the possibility of a relation to God to be independent of "objective," worldly conditions.

Now, a philosophy of the subjective standpoint is quite compatible with Marcionism. Indeed, Rosenzweig arrived at subjectivism in his 1906 reflections precisely as the consequence of considerations of world skepticism! If the Marcionist denies the world and experiences salvation only through a personal faith relation to the God who is wholly transcendent to the world, the subjectivist philosopher likewise denies any objective, worldly standard outside himself; orients himself solely according to his own subjective "center"; and holds truth to be relative to every subjectivity.

Rosenzweig's early reflections on the problematic relation between self and world suggest that if Rosenzweig indeed entered the *Leipziger Nachtgespräch* endorsing a certain form of relativism, this relativism was most probably not the historicist position of his Baden-Baden episode, but rather the subjectivist position that he had explored already in 1906.[94] In July 1913, he appears to have advocated a kind of subjectivism in both matters of faith and in matters of philosophy. The view of revelation as entailing a personal relation to the divine that elevates the individual soul beyond the world, and the view of truth as determined relative to the point of view of the individual subject, were united for Rosenzweig in an emphasis on *personal* truth and salvation at the expense of the objective and the worldly. It was this form of relativism that would have found continued support were Rosenzweig able to "bolster my dualism of revelation and world with a metaphysical dualism of God and devil."

This understanding of Rosenzweig's "relativism" finds support, finally, in his specific claim that it was "relativism *of Weltanschauung*" that he could no longer uphold after the 1913 conversation. In *The Star of Redemption,* Rosenzweig uses the terms *Weltanschauung-philosophy* and *standpoint-philosophy* virtually interchangeably, to designate that contemporary form of philosophy whose grounding in the personal standpoint of the philosopher amounts to a relativism that possesses dubious scientific status. Thus Rosenzweig asked regarding such a position, in the introduction to the second part of the *Star,* "Is this view of things, each for itself, and each one in numerous relations, seen now from this standpoint, now from that, this view whose unity lies at most in the unity of the viewer—and how questionable is this [unity] already!—still science?"[95]

2

Christian "World-Activity" and the Historical Reconciliation of Soul and World

Rosenzweig's (Near-)Conversion

HEGEL AND HYPOCHONDRIA

On February 6, 1917, Rosenzweig writes to his parents from the war front, musing over the "strange parallels to Hegel" he has "experienced in [his] life." He proceeds to explain that "1913 and 1797 is the most peculiar," "'the 27th-year of life,' insofar as Hegel made a theory . . . precisely out of this 'year of life.' Compare the beginning of 'Jena I'. I myself am thus an example for it."[1]

Rosenzweig's comments suggest that he understood the crucial transformation he underwent during the summer of 1913, in the midst of the twenty-seventh year of his life, to mirror a parallel transformation that Hegel underwent in 1797, in the midst of his own twenty-seventh year. In *Hegel und der Staat,* Rosenzweig had in fact described the period in which Hegel lived in Frankfurt, between 1797 and 1800, and which immediately preceded his move to Jena, as the "decisive moment" of Hegel's personal and intellectual development, and he claimed that it was "out of the overcoming" of the struggles of these years that Hegel "goes forth completely ripe as a human being."[2] If we seek to understand the nature of Rosenzweig's own transformation during the *Leipziger Nachtgespräch* and its aftermath, it behooves us to attend to Rosenzweig's account of the transformation Hegel underwent beginning in 1797. As he suggested to his parents in February 1917, Rosenzweig understood his own 1913 transformation to be exemplary of the theory Hegel himself had offered regarding the significance of a person's twenty-seventh year.

Rosenzweig recounts Hegel's personal transformation in his chapter on "Frankfurt" in the first part of *Hegel und der Staat,* and he recounts Hegel's analysis of the transformation the human being undergoes in his twenty-seventh year, immediately following this chapter, in the opening to the first of two chapters on "Jena." In the beginning of this first chapter on "Jena"—the "beginning of 'Jena I'" to which Rosenzweig refers his parents in his February 1917 letter—Rosenzweig draws on later comments Hegel makes describing the "hypochondria" that a human being is liable to undergo at this time in life. This "hypochondria"—a term that in Hegel's day designated a general melancholy or anxiety[3]—marks "the transition out of youth into manhood," a transition, according to Hegel, in which "the completed development of subjective individuality recoils against its dissolution [*Aufgehen*] into universality and objectivity, more a holding-in-oneself and abiding in empty subjectivity. . . . This hypochondria falls mostly in the 27th year of life."[4] In presenting Hegel's "theory," Rosenzweig stresses the personal roots of this broad claim about twenty-seven-year-old depressives. He thus cites a letter from 1810 in which Hegel writes of his own experience of such melancholy: "I suffered from this hypochondria for a pair of years to the point of debility. Every human being well has such a turning-point in life, the nightly point of the contraction of his being [*Wesen*], through whose narrowness he is pressed, and is fortified and made certain as to the security of his self, and the security of his usual everyday life."[5]

After our investigation of Rosenzweig's struggle with Marcionism and of the origins of that struggle in his perplexity over the relation between self and world, the account Hegel gives of "hypochondria" is patently familiar. According to Hegel, this anxious depression is to be understood as symptomatic of the struggle a human being goes through—typically in his twenty-seventh year—as he holds onto his "subjective individuality" over against the "universality and objectivity" of the world surrounding him. Before integrating his own unique selfhood into the world, Hegel suggests, the human being undergoes a period of resistance to such integration, seeking to protect his subjectivity out of the fear of its dissolution within the objective. This very struggle, Hegel claims, marks the "turning point in life" for the human being, the "transition from youth to adulthood." It is through the process of this struggle, Hegel suggests, that the human being becomes secure in his own selfhood even as he situates his self in the "everyday life" of the world.

Much of the chapter on Hegel's "Frankfurt" period in *Hegel und der Staat* is devoted to tracing the struggle between subjectivity and objectivity which

Hegel himself endured, in the wake of his twenty-seventh year, and to explaining its subsequent resolution. At the beginning of his Frankfurt period, according to Rosenzweig, "Hegel's personality is . . . glaringly closed off against the world," and his conception of the human being cannot accommodate any sense of a "life unity of man and world."[6] He has "climbed" to the standpoint of "'the highest subjectivity,'" but thereby experiences the world as imposing a fate upon him whose force and necessity are alien to him. According to Rosenzweig, this split between self and world that the young Hegel experiences expresses itself, moreover, in the political and theological writings of these years. Rosenzweig here cites drafts of what would later be called "The Spirit of Christianity and Its Fate," begun in 1798, in which Hegel describes the "relation of Jesus to the world" as "in part flight, in part reaction, fight against the same [i.e., the world]. So long as Jesus did not change the world he had to flee it. . . . Thus to this extent, the existence of Jesus was separation from the world and flight from it into heaven."[7]

It is noteworthy that the Jesus of "The Spirit of Christianity and Its Fate" is depicted neither as an ethical role model nor as a mediator between heaven and earth, but rather as a model of the flight from the world through which alone the individual may preserve the purity of his subjectivity. Within the context of Hegel's intellectual biography, Rosenzweig suggests, this is no accident. Hegel's Jesus reflects the very "highest subjectivity" that Hegel himself experienced during this period, and Hegel's account of Jesus' struggle with the world reflects his own first-hand insights into the nature of the struggle between self and world. It is because he himself experienced the world as alien to his own selfhood, Rosenzweig suggests, that Hegel insisted that "the Kingdom of God is not of this world" but rather "this world is actually present in opposition to it"; it is because he himself experienced the world as limiting his own freedom that Hegel declared "the fate of Jesus" to be "a loss of freedom, a restriction of life, a passivity in being ruled through a foreign power," such that Jesus "could find freedom only in the void [*Leere*]."[8]

Now, whether or not one accepts Rosenzweig's claim that the Christ of Hegel's "The Spirit of Christianity and Its Fate" embodies the struggle of subjectivity against the world which Hegel himself experienced, one should recognize at once how the Christ Hegel presents in the essay—a Christ who dies not to save to world but in order to "flee it"—must have resonated for Rosenzweig himself. Rosenzweig wrote the "Frankfurt" chapter of *Hegel und der Staat* in July 1911, months after he sent the "Young Hegel's" reflections on Hölderlin's Empedocles to Rudolf Ehrenberg, and in the very same month during which he was composing drafts of his "Shechina" and reading and commenting upon the character of Hermann in Ehrenberg's *Halbhunderttag.* Dying to the world was on his mind. At the same time, however, although Rosenzweig would later identify his own 1913 crisis and resolution with Hegel's of 1797, Rosenzweig had not yet found in 1911 a resolution to his own crisis comparable to that of Hegel. He still found himself burdened by a hypochondriacal separation from the world. It is thus fitting that in his letter of September 28, 1911 to Gertrud Oppenheim, in which he reports on having written the "Frankfurt" chapter in the preceding July, Rosenzweig suggests that the completion of the transformative process that Hegel attained still remains beyond his own personal experience: "It is the part of the book which you must read once . . . , the history of the becoming-finished of a man. I have not been able to write it out of subjective experience, because I do not yet believe to have gotten so far. If it is good, so it is 'Anticipation' in the sense in which it is the subject of *Dichtung und Wahrheit.*"[9]

When Rosenzweig later asserts that "1913 and 1797" mark a "most peculiar" parallel between a decisive moment in Hegel's life and a decisive moment in his own, there can be little doubt that he means to point to the way the conflict Hegel endured and overcame between his selfhood and the surrounding world prefigured Rosenzweig's own bout with Marcionism and its overcoming. This parallel Rosenzweig draws confirms the conclusion we reached in the last chapter that it is indeed this very struggle between self and world that stands at the heart of the *Leipziger Nachtgespräch.* But this parallel also suggests that viewing Rosenzweig as an exemplar for Hegel's theory of the twenty-seven-year-old hypochondriac should help indicate for us something about both the character of the transformation that Rosenzweig underwent over the course of the night-conversation, and the new view of self and world that he came to adopt in its wake.

As exemplary of Hegel's theory, Rosenzweig would understand his own experiences in 1913 as the "turning point in life," as the "transition from youth to adulthood," as parallel to the "decisive moment" out of which Hegel emerged "ripe as a human being." The first step in understanding the nature of the "conversion" Rosenzweig underwent on the night of July 7, 1913, I submit, is grasping this way in which Rosenzweig—following Hegel—understood the struggle of the self with the world *in itself* to be transformative in the decisive sense. Hegel's account of the twenty-seventh year suggests, that is, that there is no greater conversion that the human being undergoes than that which occurs in the struggle between one's subjectivity and the objectivity of the world. Hegel's comments suggest, moreover, two key aspects of the transformation the human being undergoes here that are to be essential to Rosenzweig's view of his own transformation. In the self's struggle with the world, in the "nightly point of the contraction of his being through whose narrowness he is pressed," Hegel suggests, the self secures itself as individual self. But at the same time, the self is reconciled to "everyday life" in the world. A reconciliation of self and world is achieved in which selfhood is not sacrificed, in which subjectivity is not dissolved into the objectivity of the world.[10]

How does Hegel attain such a reconciliation between self and world that does not reduce one to the other or dissolve one within the other? According to Rosenzweig, the answer to this question does much to illuminate the vital link between Hegel's personal development and the fundamental principle of his mature thought. The Gnostic implications of Hegel's early Christ notwithstanding, Hegel earned his place of prominence in the history of philosophy precisely by developing a dialectical method that allowed him to grasp the oppositions of nature and freedom, of life and thought, within a single systematic unity. According to Rosenzweig, Hegel's own transition from the dualism of subject and object to the dialectical monism of Spirit in his mature work can be traced back to just this moment, at the end of his Frankfurt period, when Hegel began to conceive of a *historical* reconciliation of self and world. It is *history,* according to Rosenzweig, that enters Hegel's thinking in the late texts of the Frankfurt period. "Here there grows out of wholly personal perils and doubts, the new philosophical evaluation of history," Rosenzweig writes. "The history which Hegel attained in this moment has the ethical, indeed even the religious meaning which it possessed for Hegel his whole life. It is the great basin in which man is washed clean from all guilt, it is the stream in which at once duty and bliss"—that is, the autonomy of the self and the happiness of life in the world—"are to merge for the individual."[11]

The new conception of history that Hegel adopted as he left Frankfurt and moved on to Jena, Rosenzweig suggests, allowed him to conceive of selfhood no longer as standing in fundamental tension with the world, but rather as a moment—independent and free in itself—in the historical realization of freedom in the world. This new conception of history enabled Hegel to overcome his personal struggle between subjectivity and objectivity, and to throw off his "hypochondria." It allowed him to integrate his selfhood into the world without dissolving it therein. Far more importantly for the history of philosophy, moreover, Rosenzweig sees Hegel's reconciliation of self and world within this new conception of history as clearing the decisive path to Hegel's mature thought. It lies at the ground of Hegel's insight that the contradiction between what appear to be diametrically opposed concepts can be overcome if one grasps such concepts as moments within a higher concept that transcends and at once maintains both. And it is the key to making sense of the most famous of Hegel's later dicta, to wit, that "what is rational is actual and what is actual is rational." Hegel is only able to assert the actuality of the rational and the rationality of the actual, according to Rosenzweig, because he "inserts time . . . into that double-equation." The actuality of the rational

> has not counted everywhere and for all eternity, but rather since it became an ethical demand and the standard for all human establishments through Christianity, in the idea of the Kingdom of God on earth. Since then, however, it counts for actual, and because the task is set for action to work-out reason in the world, so the task stands—since then!—before knowing, to investigate the actuality that has become since then, as reason has worked itself out in it. Only because the rational has become actual—principle of act—only for this reason now—principle of knowing—the actual is rational.[12]

Rosenzweig suggests here that Hegel only sets for himself the task of *knowing* the rationality of the actual, in his mature thought, because he grasps the working out of "reason in the world" as the "ethical demand" that has come to guide the action of free selves in the world through history. Reason has become actualized through historical action in the world, and only as a consequence can the actual now be known as rational.

Hegel's personal struggle to hold on to his "highest subjectivity" over against the objectivity of the world may thus have yielded an account of freedom as possible only in "flight from the world," and an account of the Kingdom of God as "not of this world." But in overcoming that struggle through a conception of history as that which reconciles self and world, Hegel comes to conceive of freedom precisely as demanding worldly actualization, and comes to conceive of this historical actualization as rooted in the Christian "idea of the Kingdom of God on earth."

Having traced Rosenzweig's understanding of Hegel's resolution to his personal struggle between self and world, I would like now to return to the parallel Rosenzweig draws between the decisive moment in Hegel's life and the decisive moment in Rosenzweig's own. The parallel suggests, I have claimed, that the "conversion" Rosenzweig underwent in 1913 was a conversion *to* the world, rather than the taking on of a new selfhood transcending that world. After Rosenzweig had courted Marcionism in the process of securing his selfhood in solitude with God, the *Leipziger Nachtgespräch* should have shown him the path toward reconciliation with the world. Moreover, if Rosenzweig understood Hegel to have attained a resolution to the struggle he experienced between self and world through a conception of history as the realization of the Kingdom of God on earth, then Rosenzweig would appear to direct us to view the resolution of his own struggles as similarly rooted in a kind of historical thinking. Only in coming to view revelation no longer as a means of saving the individual soul from the world, but rather as commanding the realization of the Kingdom of God in the world over the course of history—Rosenzweig's parallel to Hegel suggests—would Rosenzweig be able to overcome his Marcionist rejection of the world and reconcile his subjectivity with the objective, without at once sacrificing his selfhood in the process.

Given what we have learned about Rosenzweig's critique of history after Baden-Baden, it is indeed difficult to fathom how Rosenzweig could turn around and embrace history as the realization of the Kingdom of God. Had not Rosenzweig already rejected "history" as a solution to his perplexity over the relationship between self and world *before* he turned to the theological world denial he identified with Marcion? Had not Rosenzweig mocked both Hegel's "God in History" and the weak gods of historical relativism, in his "Young Hegel" letter to Rudolf Ehrenberg of September 1910? Had he not claimed, in a diary entry from the very same month, that all acts become "sinful" once they enter history?

It would be possible to view Rosenzweig's 1913 crisis and conversion as exemplary of Hegel's conception of "the becoming finished of a man," only if what transpired during the *Leipziger Nachtgespräch* could have led Rosenzweig to view the world not as opposed to the Kingdom of God but rather as the site in which the Kingdom of God is to be realized; and only if the conversation with Rosenstock and Ehrenberg could have led Rosenzweig to view history neither as a rational, self-judging process immanent to the world, nor as a sequence of equally valid expressions of relative human political and cultural truths, but rather as a single meaningful course toward redemption directed by the very same revelation through which the individual soul stands in relation to God.[13] The decisive conversion Rosenzweig would then have undergone during the *Leipziger Nachtgespräch* would not have been a conversion to faith, but rather a conversion back to the world, and perhaps thereby to a historical mode of thinking in which self and world, revelation and creation, could be reconciled.

Is there evidence for such a "conversion" in Rosenzweig's own account of the 1913 night-conversation? Let us now return to Rosenzweig's own statements about the *Leipziger Nachtgespräch* to find out.

CHRISTIAN WORLD-ACTIVITY

We begin by taking a closer look at the opening of Rosenzweig's famous letter to Rudolf Ehrenberg of October 31, 1913. After announcing his decision to remain a Jew, Rosenzweig recalls the events of the Leipzig night-conversation as follows:

> In the Leipzig night-conversation, where Rosenstock forced me step by step out of the last relativistic positions which I still held and forced me to an unrelativistic position, I was for that reason inferior to him from the start, because I had to affirm the right of this attack even from my position. Had I been able at that time to bolster my dualism of revelation and world with a metaphysical dualism of God and devil, so I would have been unassailable. But therein the first sentence of the Bible hindered me. This piece of common ground forced me to withstand him. It has remained even further in the following weeks the immoveable starting point. Every relativism of *Weltanschauung* is now forbidden for me.[14]

Our investigation of Rosenzweig's "Marcionism" in the last chapter makes it possible to clarify some important elements in Rosenzweig's account of the night-conversation in this letter. Rosenzweig's dual commitment to the salvation of the soul through an isolating faith-relation to the divine, and to the relative capacity of the subject to serve as its own life center, we have seen, lay the groundwork for a rejection of the world as a context in which truth or salvation are to be realized. It is this position, I have suggested, that he designates here as his "relativism of *Weltanschauung.*" Rosenzweig proceeds to tell Ehrenberg that he would have been able to defend his position against Rosenstock's attacks during their conversation, "had I been able to bolster my dualism of revelation and world with a metaphysical dualism of God and devil." What became clear to Rosenzweig over the course of his conversation with Rosenstock, this comment suggests, is that his conception of revelation as the path to the salvation of the soul and his concomitant denigration of the status of the world presupposed that the world did not share the soul's metaphysical grounding in a transcendent, beneficent God. Rosenzweig could only maintain such a position, his friends made him realize, were he indeed to subscribe to a quasi-Gnostic dualism in which the world is understood as the domain of the devil—or Marcion's creator God or Lagerlöf's Antichrist—and only the kingdom of heaven, attainable for the soul through a transcendence granted by revelation, the domain of God.

But despite his earlier flirtation with a theology of world denial, Rosenzweig shrank back from such a position on this summer night of 1913, and did so, according to his report, because of the first sentence of the Bible: "In the beginning, God created the heavens and the earth." The opening of the Bible, one may suggest, insists that God is the "common ground" of both heaven and earth, of both the "kingdom not of this world" and the "kingdom of this world alone." The monotheistic—and ultimately monistic—implications of the orthodox notion of creation rang sufficiently true to Rosenzweig at that moment, that he could not accept the metaphysical consequences of his dualism of revelation and world.[15]

The first thing Rosenzweig's October 1913 comments thereby tell us about the position to which Rosenzweig is converted during his Leipzig night-conversation is that this position entails his renewed commitment to the *world.* In his later reflections on the *Leipziger Nachtgespräch,* Rosenzweig in fact confirms this very suggestion. In 1916, we've noted, Rosenzweig writes, "What it means that God created the world and [is] *not just* the God of revelation—this I know precisely out of the Leipzig night-conversation of 7.7.13. At that time, I was on the best road to Marcionitism."[16] And in a letter to Friedrich Meinecke from August 30, 1920, in which he explains the change that he has undergone since 1913, Rosenzweig likewise writes, "I believe I stand in the world with more stability today than I did seven years ago."[17] During the early summer months of 1919, moreover, as Rosenzweig endured what he took to be the joint attempt of Rosenstock and Hans Ehrenberg to question the seriousness of his allegiance to Judaism, Rosenzweig reacts angrily to the suggestion that he has only truly been a Jew since his "rebirth" in 1913. "I am a Jew neither through nor since 1913, but rather actually, *insofar as* I am, totally from 1886 ff [i.e., since birth]. . . . 1913 increased this treasure not one penny," Rosenzweig writes. "What then did 1913 change? . . . My Judaism was *never* reborn. My worldliness was *re*born at that time, this is correct. I have been able to take the world seriously since then, because since then I took seriously the world activity of Christianity."[18]

I will address the consequences of the *Leipziger Nachtgespräch* for Rosenzweig's Judaism in chapter 3. Here I want to note how Rosenzweig's comments highlight the way that his "turn" on the night of July 7, 1913 involved a turn away from a quasi-Gnostic dualism and toward the world. In retreating from the world-denying consequences of his Marcionist position of faith, Rosenzweig has his own worldliness "reborn" and is "able to take the world seriously" again. He recognizes the world as created by the same God who reveals Himself to the individual soul. Moreover, Rosenzweig's comments at once confirm the clue we identified, in his account of the resolution to Hegel's own struggle over self and world, regarding the grounds for the new position Rosenzweig came to adopt upon abandoning Marcionism. Rosenzweig is able to take the world seriously, he writes, because he begins to take seriously "the world activity of Christianity."

Christianity acts in the world. Such a statement may appear obvious or unimportant. But for someone inclined to conceive of the individual's relation to the divine as transcending or even denying worldly action, the notion that the world be conceived as the context for Christian action amounts to a discovery of some significance. Such a discovery would demand, as Hegel's historical reconciliation of self and world in the realization of "the Kingdom of God on earth" suggests, that Rosenzweig too begin to conceive of the world not as opposed to the free act of the self, but rather as the context in which alone such free action is possible. That such a turn to a historical conception of the world demanded a change in Rosenzweig's thinking about Christianity itself can be seen, once again, in his letter to Rudolf Ehrenberg of October 31, 1913. Here Rosenzweig claims that before the night-conversation, "I had taken the year 313 for the beginning of the collapse of true Christianity, because—it opened for Christianity the opposite way through the world from that which the year 70 opened for Judaism."[19]

Before the *Leipziger Nachtgespräch,* Rosenzweig tells us here, he understood as "true Christianity" those early forms of Christianity that suffered world persecution, predating the Christian attainment of worldly political power under the rule of Constantine. That is to say, he understood Christianity to be anti-worldly in its origin. Such an understanding of "true Christianity" goes hand in hand, of course, with his early Marcionist view of the opposition between revelation and world. On this view, the moment Christianity becomes an actor in world history can only be understood as a "collapse" of the pure spirituality that Christianity maintained at its origin. While Judaism thereby left the world's political stage in the year 70, Rosenzweig had thus believed, Christianity entered into the world much to its own detriment. In a 1918 letter to Margrit Rosenstock, Rosenzweig identifies this view of Christianity once again as the view he maintained as he entered the Leipzig night-conversation. "Up until that Leipzig night . . . I let Christianity count only as 'persecuted Church' [*ecclesia pressa*]; . . . and the year 313, when it became a state-religion, counted as a fall. So I gave the true Church the look of the synagogue."[20]

The Leipzig night-conversation changed Rosenzweig's view of Christianity's relation to the world, however, and this change enabled him to reconsider his own denigration of the worldly. Moreover, Rosenzweig's account of the resolution Hegel attained to his own struggle over self and world allows us to venture a claim as to why Rosenzweig was receptive to such a re-conception of Christianity and, consequently, of the world: conceiving of Christianity as realizing its true task through "world activity," and thereby conceiving of the Kingdom of God not as divorced from the world but rather as the goal of activity in the world, enabled Rosenzweig to consider soul and world as reconcilable through this very historical course. On the one hand, the notion of realizing the Kingdom of God on earth takes seriously the opposition between soul and world; for the world must be utterly transformed through redemptive love in order for the Kingdom of God to be realized in it. But unlike Marcionism, this view of Christianity does not stop at the "antitheses" between soul and world, between mercy and stern justice, between the God of salvation and the God of creation. Rather, just as Hegel discovered, it makes it possible to conceive of the reconciliation of such antitheses through the dialectical advance of *history.*

I assert that the *Leipziger Nachtgespräch* led Rosenzweig to decide he must abandon his Judaism and convert to Christianity precisely because Rosenzweig became convinced, over the course of that night-conversation, that Christianity's world-historical mission of redemptive love offers a way of reconciling soul and world, and of thereby quelling the source of perplexity that had troubled him since his university years. Indeed, Rosenzweig tells us that as he "began to build up the world anew for myself from this knowledge" that Christianity had not ceased to be "true" after its entry into history, but to the contrary had only then begun to realize its world-historical task; "there appeared to be no place for Judaism in this world."[21]

If Christianity could be understood as reconciling soul and world through its world-historical realization of the Kingdom of God, if it offered Rosenzweig the same kind of resolution to his own personal struggles as it had to Hegel, the same could not be said for Judaism. For if Rosenzweig saw Judaism, as he implies, as having left the world stage in the year 70, Judaism did not offer the possibility of the same kind of dialectical resolution to the conflict between soul and world as did Christianity. Rosenzweig determined to convert to Christianity, I claim, not because it did not appear possible to him to experience a living faith within the Judaism of his day, but rather because Judaism, in his view, was not sufficiently *worldly* to enable the kind of reconciliation of faith and worldly life he sought. How Rosenzweig could nevertheless decide to return to Judaism given these reservations, we shall uncover in the following chapter. Once we understand the grounds for this return, moreover, we'll be in a position to say more about the structure of Rosenzweig's historical thinking, and the way he developed this historical thinking through an ongoing engagement with the questions raised by Gnosticism.

Rosenzweig's revaluation of the world, and of history as a process in which the self can be reconciled to the world, is in part rooted in the consequences he drew during the *Leipziger Nachtgespräch* from the first sentence of the Bible. But the dramatic change in his view of the relation between self and world in the wake of the *Nachtgespräch* also appears to have been rooted in something Rosenzweig experienced during the night of July 7, 1913. Rosenzweig did not experience *faith;* nor did what he experience lead him to reject the path of thinking. Rather, I will suggest, what Rosenzweig came to think over the course of the night-conversation, and what he experienced during it, came reciprocally to confirm each other in the process of his conversion. Rosenzweig never wavered, in later years, in identifying both his experience and his change in thinking over the course of and in the wake of the *Nachtgespräch,* with Eugen Rosenstock. It was Rosenstock who facilitated Rosenzweig's conversion from a commitment to a revelatory faith that denied the world to a commitment to Christianity's world-historical mission.

ROSENSTOCK AS FACILITATOR

Rosenzweig states with regularity that it was Eugen Rosenstock's presence at and participation in the *Leipziger Nachtgespräch* that made it the transformative event that it was for him. The conversion Rosenzweig underwent over the course of that night-conversation—from a Marcionism of world denial back to the world and Christianity's world-historical mission in it—was prompted by something Rosenstock said or did or represented for Rosenzweig. The myriad enigmatic references Rosenzweig later makes to his encounter with Rosenstock are, however, neither wholly clear nor wholly consistent in offering the details of his actions during the night of July 7, 1913. The task of reconstructing Rosenstock's critical role in the night-conversation for Rosenzweig is made more difficult, moreover, by the fact that Rosenstock had no idea that his words or actions had such an impact on Rosenzweig that night, until he was told so by Rosenzweig and Rudolf Ehrenberg well after the event itself. Indeed, as late as August 1917, Rosenzweig had to review for Rosenstock the details of their July 1913 conversation, because the latter still believed that the critical exchange between the two was a different conversation altogether, which occurred a few weeks afterwards(!).[22] Rosenstock's own most extensive report on the *Leipziger Nachtgespräch* appeared decades later, in 1969, long after Nahum Glatzer and others had made the story of the night-conversation famous, making Rosenstock's account of what transpired less than authoritative.

Once we accept the need for some speculation, however, the evidence at our disposal does permit us to wager on some credible possibilities for reconstructing Rosenstock's role. I will offer three such possibilities, each based both on Rosenzweig's own later reflections on Rosenstock's role during the conversation and on what can be gathered regarding Rosenstock's own personal and intellectual development during the period. I will first present the evidence suggesting that it was Rosenstock's early commitment to "the Word"—to interpersonal speech as the medium of redemptive love—that he conveyed to Rosenzweig over the course of the night-conversation. Rosenzweig's experience of Rosenstock's love for him through the conversation itself, on this account, led to the dramatic "reversal" in Rosenzweig's life from world denial to world redemption. This account of Rosenstock's role both best matches the direct evidence and best fits into the account of the transition from Marcionism to "Christian world-activity" that we have traced thus far. Questions and inconsistencies that nevertheless plague this account, however, will lead me to explore two other possible reconstructions of Rosenstock's facilitatory role. I will present the possibility that it was Rosenstock's very person, the way he combined within himself both commitment to God and commitment to the world, that modeled for Rosenzweig the possibility of such reconciliation. I will introduce evidence, finally, that by 1913 Rosenstock had already begun formulating what he would later refer to as his "calendrical thinking," and that this new mode of thinking lay at the root of Rosenzweig's change. In conclusion, I will suggest that any one of these possibilities—or any combination of them—can explain how Rosenstock facilitated Rosenzweig's conversion from Marcionism to a commitment to a Christian "world-activity" that would promise a redemptive reconciliation of self and world.

Let us begin by examining some clues Rosenzweig offers regarding the standpoint Rosenstock brought with him to the *Leipziger Nachtgespräch,* clues that appear in the letter to Rudolf Ehrenberg from July 9, 1917 which we explored earlier. In this letter, Rosenzweig suggests that Rosenstock's advantage over the Ehrenbergs and him is that Rosenstock never fell subject to the "problem" they shared—the problem of the tension between human and divine love. While concern over the threat that love of others poses to the soul's relation to the divine pushed Rosenzweig and Rudolf Ehrenberg, as we have seen, to entertain a radical denial of the world and to flirt with a "mystical solitude with the 'silent God,'" Rosenzweig explains,

> Rosenstock had mistrust toward the "silent God" from the beginning, because he has believed in the "Word" from the beginning. To want to *see* the divine "visage" is just

> paganism, however sublimated. "The voice alone you have heard." *Heard!* To want to see God is to consider Him "silent." The form would be visible even if no one were to see it, but the word is only spoken if there is someone to hear it.[23]

Rosenstock was not drawn to the kind of intimate, solitary vision of God that would take the individual soul out of the world, Rosenzweig suggests here, because of Rosenstock's commitment to "the Word" "from the beginning." The very words through which human beings express their love for each other, Rosenstock's commitment implies, are themselves of divine origin; they themselves are rooted in the primordial moment ("from the beginning") when, according to the Gospel of John, God was with "the Word." Rosenstock was unmoved by the problem with which Rosenzweig apparently still struggled entering the *Leipziger Nachtgespräch* because Rosenstock believed in "the Word" as that which mediated between the human being's love of God and love of others in the world. And Rosenstock's commitment to the "Word" implies that the individual soul is to find her saving relation to the divine not in an escape from the world, but through the very interpersonal relations of speech with others that build community within the world.

By the time Rosenzweig wrote this letter to Rudolf Ehrenberg in 1917, recalling the commitments Rosenstock brought to the *Leipziger Nachtgespräch,* he had already been introduced to the first fruits of what would be Rosenstock's life-long championing of speech and grammar as both a unique form of knowledge and a creative force of actuality. Rosenstock's 1915 "Die Sankt Georgs Reden" already found in the idea of "The word becomes flesh" the notion that speech brings together the spiritual and the worldly.[24] But Rosenstock's programmatic account of grammar came in a 1916 "Speech-Letter" to Rosenzweig that eventually formed the basis of his *Angewandte Seelenkunde* (*Applied Knowledge of the Soul*). At the center of this account of language, Rosenstock presents the relationship between the "You" and the "I" as constitutive both of individual selfhood, on the one hand, and of redemptive community *in the world,* on the other. Here, for example, is Rosenstock's description of the communal "We" forged in the speech of collective prayer to the divine: "In the genuine Ur-plural of the praying community, of every faith-filled community, . . . a piece of the world, thus third person, is fused together with pieces of You and of I. The Ur-grammar fuses together God, man, and world, in the resounding We."[25]

Rosenstock thus understood interpersonal speech to hold the key to reconciling those poles that stood in sharp tension for Rosenzweig leading up to the *Leipziger Nachtgespräch*. The tension between the individual soul, longing for solitary relation to the divine, on the one hand, and the world in whose confines the individual finds herself, on the other; between the individual's love of God and his love of others in the world, is mediated, for Rosenstock, through the "Word." Where Rosenzweig sees tension, Rosenstock sees the possibility of a community in which the soul, world, and divine could unite.

Now, for our purposes, it is important to highlight what Rosenstock understood to be the historical consequences of such mediating speech. To do so, however, we must take a brief detour through another concept that Rosenstock developed in the mid-1910s, one that likewise had an enormous influence on Rosenzweig: the notion of revelation as "orientation." Central to the notion of revelation that Rosenstock developed, largely through his exchange with Rosenzweig in 1916, is the idea that revelation does not free its recipient from the confines of the world, but rather *orients* human existence in the world: revelation orients human existence historically between past and future, and spatially between heaven and earth. Reporting on Rosenstock's notion of revelation to Rudolf Ehrenberg in November 1917, Rosenzweig writes, "Revelation is orientation. After revelation there is an actual, no longer relativized Up and Down in nature—'heaven' and 'earth'— . . . and an actually fixed Earlier and Later in time. In the revealed space-time world . . . the earth is the middle of the world, and world history lies before and after Christ."[26] These four directions of orientation that Rosenzweig cites—up, down, earlier, later—were understood by Rosenstock, as early as 1915, to be the four points of a "Cross of Actuality," which alone enables the follower of Christ to grasp her situatedness in the actual world, and which at once calls on her to act within that world.[27]

Part and parcel of Rosenstock's later understanding of the orienting power of the Cross was his view that the event symbolized by the Cross holds the key to grasping *history* as a single redemptive course, and that the very fact of our shared reckoning of time from that event reveals the way we participate in this single historical course in concrete, often tacit fashion.[28] But it is at once in the intimate confines of interpersonal speech, according to Rosenstock, that our orientation in history happens. Rosenstock suggests that when two people enter into an "I–You" relation, when they call each other by name, they both orient themselves within, and help forge *actual history.* Later in his life, Rosenstock explained this idea as follows:

> The *double character of revelation* consists in that it directs the speaker himself as well as the men whom he sees before him, to a new and at once a determined place. . . . After this experience there is a forward and a backward, a direction. Revelation is orientation. . . . Therewith a position is granted to one that one cannot give to oneself, namely an expressly offered, public and named place. There is such a place only once, and it never comes again: it is your place in the history of the human race. And for this entry into human history the name is granted to me. . . . Because speech comes into the world so that your representation of me and mine of you set us in our right places in the world-All.[29]

Here Rosenstock ascribes solely to interpersonal speech, to the calling of another by name, the power to grant the individual entry into the course of world history. Interpersonal speech for Rosenstock is a divinely rooted force—the "Word"—that pulls the individual soul, called by her personal name, into the world-All *at a particular moment in history* ("there is such a place only once, and it never comes again"), thereby reconciling the soul to the world, even while securing that soul's individuality before God. When Rosenzweig cites Rosenstock's belief in the "Word" as ground for his being impervious to the problem of the tension between soul and world that so perplexed Rosenzweig in the years leading up to the *Leipziger Nachtgespräch,* he thus points to Rosenstock's long-standing insistence that speech has the power to mediate between soul and world. This means that interpersonal relations of love, rather than forcing the soul to choose between God and others in the world, in fact unite God, world, and the soul within a common history. One may suggest, therefore, that the new sense of "Christian world-activity" which permitted Rosenzweig to take the world seriously once again after the *Leipziger Nachtgespräch,* may have been a sense of just this task of building up a world community out of interpersonal relations of love, inspired by the revelatory "Word."

Rosenzweig elsewhere suggests, moreover, that during the *Leipziger Nachtgespräch* he not only learned about the mediating power of "the Word" through history from Rosenstock, but rather *experienced* it directly from Rosenstock himself. Here we must recall not only Rosenzweig's apparent conviction that he had to choose between loving God and loving others in the world, but also Rudolf Ehrenberg's veiled critique of Rosenzweig's Marcionist tendencies in the eighteenth sermon of *Ebr. 10:25: ein Schicksal in*

Predigten. The "heretic" of this sermon, we recall, was one who "took of faith and takes not of love,"[30] one who so committed himself to a faith relationship to the divine beyond the world that he denied the redemptive effects of love in the world. If Rosenzweig had served as the exemplar of this world-denying heretic in the period leading up to the *Leipziger Nachtgespräch*, Rosenzweig's later account of that evening suggests that it was in part the *experience* of redemptive love through the exchange with Rosenstock and Ehrenberg that night which led him to change his position. On August 25, 1919 Rosenzweig thus wrote to Rudolf Ehrenberg, "In that whole time in August and September 1913 I didn't see Christ for even one moment, rather always only—Eugen, and besides him, you, to some degree. But above all, Eugen. . . . My whole experience at that time was not [of] Christ (an experience of faith), but rather [of] Christians (an experience of love)."[31]

Rosenzweig's pointed classification of his religious experience in the wake of the *Leipziger Nachtgespräch* as an experience of love rather than of faith is doubly significant for us. It serves once again to undermine the narrative of Rosenzweig's conversion that has dominated the scholarship for the last sixty years, according to which Rosenzweig was converted to a position of faith through his exchange with Rosenstock, and it is thereby consistent with my claim that Rosenzweig's conversion did not remove him from the world but to the contrary returned him to it. More illuminating still, however, is Rosenzweig's particular classification of his religious experience as an experience of love. It suggests that Rosenzweig experienced through Rosenstock and, to a lesser extent, through Ehrenberg, the very love whose redemptive effects in the world Rosenzweig had hitherto denied. In the wake of his encounter with Rosenstock, Rosenzweig now "takes of love," and not merely of a faith that would deny the status of the world. The "word" of interpersonal speech, we might suggest, has reconciled what appeared to be the irreconcilable commitments of loving God and loving others in the world. Rosenzweig evidently *experienced* this reconciliation as the recipient of the very redemptive love through which, Rosenzweig would come to believe, the historical realization of the Kingdom of God is advanced in the world.

The sense that Rosenstock's redemptive love was experienced by Rosenzweig as a *conversion* is dramatically conveyed in a letter Rosenzweig wrote to Margrit Rosenstock on June 24, 1918, nearly five years—as Rosenzweig notes explicitly—after the Leipzig night-conversation. Although our focus must remain on what this letter has to tell us about Rosenzweig's 1913 encounter with Rosenstock, it must be acknowledged that Rosenzweig wrote the letter in the midst of another transformative moment in his life. The letter was written shortly after Eugen Rosenstock had apparently learned of Rosenzweig's relationship with Eugen's wife, Margrit. I need to cite the letter at some length in order to show how Rosenzweig conveyed Rosenstock's 1913 impact upon him; but I will only address the complicated 1918 context to the extent that it helps us understand the 1913 encounter.

Troubled by Rosenstock's response to his relationship to Margrit, Rosenzweig wrote as follows:

> His feeling of self-assertion [*Selbstbehauptung*] is inconceivable to me. Against me? Against me? Against surely the first person after you who believed [in] him? And who will believe [in] him so long as—so long as we still rely on belief. And he must still only "assert" himself against me? Does he not feel what it means that *I* believe [in] him? Does he not know how hard it not only *was* but *is* to *have to* believe [in] him? How much simpler my life would be, if I did not need to believe [in] him. He is the point of reversal [*Umkehr*] in my life and thereby the chain that drags after me. It is indeed no accident that when I had the feeling that I now had to open myself up before Cohen, I had to speak of my relationship to Eugen and of nothing else at all! He became fate for me, before I became this for him. But is it not natural, that I must also become so for him? See: this is what carried me away now over the horrible feeling of knowing him jealous [*ihn eifersüchtig zu wissen*]: that he, in a wild-bodily-spiritual [*wüsten-leiblich-geistigen*] shock of his being, has only now [*da*] learned faith in me—beyond the consciousness of our "planetary" belonging-together—the actual Man-to-Man-ly [*Mensch-zu-Mensch-lich*] faith in the actuality of my existence—just as I learned by [*bei*] him in that equally harrowing penetrating-shock of that Leipzig night nearly five years ago, in and after which I have not after all designated myself as just nice to him. There is just nothing more difficult than this apparently most simple: to believe reciprocally in our *actuality*. "Love your neighbor—he is like you," yes actually like you, wholly like you![32]

Rosenzweig conveys in multiple ways in this letter how impactful and transformative his relationship with Eugen Rosenstock had been. He identifies Rosenstock as the "point of reversal in my life," as representing the moment of fundamental transformation—indeed, of conversion[33]—in Rosenzweig's life. The end of the letter alludes, moreover, to the key role that redemptive love played in that conversion. Here Rosenzweig cites Leviticus 19:18: "and you shall love your neighbor as yourself." When Rosenzweig came to cite this biblical passage in the *Star*, he translated and stressed the end of the passage, "he is like you," in the same way he does here. Rosenzweig seeks to make the point thereby that in this act of loving the other in the world one not only acknowledge the other's unique "self," but one acknowledges and confirms one's *own self:* "'like you,' thus not 'you.' You remain you and should so remain. But he should not remain a he for you, and thus only an It for your you, but rather he is like you, like your you, a you like you, an I—soul."[34] Rosenzweig's citation and comment on this passage in the letter ("'he is like you', yes actually like you . . .") suggests he already reads the passage as conveying the power of redemptive love to affirm the respective personhoods of lover and beloved. His account of Rosenstock's impact upon him, moreover, highlights this effect of redemptive love. What Rosenzweig apparently attained through Rosenstock's love, accompanied by the "harrowing penetrating-shock of that Leipzig night," was "actual Man-to-Man-ly faith in the actuality of my existence." Through the actual experience of Rosenstock's personal and personalizing love at the *Leipziger Nachtgespräch,* and through then *having to* believe in Rosenstock's actuality, Rosenzweig suggests he likewise gained faith in the actuality of his own existence in the world. Rosenzweig is troubled in this letter by his realization that Rosenstock has only now had the same experience through Rosenzweig. And he suggests that there is "nothing more difficult" than believing "reciprocally in our actuality." But his description suggests that redemptive love has the power to grant *actuality in the world,* and that it was the force of the recognition of the actuality of his own existence at the *Leipziger Nachtgespräch* that effected his conversion back to the world. He could no longer deny the world its right to actuality once he was forced to acknowledge his own actual existence in it. If we take the liberty of drawing on Rosenstock's later assertion, cited above, that interpersonal exchanges that are truly revelatory pull their participants into the world's historical course at a particular and irreplaceable moment, then we might also suggest that Rosenzweig experiences his entry into the world as bound to his particular moment within the historical course of "Christian world-activity," as well, as his "place in the history of the human race."

The depiction of Rosenzweig's personal transformation through Rosenstock's love here mirrors in important ways Rosenzweig's account of Hegel's personal integration into the world we examined earlier. For after holding his self separate from the world during his Marcionist period, this letter suggests Rosenzweig had his selfhood secured precisely through the relation of love that integrated him into the world. And just as Rosenzweig's account of Hegel suggested, such a transition from isolated subjectivity to integration into the objective world amounts to the most dramatic personal conversion Rosenzweig underwent.

Now, this account of interpersonal love, or of the "Word," as the medium through which Rosenstock facilitated Rosenzweig's conversion away from Marcionism and toward the "world activity of Christianity," may be the most compelling of the possibilities the evidence offers us for explaining Rosenstock's role in the event.[35] But there remain reasons to question its credibility. Rosenstock would later claim that the idea of the "word become flesh" occupied his thinking as early as his years in Heidelberg (from 1907 onward),[36] but the written record suggests that Rosenstock did not develop his programmatic account of speech as revelatory until *after* 1913. We must concede, therefore, that we court some degree of anachronism in ascribing to the Rosenstock of 1913 the ideas about revelatory speech he formulated only in later years. At the same time, however, Rosenzweig himself linked Rosenstock's belief in the "Word" and his 1913 opposition to Rosenzweig's Marcionism, in 1917, after he had read and discussed with Rosenstock at least the preliminary form of this later account of speech. Rosenzweig himself thus identified the position Rosenstock held during the 1913 night-conversation as at least consistent with Rosenstock's later account of speech and revelation, even if questions remain as to whether Rosenstock had articulated already in 1913 the view of interpersonal speech he put to paper in the years that followed.

Aside from the fear of anachronism, however, there is another reason to question the role that the "Word" of redemptive love may have played in Rosenstock's facilitating of Rosenzweig's conversion over the night of July 7, 1913. While the impression Rosenstock left on Rosenzweig during the *Leipziger Nachtgespräch* was dramatic, the same cannot be said about the impression the night-conversation left on Rosenstock. To the contrary, there are several indications that Rosenstock did not even realize Rosenzweig was undergoing such a transformative event at that time. Rosenzweig had to review what transpired on that night for Rosenstock in his letter of August 13, 1917, because Rosenstock acted "as if [he] knew nothing about the course of both planets after the catastrophe, and thus elicits these things piecemeal out of" Rosenzweig himself; and because Rosenstock appeared to believe that the "catastrophic" conversation between them in July 1913 occurred at the end of the month, and took its starting point from a discussion of Kierkegaard (a conversation that, on the other hand, Rosenzweig didn't remember!).[37] In the letter just cited at length from June 24, 1918, Rosenzweig likewise suggested that although he was transformed through Rosenstock in 1913, Rosenstock was only transformed through his relationship with Rosenzweig much later. Furthermore, in his 1969 introduction to the English-language publication of the 1916 correspondence between Rosenzweig and Rosenstock, *Judaism Despite Christianity,* Rosenstock himself twice emphasized that he "knew nothing of the intense resolve to which his confession of faith in the Leipzig conversation had given rise, nor of its later modification by Franz' visit to the Jewish place of worship" until Rudolf Ehrenberg mentioned this to him a few years subsequently.[38] If the transformative impact Rosenstock had upon Rosenzweig during the *Leipziger Nachtgespräch* was rooted in the idea of and the experience of redemptive love, we are led to the odd conclusion that at the heart of the *Leipziger Nachtgespräch* is an "I–You" encounter of which only one of the two participants was aware.

Questions surrounding the suggestion that the "Word" is the key to Rosenzweig's conversion to Christian "world-activity," lead us to consider two additional possible accounts of Rosenstock's role during the night-conversation. According to some of Rosenzweig's later recollections, first of all, the significance of Rosenstock's presence at the *Leipziger Nachtgespräch* lay in his very person: Rosenstock modeled for Rosenzweig a kind of Christian life in the world that Rosenzweig had hitherto taken to be impossible. On this view, we may suggest, just witnessing Rosenstock as the person that he was, without experiencing any special interpersonal connection to him, was enough to open up for Rosenzweig the possibility of living the very sort of life of the soul in the world that he had hitherto denied was possible, let alone necessary, for him.

In Rosenzweig's letter to Rudolf Ehrenberg, from October 31, 1913, in which he reviews the details of the night-conversation, Rosenzweig writes, "That a man like Rosenstock was consciously a Christian . . . , this nixed my whole representation of Christianity, but therewith of religion generally, and therewith of my religion."[39] Scholars since Glatzer have tended to read the surprise Rosenzweig conveys in his statement as directed toward the fact that he found in Rosenstock an intellectually serious person who despite his commitment to knowledge still turned to faith for answers to ultimate questions. Glatzer writes, for example:

> That a man like Rosenstock, not a naïve believer and not a romantic, but a scholar and thinker, was able to accept religion as his personal answer, showed Rosenzweig that a union of mind and faith was indeed possible. He came to see, with the clarity of conviction, that an intellectual's attitude toward the world and history can be one of religious faith. He had thought that faith existed, but not for the objective scholar. Now he learned differently.[40]

Our reconstruction of Rosenzweig's early thinking has shown us that Rosenzweig in fact had no problem, in the years before 1913, accepting "religion as his personal answer"; to the contrary, he entertained a theology of world denial in order to make a radical form of such "religious faith" possible. But this does not rule out the possibility that it was Rosenstock's combination of scholarship and religion that indeed made such a strong impression on Rosenzweig. In the light of what we now know about Rosenzweig's Marcionism prior to the *Nachtgespräch,* we might suggest that what surprised Rosenzweig about Rosenstock was the fact that "a man like Rosenstock," who accepted "religion as his personal answer," could still be a "scholar and thinker," and that a person committed to *God* could still be committed to the study of the world and its history.

Although we are accustomed to assuming that Rosenstock's commitment to faith was far more central to the impact he made upon Rosenzweig than his commitment to scholarship, this is due in large part to what we know about Rosenstock's later activity in the wake of World War I, when he began challenging the limits of the academy from the standpoint of his own religious thinking. The consistency of this commitment after the war may lead us to forget that prior to it, the public figure Rosenstock cut at the university and in his writings was very much that of a scholar. Indeed, Rosenstock himself would later suggest that before 1914, in sharp contrast to the iconoclastic position he would later take up in the academy, he had been "to a certain degree . . . a 'normal history professor'"[41]—an impression that the study of Rosenstock's *Herzogsgewalt und Friedenschutz* (1910) or his magisterial *Königshaus und Stämme in Deutschland zwischen 911 und 1250* (1914) certainly confirms. As a result, it is quite possible that before the night-conversation, during the months in which Rosenzweig sat in on Rosenstock's course on legal history, Rosenzweig had taken Rosenstock, first and foremost, as a historian, one who had become Christian in name only. Rosenzweig's recollections suggest he was genuinely surprised by Rosenstock's "confession," and this may be because Rosenstock's early scholarship on medieval German history betrayed little of the inspired program of thought and action that would later guide his writings.[42]

In an August 13, 1917 letter to Rosenstock, Rosenzweig recounts the events of the *Leipziger Nachtgespräch,* in order to remind Rosenstock himself of what transpired. He recalls that in the discussion that developed around Lagerlöf's "Antichrist book," Rosenzweig first took the role of interrogator, chiding Rosenstock "in the tone of" the prophet Daniel, who interpreted the mysterious inscription that appeared on the wall of Belshazzar's court as admonishing the king: "'[you have been] weighed, etc... [and found wanting]'" (Daniel 5:27). But Rosenstock "didn't tolerate" such rebukes from Rosenzweig. He proceeded to reveal his own "secret," and the tides were abruptly turned.[43] Rosenzweig's letter to Rudolf Ehrenberg of October 31, 1913 offers what appears to be a similar account of the exchange, suggesting that Rosenzweig was "disarmed already through Rosenstock's simple confession."[44]

Given what we now know about the Marcionist commitments with which Rosenzweig entered the *Leipziger Nachtgespräch,* and the return to the world that he underwent through it, we can offer the following possible reconstruction of the exchange that Rosenzweig describes in these letters. One can well imagine how a conversation about the relationship between the "kingdom not of this world" and the "kingdom of this world alone" would lead Rosenzweig to rebuke Rosenstock the scholar—much as Daniel had rebuked Belshazzar—for losing sight of the God beyond the world while being so singularly devoted to the study of its history. Rosenstock's subsequent "simple confession" that he is a Christian not out of convenience, but is "consciously" so would then have turned the tides on Rosenzweig. Faced now not with a mere historian, but with someone who combined a real commitment to the study of the world's history with a real commitment to Christianity, it was now Rosenzweig's turn to be rebuked, it seems, for his own denial of the world's right to redemption.[45]

This way in which Rosenstock understood Christianity to demand his own commitment to the world appears to have made Rosenzweig begin to question the motives of his own Marcionism. If we may judge from certain allusive comments Rosenzweig made to Rosenstock in letters from the fall of 1917, Rosenzweig began to question whether his former appeal to spiritual purity, to the soul's personal relation to God as the sole site of human salvation, might in fact have been merely a ruse justifying his own neglect of the world and its mores. Thus, Rosenzweig writes of his own attempt to excuse himself from responsibility for worldly indiscretions: "The alibi everywhere has the same content, and the 'spiritual' [*geistige*] is only the self-deluding justification for it." According to Rosenzweig, however, over the course of the *Leipziger Nachtgespräch* Rosenstock "tore from me my artificial self-spun alibi," and "pulled the curtain away behind which I permitted myself everything." Rosenzweig must now concede that the "unchasteness" that he had permitted himself was not "error," but rather "sin."[46] No longer able to excuse his own actions in the world as the product of the world's own immoral or undivine status, one may suggest, Rosenzweig now saw himself forced to take responsibility for such actions. If the world is conceived no longer as a context from out of which the individual soul must be saved, but rather as the context within which the individual soul must take up a redemptive vocation, then what one does in the world matters. In the final section of this chapter, we shall return to the consequences that Rosenzweig's turn away from Marcionism had for his view of the significance of human action.[47]

In later reflections on his own self-presentation at the night-conversation, Rosenstock claims that he "bore witness" during the conversation "to prayer and worship as his *prime guides to action.*"[48] That is to say, Rosenstock presented prayer and worship not as the keys to a relationship with the divine that raises the individual out of the world but rather as "guides to action" in the world. It is thus quite plausible that Rosenstock's personal reconciliation of worldly and spiritual commitments led Rosenzweig to change his "whole representation of Christianity." A commitment to spiritual devotion could be grasped as orienting life in the world, rather than as removing the devotee from it, and thus Christianity could be viewed as realizing itself in a "world activity" rather than in an escape from the world.

According to this alternative account of Rosenstock's role in Rosenzweig's transformation in the wake of the *Leipziger Nachtgepsräch,* the fact that "a man like Rosenstock was consciously a Christian" modeled for Rosenzweig the possibility of reconciling commitments to the study of the world's history, on the one hand, and to living a Christian life, on the other. Independent of whether or not Rosenstock grasped the impression he was making upon Rosenzweig, one may suggest that the very presence of Rosenstock as one who was able to reconcile spiritual and worldly commitments within his person forced Rosenzweig to question whether his radical world-denial had been self-delusion rather than spiritual purity.[49]

I want finally to introduce a third way of reconstructing the transformative impact Rosenstock had on Rosenzweig over the course of the night-conversation. As in the first possibility I suggested, here I propose that Rosenzweig's conversion was facilitated, at least in part, by ideas that Rosenstock shared with Rosenzweig. But rather than proposing that the conversation arrived at the theme of "the world activity of Christianity" through a discussion of the "Word," I suggest that another aspect of Rosenstock's later notion of "revelation as orientation" may have been introduced to Rosenzweig over the course of the evening, one that likewise emphasizes Christianity's historical realization of the Kingdom of God. I am referring to what Rosenstock later called "calendrical thinking." Let me sketch quickly the form this idea took on in the years after the *Leipziger Nachtgespräch,* before explaining why I think there are grounds for believing this idea may have already been in the air during the conversation itself.

By 1915, Rosenstock was exploring the Christian yearly liturgical calendar as one particular venue through which human beings situate themselves and their redemptive task within this historical trajectory established by the Cross of Actuality.[50] Rosenstock came to view the yearly calendar, and the way it brings together moments of natural, historical, national, and spiritual importance, as the pedagogical means through which Christians learn to take up their calling in the establishment of the Kingdom of God on earth. "The Church Year of the Christian reckoning of time is the great form of education," he writes, in his 1917 "Volkstaat und Reich Gottes." Through the calendar, one is "instruct[ed] to experience and to realize a higher unity beyond the visible state and the smoking Volk, beyond the predetermining of head and the surprising of heart: the Kingdom of God."[51]

The structure of the liturgical calendar offered Rosenstock a unique way of thinking about the historical integration of the individual soul into the course of the world's redemption, one that has important parallels to the way Rosenzweig would begin to think about a redemptive reconciliation of self and world in the wake of the night-conversation. Now, while Rosenstock would only begin thinking "calendrically" in 1915, and would only announce this calendrical thinking to Rosenzweig in 1916, Rosenstock had in fact already published a short article on the development of the Christian calendar, "Toward the Elaboration of the Festival Calendar in the Middle Ages," in 1912. The premise of this early article is that when the Roman Church set out to "preach the cross" in the world with "claims to be universal, catholic," it had to learn ways to reconcile its "new world-fleeing doctrine" with the beliefs and practices of the world's pagan communities. The Church struggled bitterly at this task, Rosenstock claimed, "until half against its will, and half unconsciously, the Church took up, piece-by piece, the old festival calendar, the old superstition, the old cult into its own calendar."[52] Primarily through a case study of changes to the Ascension Day celebrations in medieval Germany, Rosenstock's article proceeds to explore how the evolving medieval Church calendar was the context within which the missionizing Church became reconciled—at times against its will—to the world it sought to convert. By absorbing local pagan customs into its festival calendar, Rosenstock shows, the Church both conquered the world and at once became indistinguishable from it.

Although Rosenstock's article is first and foremost a work of scholarship, and thus cannot truly be considered the beginning of what Rosenstock would later call his "calendrical" philosophizing, its thematic connection both to Rosenzweig's concerns during the period of the *Leipziger Nachtgespräch* and to Rosenstock's own later calendrical thinking are significant. For here Rosenstock presents the evolving Church calendar as the site in which the historical reconciliation of the "world-fleeing" early Christian doctrine with the world itself is worked out concretely. Rosenstock ends the article, moreover, by intimating that there is an organic quality to the process of unification of world and spirit at work in the development of the festival calendar.

> Do we not experience in our day that not only the most un-Churchly, but rather even un-Christian people, even with educated capacities for reflection, adopt the use of the Christian festivals, that is, the Church doctrine become flesh, and thereby also the strictly Christian festival songs, in completely good faith in their new "Weltanschauung"? . . . Spiritual life is only possible in unity, and two so sharply different spiritual worlds . . . could not remain next to each other in the individual human head unmixed. Just as little, however, could one alone claim the field, since both carried the un-dry-up-able life force of truth, if also only in part, in itself.[53]

Rosenstock's message to his 1912 contemporaries here is clear: even in our day, no member of the Christian world can take up a life of devotion to the soul or to the world—to the churchly spirit or to the worldly spirit, in the terms of the article—while denying the "life force of truth" of its counterpart. The redemptive cause of the Church, on the one hand, and worldly life, on the other, are destined to attain that "unity" in which alone true "spiritual life is possible." It is the Church festival calendar that thereby brings together Church and world, for it is nothing less than "Church doctrine become flesh."

We thus find that less than a year before the *Leipziger Nachtgespräch,* and a mere few months before Rosenzweig began to attend Rosenstock's classes at the University of Leipzig, Rosenstock was already preoccupied with the role of the liturgical calendar in the historical advance of the Church through the world. Even before the 1913 night-conversation, then, Rosenstock conceived of the calendar in such a way that foreshadowed his later explicit declaration that the calendar instructed and guided those who lived—even unknowingly—according to it, toward fulfilling their vocation in the establishment of the Kingdom of God on earth.

There is reason to speculate that Rosenstock's ideas about the constructive role of the Christian liturgical calendar in the historical reconciliation of soul and world may have arisen in the *Leipziger Nachtgespräch* and may thereby have played some role in Rosenzweig's own radical change of attitude toward the world. The plausibility of this suggestion gains credence when we recall Rudolf Ehrenberg's participation in the night-conversation. We know that Rosenzweig was familiar enough with the early drafts of Ehrenberg's *Ebr. 25,10: ein Schicksal in Predigten* such that Ehrenberg could criticize Rosenzweig's Marcionism—presumably during the night-conversation itself—by identifying Rosenzweig with the heretic of its eighteenth sermon. We may recall, furthermore, that the sermons in Ehrenberg's book are themselves organized calendrically, according to their positions vis-à-vis the nearest festival within the Church year! Indeed, when Rosenstock later writes to Rosenzweig, in 1916, to tell him of his developing calendrical thinking, he says, "I philosophize in the form of the calendar (compare Rudi's Sermon-plan)."[54]

Thus while there is no direct evidence that Rosenstock's later "philosophizing in the form of a calendar" was instrumental in Rosenzweig's radical change of conviction on July 7, 1913, I think we are given fair grounds for speculation. One can easily imagine that as Rosenzweig, Rosenstock, and Ehrenberg engaged in a discussion that would convert Rosenzweig from the conviction that the salvation of the soul demands the denial of the world, to a commitment to the Christian realization of the Kingdom of God in the world, Rosenstock would have introduced the idea that the festival calendar serves to unite soul and world within the historical advance of the Kingdom of God. We may thus speculate that it was neither Rosenstock's personal example alone nor merely his expression of love that helped lead Rosenzweig to change his view of the possibility of reconciling soul and world. Rather, the early seeds of Rosenstock's calendrical philosophizing may likewise have played a decisive role here. Perhaps it is precisely to such hints at a philosophical position that Rosenzweig gestures in 1916, when he responds to Rosenstock's announcement of having arrived at his new form of philosophizing with the claim: "In these last years, you were never anything other than a 'philosopher' for me."[55]

Thus it may have been Rosenstock the Christian scholar whose very person awoke Rosenzweig to a revaluation of the world. It may have been Rosenstock's early ideas about revelatory speech or about the liturgical calendar that directed Rosenzweig to conceive of history as a redemptive course constructed out of and oriented by revelation. It may have been the experience of Christian love that not only demonstrated to Rosenzweig the possibility of reconciling the soul's love for God with the forging of a loving community with others in the world, but *actually* turned Rosenzweig into a participant in such a redemptive community. It may, likewise, have been some combination of Rosenstock's person, his thoughts, and his love that so impressed Rosenzweig. But it is clear that the encounter with Rosenstock during the *Leipziger Nachtgespräch* led Rosenzweig to turn away from the theology of world denial that he had entertained in the years prior, and toward a commitment to Christian world-activity as the historical process through which soul and world are reconciled. Once we grasp how Rosenstock symbolized for Rosenzweig the possibility of fusing the soul's personal relation with God with his position and vocation in the world, then we can likewise understand how troubled Rosenzweig was years later, in June 1919, to find Rosenstock struggling with the very same tension between soul and world that Rosenstock had helped Rosenzweig overcome in 1913. After reading Rosenstock's *Selbstmord Europas,* in which Rosenstock juxtaposes what he sees as Europe's suicide in the World War with a rebirth of divine presence, we recall, Rosenzweig writes to Margrit Rosenstock of being surprised at how important Rosenstock believes his essay is: "I was astounded because that which is new in it for Eugen ("God wants to have us back"), is really that from which none other than he freed me."[56] It was precisely because Rosenstock had freed Rosenzweig from a world-denying theology in the *Leipziger Nachtgespräch,* that Rosenzweig was shocked to find Rosenstock himself now touting the death of the European world as a path back to God.[57]

POST-CONVERSATION PERSONAL CRISIS: CONTINUED STRUGGLE WITH GNOSTICISM

If we judge by the extant accounts of Rosenzweig's state of mind in the aftermath of the *Leipziger Nachtgespräch,* the conversion from Marcionism to the "world activity of Christianity" that he apparently underwent during this period was anything but a source of the solace one might expect to follow from discovering the key to resolving a long-standing personal and philosophical perplexity. Rosenzweig uniformly refers to the period including and following the *Leipziger Nachtgespräch* as a "catastrophe," a period of "breakdown" in which Rosenzweig seriously contemplated suicide. Two vivid accounts he offers of his state of mind immediately following the night-conversation will suffice to highlight the seriousness of Rosenzweig's crisis. In a letter to Rosenstock of August 13, 1917, Rosenzweig claims to remember virtually nothing from the hours immediately following the night-conversation, and writes, "I was still much too near to that complete face-to-face with the nothing [*vis-à-vis du rien*] with which I had come into my room, in that morning after the night, and took my Browning 6.35 out of my desk drawer. Whether cowardice or hope at that time prevented its use, I don't know. . . ."[58]

In a letter to Margrit Rosenstock of July 15, 1920, Rosenzweig reflects further on the suicidal state in which the *Leipziger Nachtgespräch* left him:

> I cannot demand such readiness for death = readiness for suicide from everyone, as I indeed had at that time in 1913 from July to October. . . . It is [an act of] God's grace that He once has so torn me out of life in life. {From July to September 1913, I was completely prepared to die—to let everything in me die.} But this cannot be a rule. Most people live only simply their life-fate, their life-course and no further. It is the something particular in us five, or with Eduard six people (Eugen Hans Rudi Werner

> me Eduard), that God in our case has not been satisfied only to speak to us through our life; but rather once he has let the life collapse around us like the background of a theater decoration and has spoken with us on the empty stage.[59]

Scholars have tended to interpret the breakdown Rosenzweig describes in these and other comments as linked either to a difficulty he experienced in trying to break away from Judaism, or to a sudden sense that spiritual emptiness had defined his life up to that point.[60] It seems to me, however, that the account of the stakes involved in the *Leipziger Nachtgespräch* I have proposed in this study enables us to offer some new insights, as well, into the particular nature of the crisis Rosenzweig appears to have endured in its wake.

An experience of despair may indeed accompany conversion stories with some regularity.[61] Rosenzweig's description of his standing "face-to-face with the nothing" does, at least at first glance, point to a sense that the foundations that had grounded the values and direction of his life up to that point had collapsed, leaving him hovering over an abyss. But what is striking about the recollections in Rosenzweig's letter to Margrit Rosenstock of 1920 is that they describe Rosenzweig's "readiness for suicide" as in no way the consequence of despair. On the contrary, Rosenzweig recalls this suicidal period of crisis as a time in which he experienced "God's grace"! His readiness for death corresponds, he tells us, to God's having "torn him out of life within life," by allowing "the life around" Rosenzweig "to collapse like the background of a theater decoration." Here God speaks with Rosenzweig "on the empty stage."

Having uncovered the Marcionist strain in the approach to revelation and the world that Rosenzweig endorsed in the years before the *Leipziger Nachtgespräch,* it seems warranted to see in Rosenzweig's "readiness for suicide" after the night-conversation a concrete sign of his ongoing struggle with this position even after that night. For Rosenzweig here links the experience of divine grace with dying to the world; his unique relation to the divine happens not in worldly life—as he suggests most people alone have access to the divine—but rather is an experience of divine proximity in which the world drops away around him. The suicide Rosenzweig contemplates in the wake of the night-conversation, one may thereby suggest, is the suicide of *Hermann*—the self-sacrifice for God that Rosenzweig had entertained in the years prior to 1913, and from which he apparently was not wont to turn away all too easily.

The new understanding we have gained regarding the Marcionist position Rosenzweig entertained *before* the *Leipziger Nachtgespräch* thus suggests that it is not merely a feeling of despair—brought on by the magnitude of a conversion from Judaism to Christianity or by the recognition of the loss of what had hitherto been the grounding of his life—that brings on Rosenzweig's suicidal tendencies in the wake of the conversation. Rather, Rosenzweig's contemplation of suicide may be understood as a direct extension of the very Marcionist position he had entertained in the years prior, as a last serious consideration of the "death-for-God" theology to which he had been drawn since 1910–1911. We may imagine him coming to the preliminary conclusion, through conversation with Rosenstock and Ehrenberg, that if his "dualism of revelation and world" presupposed the "metaphysical dualism of God and devil," then it was incumbent upon him to take that Marcionist position with which he entered the night-conversation with the seriousness which Rosenstock and Ehrenberg may have dared him to take it. If Rosenzweig were truly serious about the incompatibility of the soul's salvation through a relation to the divine and a commitment to worldly life, then the only reasonable consequence would be to choose one or the other. Had he not already recognized that a choice for personal salvation demands putting an end to one's life in the world? Might not such suicide—and *not* the Christian path through the world advocated by Rosenstock—yet direct the individual on the true path to redemption? Had not the Christ of Hegel's "Spirit of Christianity and its Fate" found "freedom only in the void"?

Rosenzweig's 1917 recollections of his suicidal state after the *Leipziger Nachtgespräch* may likewise allude to a characteristically Gnostic moment in Rosenzweig's reaction in the conversation's aftermath. Here Rosenzweig describes having experienced a "complete face-to-face with the Nothing." Now, such a vivid description may refer, once again, simply to the loss of grounding Rosenzweig experienced when considering abandoning his Judaism, or even his Marcionism, in conversion to Christianity. But in a comment written in 1916 and published in the "Paralipomena," Rosenzweig offers musings about the "nothing" that he identifies explicitly with Gnosticism. Taking notes on J. A. Endres's *Geschichte der mittelalterlichen Philosophie im Christlichen Abendlande,* Rosenzweig reads the book's short summary of Fridugisus' fragment *De nihilo et tenebris* ("The Nothing and the Shadows"), and writes the following in his notebook: "To grasp the Nothing as reality (Fridugisus [d.]

834 by Endres 17), is really Gnosticism (since one grasps it as the *ouk-on,* and not as the *me-on*)."[62]

Rosenzweig's terse remark in his notes implies that grasping "nothing as reality," as possessing a substantiality that is independent of true "being" rather than as a relative privation of such being, amounts to Gnosticism. For Gnostic dualism does indeed posit a metaphysical grounding for the world that is opposed to the true being of the transcendent God; indeed, elsewhere in the "Paralipomena" Rosenzweig identifies the rejection of Gnosticism with the rejection of *hyle,* primordial matter.[63] Gnosticism may be said to posit the reality of the world itself, that is, as *essentially* "nothing," as rooted metaphysically in "nothing," rather than as the shadowy image of divine being.

Bearing Rosenzweig's reflections on a substantive "nothing" grounding the world in mind, one may suggest it plausible that when Rosenzweig claims to have stood "face to face with the Nothing" in the hours after that night-conversation, what he encountered there was not merely the abyss now visible where once the values formerly grounding his life lay, but rather the nihilistic consequences of his Marcionism. If Rosenstock and Ehrenberg made Rosenzweig realize that his view of revelation entailed a denial of the world, that is to say, what confronted him "face to face" afterwards was the nothingness *of the world,* and hence the demand that he take up his Browning 6.35mm and deny his very own participation in that nothingness.

The way in which Rosenzweig describes his state of mind during the months between the *Leipziger Nachtgespräch* and his eventual decision *not* to convert to Christianity thus suggests that he continued to struggle with the issues raised during the night-conversation. Even as he committed himself, in the summer of 1913, to the historical reconciliation of subjectivity and objectivity that Christianity appeared to offer him, he continued—much as he believed Hegel had—to hold onto his "subjective individuality" and to "recoil against its dissolution into universality and objectivity." He continued during those months to struggle between a Marcionist position that promised a revelatory relation to the divine that truly transcended worldly existence, and the historical vision of Christianity as realizing the Kingdom of God on earth. Rosenzweig appears to hint toward this latter position when he wonders whether it was "cowardice or hope" that kept him from pulling the trigger of his pistol. If it may have been "hope" that prevented his suicide, this suggests that the possibility of realizing a future world-community through redemptive love—a future possibility for which one "hopes"—held its own, in his mind, over against the Gnostic possibility. In chapter 3, we will indeed discover how crucial the principle of and the experience of "hope" became, for Rosenzweig, in charting out the historical reconciliation of soul and world.

"THE NECESSITY OF ACTION": MONOTHEISM AND HUMAN FREEDOM AFTER 1913

This chapter has clearly shown the extent to which Rosenzweig's metaphysical struggles in the years surrounding the *Leipziger Nachtgespräch* carried with them immediate practical consequences. The theoretical decision he faced as to which metaphysical view was most compelling—to wit, Marcionist dualism or developmental monism—could not be separated from the practical decision Rosenzweig faced as to what he should do. Were the world to be grasped as devoid of all divinity and freedom, as issuing from a source opposed to the salvific God, then it would be incumbent upon human beings to deny the world. It was in such a mindset that Rosenzweig had "taken from faith and not from love," and it was in such a mindset, I presume, that he contemplated his own personal "dying for God." Were the world to be grasped, alternatively, as created by the very God who would redeem it, were the world to be grasped as the site of the future Kingdom of God, then it would be incumbent upon human beings to engage in those acts of interpersonal love that would help redeem the world.

There is evidence to suggest that in the years that followed his crisis Rosenzweig returned again and again to reflect on this practical alternative, and that when he did so, he came to see the question of "human action" as having stood at the center of the *Leipzig Nachtgespräch*. Perhaps the centrality of this question for the Rosenzweig of 1913 is self-evident at this point: how could he take "the world activity of Christianity seriously" without clarifying for himself the significance of human action itself? Indeed, Rosenzweig's comments suggest he was concerned in this context not only with how the world-denier or the world-redeemer would answer the ethical question, "What should I do?," but he was perplexed by meta-ethical questions that arose when the world-denier or the world-redeemer answered this ethical question in one way or another. Rosenzweig was concerned, that is to say, with how one might understand the significance and indeed the very possibility of free human decision and action in the light of the world-denying and the world-redeeming worldviews respectively. The train of thought he developed out of reflecting on this alternative was to have a dramatic impact on how he would come to explain redemptive human action in the *Star*. Before proceeding to narrate the process through which Rosenzweig resolved his 1913 crisis, I pause here to consider more carefully how Rosenzweig's thinking about the possibility and significance of human action after 1913 developed in clear and conscious opposition to his early Marcionism.

Despite how radical the Marcionist prescriptions for human action might be, at first glance the Marcionist account of human action actually appears far more coherent than does the alternative. Human actions for good and for evil, human conflict, and the very possibility of inclining toward a worldly or a spiritual life can well be understood as having their basis in a corresponding metaphysical conflict between the God of creation and the God of salvation, or between God and the devil, or between spirit and matter. But how are such human decisions and actions to be understood if one assumes a single divine source of heaven and earth? What significance could human actions have, given the assumption that the one God is the ground of everything? Wouldn't the very possibility of human decision undermine the omnipotence inherent to a single divine ground? And what about human acts of evil—is the one God to be understood as the cause of these acts as well?

The conviction that "God created the world and [is] not just the God of revelation" may have directed Rosenzweig to view the world as demanding redemption, and his encounter with Rosenstock may have drawn him into those relations of interpersonal love that promised to realize redemption in the world. But neither the conviction regarding creation nor the experience of love would have any practical significance were the possibility of human action for or against redemption in the world inconceivable. Commitment to the efficacy of "Christian world-activity" requires a coherent account of the possibility of human action.

In letters and in the notes of the "Paralipomena" from 1916, we find Rosenzweig developing his views about this problem of human action under the conditions of monotheism in explicit opposition to Marcionism and through frequent references to his own crisis of 1913. We will explore these fascinating notes here in some detail, but the view that emerges from them collectively may be summarized as follows. Contrary to dualist accounts of self and world, the freedom of the self is in fact to be grounded in revelation and creation *together.* Space for human freedom in the world has been opened up by an act of divine self-limitation that was intended, from the beginning, to complement the divine creation of the world. The very purpose of the world is wrapped up in this capacity human beings have for free decision, and it is the very situatedness of human decision within a historical course that begins in creation which grants that decision its monumental significance. I will now trace the development of this position in Rosenzweig's notes and highlight both how this position responds to the challenge of Marcionism and how it foreshadows the account of human action Rosenzweig will articulate in the *Star.*

The question of the possibility of human action under monotheism was clearly on Rosenzweig's mind in 1916 as he read Tertullian's *Adversus Marcionem.* Marcion had apparently suggested in his "Antitheses" that human sin undermines the view that there is a single all-powerful, good God. For the human capacity to act against God's law suggests either that God is too weak to prevent such human action, or that this God in fact wills human sin and the punishment that follows. Doesn't our very freedom to disobey, Marcion appears to suggest, imply that there are opposing forces at work in the world?

Rosenzweig was most pleased with Tertullian's response to Marcion's attack on the God of creation. While reading Book II of *Adversus Marcionem,* Rosenzweig jotted the following note to himself: "Tert. Marc. II 5 ff. Totally the right theory of the connection of sin and freedom with the image-of-God-ness."[64] Brief as it is, Rosenzweig's note already signals those aspects of Tertullian's response to Marcion that Rosenzweig will make his own. Tertullian rejects Marcion's suggestion that the human freedom to sin undermines God's goodness and omnipotence. To the contrary, Tertullian asserts, human freedom is a clear expression of God's goodness and omnipotence. Precisely as created in the image of a God who is good and powerful, the human being is defined by her power to choose the good. Thus, according to Tertullian, the Creator's myriad laws all set the human being before the choice between "good and evil, life and death."[65] And God must be understood as thereby giving human beings the chance to exhibit goodness out of their own respective beings, out of free will rather than out of necessity.

What interest does God have in creating beings endowed with the freedom to choose good or evil? Tertullian answers this question by claiming that *God needs to be known:* "it was necessary that there should exist something worthy of knowing God" [*Oportebat dignum aliquid esse quod deum cognosceret*].[66] Only a being created, as the human being is, in "God's own image and likeness,"[67] Tertullian argues, is worthy of such knowledge. It is the freedom to decide for good or for evil, Tertullian implies, that makes the human being worthy of knowing God, and thereby capable of fulfilling God's need.

Alas, Tertullian concedes, the fiasco in the Garden of Eden reflects the downside of beings created in God's image. With the freedom to choose good comes the freedom to choose evil, and thus the capacity for sin goes hand-in-hand with the freedom that makes the human being the worthiest of God's creatures. But Tertullian insists that the human capacity for evil should in no way be viewed as a knock on either God's power or goodness. Creating human beings free was the ultimate reflection of God's goodness and power. What human beings did with that freedom was their own responsibility. "To conclude," Tertullian sums up, "God's goodness, brought into full view since the beginning of his works, will give assurance that from God no evil can have proceeded: while the man's freedom, if taken full account of, will prove that itself, and not God, was guilty of that which itself committed."[68]

In one stroke, Tertullian thus justified divine goodness and power before the reality of human sin, and explained human freedom as inherent to God's plan for creation. Rosenzweig's praise for the way in which Tertullian rooted the very human freedom to sin in his having been created in God's image, is not simply admiration from afar. In the months just prior to his reading Tertullian, Rosenzweig had already begun to formulate the notion that human freedom was not only not a threat to the Creator, but even that freedom could not be properly understood without grasping its roots in the idea of creation itself. Moreover, Rosenzweig shared with Tertullian a concern with articulating why human decision and action were *necessary* at a metaphysical level. The divine need for human action had indeed been a theme Rosenzweig and his cousin had explored before the *Leipziger Nachtgespräch,* when they considered the human act of world denial as contributing to God's own redemption—to God's reunification with the Shechina, for example. The "Paralipomena" show Rosenzweig edging toward Tertullian's view, to the contrary, that God required human freedom because God required recognition, a recognition that was only of value if it came from free others. As we shall see, it was indeed this view that Rosenzweig would articulate later in the *Star.*

Let's now examine the series of notes from the "Paralipomena" in which Rosenzweig began to formulate the view that human freedom is rooted in—and is demanded by—the notion of the createdness of the world. Here is a note Rosenzweig wrote to himself on January 29, 1916:

> He who does not simply ignore the ethical (thus he who doesn't pantheize), he is compelled to posit a restriction or limitation [*Beschränkung*] in God Himself. As metaphysician, he will then posit evil as independent counter-divine power and misplace [*verlegen*] the restriction already in the first concept of God. Or he can maintain the "first" concept in the utmost purity, but then must posit the restriction itself as a "second" [concept]: revelation. So—once the consideration of the ethical is assumed—creation (i.e., the denial of all *hyle* [matter]) is the necessary correlate of revelation. Since now the ethical can only be eliminated by force (because it is posited through the subjective side of thinking together with the thought of the true), so in fact there is only the alternative of either positing God as restricted (thus not as *God*) or as self-restricting (thus revealed). *Tertium non datur.* And for this reason it is rightly said of the pagans that they "know nothing of God"; the Aristotelian *let there be one Ruler* only makes God into the *Lord* but not into the *Origin* of *hyle.*[69]

Rosenzweig's musings in this note center around the same question he would soon find Tertullian had grappled with in his polemic against Marcion: How can the possibility of human action be reconciled with the concept of an all-powerful God? Rosenzweig's response is that the "ethical" realm of human action can indeed only be maintained if God is conceived as limited or constrained. Rosenzweig entertains two ways of conceiving of such divine limitation. One can take the route of Marcion and ground God's limitation metaphysically in "an independent counter-divine force," Rosenzweig considers. But although noting this as a coherent alternative, here he rejects this metaphysical dualism as a "misplacement" [*verlegen*] of the restriction required for thinking human action within the very concept of God itself. It is the other alternative that now captures Rosenzweig's interest. One can reconcile the possibility of human action with the concept of an all-powerful God, he now suggests, if that God is conceived as "restricting Itself" [*sich beschränkend*] through revelation and thereby clearing space for human beings to act ethically. The important but perhaps counter-intuitive consequence that Rosenzweig draws from these considerations is that the possibility of human action under this alternative depends not on revelation alone but rather "once the consideration of the ethical is assumed, creation (i.e., the denial of all *hyle*) is the necessary correlate of revelation."[70]

Why does Rosenzweig conclude that the realm of the ethical can only be reconciled with God if one posits creation and revelation together? I think he answers this question as follows: only if God is grasped as the absolute ground of all that is, can God's self-restriction and revelatory call be conceived as making human selfhood and free action possible. For so long as the world is conceived as grounded in something other than God—whether it be "matter" or a counter-deity—then human action will always be rooted causally in one of two metaphysical grounds, either in the good God or in matter or evil. Only if God is first conceived as Creator of all, and *then* conceived as restricting His own Being, is there a space opened up within which, as it were, there is no metaphysical grounding and hence within which human beings can freely determine their own actions. For revelation to do its job—to awaken its recipient to her individual, free selfhood—then it must come from the God who is the sole "*Origin* of matter"; it is not enough for it to come from one "Lord" among many. Said differently, the possibility of human freedom depends on the presupposition that the world is a place that is amenable to free, ethical action; and the world can be thus conceived if it has been created by the same God who awakens human beings to freedom through revelation.

We thus find that Rosenzweig's discovery at the *Leipziger Nachtgespräch,* to wit that "God created the world and [is] not just the God of revelation," holds the key to a new account of the possibility of human action: creation and revelation must be thought of in unison if one is to articulate the grounds of human freedom. Rosenzweig formulates this account, as we see, through an ongoing struggle with the Marcionist position, and a clarification of its strengths and weaknesses. I have designated this view as "counter-intuitive" because the notion of an all-powerful God who is the ultimate cause of all things certainly appears, at first glance, to leave no room for human freedom. But Rosenzweig, apparently drawing on the Kabbalistic notion of *tsimtsum,* not only reconciles human freedom with an all-powerful God, but goes so far as to suggest that human freedom can only be grasped on the grounds of an all-powerful God who is both Creator and Revealer.

Further notes in the "Paralipomena" show Rosenzweig refining his developing view of the relationship between creation, revelation, and human freedom, and continuing to do so through a reflection on Gnosticism. Thus, in a note from his "Paralipomena" from July 1916, he writes:

> Gnosis, in that it made the world and revelation itself, at least of the Old Testament, into their own *archai,* even if they come out of the All-father, is *still* polytheism; because even if it claims a unity of the *standing principles*—God is withdrawn from the *course* of the world, [i.e.,] the effects of these principles. God *in*tervenes afterwards through revelation in the New Testament. But this revelation is now over against the world itself again only a stiff *Über*world, not a new and conclusive demand on the world created by God from eternity on toward this end, to *decide. Freedom* gets tonelessly lost here, while where revelation was already God's essence in creation (!בין השמשות), it is the meaning of the world from the beginning. The world is created for the sake of the *decision*—who else could have created it thus but God himself![71]

In this remarkable comment, we find Rosenzweig testing out his newfound conclusion that human freedom depends just as much on creation as it does revelation. He critiques the notion of freedom that emerges from a Gnostic dualism of world and revelation, even one that roots both the creator of the world and the agent of salvation in an ultimate "unity of the *standing principles.*" Precisely because it takes care not to reduce the fact of freedom to an aspect of worldliness, such dualism would *appear* to offer a compelling account of that freedom. Freedom, on this view, is freedom *from* the world made possible by the intervention of the transcendent divine into the world through revelation—Christ's "freedom only in the void" from the early Hegel. But Rosenzweig here argues, to the contrary, that just revelation's transcendence to the worldly in the Gnostic account eliminates any context within which such freedom might have been effective: a "stiff *Über*world" of revelation frees the soul, ironically, from the only world in which her freedom could be meaningfully enacted. Contrary to appearances, Rosenzweig thus once again argues, it is precisely when that human freedom that stands in tension with the world is grasped, all at once, as rooted in what was "already God's essence in creation," that it can be conceived as realizable. Indeed, Rosenzweig reiterates his earlier suggestion that revelation can be conceived as awakening the self to freedom only under the presuppositition that the God of revelation is at once the absolute creator of all. "Who else could have created" a world in which revelation awakens the individual self to freedom, Rosenzweig muses, "than God himself!"—the God who is the absolute ground of all that is.

But Rosenzweig doesn't simply declare human freedom to depend on creation here. He asserts that the human freedom to "decide" must be grasped as the very purpose of creation as a whole. Revelation "is the meaning of the world from the beginning," he writes. "The world is created for the sake of the *decision*."[72] Just as Tertullian had suggested that it was the quality of freedom that made human beings worthy of knowing God, Rosenzweig hints here that free human selves have a crucial role to play in the divine plan. Will human beings freely choose the good, will they freely choose to advance God's redemptive plan in the world, will they freely choose to realize their image-of-God potential? It is the biblical account of creation as the beginning of a historical process in which the Kingdom of God is realized *through free human action,* Rosenzweig suggests here—citing the saying from the fifth chapter of *Pirke Avot* to the effect that the tablets of the Ten Commandments were created at the end of the six days of creation—which makes human freedom effective and meaningful. For free human beings are thereby invested with the responsibility of making decisions that forward the advance of redemption in the world—or that fail to. If one bears in mind Rosenzweig's account of divine self-limitation from his January 1916 note, moreover, one is inclined to suggest that in his developing view, God limits God's self *so that* the human being will face that free decision in which the purpose of the world stands to be realized. *Why* God creates a world that requires free human beings for its redemption—this is a question for which Rosenzweig owes us an answer. But Rosenzweig's praise for Tertullian certainly suggests, at this point, that he shares Tertullian's view that God demands to be known, or recognized by others. We will return to this question as we proceed; indeed, it will call for our earnest attention when we address *The Star of Redemption* itself in the final chapter of this book.

I turn now to one final note from the "Paralipomena," which is included under the same July 20, 1916 date as the comment we have just examined. Here Rosenzweig reflects once again on the possibility and significance of human freedom under monotheism, this time contrasting the experience of revelatory command with stoic natural law:

> The ground-paradox of revelation is that the human being is summoned to abandon his nature, and is summoned to do so by the God who is Himself the Creator of this nature. In this already consists the double myth of the original sin of man and the descent of God (the one necessarily a pre-historical myth, the other a historical).
>
> This connection of the pre-historical and historical myth generates the characteristic feature of revelation: the *pathos of the moment.* The stoic natural law (Cicero, *De Republica,* p. 344) doesn't have this. The *lex Dei* is eternal and corresponds quintessentially to the nature of the human being. The תורת ה' [Torah of God] is חיים [life] and demands a *choice* between חיים [life] and מוות [death].[73]

The holding-together of creation and revelation in which, we have seen, Rosenzweig has come to ground the possibility of freedom, is deemed "the paradox of revelation" in this passage. For through revelation, Rosenzweig explains, the human being is "summoned to abandon his nature," to transcend his creaturely being and realize his free selfhood, by the very "God who is the creator of this nature." This paradox is expressed, Rosenzweig suggests, in the twin myths of the Original Sin of the primordial human being and of the "descent of God" in revelation (at Sinai or Golgotha). One might suggest that the former is "pre-historical" insofar as it roots both the possibility of human freedom vis-à-vis God and the need for human self-transcendence, in a divinely created human *nature,* while the latter is "historical" insofar as it points to a divine intervention into nature at a historical point that initiates a *historical process* through which nature is transcended. And Rosenzweig claims here that this paradoxical synthesis of a divinely created human nature and a divine command upon the human being to overcome that nature in time forges the decisive character of human experience: "*the pathos of the moment.*" The sense I have, Rosenzweig implies here, that the decisions I am called on to make at key moments in my life are truly of crucial significance, is rooted in this paradox of revelation. What a person decides to do in the "moment" she is summoned by God matters, Rosenzweig implies, because such decisions are not predetermined by human nature, and because—occurring as they do within the flow of historical time—they present opportunities for self-transcendence that will not return. On other hand, were these opportunities for self-transcendence not at the same time still tied to the worldly nature out of which they emerge, they would not be *moments,* or points in a shared temporal course of development, but rather isolated and nontemporal experiences of transcendence, of the kind Rosenzweig appears to have entertained when he still inclined toward Marcionism.

Unlike in the Stoic account of natural law, according to which the law I must follow directs me to realize my own nature, Rosenzweig asserts further, the revelatory divine law that summons me to transcend my nature demands, as Tertullian had noted, "a choice between life and death."[74] But if we recall Rosenzweig's previous comment, written on the same date, to the effect that "the world is created for the sake of the *decision,*" then we can also suggest that this life-or-death choice between accepting the vocation to which God summons the individual and shirking that vocation grants the moment "pathos" because the whole purpose of creation is tied up with that decision. The fate of the world "depends," as it were, on whether or not human beings freely take on the redemptive task God has summoned them to adopt. Let me note, finally, that Rosenzweig's account of the "pathos of the moment" here parallels Rosenstock's assertion, examined earlier, regarding the actualizing force of revelation: "there is such a place [i.e., "your place in the history of the human race"] only once and it never comes again."[75]

If we consider together now the three different passages about creation and revelation we've examined here, the following account of human action in the world emerges, which Rosenzweig has formulated in clear opposition to the Marcionist worldview to which he was drawn before the *Leipziger Nachtgespräch.* The possibility of free human action depends on and is grounded in the concept of a God who is the absolute creator but who has limited Himself in order to open up a space within which human beings can act. Indeed, God has created the world *so that* the human being is faced with the free decision between life and death, between accepting or not accepting the vocation to which God summons the human being in the midst of the world and its history. The moments in life during which the human being is thereby summoned to decide are invested with dramatic significance *because* the life of the individual and the fate of the world appear to depend on what the human being decides in these moments.[76]

I want to note one particular characteristic of the view of freedom Rosenzweig arrives at here, in his reflections on thinking creation and revelation together as the alternative to Marcionism. The freedom Rosenzweig articulates here is not the capacity to decide between myriad possibilities. It is a binary choice between life and death, between "Yes and No," between taking up the divine vocation to love others in the world or not. Thus when Rosenzweig says, "the world is created for the sake of the *decision,*" he does not mean to suggest that the world exists so that the human beings in it can have the freedom to make of it whatever they so choose. He means that whether or not the world will be redeemed depends on whether human beings decide to take up their redemptive vocation. This narrowing of the scope of human freedom remains central to Rosenzweig's account of freedom in the *Star* and, as we shall see, lies at the heart of his critique of Kantian autonomy in II 3 of the *Star.*

One final source will bring us full circle in our investigation of Rosenzweig's response to those questions regarding the possibility and significance of human action that emerged for him in his struggle against Marcionism. In early 1917, Rosenzweig wrote two excited letters to Rudolf Ehrenberg while reading a book by Ricarda Huch, entitled *Luthers Glaube: Briefe an einen Freund.* The book, Rosenzweig tells Ehrenberg, "deals not at all with Luther but rather with the matter itself, with our matter" even though "she dresses it in the language of pantheism."[77] He suggests the book shares its theme with Ehrenberg's *Ebr. 10, 25: Ein Schicksal in Predigten,* and then attempts to use the themes of Huch's book in order to identify the issues that were at stake in the *Leipziger Nachtgespräch* itself:

> "Luther" was then the opportunity [for Huch] to bring together the theme of the novel (Lucifer and the one who acts [der Handelnde]) with the theme of life ("Nature and Spirit" . . .). But the connection must now not be coincidental. Because while my meeting with Rosenstock in 1913 occurred on the ground of the "theme of the novel," our correspondence of 1916 concerned the "theme of life." It is totally clear, indeed, that the former must come first. One must first believe in the necessity of *action* before one has qualms over *intentionality.*[78]

Rosenzweig here first situates Huch's *Luthers Glaube* vis-à-vis another one of her writings, *Natur und Geist,* and suggests that Huch's Luther book brings together its own main theme—"Lucifer and the one who acts"—with the "theme of life" that had been at the heart of Huch's *Natur und Geist.* What interests us in this letter is how Rosenzweig's discussion of Huch immediately leads him to identify the core issue of the *Leipziger Nachtgespräch,* but to do so in terms of the question of human action we have been examining. Rosenzweig claims that his "meeting with Rosenstock in 1913 occurred on the ground of the 'theme of the novel,'" that is, the theme of "Lucifer and the one who acts," and indeed that only because he came out of that conversation believing in "the necessity of *action,*" could he later correspond with Rosenstock over "intentionality."

Let me offer a very brief overview of Huch's *Luthers Glaube* so that we can make some sense of Rosenzweig's comments here. Huch's book is composed as a series of passionate and intensely spiritual letters to a "friend" whose cultivation of moral purity leads him to avoid action in the world. The letters offer an account of the world as a single whole of which God represents the center and spirit. It is the task of individuals, according to the letters, to merge their respective wills and minds with that of the divine whole. Thus, however pure his intentions, when the letters' addressee spurns action in the world, according to the writer, he isolates himself from God and opposes himself to God's utmost intentions. He is "like Lucifer, the most beautiful among the angels who became through his beauty the most supreme devil."[79] "Nothing and no one appears beautiful enough to you to seduce you to sin," the letters' author complains. "Thus you worship yourself and you—who don't want to sin, seduce others to it, to the sin of worshipping you."[80]

As Rosenzweig notes, the worldview Huch presents in *Luthers Glaube* is far more akin to pantheism than Gnosticism. But the manner in which the addressee of the letters, like "Lucifer," refuses to act in the world for fear that it will undermine his own purity as an individual, certainly recalls the world denial Rosenzweig entertained as he entered the *Leipziger Nachtgespräch.* Indeed, Rosenzweig surely found his own earlier withdrawal from action in the world, his having been deemed a heretic worthy of God's rejection for the way he "took from faith and not from love," echoed in Huch's depiction of Lucifer as the one who "sins against love; that is the sin which God damns."[81] But over the course of the *Leipziger Nachtgespräch,* Rosenzweig writes to Rudolf Ehrenberg, he came to believe in "the necessity of *action*" in the world. Indeed, as we have seen, Rosenzweig came to view the human decision to enter into relations of love in the world as both made possible by creation and revelation in tandem, and as necessary to advance the redemptive process through which self and world can hope to find reconciliation.

If Rosenzweig's commitment to the "necessity of *action*" was in part the fruit of his experience of redemptive love through Rosenstock over the course of the *Leipziger Nachtgespräch,* then his excitement over *Luthers Glaube* may be linked to this aspect of his conversion as well. As part of her pleading in *Luthers Glaube* that her addressee enter into the divine orbit of the world, rather than remain aloof from it, the letter-writer suggests that Luther himself endured a similar period of isolation.[82] But Luther's personal estrangement from the world was overcome, she proceeds to explain, through the very experience of redemptive love we have suggested Rosenzweig experienced through Rosenstock at the *Leipziger Nachtgespräch*. Thus she claims that "the little hint that Staupitz gave him, that God's essence is love, and the circumstance that this love was now also at once represented sensibly [*sinnenfällig*] in Staupitz, tore him loose from his self and prepared the change-in-direction, the *metanoia*, in him."[83]

Rosenzweig did not come to a resolution to the crisis that he experienced in the wake of the *Leipziger Nachtgespräch* until he reached the conclusion to remain a Jew, in October 1913. It is unlikely that this is mere coincidence. It suggests, to the contrary, that his questions about his own Judaism played a more intimate role in his quest to arrive at a coherent and compelling account of the relation between soul and world than we have hitherto suggested. In the following chapter, I will reconstruct Rosenzweig's thinking about Judaism during the period of the *Leipziger Nachtgespräch* and its aftermath. I will try to determine the extent to which Rosenzweig understood his Judaism to be consistent with the faith-position with which he entered the night-conversation, and the extent to which Rosenstock's and Ehrenberg's challenge to Rosenzweig that night was at once a challenge to his Judaism. More significantly, however, examining Rosenzweig's reflections on Judaism in the wake of the *Leipziger Nachtgespräch* will make it possible to offer a new explanation for *why* Rosenzweig reversed his decision to convert to Christianity, and determined to recommit himself to Judaism. This explanation, we shall find, is rooted in the very struggle with Marcionism at the heart of the *Leipziger Nachtgespräch*.

3

"Ich bleibe also Jude"

Judaism, Redemption, and the World

A YOM KIPPUR EXPERIENCE?

Why did Rosenzweig return to Judaism? After the transformative conversation of July 7, 1913, in which he was forced to examine the Marcionist consequences of his faith position, and in which he determined to convert to a Christianity that would resolve his long-standing perplexity over the relation between soul and world, what could have led him to decide to recommit himself to Jewish life?

The answer that has dominated the scholarship for the last sixty years suggests that the key to Rosenzweig's reversal was a transformative experience at a traditional Day of Atonement prayer service. Stéphane Mosès claims that "before taking the decisive step" of conversion to Christianity, "Rosenzweig decided to attend the Yom Kippur service in a small synagogue in Berlin. It is there that his real conversion occurred, the conversion that brought him back to Judaism. Rosenzweig does not mention explicitly this experience in any of his writings, but without a doubt, it is the decisive event of his spiritual biography."[1] "Having witnessed, perhaps for the first time, a traditional Day of Atonement service," Paul Mendes-Flohr likewise narrates, "Rosenzweig concluded that Judaism was not spiritually moribund as he and his friends had assumed. Reversing his decision to enter the Church, he thus affirmed that a meaningful life of faith may be pursued within the precincts, as he put it, of the Synagogue."[2] And Eugen Rosenstock himself writes, in 1969, that "in September [*sic*] 1913, Franz attended services of the highest Jewish holidays, and his participation in this act of divine worship convinced him, much to his own surprise, that he could remain, that he would *have to remain,* a Jew—but on a different basis than before. He was, in effect, converted to Judaism as the guiding force of his life."[3]

This common account of Rosenzweig's 1913 Yom Kippur experience, which nearly all scholars of Rosenzweig's work retell, has its origins, if I am not mistaken, in Nahum Glatzer's 1952 essay, "Franz Rosenzweig: The Story of a Conversion,"[4] which was reprinted as the introduction to Glatzer's *Franz Rosenzweig: Life and Thought* (1953).[5] In this essay, Glatzer claims "Rosenzweig's biography indicates" that Rosenzweig's "call . . . back to Judaism" after his decision to convert to Christianity "happened during the service of the Day of Atonement, 1913. . . . The experience of this day was the origin of his radical return to Judaism."[6] Glatzer acknowledges that Rosenzweig himself says nothing about such an experience of communal prayer directly. Indeed, he cites the fact that Rosenzweig "never mentioned this event to his friends and never presented it in his writings" as evidence for how deeply and personally important it must have been for him ("He guarded it as the secret ground of his new life.").[7] Glatzer suggests that his account is based on a report given to him by Rosenzweig's mother, but that "the mother's contention could only be convincing if confirmed by some internal evidence."[8] By way of such confirmation, Glatzer adduces three bits of evidence: 1) the dates of Rosenzweig's announcement to Rudolf Ehrenberg (October 31, 1913), written less than three weeks after Yom Kippur that year (October 11), and of a letter to his mother hinting at his decision to return written even earlier (October 23); 2) the obvious centrality of the Yom Kippur liturgy within Rosenzweig's account of the Jewish people in *The Star of Redemption*, in which Rosenzweig identifies Yom Kippur as the climactic point of the liturgical year in which the Jew experiences eternity within the praying community;[9] and 3) the radical character of Rosenzweig's reversal, which appears to have occurred with the "suddenness and in that spirit of absolute finality reported in great conversions," and which bespeaks, according to Glatzer, of "a certainty that does not come to a man through thinking; it points to a profound, instantaneous event."[10]

Now, let me concede that I have no new evidence to present that would either confirm or undermine the Yom Kippur hypothesis that has become such a central part of the Rosenzweig legend. And while the circumstantial evidence that Glatzer provides hardly seems to me to supply the kind of foundation that would justify the staying-power the Yom-Kippur hypothesis has had in the scholarly literature, I see no reason—barring unforeseen new evidence—to rule out the possibility that a visit to the synagogue on Yom Kippur played some role in Rosenzweig's decision to remain a Jew.[11]

But the considerations that lead Glatzer to champion the Yom Kippur story deserve our attention. Glatzer's account of Rosenzweig's reverse conversion makes an assumption that I think many scholars of religious thought and of intellectual history might be inclined to share: radical insights are most often the result of radical events or experiences. There is no question, moreover, that the manner in which Rosenzweig would recall the period of the *Leipziger Nachtgespräch* itself for the rest of his life—as an experience of intimacy with God transcending the world, as an experience of Rosenstock's redemptive love—encourages this approach in the scholarly attempt to understand him, in particular. But we must be wary of adopting this assumption indiscriminately. It runs the risk, among other things, of reducing all ideas to psychological or physiological grounds.[12] When it comes to recalling his decision to remain a Jew, furthermore, Rosenzweig insists more than once that such a decision was *not* solely or even primarily the result of experience, but rather was the result of a conclusion reached through *thought*. In his letter of October 31, 1913, Rosenzweig tells Ehrenberg that he has reached his decision to remain a Jew "after long and, as I see it, fundamental consideration."[13] He reports to Martin Buber, on May 21, 1924, that his own "theory of Jews and Christianity" was a "saving thought" which he found in 1913.[14] Two months later, he clarifies this comment as follows:

> The great reversal [*Umkehr*] in my own life reflected itself precisely in thoughts. Of course acts also depend on thoughts: what was permitted or even commanded before was afterwards no longer permitted. But that was only consequence, and if I looked back afterwards to the before, so it was not the acts which alarmed me, which were just only consequences, but rather the whole circle of intuition, in which I lived at that time—a kind of Barthianism, as I well already told you once.[15]

Rosenzweig's comments to Ehrenberg and Buber are important because they suggest the predominant role that thinking played for Rosenzweig in the process of leaving his early "Barthianism"[16] and then committing himself, first to Christian world-activity, and then to Judaism. As we shall see, this insistence on "thought" as the medium through which Rosenzweig reached his decision to remain a Jew is not meant to exclude experience as complementing or confirming or contributing to his thought-process. Indeed, we shall suggest that an experience Rosenzweig does report having had in Berlin in the fall of 1913—an experience of *hope* rather than of *faith*—serves precisely to confirm a line of thought Rosenzweig had entertained from the moment of the *Leipziger Nachtgespräch* itself. But Rosenzweig's insistence in this case warns against placing too much emphasis on a Yom Kippur experience that Rosenzweig never mentions.[17]

I hope to show, moreover, that one of the great benefits of recognizing the struggle with Marcionism in which Rosenzweig was embroiled during the summer of 1913, is that it enables us to offer a credible explanation for Rosenzweig's decision to return to Judaism, in October 1913, that does not *depend* on a Yom Kippur experience. Both Rosenzweig's announcement of his decision to return to Judaism in the fall of 1913, and the new account of the complementary roles to be played by Christianity and Judaism in the redemptive process that accompanies that announcement, can best be understood, I will claim, as the consequence of a new conclusion Rosenzweig reaches in his thinking in the fall of 1913: without the Jewish people performing the unique redemptive role they exist to perform, Christianity cannot realize the historical reconciliation of soul and world that would signal the true overcoming of Gnostic dualism. As we shall see, Rosenzweig's return to Judaism is, remarkably, a consequence of the very turn from Marcionism to history that first directs Rosenzweig to Christianity.

ROSENZWEIG'S EARLY VIEW OF JUDAISM

Before exploring the new view of Judaism and Christianity reached by Rosenzweig in the fall of 1913, I want to attempt at least a partial reconstruction of Rosenzweig's view of Judaism both leading up to and immediately following the *Leipziger Nachtgespräch.* This is not a straightforward task, unfortunately, as Rosenzweig's sparse comments about Judaism prior to the summer of 1913 give us precious little material to work with. To lay the background for Rosenzweig's later explicit views, however, I will offer a conjecture about how Rosenzweig conceived of Judaism upon entering the Leipzig night-conversation, what role his Judaism may have played in the conversation itself, and finally the ways in which that conversation changed how he thought about Judaism and his own relation to it.

In his letter to Rudolf Ehrenberg of October 31, 1913, Rosenzweig gives us a few clues about the conception of Judaism he held before his Leipzig night-conversation, and why that conversation initially changed his attitude toward Judaism. Immediately after pointing to the first sentence of the Bible as providing the beginnings of a new standpoint, opposed to the Marcionism with which he entered the conversation, Rosenzweig offers the following reflection, parts of which we have already encountered:

> What forced me . . . to follow further [i.e., along the path opened up by the first sentence of the Bible], this you well know, and have expressed it in the *Predigten* (the one about the heretic): that I Christianized my Judaism conceptually, that I shared or at least intended to share with you [plural] the community of faith. For this reason I was at that time disarmed at once already through Rosenstock's simple confession, with which his attack began. That a man like Rosenstock was consciously a Christian . . . this nixed my whole representation of Christianity, but therewith of religion overall, and therewith of my religion. I had believed to have Christianized Judaism. In truth, I had done the reverse, that is, Judaized Christianity. I had taken the year 313 for the beginning of the collapse of true Christianity, because it opened for Christianity the opposite way through the world from that which the year 70 opened for Judaism. I had resented the Church for its ruling-staff, because I saw that the Synagogue held a broken staff. You were witness to how I began to build up the world anew for myself from this knowledge. In this world . . . there appeared to be no place for Judaism.[18]

This passage as a whole will occupy us for some time, but I want to begin by focusing on Rosenzweig's initial assertion that he had believed to have "Christianized" his "Judaism conceptually," and in doing so "intended to share" with Rosenstock and Ehrenberg "the community of faith." Obscure as this statement is, it suggests that, according to Rosenzweig's earlier views regarding the task and essence of Judaism and Christianity, respectively, he entered the *Leipziger Nachtgespräch* under the impression that the Judaism to which he was able to pledge allegiance bore typically Christian features. Such a commitment to a "Christianized Judaism" appears to have led Rosenzweig to believe that he could participate, despite his Judaism, in the "community of faith" shared by Ehrenberg and Rosenstock.

What exactly was this "Christianized Judaism" Rosenzweig believed himself to have espoused?

We take a step toward clarifying Rosenzweig's meaning, in fact, by reviewing what we've learned about the way his view of Christianity changed over the course of the *Leipziger Nachtgespräch*. Rosenzweig had believed to have "Christianized Judaism," but discovered that he had instead "Judaized Christianity." He had done so, we may presume, insofar as he had taken "true Christianity" to be that Christianity that preceded its involvement in "world activity," when it still represented, for Rosenzweig, a path of faith—with Marcionist ramifications—rather than a path through the world.[19] If Rosenzweig thus viewed true Christianity as directing believers outside the world rather than to a vocation within it, then we might suggest, preliminarily, that a "Christianized Judaism," according to this earlier view, would likewise define Judaism as a mode of relation to the divine through faith, rather than, say, through ritual and works within the world.

A diary entry of Rosenzweig's from September 1, 1910 may help further decode what Rosenzweig intends by the designation, "Christianized Judaism":

> My Judaism is dogmatically foreign in every way to present-day Judaism. I believe in sin and in the necessity of the mediator (of "am yisrael"). But that God in fact forgives the individual sinner if he calls to Him in the choir of Am Yisrael, that God has chosen this people in order to redeem the whole of humanity, and His own limb as well, through it—that is a dogma so outrageous, so beyond all reason, that even Christian dogma cannot be "more absurd."[20]

Rosenzweig's comment here identifies his own conception of Judaism as deviating significantly from the prevailing Jewish doctrine of his day. This deviation appears to turn on the question of the redemptive role of Am Yisrael, that is, the Jewish people. Rosenzweig apparently assents to the view that the Jewish people as a unit fulfills a need for mediation individual Jews have: given their sins, Jews require such mediation presumably in order to achieve a relation to the divine. But Rosenzweig here rejects views he takes to be central to contemporary Jewish belief: the view that such mediation through the Jewish people serves to "forgive" individual Jews their sins; and the view that the Jewish people is *chosen* to fulfill a redemptive task both in the world and for the divine Itself.

Rosenzweig pens this comment at what we now know to be a significant moment in his development in the wake of the Baden-Baden experiment, and this context can help us shed some interpretive light on his words. September 1910 was the very month during which Rosenzweig wrote both his "Young Hegel" letter to Rudolf Ehrenberg, in which he first explores the notion of dying for God, and the letter to Hans Ehrenberg in which he points to the "God of religion" as the sole means of redeeming the individual from the sinfulness of the historical world. Since we now know Rosenzweig at that time to have understood the soul's relation to the divine as demanding the denial of the world, we may infer that Rosenzweig would have viewed it as the task of religion to make possible such a relationship to the divine. Since, moreover, the theology of world-denial that Rosenzweig entertained would have indeed assumed the sinfulness of the world, then it is not surprising that Rosenzweig would have believed in "the necessity of the mediator (of 'am yisrael')," without which the individual would be unable to transcend the sinfulness that adheres to him as part of the world. We might suggest that one aspect of the "Christianized Judaism" to which Rosenzweig later claimed he could commit was precisely this need for mediation. His belief demands that his Judaism be structured in a manner parallel to Christianity, with Am Yisrael playing the role of Christ, as salvific mediator who makes it possible for the individual to enter into a relation with the divine despite the sinfulness of the world he inhabits.

On the other hand, according to the September 1910 diary entry, Rosenzweig finds the notion of Jewish chosenness "outrageous." He cannot accept that the Jew within Am Yisrael stands in a unique position of being able to be forgiven his sins by God, perhaps because he holds that in a world inherently sinful, a mediator may serve to remove an individual from his sinful context, but such a mediator cannot achieve the "forgiveness" of such worldly sinfulness. More pointedly, Rosenzweig finds it absurd to imagine that Jews play a fundamentally unique role in a process that redeems both the world and the divine itself. He finds it absurd, we may conjecture, because his view of religion as enabling the soul to transcend the world has no place in it for the notion that particular actors or particular actions within the world can redeem it. To believe that the world is inherently sinful is to believe that it *cannot* be redeemed, and that the soul's redemption can come solely from escaping it. Nor does Rosenzweig appear to believe, at this stage in his thinking, that any action in the world could serve to redeem God's "own limb"—any action, that is, besides the negation of the worldly itself. Recall how the "Shechina" sonnets, which Rosenzweig wrote in the year following this diary entry, assign to the act of human death alone the power to redeem God that Rosenzweig here denies to Jewish ritual action.

If Rosenzweig thereby saw his denial of the efficacy of Jewish action in the world, and of the chosenness of Jews to perform such actions, as contrary to the doctrine of mainstream Judaism; and if he emphasized instead the way Judaism shares in religion's general task of mediating the individual soul's relation to the divine, then we may suggest that when he entered the *Leipziger Nachtgespräch,* he would have understood his Judaism to offer a kind of faith experience, and a kind of personal path of salvation, that he likewise understood to be central to Christianity. He thereby would have understood himself to have "Christianized Judaism."

Our exploration of the Marcionism Rosenzweig advocated during this period permits us to speculate further. If Rosenzweig indeed understood revelation at the time as a relation the soul has to the divine that transcends or even negates the worldly, then he could very well have been able to ignore the differences he would later emphasize between the *worldly* forms and tasks of Judaism and Christianity, respectively. Such a view would have permitted him to believe that he could "share" a "community of faith" with Rosenstock and Ehrenberg, despite the fact that he still held to his Judaism, while they were Christians. Rejecting Jewish chosenness would thus have enabled Rosenzweig to share in a faith community beyond the limits of Am Yisrael. The rebuke of the eighteenth sermon of Ehrenberg's *Predigten,* which we examined earlier, does indeed appear to imply a criticism of Rosenzweig on this very point. Rosenzweig writes, in his letter to Ehrenberg of October 31, 1913, that Ehrenberg had "expressed . . . in the *Predigten* (the one about the heretic): that I Christianized my Judaism conceptually, that I shared or at least intended to share with you [plural] the community of faith." Ehrenberg's sermon includes no direct comment on Judaism; but its attack on the heretic who "takes of faith and not of love," an attack we have understood thus far as directed against Rosenzweig's Marcionist emphasis on faith at the expense of the world, may be understood as chiding Rosenzweig for his view of Judaism as well. It suggests that Rosenzweig is wrong to think that he can adopt a faith he understands to be common to Judaism and Christianity, without taking up one of the very distinct worldly vocations that Judaism and Christianity, respectively, demand. Rosenzweig the heretic, Ehrenberg's pastor may be said to claim, wishes to share in Christian faith without participating in Christian "world-activity."

Now if, as we've seen, Rosenzweig left the *Leipziger Nachtgespräch* convinced that the "world activity" of Christianity offered him a way of taking seriously the conflict between self and world that had perplexed him, while at once pointing to the dialectical resolution of this conflict through history; if then he became open to committing himself to taking his place within that historical advance; then Judaism—as he then understood it—appeared only as a barrier to such resolution. For while Rosenzweig now came to understand "true Christianity" no longer through Marcionist eyes, he continued to grasp Judaism as no less foreign to the world than he formerly viewed Christianity. "In this world" in which Christianity took up the task of realizing the Kingdom of God through redemptive love, Rosenzweig thus concluded, "there appeared to be no place for Judaism." While Rosenzweig had thought that he was guilty of "Christianizing Judaism," he realized through the *Leipziger Nachtgespräch* that he in fact had been "Judaizing Christianity." He had attributed to Christianity the anti-worldly comportment that he now saw as characteristic solely of Judaism.

Strange bed-fellows though they certainly are, Judaism and Marcionism thus came to be identified in Rosenzweig's mind as the twin doctrines he must turn away from in converting to a Christianity that acts in the world. For all that Judaism and Marcionism disagree on the most essential question—which God is which—"the year 70 opened for Judaism" the way out of the very world that its God had created. The Synagogue "held a broken staff," and thus had no role to play in the historical realization of the Kingdom of heaven on earth. This proximity of Judaism to Marcionism in Rosenzweig's thinking will continue to occupy us in what follows.

Rosenzweig may thus be understood to have reached the decision to abandon his own Judaism—as the flipside of his decision to adopt Christianity—not merely because he found the Judaism of his time to be "spiritually moribund,"[21] or because he doubted that "Judaism could be existentially lived"[22] in his day, or because he was not able "to counter the faith of the Christian with the faith of a Jew."[23] To the contrary: the line of thinking we have followed here suggests that it is not at all the spiritual side of Judaism that Rosenzweig found lacking, but rather its *worldly* side. Only Christianity appeared to offer Rosenzweig that means of reconciling self and world.

Yet, on October 31, 1913, Rosenzweig wrote Rudolf Ehrenberg to tell him that, "after long and, as I see it, fundamental consideration, I have decided to take back my decision. It appears to me no longer necessary and therefore, in my case, no longer possible. So I remain a Jew."[24] Here we return to the questions with which we opened this chapter: what could have led Rosenzweig, during the months in which he struggled between Marcionism and Christian world-activity, to decide to remain a Jew?

We know, first of all, that Rosenzweig made an important decision, shortly after the July night-conversation, regarding the process that was to lead up to his conversion. Rosenzweig's decision to convert to Christianity included the "personal caveat," as Rosenzweig later reminded Rudolf Ehrenberg, that he "be able to become Christian only as *Jew,* not through the between-stage of paganism."[25] Although Ehrenberg apparently approved of Rosenzweig's decision to practice Judaism during the months before his conversion "in recollection of the original Christianity," that is, as tribute to the way the early Jewish converts to Christianity were urged to "live true to the law during the time of preparation up to the moment of baptism," Rosenzweig insisted his caveat was "purely personal."[26] We might suggest that this insistence was based on the new seriousness with which Rosenzweig began approaching his own worldliness after the night-conversation. We recall that Rosenzweig no longer found himself justified in sweeping the Judaism of his birth under the rug in order to share with Ehrenberg and Rosenstock "a community of faith," despite his Jewishness. If the position to which Rosenzweig was to convert demanded he take the redemptive activity of Christianity in the world seriously, it also demanded that he take seriously the worldly character of the person away from which he was converting. He could not arbitrarily consider himself a pagan, when the very world that demanded his redemptive action was the world in which he had been born a Jew.

Rosenzweig's "personal caveat" suggests that rethinking Judaism was an *immediate* consequence of the *Leipziger Nachtgespräch,* one he understood to be demanded even by his decision to convert to Christianity. Rosenzweig's own reports likewise suggest that the process that led to his ultimate resolution to remain a Jew began during the July night-conversation. The first extant letter we posses that Rosenzweig wrote in the wake of his decision to remain a Jew was addressed to his mother, on October 23, 1913—eight days before he announced his change of mind to Rudolf Ehrenberg. Rosenzweig ended this letter by noting that his mother "will have gathered from this letter that I hope to have found the way back [*Rückweg*], which I had been brooding over [*zergrübeln*] in vain for almost three months."[27] Rosenzweig suggested, thereby, that he had already begun reconsidering his conversion to Christianity in the immediate aftermath of the *Leipziger Nachtgespräch*. Rosenzweig likewise tells Rosenstock, on January 15, 1920, "I date my Jewish return [*Einkehr*] not from that day in Berlin, in October 1913, but rather from our Leipzig night."[28]

Since the process of Rosenzweig's return to Judaism thus appears to have begun immediately following the *Leipziger Nachtgespräch*, there is good reason to suspect that the considerations that led him ultimately to "return" to Judaism were rooted in the very same fundamental questions that Rosenzweig was forced to ask himself at the conversation itself. I have thus proposed that the key to explaining Rosenzweig's decision to remain a Jew be sought out in the very same course that Rosenzweig's thinking took in the wake of the *Leipziger Nachtgespräch*, from a Marcionist faith in revelation as that which grants the soul salvation from the world, to a Christianity committed to the realization of the Kingdom of heaven *on earth*. Indeed, it is precisely in the case of explaining Rosenzweig's return to Judaism that the new account of the Leipzig night-conversation I am offering is most illuminating.

MARCIONISM AND RETURN: CHRISTIAN TEMPTATIONS AND JEWISH CHOSENNESS

Let us then explore how Rosenzweig's return to Judaism was rooted in his struggle with Marcionism. The Marcionist background to his decision to remain a Jew is already evident, in fact, in the very letter to his mother from October 23, 1913, in which he first alludes to this decision. Here Rosenzweig responds to his mother's report on a conversation she evidently had with a local pastor named "Jaeckh." Rosenzweig is clearly wary in the letter of what he takes to be Jaeckh's supercessionist attitude toward Judaism, and this prompts him to offer a first articulation of his newly formulated view of the relation between Judaism and Christianity:

> The vitality which J[aeckh] concedes to Judaism is just that which the whole Church concedes to it and which the Church has fought through in the most difficult inner struggle for its existence (the struggle with the Gnostic heresy) and so for its own sake cannot relinquish: that the Old Testament is "God's Word," that "salvation" has come from the Jews (as Paul says), and the God, who "created Heaven and Earth," the "God of Abraham and the God of Isaac and the God of Jacob," the God who named his "name" to Moses, and gave his spirit to the prophets—that this God is the

> "Father of Jesus Christ." This the Church has fought through against the Gnostics, who refused to believe this, and explained the God of the Old Testament as being one with the Devil or in the best case as an angel or under-God. No sensible Jew will not be thankful to it for this. But the consequence, that now his own development leads through Jesus, that Jewish religion can "live itself out and fulfill(!)" itself in him, *this* [consequence] Judaism has *not* drawn. To the contrary, it rejects as roughly as possible that he in whom its world-historical calling could *fulfill* itself, *has* already come. It still waits for him and will wait, so long as it *remains* Judaism.[29]

Rosenzweig's letter attributes to Judaism an essential function in the historical development of the early Church, through the latter's struggles to define its doctrinal identity. Having come to recognize Rosenzweig's own struggle between Marcionism and a commitment to Christian world-activity, it is perhaps not surprising to discover that Rosenzweig understands "the most difficult inner struggle" which the early Church endured "for its existence" to be a struggle with "Gnostic heresy."[30] In this struggle, Rosenzweig implies, it was the "vitality" of Judaism to which the early Church fathers pointed in their insistence, against those Christian Gnostics, that "'salvation' has come from the Jews," that "the 'God of Abraham . . . Isaac and . . . Jacob'" is "the 'Father of Jesus Christ.'"[31] Against the Gnostic view that "the God of the Old Testament" is "one with the Devil or in the best case an angel or under-God," Rosenzweig thereby shows, the developing Church doctrine insisted that the God of creation and the God of salvation are one and the same, that the "God who 'created Heaven and Earth'" was none other than "the Father of Jesus Christ." Indeed, Rosenzweig suggests here that the Gnostic position of theologians like Marcion highlights, by way of distinction, the shared commitment of Judaism and Christianity to a salvation that does not deny the world and its history, but rather that situates its own activity along the path that leads from creation to salvation.[32]

However, Rosenzweig demurs, this shared commitment to a salvation that would accommodate both the soul and the world does not entail that the "Jewish religion . . . fulfills itself" through Jesus. In contradistinction to the Christians, Jews continue to "wait" for the coming of the world redeemer. Indeed, such waiting is demanded by their "world-historical calling."

Rosenzweig's letter to his mother implies, furthermore, that the role Judaism played in securing the Christian commitment to redeeming the world did not come to an end with its bolstering of early Christian orthodoxy in the latter's struggle with Gnosticism. "The Jew must remain Jew," Rosenzweig writes to his mother, "in order to awaken for each Christian his Christianity again if he has forgotten it."[33] Here Rosenzweig intimates a thought that was to become the centerpiece of his account of the relationship between Judaism and Christianity in *The Star of Redemption:* it is the Jew's very existence that ever reminds the Christian that the world still needs to be redeemed. In Rosenzweig's letter to Ehrenberg of October 31, 1913, Rosenzweig asserts that the danger that threatens to cause the Christian to forget her task in the world lies in the fact that she is "sent to all," and thus might "lose herself in the universal."[34] But in a number of later formulations, the explanation Rosenzweig offers suggests that the existence of the Jew serves the vital function of ensuring that Christianity not fall into those Gnostic tendencies from which, apparently, it is never truly immune. Thus Rosenzweig asserts, in his "Paralipomena," that "Judaism is the crude factuality through which Christianity is hindered from a dissolution of its eschatology into the pneumatic, to which it always tends. We are the impetus for the Church to be visible."[35] And Rosenzweig makes this same point in a letter to Gertrud Oppenheim, on May 1, 1917, by suggesting that the danger inherent to Christianity is its tendency to blur the distinction between the first coming of Christ and the ultimate redemption. "They don't know the difference between first and last men," Rosenzweig writes:

> They believe that the choice is already the accomplishment, that redemption already happens in faith. . . . Then comes the Jew, the eternal *enfant terrible* (eternal infant—he was there when the matter began) of Church history, and cries: the robe has been stolen! It belongs to the *last* man, the world is *not* yet redeemed. Men are *on the way,* faith makes them into men, but not into more than men. . . . Humanity still *waits* for redemption. . . . Without the eternal admonisher, the eternal *enfant terrible,* the effectiveness of the first man would expire in his presumed already-finishedness, and the world would never be finished.[36]

Rosenzweig's explanation of the indispensable role the Jew plays in the world's redemption here is striking for the way it recalls the very terms of the struggle with Marcionism that Rosenzweig himself endured. Redemptive as Christian world-activity may be, Rosenzweig suggests, there are risks involved in the Christian vocation. Christians are called on through belief in an actual redeemer to complete the task of redeeming the world, of realizing the Kingdom of God on earth. But precisely insofar as the call to act redemptively in the world rests on a faith in a redeemer who has *already come,* Rosenzweig implies, the Christian always runs the risk of believing that "redemption already happens in faith." The Christian thus courts the danger, throughout world history, of celebrating the redeemer and the experience of having been redeemed that accompanies faith, and forgetting that "the world is *not* yet redeemed," but rather still calls for redemptive action. Christianity, Rosenzweig thereby implies, *is always at risk of falling back into Marcionism.* And this is where the Jewish people comes in. The Jewish people's very existence, according to Rosenzweig, "admonishes" the Christian lest she forget the world still needs redeeming, lest she forget that the salvation of some is not the salvation of all, that the reality of the Church as the community of faith is not the same as the reality of the Kingdom of God on earth.[37]

Two aspects of the Jewish people's role as "eternal admonisher" for Christians should be emphasized and elaborated upon here. The first of these we have in fact already touched on. The existence of the Jewish people "chosen" by the God of creation—the very God understood by Christians to be the "Father" of Jesus Christ—serves as a perpetual reminder to the Christian that the God of creation and the God of salvation are one and the same, and hence that creation and redemption are intertwined. The existence of the Jew ensures, that is to say, that the Christian grasps redemption as the *fulfillment* of the creation of the world, and hence as unthinkable for the individual soul independent of the world as a whole. As we shall explore further in this chapter, thinking creation and salvation together is essential to Rosenzweig's developing view of history, and Rosenzweig understands the promise–fulfillment relationship between creation and salvation to be determinative for the kind of knowledge the Bible makes possible. "With the knowledge of the mere *createdness* of things, nothing is really known," Rosenzweig thus writes in a letter to Gertrud Oppenheim on May 30, 1917. "Only that the 'created' . . . things are 'created' for the sake of the *End* and He who is the First is also the Last (as Isaiah 44:6, 48:12), or the Alpha *and* the Omega (as John says [Revelation 1:8, 21:6, 22:13]), only this gives knowledge."[38]

This notion that creation, on the one hand, and revelation and redemption, on the other, stand in a relation of promise and fulfillment to one another had far-reaching consequences for Rosenzweig's mature thought. In the following chapter, we will have an opportunity to explore how Rosenzweig orders much of *The Star of Redemption* according to this promise–fulfillment structure. There I will suggest that Rosenzweig's account of revelation and redemption as promised or prophesied in creation has its roots in his reading of the Church Fathers, and of Tertullian and Augustine in particular. Indeed, it is to the arguments of Tertullian and Augustine—to the effect that the credibility of Christ's mission depends on its having been promised in the Hebrew Bible—that Rosenzweig alludes in his letter to his mother of October 23, 1913.[39] Moreover, the manner in which Rosenzweig describes the early Church's determination that "the Old Testament is 'God's Word,'" and that "the God who 'created Heaven and Earth' . . . is the 'Father of Jesus Christ,'" permits us to contextualize his developing view of the complementary redemptive tasks of Jews and Christians within another contemporary discussion involving Marcionism, to wit, that concerning the proper scope of the Christian Scriptural canon. For the practical decision to which Rosenzweig alludes when he writes of the early Church's concession that the "Old Testament is 'God's Word,'" is the Church's decision to include the Hebrew Bible *qua* Old Testament within its canon.[40] In line with his rejection of the Creator God of the Hebrew Bible, Marcion had advocated a much more narrow canon, composed primarily of the gospel of Luke and the letters of Paul, and he held all statements in the Christian Scripture that appeared to fulfill or complement teachings of the Hebrew Bible to have been the corrupt interpolations of Judaizers.[41] Rosenzweig's letter to his mother suggests Jews should be "thankful" that the early Church rejected Marcion's narrow canon and the world-denying theology supporting it.[42] But interestingly enough, Marcion's vision of a Christian canon that could stand free of the Old Testament had gained renewed traction in Rosenzweig's day, and precisely among some of those whom Rosenzweig associated with Marcion's theology. Schleiermacher had already questioned the canonical status of the Old Testament, and viewed the argument to the effect that the credibility of belief in Christ depended on Old Testament prophecies as reflecting a distorted understanding of faith itself. He went so far as to suggest that "we have to thank the dogmatic attachment to the Old Testament for much that is bad in our theology; and if Marcion had been correctly understood and not denounced as a heretic, our doctrine of God would have remained much purer."[43] In Rosenzweig's own time, moreover, none other than Harnack took up the torch of removing the Old Testament from the Christian canon. Historically and religiously important though the Old Testament may be, Harnack argued, its *canonical* status within Christianity is a dead vestige of early Church history. As Harnack writes in his monograph on Marcion, "To dismiss the Old Testament in the second century was a mistake which the Great Church rightly rejected. To retain it in the sixteenth century was a fate which the Reformation did not yet want to abdicate. But to conserve it still as a canonical document in Protestantism since the nineteenth century is the consequence of religious and ecclesiastical paralysis."[44]

In *The Star of Redemption,* Rosenzweig would later chastise "the disguised enemies of Christianity, from the Gnostics to the present day, who wanted to take from it its 'Old Testament.'"[45] He continues to identify the Christian temptation toward spiritualization, and its concomitant tendency to forget the world in need of redemption, with the recurring struggle within Christianity over the status of the Old Testament. And the Jewish people continues to serve the role, in the *Star,* of reminding the Christians that the world is *created* and thus still requires and merits redemption. When Rosenzweig first begins to articulate his account of the complementary roles of Christians and Jews within the economy of redemption, in his October 1913 letter to his mother, he thus takes up a position that explicitly opposes both the Marcionist narrowing of the Christian canon and the theology of world-denial upon which it is based.[46] The Jewish people, whose covenant with the divine promises worldly redemption, reminds Christians that "God created the world and [is] not just the God of revelation," and hence tasks Christians with fulfilling the redemptive course begun in the world's creation.

In his letters from the fall of 1913, Rosenzweig also points to a second aspect of Jewish people's role in reminding Christians to attend to the world's redemption. The Jewish people ensures that the Christian fulfill her task in redeeming the world by anticipating, through its communal prayer and practice, that ultimate redemption toward which Christianity is called on to guide the world as a whole. Hence Rosenzweig writes, in his October 1913 letter to Ehrenberg:

> The people Israel, chosen by its Father, stares fixedly over the world and history to that last furthest point, where its Father, this same, the One and Only will be—"All in All"! . . . Up to this day . . . it is Israel's life, to anticipate this eternal day in confession and action, to stand there as a living sign of this day, a people of priests, with

> the law, to make the name of God holy through its own holiness. How this people of God stands in the world, which outer (persecution) and inner (stiffness) suffering it assumes through its separation—in this regard we are again in agreement.[47]

Rosenzweig asserts here that what is unique about the Jewish people is the way in which its life of "confession and action" anticipates the redemptive goal toward which the world strives. While the Jewish people "stands in the world," it at once "stares fixedly over the world and history" at the ultimate redemption, and thereby ensures that the Christian not be misled into thinking that any given present state of affairs in the world is redemptive. By anticipating the future redemption of the world as a "people of priests," the Jewish people ensures that Christianity continues to direct itself toward the world's redemption.

When we consider together these two aspects of the Jewish people's role in the world's redemption, we may characterize their collective impact as follows. By insisting that the divine act of creation finds its fulfillment in the world's redemption, and by insisting that this redemption still lies in the future, the existence of the Jewish people ensures that the realization of the Kingdom of God on earth be conceived *historically,* and that the present moment be grasped as standing between that beginning of world history in creation, and its ending in redemption.

I shall have more to say about the roles Rosenzweig attributes to Judaism and Christianity in ensuring the historical realization of the Kingdom of God shortly. But let us first return to Rosenzweig's decision to remain a Jew. Rosenzweig's initial decision to convert to Christianity was rooted, I have claimed, in the conviction he arrived at during the *Leipziger Nachtgespräch,* that "true Christianity" did not promise the salvation of the soul at the expense of the world, but rather was committed to redeeming the world, to realizing the Kingdom of God on earth. Grasping this redemptive process historically made it possible for Rosenzweig to conceive of a reconciliation of soul and world. The conditions of life in the world may indeed be diametrically opposed to the salvation of the soul; but this opposition may be conceived as to be overcome through the historical process of the realization of the Kingdom of God.

By October 1913, however, Rosenzweig had arrived at a critical conclusion. This historical reconciliation of soul and world—the only viable alternative, to Rosenzweig's mind, to Marcionism—although carried out actively by those of the Christian faith, could not be realized unless the Jew *remained* a Jew. For without the Jewish insistence that redemption is the fulfillment of the creation of the world—and not the escape from it—without the Jewish insistence that redemption has not yet come, but is still to be realized, no such historical reconciliation of soul and world would be achieved.

Rosenzweig came to the decision to "remain a Jew," I suggest, not because of a Jewish faith experience, but because he became convinced that only if Jews remain Jews can the historical realization of the Kingdom of God come about which promises the reconciliation of soul and world. Remaining a Jew meant taking the world seriously—even as the Jew's respective role in the redemptive process held him outside the world's history—as the context within which redemption was promised to unfold. The arrival at this conclusion "after long and . . . fundamental consideration" meant that conversion to Christianity, as Rosenzweig explained to his cousin, was not simply "no longer necessary" but more importantly, was now "no longer possible." As a Jew, committed now to the realization of the Kingdom of God on earth, Rosenzweig *could not* convert. For his Jewishness demanded of him, as he now understood things, that he fulfill a unique task in the redemptive process.

If we wish to explain Rosenzweig's decision in more pithy terms, we may say that Rosenzweig came to the decision to remain a Jew because he became convinced the Jewish people is *chosen.*[48] Prior to the *Leipziger Nachtgespräch,* we recall, Rosenzweig had found "absurd" and "outrageous" the dogmatic Jewish notion that the Jewish people had been chosen by God to fulfill some redemptive vocation in relation to God or to the world. But Rosenzweig's new conviction regarding the essential role the Jewish people must play in the redemptive process now serves to align his thinking with the traditional Jewish dogma. "I find myself in complete—and unintentional . . . —agreement with the Jewish doctrine whose demonstrability in Jewish ritual and life I earlier denied," Rosenzweig tells Rudolf Ehrenberg, in his October 31, 1913 letter. "I now recognize [that Jewish doctrine] in its most important points, and above all the doctrine of sin, from which I expressly deviated up to now."[49]

That the Jewish people now could be understood as playing a vital role in the redemption of the world assumed, in the first place, that the world was redeemable—that it was no longer conceived as utterly and inherently sinful. But the conviction regarding Jewish chosenness at which Rosenzweig arrived by the fall of 1913 also involved the more dogmatic belief that the communal life of prayer and ritual through which the Jewish people reminds Christians of their redemptive vocation in the world at once shields the Jew from the world's sinfulness. Unlike all others in the world, the Jew does not "need to come to the Father, because he *is* already with him." And if the individual Jew does deviate from the proper path of "confession and action," according to Rosenzweig, he does not need to undergo the same process of conversion through which all others are reconciled to the redemptive process. Thus Rosenzweig writes, in his November 4, 1913 follow-up to the letter in which he announced his decision to remain a Jew: a Jew's distance from God is "just disloyalty and not an original distance from God ('Adam's sin'!); [it is] healed only through return, and not through conversion [*Umwandlung*]."[50]

The Jew need not convert, Rosenzweig now believed. *He need only return.*

HOPE AND HISTORY

One of my aims in tracing the process through which Rosenzweig turned back from the precipice of conversion to Christianity and returned to Judaism has been to emphasize that this process occurred, first and foremost, as the unfolding of a train of thought. I will turn, shortly, to discuss the coherence of this train of thought. But before doing so, I want to examine how this train of thought appears to have been confirmed for Rosenzweig in an *experience* Rosenzweig alludes to having had in October 1913. I have repeatedly noted the fact that Rosenzweig never mentions a 1913 Yom Kippur experience, nor does he anywhere associate his transformation over the summer and fall of 1913 with an experience of faith. But in a few letters, Rosenzweig does hint at having had some kind of experience upon arriving in Berlin at the beginning of October 1913. One of these hints comes in an important letter to Rudolf Ehrenberg, from August 25, 1919, part of which we had occasion to discuss in the last chapter:

> In that whole time in August and September 1913 I didn't see Christ for even one moment, rather always only—Eugen, and besides him, even you to some degree. But above all, Eugen. Were it otherwise, then I would well, for all I know of it, already be a Christian. But it just wasn't so. My whole experience at that time was just not of Christ (an experience of faith) but rather of Christians (an experience of faith). My experience of faith remained as you well know actually unchanged for me that whole time as Jewish. And in that moment where I, in the first day in Berlin,

> experienced the hope for the first time (and once and for all), the objective principle (the point of intersection in infinity) was found, on which the unbearable contradiction between my experience of faith and my experience of love (thus between that which I possessed from childhood on as my oldest and most treasured possession and between that which I from 1909, namely from Hans's baptism onward—then came you in 1910, Eugen in 1913—have experienced in a "quarrel" with God which I never knew before) thus the contradiction between the two experiences was settled there. Everything for me since then stands on these principles, up to and including the *Star,* which is not just called the Star of *Redemption* for nothing, because it stands toward [*auf*] the heaven of the *future,* for which one "hopes."[51]

In this fascinating letter, Rosenzweig uses a distinction between kinds of experiences in order to explain the transformations he did and did not undergo in the wake of the *Leipziger Nachtgespräch.* Rosenzweig's encounter with Rosenstock and Ehrenberg during that night did not precipitate an "experience of faith," as we've long stressed. Had he actually experienced the divinity of Christ through his encounter with Rosenstock in particular, Rosenzweig now claims, he would have no doubt already become a Christian. Rosenzweig's experience during the night-conversation was rather an experience of love, which we have understood as the interpersonal connection between an I and You that Rosenstock would come to proclaim as the path into the world's redemptive historical course. Rosenzweig now suggests, furthermore, that this experience of love stood in tension for him in the wake of the night-conversation with a Jewish "experience of faith" that he identifies as having remained "unchanged." Although the changes we have just traced in Rosenzweig's understanding of Judaism make me less certain of Rosenzweig's intention in this case, I am inclined to understand by Rosenzweig's "Jewish" experience of faith the very account of faith that Rosenzweig had concluded, in the fall of 1913, had been a product of his "Judaized Christianity"—that is, the experience of intimacy with God that hovers beyond the world, or even takes the individual out of the world. That is to say, the account of faith Rosenzweig elsewhere identifies as "Marcionism," Rosenzweig here appears to identify as a Jewish experience of faith, a relation to God outside the world. Once again we must defer the question of the proximity between Rosenzweig's respective views of Judaism and Marcionism. If I'm correct in this interpretation, however, then the tension Rosenzweig reports on having experienced after the 1913 night-conversation, between a Jewish faith experience and a Christian love experience, is identical to the tension between faith and love, or between love of God and love of others in the world with which we know Rosenzweig struggled in the years leading up to the night-conversation. Thus Rosenzweig speaks of having endured through his exposure to Christianity through Hans and Rudolf Ehrenberg, and then through Rosenstock, "a quarrel with God which I never knew before," the quarrel, we may presume, between loving God and loving others in the world. But here, Rosenzweig identifies his own faith relation to God with Judaism, and his experience of love in relation to others in the world with Christianity.

This tension is bridged for Rosenzweig, according to his letter, through an experience of *hope* Rosenzweig had in Berlin. Hope marks, for him, "the point of intersection in infinity" of the two opposed experiences. We may formulate Rosenzweig's comment about hope in the terms with which we've become familiar: a comportment toward the future redemption makes it possible to reconcile the soul's faith relation to God with the world's need for love. That is to say, the hope that Rosenzweig experiences captures the very commitment to a historical realization of the Kingdom of God that we've claimed he adopts in the wake of the *Nachtgespräch*. Hope points to a future redemption in which faith and love will be reconciled; it thereby points to the goal that Judaism and Christianity share. But in the way the experience highlights the *future* character of the reconciliation between soul and world which redemption will bring, "hope" also captures the specific role Rosenzweig assigns to the Jewish people in the redemptive process: reminding the Christian that redemption has not yet occurred, but is still a goal toward which Jews and Christians together must direct their sights and actions. It was on just such a principle of hope, Rosenzweig suggests in his letter, that everything since has stood—including the monumental book he had just completed, which, Rosenzweig insists, was not called "The Star of *Redemption* for nothing."

One may thus suggest that Rosenzweig found in the experience of hope to which he alludes in the letter of August 1919 a kind of concrete manifestation of the conclusions he had reached in thinking about the possibility of a redemptive reconciliation of the soul and the world. But offering an account of the *meaning* of Rosenzweig's hope experience, and the way it would have made sense for him within the context of his thinking, hardly amounts to an explanation of the experience itself. What was the experience of "hope" that Rosenzweig underwent in Berlin? Could Rosenzweig be referring here allusively to the very anticipation of redemption in the Yom Kippur liturgy that he would describe in such vivid terms in *The Star of Redemption*?

As I have noted, I see no reason to reject the possibility that Rosenzweig experienced something over the course of Yom Kippur in 1913 that contributed to his decision to remain a Jew. But as Rivka Horwitz has pointed out in her careful reading of this part of the letter from August 25, 1919, Rosenzweig writes that he experienced hope "in *the first day* in Berlin." Horwitz notes that, according to Rosenzweig's mother's account, Rosenzweig had traveled from Kassel to Berlin, between Rosh Hashanah and Yom Kippur that year. "Rosenzweig provides as the decisive date for his decision to remain a Jew the day of his arrival in Berlin," Horwitz concludes. "He must have found the solution before Yom Kippur, which is not mentioned in the letter to Rudolf Ehrenberg." Horwitz goes on to suggest that a visit to a synagogue on Yom Kippur may indeed have confirmed for Rosenzweig the decision he had made. But it could not have made it for him.[52]

Now, as we have noted, Rosenzweig came to "date" his "Jewish turning inward not from that day in Berlin October 1913," as he wrote to Eugen Rosenstock on January 15, 1920, "but rather from our Leipzig night."[53] My reconstruction of Rosenzweig's personal and intellectual development, from the *Leipziger Nachtgespräch* in July 1913 to his October 1913 decision to remain a Jew, has aimed to show how this decision was grounded in the very struggle with Marcionism in which Rosenzweig was engaged over the course of the Leipzig night-conversation and in its wake. I want now to assert that this grounding was not merely biographical: there is a coherence to the line of thinking that leads Rosenzweig from his struggle with Marcionism to his decision to remain a Jew that I would like to make explicit at this point. The premise of this line of thought, if I'm not mistaken, is that historical thinking depends on the thinking together of creation and salvation. Only when creation is conceived not as complete in itself, but rather as the beginning of a process that will culminate in redemption; and only when redemption is conceived not as wholly independent of what transpires in the world, but rather as the fulfillment of what the world has been since its creation, does the historical view of selves in the world become possible and necessary.

It is because Rosenzweig holds this to be the case, I submit, that the turn away from Gnostic dualism and the turn toward a historical worldview are fundamentally intertwined in his thinking. In rejecting the Gnostic dualism of the created world, on the one hand, and of the soul eligible for salvation from the world, on the other, Rosenzweig insists on the identity of the God of creation and the God of salvation. Since he understands this holding together of creation and salvation to be the root of historical thinking, his turn away from Marcionism is at one and the same time a turn toward history. The possibility of a historical conception of the world is thus already implicit within the turn away from a Gnostic dualism of created world and redeemed soul, and toward a view of salvation unfolding from out of creation.

This conviction that human beings only begin to think historically when they grasp the creation of the world and the salvation of their souls as intertwined is at the heart of Rosenzweig's repeated insistence, in the years after the *Leipziger Nachtgespräch,* that the struggle *against* Gnosticism is at once the struggle *for* history. While reflecting on the struggle of the early Church over the status of the Hebrew Bible, Rosenzweig writes, in his "Paralipomena,"

> The historical solution to the opposition between *nomos* and *physis* was scarcely possible for the Greeks themselves. Here it appears, though, how the struggle of the Church against Gnosticism surrounding the Old Testament, *really* was a struggle against philosophical paganism . . . which wants to allow no *actual history.*[54]

Moreover, while reading Tertullian's *De Praescriptione Haereticorum* in 1916, he writes the following note to himself:

> It is always the same points in which the "heresy" of the first century moved. That Christ did not become an *actual* man, that the flesh is not fit to be resurrected, that the lawgiver and the world-creator could only be an under-god (consequently a counter-God for Marcion, even if this was also wholly *un*Pauline). It comes down everywhere to the dehistoricization of faith.[55]

In these passages, Rosenzweig understands the Gnostic rejection of the world as the site of meaningful action as a sub-case of the general inability of pagan thought, to his mind, to conceive of a historical reconciliation of the "*physis*" of the human being with the divine "*nomos*" addressed to human freedom. Only the Church's insistence on the centrality of the "Old Testament" within its canon, only its insistence on grasping creation, that is, as the prophecy of salvation, makes the historical reconciliation of freedom and nature, of self and world, possible. Thus when Marcion rejects the identity of spirit and flesh, when he rejects the identity of the God of creation and of salvation and instead declares the "world-creator" to be a "counter-God," these rejections are in and of themselves rejections of an historical account of faith. Insofar as it can be understood to sever the link between creation and salvation, the Gnostic dualism of soul and world removes the conditions that make history thinkable.

Now, as we've seen, Rosenzweig claims in his letter of October 31, 1913, that he arrived at his decision to remain a Jew "after long and . . . fundamental consideration."[56] He tells Eugen Rosenstock that he "dates" his "Jewish return [*Einkehr*] not from that day in Berlin, in October 1913, but rather from our Leipzig night."[57] If we take such statements seriously, it appears to me, our reflections on how the turn away from Gnosticism in itself amounts to a turn toward historical thinking permit us to wager that Rosenzweig's "return" to Judaism in October 1913 was already predetermined at a particular moment in his deliberations over his Marcionism in the wake of the *Leipziger Nachtgespräch*. In the "Paralipomena," we recall, Rosenzweig writes, "What it means that God created the world and [is] *not just* the God of revelation—this I know precisely out of the Leipzig night-conversation of 7.7.13. At that time, I was on the best road to Marcionitism."[58]

When did Rosenzweig learn that the God of creation and the God of revelation are one and the same? We recall that Rosenzweig tells Rudolf Ehrenberg, in his letter of October 31, 1913, that he would have been able to ground his "dualism of revelation and world with a metaphysical dualism of God and devil," had not "the first sentence of the Bible" stopped him.[59] When we first examined this statement, we understood Rosenzweig to find in the first sentence of the Bible a compelling claim against Marcionism, insofar as it asserts the same God as creator of "heaven and earth," and thereby denies the opposition between the "kingdom not of this world" and the "kingdom only of this world." But Rosenzweig's attendance to the first sentence of the Bible may be said to have determined in a more far-reaching sense the whole line of thought he would embark upon, leading away from Marcionism, through the decision to convert to Christianity, to his ultimate decision to remain a Jew. For the first sentence of the Bible would have made explicit for Rosenzweig the way in which the very book of revelation, the Bible, which directs its readers on the path toward their salvation, locates the starting point of that path to salvation in God's creation of the world itself. The first sentence of the Bible already presents creation, that is to say, as the promise of salvation, as the beginning of the realization of the Kingdom of God on earth and thus already presents what Rosenzweig understands to be the conditions for a historical conception of the realization of the Kingdom of God. Moreover, since Rosenzweig will reach the conclusion that Judaism alone ensures that Christianity not forget the identity of the God of creation and the God of salvation, Rosenzweig's later decision to remain a Jew is likewise rooted in this premise about the thinking together of creation and salvation as the condition for history.

When the first sentence of the Bible led Rosenzweig to turn away from the full consequences of his Marcionist tendencies, it did not merely lead him to embrace the world, as we have seen, and it did not merely open up for him the *possibility* of a historical reconciliation of self and world. Rather, Rosenzweig's understanding of the significance of the first sentence of the Bible already predetermined, in that moment, his commitment to a historical conception of the Kingdom of God, and—since in his view only the continued existence of Jews as Jews could ensure that Christians remember that the God of creation and the God of salvation are one and the same—his return, in October of that year, to Judaism. In this very moment of rejecting Gnostic world-denial, Rosenzweig already *had* to become committed to a historical account of the reconciliation of self and world in which Judaism and Christianity have necessary and mutually supportive roles.

The new position that Rosenzweig adopts, in October 1913, regarding the respective roles Judaism and Christianity serve in redemption, is likewise illuminated in important ways when viewed as a consequence of his turn away from Marcionism. According to Rosenzweig, we have seen, both Christianity and Judaism have unique roles to play in the process of the world's redemption, but it is only insofar as these roles are carried out in tandem that the process of redemption is advanced. Given the appeal Marcionism held for him during the summer of 1913, Rosenzweig's emphasis on the "world denial" of the Jewish people, in his letter to Rudolf Ehrenberg of October 31, 1913, is particularly striking. In anticipating the ultimate redemption, Rosenzweig claims, the Jewish people "stares fixedly over the world and history" and "must deny itself all work in the world." Rosenzweig's Jew does not need "to come to the Father, because he is already with him." Moreover, to the degree to which the Jewish people nevertheless "stands in the world," as a "living sign" of the world's future redemptive state, the separateness of its existence yields, according to Rosenzweig, "outer (persecution) and inner (stubbornness) suffering."[60]

By October 1913, Rosenzweig has indeed come to see the Jewish people in the same Marcionist light as he had presented "true Christianity" before the *Leipziger Nachtgespräch.* The Jewish people are now grasped as a kind of foreign presence in the world. The Jew negates the world even as she lives in it, and her life is directed toward the anticipation of a redemption that is beyond the present world. No wonder Rosenzweig could describe his early faith position as *Jewish,* in his letter of August 25, 1919, to Rudolf Ehrenberg, even as he gestured thereby to the very world-transcending faith position he otherwise identified with Marcion.

But as soon as we identify the clear parallels between Rosenzweig's early Marcionism and the view of Judaism that he developed in the wake of the *Leipziger Nachtgespräch,* the vital difference between these two positions likewise becomes clear. Rosenzweig's Jew may deny the worldly, and she may set her sights on a life of intimacy with God beyond the world—just like the Marcionist. But the beyond toward which Rosenzweig's Jew directs her sights represents the *future* of the world. As such, the redemption that Judaism anticipates is not the "stiff *Überworld*" Rosenzweig attributes to the Gnostic, but rather precisely a "demand on the world" that it realize the future that the Jewish people anticipates.[61]

The historical trajectory that this anticipation of the future redemption endorses, we have seen, ultimately overcomes the opposition between the Kingdom of God and the Kingdom of this world to which the Marcionist holds firm. Thus Rosenzweig writes, "since these sufferings of world negation are taken up by the synagogue in the same hope-of-the-end as the sufferings of world affirmation are taken up by the Church . . . , Church and Synagogue depend on each other."[62] Even in its denial of the world, Rosenzweig thereby suggests, the Jewish people serves the very redemption of the world that the Church takes on through its world affirmation. Both Jew and Christian suffer in their respective tasks. In order to anticipate the ultimate redemption even in the present, the Jew must endure an existence in which she is never truly at home in the world. In order to carry out the very "world activity" that will realize the Kingdom of God on earth, the Christian must ever defer the experience of salvation itself.

In the account of Judaism and Christianity that Rosenzweig develops after the *Leipziger Nachtgespräch,* both Jew and Christian are grasped as experiencing the tension between self and world, between the opportunity for personal salvation and the thwarting of such opportunity through worldly existence. Both Jew and Christian experience and substantiate, that is to say, the very tension between soul and world at the core of Rosenzweig's earlier struggle with Marcionism. But the joint efforts of Jew and Christian at once point toward an ultimate redemptive resolution to this conflict. Jew and Christian share the "same hope-of-the-end," as Rosenzweig writes. This shared hope creates history.

RECONCILING CHRIST AND ANTICHRIST

The last chapters of Rosenzweig's *Hegel und der Staat* include an account of the development of German politics from Hegel's time down to Bismarck's. At the close of a discussion of Marx's program of world transformation, Rosenzweig alludes to the possibility of an imminent historical reconciliation of church and society after Marx, and writes, "As in the profound parable of the great Christian poetess of the north, now the copy image, whose kingdom is only of this world, could be brought home into the Church to the genuine image, whose kingdom is not of this world."[63]

The "great Christian poetess of the north" to whom Rosenzweig refers at this point in *Hegel und der Staat* is none other than Selma Lagerlöf, and the "profound parable" of reconciliation that Rosenzweig recalls—in which the copy, "whose kingdom is only of this world," is reunited with "the genuine image, whose kingdom is not of this world"—is articulated in the final chapter of her *Antikrists mirakler.* In closing this chapter, I want to return to *Antikrists mirakler,* the novel which sparked the 1913 night-conversation that would so utterly transform Rosenzweig's life and thought, and recount the vision of reconciliation that Lagerlöf paints there.

As socialist revolts erupt around them, the people of Diamante in *Antikrists mirakler* unite in their shared worship of the Christ child icon they have discovered, and in their shared experience of its miracles. In so doing they become, for at least a short time, a model of a community held together by neighborly love. But when word of these miracles spreads to Rome, a Father

Gondo sets out with a group of pilgrims to pay homage to the Christ child of Diamante. Gondo—who himself grew up at Aracoeli—recognizes the icon as the false figurine thrown off the hill at the Capitol years earlier. He reveals the inscription upon its crown, and chastises the people of Diamante for failing to distinguish between Christ and Antichrist. "You yourselves say that the image has given you everything for which you have prayed. Has no one in Diamante in all these years prayed for the forgiveness of sins and the peace of the soul?" he rails. "You have had Antichrist among you, and he has got possession of you. You have forgotten heaven. You have forgotten that you possess a soul. You think only of this world."[64]

But *Antikrists mirakler* does not end with this pronouncement of Father Gondo—a pronouncement that leaves the reader just as perplexed about the relation between world and spirit, and between Christ and Antichrist, as it does the people of Diamante. The closing chapters of the book recount Father Gondo's visit to the Pope, where he reports "how he had found Antichrist in the likeness of Christ, how the former had entangled the people of Diamante in worldliness and how he, Father Gondo, had wished to burn him."[65] Much to Gondo's surprise, however, rather than praise him for his struggle for the sake of the kingdom of heaven, the Pope reproaches him for his reaction to the false icon and for his treatment of the people who worshipped it:

> "Father Gondo," said the Pope sternly, "when you held the image in your arms you wished to burn him. Why? Why were you not loving to him? Why did you not carry him back to the little Christchild on the Capitolium from whom he proceeded? . . . You shall let him go his way through the ages. We do not fear him. When he comes to storm the Capitol in order to mount the throne of the world, we shall meet him, and we shall lead him to Christ. We shall make peace between earth and heaven. But you do wrong," he continued more mildly, "to hate him. You must have forgotten that the sibyl considered him one of the redeemers of the world. 'On the heights of the Capitol the redeemer of the world shall be worshipped, Christ or Antichrist.'"[66]

For the reader who has borne witness to the struggles throughout *Antikrists mirakler* between Christ and Antichrist, between the Church and socialism, between the "kingdom not of this world" and the "kingdom of this world alone," the Pope's reproach of Father Gondo at the end of the book offers a surprising vision of reconciliation. Seen through the eyes of the wisest and most powerful of the Church's representatives, the forces of the world that appear to threaten the realization of the kingdom of heaven are not to be feared. For over the course of time, the Pope suggests, peace shall be forged between earth and heaven, Antichrist is to be led back to Christ, and both are to be considered "the redeemers of the world."

If Lagerlöf's book thus posed for Rosenzweig and his interlocutors the problem of soul and world that occupied them during their discussions of the *Leipziger Nachtgespräch,* it also offered a model of their historical reconciliation that Rosenzweig would soon advocate as his own. Jew and Christian, monk and socialist, those who take from faith and those who take from love: "over the course of time," the cumulative labor of both will together bring redemption.

The first three chapters of this study have offered a new account of the transformative moment in Leipzig, July 1913, in which Rosenzweig left behind his early Marcionist intuition that the salvation of the soul demands denial of the world. He was then "converted" to the view that soul and world are reconciled in the historical realization of the Kingdom of God, a historical realization that demands that Christians and Jews fulfill their respective redemptive vocations. The account I have proposed rests, I have claimed, on a more careful study of Rosenzweig's own description of this personal event than has been carried out up until now. It has permitted us to trace Rosenzweig's perplexity over the relationship between self and world from his early world-skepticism, through his flirtation with Marcionism, up to the period, in 1913, when he arrived at a resolution to his perplexity that would prove central to his mature thought. What remains for us to show is how some of the most important and most familiar aspects of Rosenzweig's mature thought are rooted in the complex of questions Rosenzweig raised and responded to during his personal and intellectual crisis of 1913. Now that we understand Rosenzweig's conversion not as a move away from a commitment to philosophy and toward a commitment to faith, but rather as a move from Marcionism to a commitment to the historical reconciliation of self and world, we are in a position to shed light on *The Star of Redemption* in ways that have hitherto not been possible. The *Star*'s opening insistence on the philosophical import of the fear of death; its account of the advance of God, world, and the self, through interrelations, from creation to redemption; its account of the role the human being plays in confirming and actualizing divine unity; its depiction of the respective redemptive vocations of Judaism and Christianity; and indeed, the very fact that Rosenzweig elaborates all these thoughts as part of an overarching "system of philosophy"—these noteworthy themes in Rosenzweig's later thinking may be traced back to the questions he posed for himself during, and in the wake of, the *Leipziger Nachtgespräch*.

4

World Denial and World Redemption in *The Star of Redemption*

THE STAR OF REDEMPTION offers a philosophical account of "the All"—the whole of what is—that is forged out of the relations between three fundamental kinds of beings: God, the world, and human selves. The first part of the *Star* shows how each of these three "elemental" beings may be conceived as constructing itself out of its own particular "nothing"; and the second part of the book articulates the course of relations between them—creation, revelation, redemption—which both generates our actual experience and points toward their future unity in redemption. We find ourselves, Rosenzweig suggests, in the middle of this course of the All where we are in a position to experience and to participate in the relations that will ultimately realize redemptive unity. Insofar as we are part of the network of things that exist in the world, we experience "creation" as the always-past origin of that world in its primordial relation with God. Insofar as we come to recognize ourselves as individual persons—as "I"s—we discover our individual selfhood to be awoken in us through the summons of divine revelation. We experience redemption, finally, as the task we must take up for the future; for the course that leads to the ultimate redemptive unity of all beings is advanced through the interpersonal relations into which we enter in the world. Jewish and Christian communities play different but complementary roles in the economy of redemption: together they accelerate the redemptive process, each granting its members an anticipatory glimpse of the unity of the All that redemption will bring.

The redemption toward which *The Star of Redemption* directs its readers, and after which the book is named, is thus the ultimate unifying goal of existence. All particular beings achieve their shared unity in redemption; all the oppositions of actual existence are overcome in it; all actions by and relations between God, human beings, and the world, are fulfilled in it. Precisely by identifying redemption as the unifying *goal* of actual existence, however, Rosenzweig calls attention in the *Star* to the fact that such redemptive unity is *not yet* actual in the present. To the contrary: actual life is fraught with tension and conflict. Indeed, redemption would not represent the monumental cosmic task that it does for Rosenzweig, did life not constantly confront us with our unredeemed state, were the need for redemptive actions not so urgent in his eyes.

At the root of our experience of the present as unredeemed, the *Star* suggests, is the fundamental opposition between selfhood and worldliness. The very moment in which I come to recognize myself as an independent, individual "I," Rosenzweig claims, I feel myself torn out of the world in which I have otherwise been at home. That very worldliness, on the other hand, appears to prevent me from realizing my free selfhood to the fullest, and it appears to disrupt my revelatory connection to the divine. Free but determined by the laws of nature; a subject but also an object; an unique person called by name, intimate of God, but at once a thing among things, a creature like all other creatures in the world—so internally conflicted is my experience of selfhood in the world, that Rosenzweig finds in this conflict evidence that the selfhood and worldliness awkwardly united in me are each to be conceived as deriving from a fundamentally different elemental root.

As Rosenzweig sets out to show in the *Star,* it is this fundamental conflict we experience in ourselves between our selfhood and our worldliness that alerts us to redemption as the goal of our actions and relations in the world. Or rather, Rosenzweig presents the task of redemption in the *Star* as the proper response to a set of questions that arise for human beings out of this inner conflict: what is the meaning of this tension we experience and how are we to respond to it? What does this tension between selfhood and worldliness demand of us as human beings? How are we to *live* in the face of this tension? In taking this conflict between self and world seriously, Rosenzweig is quick to reject those responses to it that identify solely with one side of the conflict at the expense of its other. Throughout the *Star* he thus has harsh words for those philosophers who direct their readers to the eternity of the soul "beyond" this world at the expense of the body, and for "mystics" and "sinners" who deny the world in the hopes of preserving selfishly their own respective

"I"s or their own respective intimate revelatory relation to the divine. He likewise chides those who, instead of turning toward others in redemptive love, seek to dissolve their selves pantheistically into the world. Both our selfhood and our worldliness are essential to our being and our vocation; both our selfhood and our wordliness are rooted in relations we have to the divine; both our selfhood and our worldliness are integral to the redemptive task that alone promises resolution to the conflict we experience between them.

In the light of all that we have learned about Rosenzweig's personal crisis of 1913, this course the *Star* charts toward redemption takes on a new resonance. For we recognize in the conflict between self and world at the heart of the *Star* the very dualism Rosenzweig identified with "Marcionism," and toward which he was inclined in the years leading up to his 1913 crisis. The *Star* as a whole may indeed be understood as nothing less than the comprehensive articulation of the personal and metaphysical response to Marcionism that Rosenzweig developed in the wake of the *Leipziger Nachtgespräch*. The dramatic contours of Rosenzweig's 1913 crisis, and the key insights at which he arrived through it, find expression in the structure, the argument, and the imagery of the *Star*. The *Star* thus opens with the human being standing "face-to-face with the Nothing," in a confrontation with death that reveals both our inherent worldliness and at once our capacity—even our inclination—to separate from the world. The realization that "God created the world and [is] *not just* the God of revelation" governs the whole of the *Star*'s account of cosmic reality: the revelatory relation between God and self may be central to the course of redemption, but only because it complements creation perfectly in that course. The advance to that ultimate future redemption which will reconcile self and world occurs in the *Star*, moreover, both at the individual level through the medium of interpersonal relations—love and speech—that Rosenstock conveyed to Rosenzweig during the night-conversation, and at the global level through a Christian "world-activity" that is oriented by the Jewish community's anticipation of the world's redemptive goal.

The aim of this chapter is to show how the new account of Rosenzweig's 1913 near-conversion and return I have presented illuminates the philosophical claims of his magnum opus in important and hitherto unidentified ways. I seek here both to show how integral the problem of Marcionism is to the systematic concerns of the *Star*, and to highlight the *traces* of Rosenzweig's personal struggle with Marcionism that mark the pages of the *Star.* I suggest, furthermore, that the *Star* explores the full ramifications of Marcionism and its overcoming, and draws conclusions from the problematic of Marcionism that remained below the surface for Rosenzweig himself in 1913. The most radical of these consequences concerns the problem of divine unity. For while redemption in the *Star* will indeed reconcile self and world, and while it will bring salvation to the soul beloved of God only through world activity, ultimately redemption in the *Star* is the redemption of *God.* Prior to redemption, the question of the identity of the God of creation and of revelation is no less problematic for God than it is for the human being who experiences the grounding of her worldliness and her selfhood respectively, in one or the other. The metaphysical dualism Rosenzweig attributes to Marcionism is thus shown to have some basis for justification: God is in fact "not yet" one. But here too Rosenzweig will present the lack of unity as at once the call for unifying activity: the redemptive activity human beings are called upon to carry out in the world has as its ultimate goal the unification of God.

This chapter will be divided into six sections, each of which will address the way Rosenzweig's struggle with Marcionism illuminates a different key moment or theme in the *Star.* We will begin with a discussion of the book's opening reflection on the fear of death, and of how the fear of death reveals the conflict between selfhood and worldliness. Resisting the temptation to preserve the self through a denial of the world and our existence in it, Rosenzweig here insists that the healthy human desire to *remain* in the world with the fear of death directs us toward a path to redemption that leads through the world rather than out of it.

The second section will explore how the *Star*'s relational concepts of creation, revelation, and redemption begin to explain both the basis of the tension we experience between self and world, and the path to overcoming that tension. Two aspects of the course from creation to redemption will be examined here in particular. We will first look at the way Rosenzweig depicts the relation between creation and revelation as that of promise and fulfillment. We will then examine how creation and revelation demand and find their unity in redemption.

By presenting the *Star*'s account of the course from creation to redemption as that course upon which self and world strive for reconciliation, the second section of the chapter offers an overview of the *Star*'s alternative to

Marcionism. Once we have sketched out the scope of this alternative broadly, we will be in a position to explore, in the sections that follow, some especially important examples of how Rosenzweig's 1913 struggle with Marcionism informs key developments in the book. The third section will focus on the dialectic of divine love and human freedom that plays out between revelation and redemption. Hearkening back to Rosenstock's account of the "Word" as mediator between human love of God and love of others, I will highlight here Rosenzweig's account of the divine command to love, and how this command at once points toward redemptive action in the world. As we shall see, however, human beings exhibit their freedom in the ways they respond to God's command. As the case of the mystic shows, Rosenzweig conceives of this moment of human decision between revelation and redemption in terms that draw vividly from his own struggle with Marcionism.

The fourth section of this chapter will present Rosenzweig's account of Judaism and Christianity in the *Star*, and explore the different ways in which Rosenzweig builds on and deviates from that conception of the complementary redemptive tasks of these two communities that guided him in his return to Judaism in 1913. Here we will examine in particular the way he continues to describe the role the Jewish people plays in orienting Christians in their redemptive work in the world as that of combating the Christian temptation to Gnosticism.

The fifth section will turn to the theme of divine unity in the *Star*. God only becomes One, Rosenzweig suggests, at the end of the course to redemption. Since Marcionism, as Rosenzweig understood it, is first and foremost a doctrine of metaphysical dualism, Rosenzweig's account of divine unity as a unity that becomes out of a state of divine division will interest us for the way it both takes seriously Marcionist metaphysical dualism and at once overcomes that dualism. But making sense of God's course to unity in the *Star* will demand that we address the weighty question of *why* God, in order to attain unity, must undergo a process of relations with others through which God depends on human redemptive activity in the world.

The sixth section will conclude this chapter by addressing Rosenzweig's account of creatureliness and truth at the end of the *Star*. Rosenzweig here declares that those opening words of the Bible, "God created," which had in 1913 stopped him from committing to a metaphysical dualism of God and devil, remain true along the whole course to redemption. The tension we experience between self and world is thus, in the last instance, an expression of our fundamental creatureliness. As we shall see, Rosenzweig suggests that we actualize that creatureliness in the fullest sense when we decide between death and life, between world denial and world redemption.

My hope is that these discussions of key moments in the *Star* will give the reader a clear sense of the overwhelming importance of the problem of Marcionism for the *Star* as a whole. If I have not presented a comprehensive interpretation of the *Star*, this is in large part because I have attempted to produce such an interpretation elsewhere, in my *Franz Rosenzweig and the Systematic Task of Philosophy*. Although I introduce in this chapter some very different readings of the *Star* than I offered in that book—and in a few places, different readings of the same passages I interpreted in that book—I view the arguments I make in this chapter to be quite consistent with those of the book. Indeed, the account of all beings striving for redemptive unity out of difference through relations, which I present here as Rosenzweig's alternative to Marcionism, is none other than the "systematic task" that I claim governs the book as a whole in *Franz Rosenzweig and the Systematic Task of Philosophy*. When appropriate in what follows, I will thus rely on and point readers to arguments I have made in that book to help support and clarify my claims here.

REMAINING IN THE FEAR OF THE EARTHLY

The opening of *The Star of Redemption* identifies death, and our fear of it, as a fundamental human perplexity. The book goes on to show that proper comportment toward and response to this perplexity makes possible both comprehensive "knowledge of the All" and a redemptive engagement with God in the world. Misguided responses to this perplexity, on the other hand, are at the root of philosophical delusion and of a sense of futility in the face of life in the world.

I will show in this section that the perplexity that confronts human beings in death, according to Rosenzweig, is the very perplexity over the relation between self and world that we now know stood at the heart of Rosenzweig's 1913 crisis, and which he came to identify with Marcionism. The opening pages of the *Star* thus announce Marcionism as the basic problem with which the book as a whole is concerned. In what follows I will explore how Rosenzweig presents the problem of self and world in the opening paragraphs of the *Star,* and how he articulates the book's argument with the philosophical tradition around this problem. I will show how Rosenzweig identifies the problem of self and world as lying at the root of both the human fear of death and the human propensity for suicide. I will attend to the ways he illustrates his claims, moreover, by drawing on four classic Western literary sources that convey the struggle over selfhood and worldliness that accompanies the contemplation of death in especially vivid and influential ways. For reasons I shall explain, I will address three of these sources—Plato's *Phaedo,* Paul's "First Letter to the Corinthians," and Schiller's "Das Ideal und das Leben"—together in the context of Rosenzweig's discussion of the fear of death, and I will address the fourth source—the "Night" scene at the beginning of Goethe's *Faust*—in the context of Rosenzweig's discussion of suicide. I will note, finally, how the opening of the *Star* alludes explicitly to Rosenzweig's own personal crisis of 1913 in order to convey to his readers both the urgency and the universality of the problem of Marcionism, as well as to hint at the path to its overcoming the *Star* will lay out.

The opening of the *Star* suggests that what comes into question when a human being confronts his or her own death is the relation between her unique selfhood and the world. An impending death leads the human being to sense "violently, inescapably, what he otherwise never senses: that his I would only be an It if it died."[1] The "I" with which I name my self uniquely is lost in death, Rosenzweig suggests, and what remains of me in place of my "I" is an "It"—corpse, matter, thing—that merges with or lies among all other "Its" in the world. Insofar as I lose my "I" and become part of the world of "Its" in death, such a description implies, fearing death makes manifest to me the way in which my "I-hood" is fundamentally different from the world. Rosenzweig reiterates this point, moreover, when he suggests that in confronting the possibility of suicidal death, the human being feels himself "in his terrifying poverty, loneliness and torn-ness from the whole world" (4/10).[2]

At the same time that death highlights the fundamental difference between my selfhood and my worldliness, however, death also suggests my selfhood and worldliness are inextricably intertwined. If my "I" becomes an "It" when I die, then this suggests my selfhood is thoroughly dependent on my bodily, worldly existence. Such a dependence emerges throughout the opening paragraph of the *Star.* Thus Rosenzweig identifies the fear of death as "fears of the earth" and "fear of the earthly" (3/9). I fear death, that is to say, insofar as my earthly existence leaves me subject to that corruption to which everything earthly is subject. Moreover, Rosenzweig links the fear of death together with one's very birth as an individual in the world: "Everything mortal lives in this fear of death, each new birth increases the fear by one new ground because it increases the mortal. Without stopping, the womb of the indefatigable earth gives birth to the New, and each one is to fall to death [*dem Tode verfallen*]" (3/9). The same confrontation with death that grants me a sense of my inherent uniqueness as a "new" self, we see, reveals that very selfhood—and our fear of its loss—to be rooted in a birth out of the "womb of the indefatigable earth" into a world that I share with others.

While provoking our fear, death thereby confronts the human being with a puzzle: my "I would be an it" if I died. I am an "I"—a self—and thereby I am more than, different from the "Its" of the world. But my selfhood emerges as a consequence of my birth into the world, and it is lost through my earthly death. How can I be both more than the world and yet still part of the world? How can I transcend the world as a unique self, on the one hand, and at the same time be subject to the generation and corruption that governs the world? How can my worldliness both lay the ground for my selfhood and have the power to put an end to my selfhood at the same time? And, practically speaking: What am I to do about it?

Such is the perplexity that confronts us in the fear of death. I've suggested that Rosenzweig views this perplexity as fundamental: the *Star* in its entirety will show how a proper response to the fear of death will yield comprehensive knowledge and participation in the course of redemption.[3] But in the opening paragraphs of the *Star,* Rosenzweig introduces the path his book will take, in responding to the perplexity of self and world, only by way of contrast to the approach to the fear of death he claims has been championed by the philosophical tradition. Rather than take the fear of death seriously as the clue to the human being's inherently twofold nature, according to Rosenzweig, philosophy denies the fear of death by denying the "earthly" altogether:

> Philosophy presumes to throw off the fear of the earthly, to take from death its poisonous sting [*Giftstachel*], from Hades its pestilential breath. . . . Philosophy denies these fears of the earth. . . . She lets the body fall to the abyss [*dem Abgrund verfallen sein*], but the free soul flutters away over it. That the fear of death knows nothing of such a division into body and soul, that it howls "I I I" and doesn't want to hear

> anything about a diverting of the fear onto a mere "body"—what does philosophy care about that? . . . Philosophy laughs its empty laugh at all this need and points with outstretched index finger showing the creature, whose limbs tremble in fear for his here-and-now [*Diesseits*], to a beyond [*Jenseits*] about which he doesn't want to know anything at all. Because man doesn't want to escape any kind of fetters at all, he wants to remain, he wants—to live. (3/9)

Philosophy copes with the fear of death, and with the self-world perplexity with which death confronts us, Rosenzweig suggests, by identifying the essence of the human being with only one side of the human being's twofold nature. The human being is essentially "soul," Rosenzweig has the philosophical tradition teach, while the "body" is reduced to no more than a network of "fetters" holding the soul temporarily in the worldly realm. Were such the metaphysical case, the "sting" of death would be removed, the "fear of the earthly" disposed of: death would no longer be something to fear, but would rather be precisely the freeing of the soul from the earthly, permitting it at long last to realize itself. Selfhood would be fulfilled rather than lost in its exit from the world.

Human beings who fear death, Rosenzweig nevertheless claims, do not find solace in philosophy's doctrine of the division of soul and body. They are not so consoled, Rosenzweig intimates, because what they "sense" in the fear of death is not accounted for in this philosophical doctrine. Fear of death "knows nothing of such a division into body and soul"; the human being cries out for her "I" when confronted by death in recognition of the rootedness of her "I-hood" in her worldly, bodily form. The promise of immortality for the soul thus does not console "the creature whose limbs tremble in fear for his here-and-now [*Diesseits*]." For the human being recognizes herself just as essentially as "creature"—i.e., as part of the created world—as she recognizes herself to be a unique "I." The human being who fears death wants "to remain"; for only as an embodied individual in the world can she continue to be a self.

The will to "remain" that emerges in the fear of death will turn out to be the key to directing the *Star*'s readers on the proper path toward redemption. Before addressing this vital point, however, I want to pause to highlight the first three literary sources Rosenzweig draws upon in the first paragraph of the *Star* while illustrating the self-world perplexity that arises in our confrontation with death: Plato's *Phaedo,* the fifteenth chapter of Paul's "First

Letter to the Corinthians," and Schiller's "Das Ideal und das Leben." Different as these texts are from each other, each engages the problem of self and world, and each exemplifies the tendency to respond to this problem by denying one's this-worldly existence and by imagining a philosophical, a spiritual, or an aesthetic realm beyond this world in which the self will find peace. Collectively, the allusions to these texts convey the urgency of the problem of self and world by suggesting that the human struggle with this problem has been pervasive in Western culture across time and forms of literary expression.

When Rosenzweig ascribes to "philosophy" the view that the soul separates from the body in death, when he describes philosophy as mocking the human fear of death and as directing us, instead, to a "beyond" in which our soul will "escape" the "fetters" of the body, he is alluding to the central claims of Plato's *Phaedo.*[4] In the *Phaedo,* Plato depicts Socrates discussing death and the pursuit of wisdom while in his prison cell, in the hours leading up to his execution. Socrates faces his impending death without fear, he suggests, because his lifelong pursuit of philosophy has prepared him for death. "A man who has truly spent his life in philosophy is probably right to be of good cheer in the face of death and to be very hopeful that after death he will attain the greatest blessings yonder," Socrates explains to his disciples. Indeed, "the one aim of those who practice philosophy in the proper manner is to practice for dying and death."[5]

How is philosophy a propaedeutic for dying? Why does the philosopher have good reason to be cheerful facing death? Socrates argues as follows. Death is nothing but the "release and separation of the soul from the body."[6] The philosopher's quest for wisdom during his lifetime, moreover, depends on his ability to transcend the materiality, the needs, the desires, and the distractions of his body. The philosopher thus "turns away from the body towards the soul as far as he can,"[7] during his lifetime, whenever he strives to know things as they are. "He will do this most perfectly," Socrates explains, "who, using pure thought alone, tries to track down each reality pure and by itself, freeing himself as far as possible . . . from the whole body, because the body confuses the soul and does not allow it to acquire truth and wisdom whenever it is associated with it."[8] Since the philosopher can only attain truth, to the extent possible during his life in the world, by "freeing himself as much as possible" from the body, since "as long as we have a body and our soul is fused with such an evil we shall never adequately attain . . . truth,"[9] it stands to reason—says Socrates—that "if we are ever to have pure knowledge, we must escape from the body and observe things in themselves with the soul by itself," something we shall only attain "when we are dead."[10] Philosophy is thus nothing other than preparation for death, for the moment in which the soul will finally be "freed, as it were, from the bonds of the body."[11] And it is reasonable for the philosopher to look forward to death as an event that will finally make possible the attainment of wisdom he has long sought. "Those who practice philosophy in the right way are in training for dying and they fear death least of all men," Socrates declares. "If they are altogether estranged from the body and desire to have their soul by itself, would it not be quite absurd for them to be afraid and resentful when this happens?"[12]

The *Phaedo*'s vivid account of the metaphysical split between soul and body has had, of course, a profound influence on the history of Western philosophy, such that—generalize though he does—Rosenzweig has grounds for depicting Plato's response to death as definitive for "philosophy" as a whole. Although Rosenzweig likewise sees death as making manifest the human being's twofold nature, however, we have seen that Rosenzweig rejects Plato's response to the fear of death as one-sided in its denial of the body, and thereby as failing to address what is really of concern in the fear of death: the loss of *this life* in which selfhood and worldliness are perplexingly intertwined.

We find a strikingly similar theme at the heart of the second source Rosenzweig draws upon in the opening pages of the *Star.* When Rosenzweig suggests philosophy seeks to "take from death its poisonous sting, from Hades its pestilential breath," in the book's second line, and when he points one page later to philosophy's illusory desire to have "death devoured, if not in the eternal victory" (4/10) then at least in conceptual nothingness, he is alluding to the culminating lines of the fifteenth chapter of Paul's "First Letter to the Corinthians."[13] Of concern in the fifteenth chapter of this letter is the resurrection of the body after death. But just as we found in the *Phaedo,* the discussion of death here in Paul raises a whole set of questions about the relationship between the earthly and the heavenly, the bodily and the spiritual. Some of Paul's correspondents apparently deny the possibility of the body's resurrection. Paul writes, "If Christ is proclaimed as raised from the dead, how can some of you say there is no resurrection of the dead?" (I Cor. 15:12) and his rhetorical questions over the details of the resurrection—"Someone will ask, 'How are the dead raised? With what kind of body do they come?' Fool!" (I Cor. 15:35–36)—suggest he is responding to mockery of resurrection among the Corinthians. A number of scholars have suggested that the Corinthian rejection of resurrection rests on the same kind of flesh–spirit dualism we have become familiar with: these Corinthians denigrate the worldly to such a degree that they cannot fathom the *body* attaining salvation through Christ.[14] Paul's response, on this reading, is to combat this categorical split of spirit and body with an account of resurrection as a *future redemptive transformation of body into spirit,* a redemptive transformation in which the redeemed dead will yet participate.[15] Paul writes,

> The trumpet will sound, and the dead will be raised imperishable, and we will be changed. For this perishable body must put on imperishability; and this mortal body put on immortality. When this perishable body puts on imperishability, and this mortal body puts on immortality, then the saying that is written will be fulfilled:
>
> "Death has been swallowed up in victory."
> "Where, O death, is your victory?
> Where, O death, is your sting?"
>
> The sting of death is sin, and the power of sin is the Law. But thanks be to God, who gives us the victory through our Lord Jesus Christ. (I Cor. 15: 52–57)

Paul here foretells that the redemption brought by Christ will yield the miraculous transformation of flesh into spirit, in which "this perishable body" will put on "imperishability" and "this mortal body" will put on "immortality." In this redemptive moment, death will be defeated, and the worldly powers Paul links with death—sin and the authority of the Law—will likewise be overcome in "eternal victory." Paul clearly sees the spiritual being believers will assume in redemption to carry a higher ontological status than does earthly being. But it is precisely because human beings are both body and spirit at present, Paul may be said to argue, that redemption can only come to human beings through the miraculous transformation of the body. Victory over death would lose its miraculous character were the body simply shed as if it were always inessential, were the body left to "fall to the abyss" while the "soul flutters away over it." Death has not yet been defeated, and believers should not deduce from Christ's ascension that the earthly existence of the body is inconsequential. Victory over death and the powers of the world *will* be demonstrated, according to Paul, at the final resurrection, and through the transformation of the perishable and mortal into the imperishable and immortal.

We might thus understand Paul's account of the body's resurrection in the "First Letter to the Corinthians" as rejecting *tout cort* the kind of spirit–body dualism we found in the *Phaedo* and which some scholars attribute to his Corinthian correspondents. Rosenzweig's complaint regarding philosophy's attempt to remove the "sting" of death through a dualism of soul and body would then mirror Paul's retort to the Corinthians: the "sting" of death will not be overcome through the split of spirit and body, but only through a redemptive process that will occur in the world. Yet Paul's rhetoric in the fifteenth chapter of First Corinthians has left plenty of room for alternative interpretations. Paul begins his description of the redemptive moment in which the perishable body will "put on imperishability" by proclaiming: "flesh and blood cannot inherit the kingdom of God, nor does the perishable inherit the imperishable" (I Cor. 15:50). None other than Marcion himself appears to have read this statement as evidence that Paul flatly rejected the earthly realm, its Creator, and the Law that Creator-God gave to the Jews, as inimical to the redemptive kingdom toward which Christ pointed. The extent to which Marcion's reading of this passage in First Corinthians threatened the emerging Church establishment can be gathered by the lengths Tertullian goes to interpret away Marcion's view. According to Tertullian, Paul must mean that "it is to the works of the flesh, not the substance of the flesh, that under the name of flesh the kingdom of God is denied: for condemnation is passed not on that in which evil is done, but on the evil which is done."[16] That is to say, when Paul claimed that "flesh and blood" cannot attain redemption, according to Tertullian, he meant to exclude from redemption not fleshly bodies themselves, but rather those whose souls made use of their bodies to engage in fleshly *works*. And what could better prove Paul was committed to the continuity between the God of creation and the God of Christ, than the fact that Paul uses the words of the Hebrew Bible to depict the victory over death redemption will bring: "So if *then will be brought to pass the word which is written* in the Creator's scriptures, *O death where is thy victory . . . ? O death where is thy sting?—and* this is a word of the Creator, spoken by the prophet—the fact itself, the kingdom, will belong to him whose word will come to pass in the kingdom."[17]

It is significant, then, that in addition to drawing explicitly on the *Phaedo*'s account of the separation of soul and body, Rosenzweig opens the *Star* with allusions to a Pauline account of resurrection that highlights the question of whether the denial of the flesh can truly remove the "sting" of death, an account that has evoked both dualistic and anti-dualistic interpretations within the Christian tradition. The opening paragraphs of the *Star* allude to a third source, moreover, which conveys this tension between world and spirit. When Rosenzweig claims "philosophy has the presumption to throw off the fear of the earthly," and when he has philosophy tout death as the opportunity to "escape the narrow of life," Rosenzweig is drawing on the third stanza of Friedrich Schiller's "Das Ideal und das Leben."[18] The relationship between "ideal" and "life" represented in Schiller's poem is once again one of opposition. The poem opens by juxtaposing the peace and harmony, the bliss and eternity of the gods of Olympus with the limitations of human life on earth. Life in the earthly "realm of death" is transient and toilsome, and is fraught with tensions that are irreconcilable within the earthly domain. While the mythic realm of the gods presents us with a model of harmony between spirit and pleasure, the poem suggests, human beings are given merely the *choice between* the two: "Between the bliss of the senses [*Sinnenglück*] and the peace of the soul [*Seelenfrieden*] there remains for man merely the anxious choice."[19] Again we find Rosenzweig has drawn our attention to a source that highlights the tension between self and world, here posed as the irreconcilability of worldly pleasure and spiritual peace.

How then, the poem asks, can one "on earth equal the gods, be free in the realm of death"?[20] Human beings have the capacity to approximate such godly harmony only if they overcome their sensible attachment to the world and transcend it through an aesthetic comportment. Aesthetic contemplation permits the human being to see through the actual worldly body or thing he gazes upon, as it were, and to gain access to the ideal form within it, which Schiller variously names the object's "appearance," "figure [*Gestalt*]," or "form."[21] The opposition between worldly thing and ideal figure, between body and form is perhaps most clearly delineated in the third stanza of the poem, to which Rosenzweig twice alludes in the opening of the *Star:*

> Only the body is subject to those powers [*eignet jenen Mächten*]
> Which dark fate weaves;

But free from any force of time,
The playmate of blessed natures
Wanders above in the plains of light,
Divine among the gods, figure [*Gestalt*].
If you want to soar high on its wings
Throw off your fear of the earthly!
Flee out of *the narrow,* dull *life*
Into the realm of the ideal![22]

As did Plato and Paul before him, Schiller here identifies the body as that part of our being that roots us in the earthly, governed here through powers instituted by "dark fate." The "Gestalt" of objects, the form in which their beauty consists, dwells far beyond the worldly, "divine among the gods." Sharing in the divinity of beauty, flying on the "wings" of form, demands—in the words Rosenzweig cites in the opening of the *Star*—that one "throw off the fear of the earthly," that one flee *life,* "narrow" and "dull," and rise through aesthetic contemplation "into the realm of the ideal!"[23]

Schiller's "Das Ideal und das Leben" does not envision the soul's intellectual perfection after death or the resurrection of believers after death in the miraculous transformation of their flesh into the form of spiritual bodies. But his poem shares with the other texts we've reviewed a clear denigration of the earthly, and it likewise calls on its readers to transcend the earthly in search of a form of bliss suited solely for their unworldly selves. By alluding to all three texts in the opening paragraphs of the *Star,* Rosenzweig bombards the reader with the human perplexity of self and world that emerges most sharply in the face of death, and he conveys the pervasiveness of the specific response to this problem that he seeks to combat. For we who have now traced Rosenzweig's own crisis of 1913, the problem of self and world highlighted in these texts is familiar. We can now recognize the position against which Rosenzweig quarrels in the opening of the *Star* to be the very dualistic position of world denial to which Rosenzweig himself was drawn leading up to the *Leipziger Nachtgespräch,* and which he overcame in its wake. But Rosenzweig now shows this world denial to have had a far more broad and compelling appeal and influence over human history than it would have had were it articulated solely by a marginalized second-century Christian theologian like Marcion. Philosophers, religious charismatics, and poets, stretching from the ancient Greeks through the founding of Christianity up to the great period of German romanticism, have alike responded to the human "fear of the earthly" by directing the gaze of human beings beyond the earthly, by promising intellectual, spiritual, or aesthetic salvation for the self through the denial of the worldly.

And yet, we've seen, Rosenzweig claims human beings who fear death find little solace in such promises of a "Beyond." The human being who fears death does not want "to escape any fetters, he wants to remain, he wants—to live." As "creature," he senses that his selfhood is bound up with this world, that it is thus unnatural to deny the world in order to save the self. When philosophy "touts death . . . as the great opportunity to escape the narrow of life," Rosenzweig thus now recognizes, philosophy has nothing to recommend but "suicide" (3–4/9).[24]

Rosenzweig's opening discussion of the fear of death, and of the tendency in Western philosophy, religion, and culture to respond to the fear of death by denying the world, thus leads him to confront suicide as the most extreme case of world denial. It is important to note that Rosenzweig sees the human being's temptation to take his own life as rooted just as squarely in the self-world perplexity as is the human fear of death. Thus, while he defines suicide as "not natural death, but rather a death that is quintessentially counter to nature [*widernatürliche*]" (4/10), he proceeds to note that the temptation to respond to the tension between one's selfhood and one's worldliness through the ultimate act of world denial is inherent to—and unique to—human experience. "The horrifying capacity for suicide is what distinguishes the human being from all other beings," Rosenzweig writes. "It designates precisely this stepping out from all that is natural" (4/10). Once again, Rosenzweig here places the reader of *Star*'s opening lines before the human being's split character as it emerges in the confrontation with death. The world-denial that philosophy recommends is "counter to nature," because human selfhood is wrapped up in worldliness, and thus for a human being to deny his own worldliness is to deny his own nature. At the same time, however, the human propensity to commit suicide reflects the extent to which human selfhood *does* transcend the worldly; it reflects the fact that as an "I," the human being is defined by an unique ability to "step out from all that is natural." As Rosenzweig proceeds to articulate how the perplexity over self and world tempts human beings universally with an unnatural world denial, his reflections draw on allusions that demand our analysis:

> It is well necessary that the human being step out once in his life; once he must take down the precious vial full of devotion; once he must have felt himself in his terrifying poverty, loneliness and torn-ness from the whole world, and for one night long be stood eye-to-eye with the Nothing. But the earth demands him again. He may not drink up the brown potion in that night. For him there is determined another way out of the narrow-pass [*Engpass*] of the Nothing, than this plunge into the yawn of the abyss. The human being should not throw from himself the fear of the earthly; he should *remain* in the fear of death. (4/10)

As "counter to nature" as is suicide, and as unnatural therefore as is philosophy's celebration of death as a chance for the soul to flee the constraints of the body, Rosenzweig suggests here that such world-denial is understandable, given the human being's divided experience of his own selfhood in the world. In order to convey what he claims is the universality of this human propensity for suicidal deliberations, Rosenzweig draws on one of the opening scenes of Goethe's *Faust,* "Night."[25] It is Faust who "takes down the precious vial full of devotion," but who ultimately does not "drink up the brown potion that night" because "the earth demands him again."[26] The Faust we meet in the "Night" scene is tortured by the limitations of his own humanity, and in particular by his inability to attain divine or spiritual wisdom despite his lifetime of devotion to the quest. Torn between the feeling that he is God's equal and the feeling that he is but dust, Faust is drawn to the vial of poison on his shelf as a means of freeing himself from his worldly limits. He imagines the divine life that awaits him for turning his back on the world, overcoming his fear of death, and deciding resolutely to negate his earthly being. As he handles the vial, Faust announces himself "ready / to press through to the ether on the new course, / to new spheres of pure activity / This high life, this joy of the gods!"[27] He directs himself simply to "turn your back resolutely / on the sweet suns of the earth," to "tear open the gates / Before which everyone else hesitates," "to decide clearly for this step / and, dangerous though it be, fly therein into the Nothing," for "it is time to prove through acts / that the dignity of man does not fall before the height of the gods."[28]

It is noteworthy, given what we will shortly recall from Rosenzweig's own 1913 crisis, that Faust's flirtation with suicide at the opening of the play is not the result of the loss of his will to live. Faust does not court suicide because he despairs of ever attaining spiritual wisdom. Rather, Faust wishes to die because of what he imagines his life will be once he is freed from the limits of the world, because he imagines that being freed from his dust-bound body will finally raise him to the stature of the gods.

The *Faust* "Night" scene to which Rosenzweig alludes here thus shares the world-denying tendencies of the other literary sources upon which Rosenzweig draws in the opening of the *Star.* Faust's step toward a suicide that would free him from the dust of the world and grant him access to the spiritual delights of the gods illustrates the extremes to which the self–world dualism shared by these sources leads. It is also sharply reminiscent of the reflections on dying for God which Rosenzweig and his cousin entertained in the years leading up to the *Leipziger Nachtgespräch.* But Rosenzweig draws on the "Night" scene not merely to provide yet another example of the problem of self and world. Rather, the end of the "Night" scene also projects for Rosenzweig the path he will recommend toward overcoming the dualism of self and world. Just as Faust is about to take his "last drink . . . with whole soul," he is called back "into life" in the world by the bells, the choral song, and the redemptive hopes of Easter morning. Faust tearfully announces: "the earth has me again!"[29]

The arc which Faust's deliberations form in the "Night" scene leads him from anguish over the limitations of human existence in the world, to a flirtation with the possibilities of realizing his selfhood through the denial of his worldliness, and then back to a reclaiming of his place in the world. The denouement of the scene indicates, for Rosenzweig, that there is for human beings another response to the problem of self and world besides the denial of the world. This was, of course, the decision that Rosenzweig himself reached in the wake of the *Leipziger Nachtgespräch* in 1913. There are a number of allusive turns of phrase in the *Star*'s first paragraphs that strongly suggest, furthermore, that Rosenzweig has his own personal decision between world denial and world redemption in mind, as the basis for his account of death and suicide at the beginning of the *Star.* When Rosenzweig writes, for example, that for human beings there "is determined another way out of the narrow-pass of the Nothing," he alludes to the human decision between "life and death" upon which, Rosenzweig had suggested in his "Paralipomena," the whole of creation depends. In that discussion of human freedom under the conditions of monotheism, recall, Rosenzweig had suggested that "the world was created for the sake of the *decision,*" and he had suggested that by creating the world in the way that He has, God has "set the human being in the narrow-pass of this one but absolute decision," that "between 'life' and 'death.'"[30] Parallels are implied here that will receive confirmation as the *Star* unfolds: the absolute decision set in the hands of human beings upon which the redemptive course of the world depends *is* the decision between escaping the world through some form of suicide or remaining in the world—precisely the decision Rosenzweig faced personally in the wake of the *Leipziger Nachtgespräch*.

Knowing what we do now about the course of Rosenzweig's own personal crisis in 1913, moreover, allows us to illuminate another crucial phrase in the passage on suicide from the opening of the *Star*. Rosenzweig's claim that "once in his life," every human being must "for one night long be stood eye-to-eye with the Nothing" is evidently a reference to his own crisis of July 7, 1913, in the aftermath of his conversation with Rosenstock and Ehrenberg. In chapter 2, I cited Rosenzweig's letter to Rosenstock, of August 13, 1917, in which Rosenzweig recounts what transpired for him in the hours after their conversation: "I was still much too near to that complete face-to-face with the nothing [*vis-à-vis du rien*] with which I had come into my room, in that morning after the night, and took my Browning 6.35 out of my desk drawer. Whether cowardice or hope at that time prevented its use, I don't know. . . ."[31] Rosenzweig draws on his own night-long moment of standing "face to face with the nothing" in the wake of the *Leipziger Nachtgespräch* here, in the opening of the *Star*, in his claim that every human being must at one point in his life experience the split between his own selfhood and worldliness so severely that he seriously contemplates taking his own life. His own crisis of 1913, properly understood, here shows itself to be the biographical basis for the very struggle with death with which the *Star* begins.[32] The references suggest, moreover, that Rosenzweig has come to see his own 1913 crisis as both necessary and as universal, much as we've seen he shared Hegel's view that every person must undergo an extreme subjective melancholy before being reconciled with the world. Indeed, just as Rosenzweig found himself drawn away from his world-denying dualism in the wake of the 1913 night-conversation, and toward the view that redemption must occur in the world, here too, in the opening pages of the *Star*, Rosenzweig claims that the experience of separation from the world must not lead to suicide: "the earth demands him again."

The path the human being is called on to take out of "the narrow-pass of the Nothing," out of the "narrow . . . life," is not the path of extreme world-denial. It is a path that demands that the human being "remain" in the world. It is no exaggeration to suggest that the whole of the *Star* is wrapped up with elaborating the significance of "remaining" in the world, and of the demands for redemptive action implicit within the call to remain.[33] This call too, however, appears to hearken back to the resolution of Rosenzweig's 1913 crisis in a crucial manner. Rosenzweig's own decision to remain in the world, of course, was ultimately a decision to "remain a Jew," and hence to act redemptively in the world within the worldly community into which he had been born.

If Rosenzweig thereby confronts his readers with the problem of self and world in the opening of the *Star*, the *Star* will proceed to show that accepting one's twofold identity—remaining as a self in the world—and grasping the ramifications of that twofold identity will have redemptive consequences. As the next section will show, the *Star*'s relational categories—creation, revelation, redemption—situate the tension the human being experiences along a course whose goal is the reconciliation of self and world. But arriving at this goal will demand that the human being engage in redemptive work in the world itself.

CREATION, REVELATION, REDEMPTION: THE COURSE RECONCILING SOUL AND WORLD

In the first part of *The Star of Redemption*, Franz Rosenzweig offers a philosophical construction of what he asserts to be the three fundamental kinds of beings we encounter in experience: God, world, and selves. In the second part of the *Star*, Rosenzweig offers an account of the relations between these fundamental kinds of beings—creation, revelation, redemption—whose course realizes "the All." As the relation between the elemental God and the elemental world, creation produces existing things in the world, things that exist as multiplicities—such as trees or animals or stones—and find their grounding in God's power as Creator. As the relation between the elemental God and the elemental self, revelation awakens the self to her unique "I-hood" through the personal summons of a loving God. As the culminating relationship between elemental self and elemental world, redemption unfolds as the infusing of "I-hood" through the whole network of things in the living, created world, producing a totality of individuals each of which is an "I," and each of which recognizes all others as sharing equally with it in the Kingdom of God.

In this section, I will suggest that Rosenzweig's sweeping narrative of cosmic relations stretching from creation through redemption amounts to a response to the perplexity of self and world to which we have been introduced in the opening of the *Star.* The outline of this response will be familiar to us, for it mirrors in basic ways the ideas Rosenzweig adopted in the process of overcoming his own tendency to Marcionism in the summer and fall of 1913. Although we will explore a number of different aspects of creation, revelation, and redemption as we proceed, the idea at the core of Rosenzweig's reconciliation of self and world through these cosmic relations may be formulated as follows. The human being's unique selfhood, awakened to "I-hood" in revelation, is indeed opposed to her nature as part of the created world. This opposition within the human being is real; but it is not static. Rather, the opposed sides of my being—world and self, creature and recipient of revelation—can be grasped in their unity if they are grasped as part of a movement developing toward their ultimate reconciliation. The second part of the *Star* shows how my selfhood and worldliness, opposed as they are, depend on each other and complete each other within the course of development from creation to redemption. In this context, moreover, the experience of internal tension between selfhood and worldliness is presented as a call to engage in those redemptive actions that will reconcile self and world and will realize the redemptive Kingdom of God. No opposition, no action, no advance toward redemptive reconciliation.

One of the key bits of evidence I presented to suggest Rosenzweig's 1913 Leipzig night-conversation centered on the problem of self and world, and not on the viability of revelatory faith in the modern world, was Rosenzweig's 1916 note: "What it means that God created the world and [is] *not just* the God of revelation—this I know precisely out of the Leipzig night-conversation of 7.7.13. At that time, I was on the best road to Marcionitism."[34] We understood this note to indicate that the metaphysical insight Rosenzweig took away from the 1913 night-conversation was that the God of revelation and the God of creation are one and the same, and thus that the human being's worldliness is just as essential to her being and to her relation to God as is her spiritual selfhood. Rosenzweig's formulation for the content of his discovery of July 7, 1913—"God created the world and is *not just* the God of revelation"—may as well be the epigraph for the whole second part of the *Star.* The consequences of this discovery unfold in myriad ways throughout the *Star*'s second part. The first two books of the second part explore creation and revelation, respectively; the third book of the second part presents redemption as the uniting together of the created world and the soul or "I" awoken in revelation. Since Rosenzweig depicts creation and revelation as part of a cosmic process that culminates in redemption, nearly every detail of his account of the course from creation to redemption in the second part of the *Star* might be shown to reflect Rosenzweig's turn, in 1913, away from Marcionism and toward a view of redemption as reconciling self and world. I limit myself in this section to addressing two particular claims he makes in his account of that course stretching from creation to redemption, each of which reveals a different side of the *Star*'s general response to the problem of self and world. The first claim is that while world and selfhood are indeed elementally distinct, and while creation and revelation indicate distinct relationships to the divine, creation in general, and my experience of being a creature, in particular, should be understood as a "promise" or "prophecy" whose fulfillment begins with the revelation that awakens me to my particular selfhood. This claim, and the promise–fulfillment structure upon which it is based, is central to the second part of the *Star.* I will suggest that Rosenzweig's view that creation be understood as promising revelation is rooted in conclusions he reaches in the summer and autumn of 1913, in particular in his affinity at that time for the response of the early Church to Marcionism. The second claim is that although self and world, revelation and creation, are, again, distinct and opposed in the second part of the *Star,* each is at once shown to be driven through internal motivation toward reconciliation with the other. Redemption, as Rosenzweig depicts it, is not only the ultimate reconciliation of creation and revelation; it reconciles creation and revelation by showing that *each can only truly fulfill itself through such reconciliation.* In response to the self–world perplexity he introduces in the opening of the *Star,* we will thus see, Rosenzweig directs his reader to recognize that 1) despite the tension between her selfhood and worldliness, her selfhood is promised or prophesied by her worldliness; and 2) her selfhood, her worldliness, and the opposition between them all demand (but thereby promise) redemptive action in the world that will reconcile them.

By attending to these two claims regarding the relations between creation, revelation, and redemption in the second part of the *Star,* I hope to be able to provide an overview of the *Star*'s alternative to Marcionism. After we have sketched out the broad course across which Rosenzweig shows creation, revelation, and redemption to respond to the problem of Marcionism, we will be in a position, in the sections that follow, to address specific aspects of Rosenzweig's account of redemption in detail, namely human freedom, divine unity, and the complementary roles of Judaism and Christianity in the actualization of redemption in the world.

Creation and Revelation as Promise and Fulfillment

Let us first address the way the structure of promise and fulfillment governs the *Star*'s account of actuality, and of the relationship between creation and revelation, in particular. Creation and revelation, philosophy and theology, world and self—the *Star* presents the former of each pair as promising or as prophesying the latter, and as finding fulfillment in it. Building on my account of the second part of the *Star* in *Franz Rosenzweig and the Systematic Task of Philosophy,* I want to explain in what follows how the relationship of promise and fulfillment allows Rosenzweig to grasp world and self in their difference and their shared identity. I will suggest that Rosenzweig's understanding of the relationship between creation and revelation draws heavily on the insights of those Church Fathers, Augustine and Tertullian, whom Rosenzweig understood to have been responding both to Marcion's dualism and to his excision of the Hebrew Bible from the Christian Scriptural canon.

The notion that "God created the world and [is] *not just* the God of revelation" first plays a role in the argument of the *Star* in the form of an intervention into contemporary theology. In the introduction to the second part of the *Star,* Rosenzweig presents the modern embarrassment over the concept of "miracle" as a sign of the crisis of Protestant theology in his time and as evidence, more specifically, that contemporary theology does not know what to do with the world. According to their original meaning, Rosenzweig asserts, miracles were not essentially inexplicable occurrences or events contradicting the laws of nature, but rather miracles were the *fulfillments of prophecies.* Miracles were events that could be taken as revealed "signs" of the divine providential order of things in the world, precisely because they had been prophesied prior to their occurrence (103–05/103–04).

Now, once upon a time, Rosenzweig recounts, claims about miracles were not the source of theological embarrassment that they are today. To the contrary: miracles were once brought forward as the best way to *demonstrate the truth* of one doctrine or worldview over others (104/104). But with the rise of the modern enlightenment and its critique of the "gullibility of experience" (109/108), miracles began to fall out of theological favor. The crowning centerpiece of contemporary theology, Rosenzweig claims, is its conception of faith as the "personal and momentary" experience of revelation oriented by the hope for an ideal future (110–11/110).[35] According to Rosenzweig, because such an account of faith turns away from traditional claims regarding the miracles of the past, because it thereby sidesteps questions of divine providence in the world, it leaves revelation hovering in the air with no objective grounding. For hereby the experience of revelation as "miraculous" is transformed from the *fulfillment* of a prior constitutive moment of prophecy, in which the very consonance of the two moments attests to the credibility of the miracle, into a free-floating, ephemeral experience, open to any and every interpretation. Without a clear grounding in the "predetermined lawfulness of the world," Rosenzweig suggests, faith experience has no claim to *truth.* Without a clear account of its relation to the world, moreover, the faith experience of the present moment lacks any site within which it can realize its ideal future.

Rosenzweig's response in the *Star* to the crisis from which he claims contemporary theology suffers on account of its one-sided celebration of faith experience, is to articulate, in so many words, what he learned back in the summer of 1913: "God created the world and is not just the God of revelation." According to Rosenzweig, contemporary theology's crisis of groundless faith shows that theology is in need of renewed collaboration with philosophy, and that the notion of revelatory experience demands renewed grounding in creation. The following two passages express these claims in successive paragraphs in the introduction to the second part of the *Star:*

> Precisely if one . . . wants to hold onto . . . the orientation of the personal and momentary experiencing faith by [*an*] the pole of certainty that "the kingdom of the noble finally comes," precisely then the claims of knowledge must be more fundamentally

> and above all more immediately satisfied, than just through the powdering up of the past. Knowledge of the world in its systematic wholeness . . . thus philosophy, must prepare itself to work together with theology. (113/112)
>
> Thus creation must again be set, in the full gravity of its objectivity, next to the experience of revelation. Indeed still further: revelation itself and its tie to and its grounding in the confidence in the coming of the ethical kingdom of the ultimate redemption, this whole connection sensed today to be the real core of faith . . . itself must again be built into the concept of creation. Revelation too, redemption too are precisely creation in a certain, not yet to be argued-out way. And so here lies the point out of which philosophy can erect the whole building of theology anew. It was creation that theology in the nineteenth century had neglected in its craze over the notion of the living present revelation. And precisely creation is now the gate through which philosophy enters into the house of theology. (114/113)

The first of these quotations conveys Rosenzweig's view that theology cannot free faith from the world simply by sweeping past claims about divine miracles under the rug. A theology that celebrates revelatory experience and ignores the status of the world will not in the end avoid the critical question of the *truth* of faith claims. A compelling response to such a question demands that faith grasp itself within the totality of a "knowledge of the world in its systematic wholeness"; it demands an account of the status and meaning of revelatory experience within the whole of what is. Rosenzweig understands this demand on the part of theology to be met by philosophy.

The second passage suggests that philosophy can situate theology's account of faith within the whole of what is precisely by restoring to good standing that notion of creation, "in the full gravity of its objectivity," which contemporary theology has neglected, and by grasping properly the relationship between creation and revelation. It suggests, moreover, that the whole within which theology must grasp revelation in relation to the world is a whole that unfolds out of *creation*. The "living present revelation," and its directedness toward a redemptive future, must be grasped as *already there* in some way in creation itself.

How are revelation and redemption to be grasped as "precisely creation in a certain . . . way"? Rosenzweig suggests that the key to overcoming contemporary theology's crisis of free-floating revelatory experience lies in grasping revelation as the *fulfillment* of what has been promised in creation. The present experience of revelation and its directedness toward a redemptive future are to be understood as already present within creation *as their prophecy:*

> Philosophy thus contains the whole content of revelation, but this content not as revelation, but as the precondition of revelation. . . . In creation, revelation in its whole content, and precisely according to the concept of faith of the contemporary epoch thus including redemption as well, is "providentially foreseen [*vorgesehen*]." Philosophy, as practiced by theologian, becomes the prophecies of revelation, so to speak the "Old Testament" of theology. With this, however, revelation attains before our astounded eyes the genuine character of miracle once again—genuine, because it becomes wholly fulfillment of the promise that occurred in creation. (120/118)

Revelation becomes miraculous once again, Rosenzweig argues here, when philosophy shows it to be part of the fulfillment of the "promise that occurred in creation," when creation is grasped as providentially foreshadowing the redemptive process tied to revelation. "Creation is the prophecy [*Weissagung*], which is only confirmed in the miraculous sign of revelation" (149/146), Rosenzweig reiterates elsewhere. This promise–fulfillment structure of the miracle turns out to be central to the philosophical method and the movement of the *Star* as a whole.[36] It is on the basis of this promise–fulfillment structure, moreover, that we can return to the perplexity of self and world with which the opening of the *Star* confronted us. Rosenzweig's notion of creation as prediction or prophecy of revelation and redemption begins to provide us with a response to this perplexity.

Rosenzweig's argument for how the tension between self and world is eased through the promise–fulfillment relationship between creation and revelation may be summarized as follows. As part of the world, I experience myself as creature, as a member of the network of existing things grounded in God's creative act. As a unique self called by a personal name, aware of myself as an "I," and capable of entering into personal relations with others, I experience myself as the recipient of God's revelatory love. Creation and revelation—and my experience of each—are different, even opposed. But at the same time, my self-consciousness as creature points as a kind of prophecy to a process of self-realization that demands both my awakening to a sense of myself as "I" in revelation, and my ultimate turning as "I" toward others in the world, as part of the course of redemption. Moreover, the experience of being called by God directs the self to review his past life in the world as laying the groundwork for this unique revelatory relationship to God.

Let us now examine how Rosenzweig spells out this argument, through a few examples from the second part of the *Star.* First I will highlight some passages in which Rosenzweig describes the tension between self and world in the vocabulary of creation and revelation, and then I will turn to passages in which he shows that tension to be mitigated once creation and revelation are grasped as related through promise and fulfillment.

When Rosenzweig depicts the awakening of the individual soul as "I" through the divine call of revelation, he describes this process as one in which the self is singled out by God through his or her personal name, or is addressed as a "You" by the divine "I." Along the way, Rosenzweig stresses how becoming an "I" tears the person addressed by the divine out of the created world in which she has previously felt at home:

> The I or the You, seen thus in its objectivity, is quintessential individual, not individual through the mediation of some multiplicity. It is no "the" because it is an "a," but rather individual without species. In the place of the article, here steps the immediate determinateness of the personal name. With the call of the personal name, the word of revelation entered into the actual exchange of speech. In the personal name a breach has been set into the firm wall of thingness. What has a personal name, can no longer be thing, no longer everyman's matter. It is incapable of going without remainder into the species of which it belongs, because there is no species to which it belongs: it is its own species. (208/201)

Once the human being is identified as a unique "I" through God's revelatory summons, once the human being has a personal name, this passage suggests, the human being "can no longer be a thing." The "I" beloved of God is no longer defined as a member of the collective of things in the world. The "I" is not determined by its indirect relation to the divine through his "species," but rather is its own species. The personal name of revelation sets a "breach" into the "wall of thingness."

Rosenzweig suggests that the awakening self experiences this being torn from the world that accompanies divine revelation in stark, painful fashion. It leads him to view the entirety of his life in the world up to that point—the life he had before the self-recognition that has now come to him through revelation—as a life of sin. In response to God's loving summons, the soul thus confronts his past worldly life in the form of a confession of sin:

> Love would not be the shocking, seizing, tearing that it is, if the shocked, seized, torn soul were not conscious of itself as having been up to this point un-shocked, un-seized, un-torn. . . . And the soul is ashamed of its past self, and that it had not broken the spell in which it lay by its own power. . . . And so the soul to whom God calls out his command of love is ashamed of itself, ashamed to confess its love to him; because it can only confess its love in that it confesses its weakness along with it. To the "You shall love" of God, it answers, "I have sinned." (200/194)

As exalting as is the experience of being awakened to one's unique selfhood through the divine loving command, Rosenzweig suggests here, this experience casts a shadow of darkness and shame over one's previous life in the world. Indeed, the opposition between one's present selfhood and one's past life is so sharp that it seems to provide experiential evidence for a Gnostic view that revelation saves the faithful soul from an evil world.

But Rosenzweig does not let this standoff between one's created past and one's faithful present remain static. As stark as is the opposition between my worldliness and my selfhood, between creation and revelation, Rosenzweig claims, I can come to see that a "miraculous" relationship holds between them. My worldliness, my createdness, must be grasped as grounding my selfhood, as a prophecy that finds its fulfillment in my unique selfhood. Rosenzweig makes this claim in an especially clear manner when speaking of the providential form of God's relation to the things in the world through creation. Rosenzweig asserts that this providence amounts to a prophecy of the more intimate relation to individual selves God will have in revelation:

> For the Creator, . . . things present themselves only in the universal context of the whole of existence. Only through this, does his creation grasp them "each one according to its species." . . . Here too the genuine concept of creation points to its fulfillment in the miracle of revelation. The human being well appears as creature among creatures and creaturely is affected as particular existence by the providence directed to all existence in general. But this his creaturely relationship to God is yet only "prophecy," too. The human being as God's creature is the portent of human being as God's child. Fulfillment is more than omen [*Vorbedeutung*], sign [*Zeichen*] is more than portent [*Vorzeichen*],—child is more than creature. (135, 137/133, 135)

On the one hand, this passage explains, the human being's creaturely existence situates him as a thing like all other things in the world, a "creature among creatures," related to God solely through the mediation of his species. It is this thingly identity that the human being in the world will have shattered through the revelation that awakens him to selfhood. But as contrary as thing and self may be, the relation of general providence that holds over the things of creation "points to its fulfillment" in the revelatory, loving relation to God through which the human self will awaken to his unique "I-hood." When the human being comes to experience himself as "God's child" in revelation, Rosenzweig suggests here, he doesn't merely experience a "breach" in his creaturely existence, but rather experiences the fulfillment of the prophecy encapsulated in his already having been God's creature in the world.

Rosenzweig's depiction of the revelatory encounter with God that led the human being to lament the sinfulness of his past worldly existence likewise suggests that one's experience of the opposition between one's worldliness and one's selfhood is mitigated when one learns to view one's past in the world as having prepared the way for one's present selfhood. In Rosenzweig's account of the exchange between God and the individual soul, it is God who indicates to the soul the divine involvement in the world that prepared the way for revelation:

> The past creation is proven from out of the vitally present revelation. Proven—that is to say, pointed to [*Bewiesen, nämlich gewiesen*]. In the shine-of-light of the experienced miracle of revelation a past preparing and providentially foreseeing [*vorsehend*] this miracle becomes visible. The creation that becomes visible in revelation is the creation of revelation. (203/197)

In the course of the revelatory encounter between God and the soul, Rosenzweig claims here, God shows the soul that his past worldly life, which appeared so starkly opposed to his experience of being a self beloved by God, was itself the providential preparation for revelation. The human being can only come to know creation as the promise fulfilled through revelation, Rosenzweig asserts, from the standpoint of revelation itself. But it is because the individual recipient of revelation can now grasp that "God created the world and is not just the God of revelation," that he can come to see the history of the past as littered with "prophecies" of that intimate relationship in which he now stands to the divine. Looking back at my creaturely life from the perspective of revelation gives me reason to trust my experience of revelation as a true relation to God, since it is a relation that I can now see is grounded in the created world of which I am a part, in the same way that I can now see my own possession of a personal name as the fulfillment of an identity predicted through the divine providential governance of the species in the created world. My experience of revelation's rootedness in creation thus amounts to the experience of a "miracle," and serves as evidence of the truth of my faith experience.

Thus, by the time Rosenzweig writes the *Star*, he understands "God created the world and is not just the God of revelation" to mean that revelation, and the awakening of human selfhood through the human being's revelatory relation to the divine, must be grasped as a moment in the fulfillment of a cosmic process that begins in creation. It is thus that the promise–fulfillment structure articulates the identity and difference that holds between world and self. My worldliness finds fulfillment through a process that demands as one of its moments the negation of the worldly. The awareness of my "I" that comes to me through the revelatory encounter with God finds its grounding and preparation in a worldly past from which it nevertheless has been torn. Self and world are not held here in static opposition, but neither is their opposition denied. Rather, the promise–fulfillment relationship between creation and revelation points to a process of opposition and reconciliation. As the next part of this section will show, it is a process that will only reach its conclusion in redemption.

Before turning to redemption, however, I want to take a closer look at Rosenzweig's assertion that we should grasp creation and revelation as linked together as prophecy and fulfillment in the light of his 1913 crisis. We may recognize this assertion, generally speaking, as grounded in Rosenzweig's decision, on the night of July 7, 1913, to take "the first sentence of the Bible" as the starting point for his own reconciliation of self and world. We understood from Rosenzweig's declaration that he had come to see creation as the beginning of a process that summons the individual recipients of revelation to redemptive activity in the world. And we claimed that the thinking together of creation and redemption was the condition for conceiving redemption as a process that unfolds through history. I would like to suggest now that the account of miracle, and the structure of promise and fulfillment that governs much of the philosophical movement of the *Star* and allows Rosenzweig to begin to reconcile creation and revelation within it, owes a more specific debt to developments in Rosenzweig's thinking in the wake of the *Leipziger Nachtgespräch.* In the first letter to his mother from October 1913, in which he announces that he has found his way back to Judaism, Rosenzweig recalls the manner in which the early Church overcame its struggle with Gnosticism by insisting on the "vitality" of the Jews as evidence for the identity between the "God who created Heaven and Earth" and "the Father of Jesus Christ":

> the vitality which J[aeckh] concedes to Judaism is just that which the whole Church concedes to it and which the Church has fought through in the most difficult inner struggle for its existence (the struggle with the Gnostic heresy) and so for its own sake cannot relinquish: that the Old Testament is "God's Word," that "salvation" has come from the Jews (as Paul says), and the God, who "created Heaven and Earth," the "God of Abraham and the God of Isaac and the God of Jacob," the God who

> named his "name" to Moses, and gave his spirit to the prophets—that this God is the "Father of Jesus Christ." This the Church has fought through against the Gnostics, who refused to believe this, and explained the God of the Old Testament as being one with the Devil or in the best case as an angel or under-God. No sensible Jew will not be thankful to it for this.[37]

As we noted in chapter 3, this revealing passage suggests Rosenzweig understood that early Christian orthodoxy's relationship to Judaism and to the Hebrew Bible was forged through its "inner struggle" with Gnosticism. Against the Gnostic view that the God of the Old Testament is "one with the Devil," the early Church came to insist that the "Old Testament is 'God's Word,'" and that the God "who 'created Heaven and Earth,' the 'God of Abraham and the God of Isaac and the God of Jacob'" is none other than "the 'Father of Jesus Christ.'" As Rosenzweig understood it, we found, this doctrinal move to root the revelation of God through Christ in God's relation to the world and to the Jewish people, as recorded in the Hebrew Bible—the identification thereby of the God of creation with the God of revelation—linked Christians to Jews in the economy of redemption. From the Christian perspective, Christianity had no doubt come to supersede Judaism. But in Rosenzweig's view, this did not make the grounding of Christ's revelation in the prophecies of the Hebrew Bible any less essential to early Church doctrine.[38]

What Rosenzweig identified then, already in 1913, as essential to early Christianity and its link to Judaism, was that the early Church fathers argued for faith in Christ by claiming that Christ was the *fulfillment* of the teachings of the Hebrew Bible, from its account of Creation through its account of God's special relation to the Jewish people. That is to say: the precedent for Rosenzweig's claim that creation must be understood as prophecy fulfilled through the course of revelation and redemption is to be found in the arguments he uncovered in 1913 through which the early Church fathers struggled against Marcionism.[39] We indeed find, for example, that Augustine makes the claim, in the *City of God,* that the continued existence of the Jews—dispersed as they are around the globe—bears witness to this very relation of promise and fulfillment that holds between creation and salvation, and thereby serves to demonstrate the credibility of Christian belief:

> This mystery of eternal life has been made known . . . from the very beginnings of the human race. . . . Later, the Hebrew people was gathered and united in a kind of community designed to perform this sacred function of revelation. In that people

> the future course of events, from the coming of Christ to the present day, and even beyond, was prophesied. . . . In the course of time, this people was scattered among the nations to bear witness to the Scriptures, which foretold the coming salvation in Christ. For not only all the prophesies contained in words, not only all the precepts for the conduct of life which shape men's character and their piety and are contained in the Scriptures, but . . . everything which is concerned with the homage due to God—all these were symbols and predictions that find their fulfillment in Christ, so as to give eternal life to those who believe.[40]

Augustine here asserts that the very relationship which Rosenzweig later claims holds between creation and revelation must be grasped as linking the Hebrew Bible and the course of salvation through Christ. Who are the believers who are worthy of "eternal life"? Augustine suggests salvation is to come to those who know how to read "the Scriptures"—its words, its pious precepts, its praise of God—as "symbols and predictions that find their fulfillment in Christ." Recognizing the Hebrew Bible as the Old Testament, as the promise fulfilled in the New, is essential to Christian faith.

This early Christian account of the Hebrew Bible as prophesying the salvation that will come through Christ is likewise to be found in Tertullian, from whom Rosenzweig draws in even more detailed fashion. In his *Adversus Marcionem,* Tertullian rejects Marcion's account of Christ as the manifestation of a distant God come to save those believing souls from the God of Creation, by suggesting that there is *no argument* that can be made on behalf of such a view of Christ. On the other hand, an understanding of Christ that views him as the *fulfillment* of prophecies recorded in the Hebrew Bible amounts to a compelling argument in support of faith. As precedent for Rosenzweig's claim that the promise–fulfillment structure of the miracle grounds theological doctrine in a way that faith experience alone, divorced from the world, cannot do, Tertullian argues the following:

> Here [in Marcion's teaching] you have a son unexpected, an agent unexpected, a Christ unexpected. But I suggest that with God nothing is unexpected, because with God nothing exists unordained. If then it was ordained beforehand, why was it not also announced beforehand, so that the announcement might prove it ordained, and the ordaining prove it divine? And surely there is another reason why so great a work, one taken in hand for man's salvation, could not have been unexpected—that it was to become effective through faith. It had to be believed, or remain ineffective. And so it required preparatory work in order to be credible—preparatory work built upon foundations of previous intention and prior announcement. Only by being built up in this order could faith with good cause be imposed upon man by God, and shown

> towards God by man—a faith which, since there was knowledge, might be required to believe because belief was a possibility, and in fact had learned to believe by virtue of that previous announcement.[41]

Faith in Christ can only be demanded by God, Tertullian argues, because such faith is credible given the "preparatory work" God has done through his "previous announcement," the Old Testament. What can be said, Tertullian asks, in favor of Marcion's Christ, who appears out of nowhere, unannounced, unexpected? *Nothing.* Tertullian here presents the model of argument that Rosenzweig adopts, in the introduction to the second part of the *Star,* when he claims that faith alone, divorced from the world, is groundless and can make no claim to truth. The argument *per miraculum* that Rosenzweig seeks to revive on philosophical grounds, grasping creation as the promise fulfilled through revelation, is none other than the argument Tertullian offers here: only when revelation (Christ) is grasped as the fulfillment of a prophecy to which we have access through other means (Scripture), can faith in revelation be compelling.

In passages throughout the introduction to the second part of the *Star,* Rosenzweig identifies this early Church position regarding the relation between Old Testament and New, which he came to see in 1913 as having emerged through the struggle against Gnosticism, as a source of his argument regarding the promise–fulfillment relation between creation and revelation. He alludes to the arguments of Augustine and Tertullian when he claims that "when Augustine or any other Church father had to defend the divinity and truth of revealed religion . . . he hardly neglected to point to miracles. They were the most forceful argument" (104/104). Asserting the promise–fulfillment relationship that should hold between philosophy and theology, Rosenzweig envisions how "philosophy, as practiced by the theologian, becomes the prophecy of revelation, the 'Old Testament' of theology, so to speak" (120/118). And when he explains the original meaning of miracle as the fulfillment of prophecy, Rosenzweig exemplifies his view by noting that "both the Holy Scriptures and the New Testament place great value on granting the character of sign to their miracle of revelation, the former through the promise to the patriarchs, the latter through the prophecy of the prophets" (107/106). These passages indicate that the affinity Rosenzweig felt for those early Christian arguments against Marcionism that were based on the assertion that creation—and the account of it in the Hebrew Bible—must be grasped as the prophecy for revelation, finds expression in some of the central arguments, and indeed in the basic structure of the *Star.* The relationship between creation and revelation, as Rosenzweig presents it in the *Star,* has its roots in the arguments regarding creation and revelation to which Rosenzweig was drawn in the months after the *Leipziger Nachtgespräch.* Indeed, the very method of promise–fulfillment that is so central to the movement of the book as it articulates how God, world, and self only find the fulfillment of their respective being through the relations among them that realize the redemptive "All"—this method can be understood as the broadest systematic application of an argument Rosenzweig came to adopt during the course of his personal overcoming of Marcionism.

The Redemptive Reconciliation of Creation and Revelation

Rosenzweig's response to the opposition between self and world in the *Star,* I have suggested, is not to take this opposition as evidence of a fundamental dualism, but rather to show how that opposition must be understood as part of a movement toward unity. The redemption toward which God, self, and the world strive, according to Rosenzweig, is none other than the unification of creation and revelation; it is the bringing together of those beings and those ways of being that emerged out of the relation between God and the world on the one hand, and God and the self, on the other. This redemptive reconciliation of creation and revelation shows the tension between self and world we experience to be transitory. We are called on, moreover, to take up the kind of redemptive activity in the world that will advance their reconciliation.

Thus far in this chapter, we have examined both the perplexity of self and world, as Rosenzweig introduces it in the opening of the *Star,* and the way Rosenzweig begins to respond to this perplexity through a developmental account of the relationship between these two poles of our experience, by conceiving of the world's creation as a prophecy that begins to be fulfilled through revelation. I will focus my discussion here on Rosenzweig's account of redemption as the ultimate reconciliation of self and world, thus as the ultimate solution to the problem that plagued him during his 1913 crisis. We will recognize at the root of the *Star*'s depiction of redemption, the very account of the realization of the Kingdom of God on earth that Rosenzweig adopted in the wake of his 1913 *Leipziger Nachtgespräch.* But as we shall see, Rosenzweig's systematic presentation of the relations between God, self, and world in the *Star* allowed him to offer explanations for both the opposition between self and world and for their ultimate reconciliation, which he could not yet have formulated in 1913.

As the third book of the second part of the *Star* shows, redemption engages soul and world in a process of reciprocal activity that results in their union. Rosenzweig regularly suggests that soul and world are redeemed through this reciprocal, unifying activity, and that even God earns redemption through the process. "In the redemption of the world through the human being and of the human being by [an] the world, God redeems Himself" (266/256), Rosenzweig writes:

> From God to the world, from God to the human being—this was each time a movement in unambiguous direction. God had to create the world, so that it could snuggle up as enchanted creature under the wings of His providence. God had to call the human being by name, so that as opened soul he could open his mouth. Here alone [i.e., in redemption] the two poles referred to each other from the beginning and everything that happens between them, happens in both at the same time. . . . The redemption of the soul by the things, of the things through the soul happens in the same-breath duet of both. . . . In redemption, the great And completes the arch of the All. (255/245–46)

Redemption for the individual soul and for the things of the world occurs through their united reciprocal activity. We will address the meaning of God's redemption below; but note here how the reconciliation of soul and world, according to these passages, both completes "the All," and is the means through which God redeems Himself. How does this redemptive process occur? Recall that the created world amounts to an expansive network of things governed by the providential laws enacted by the Creator, and that revelation amounts to the awakening of "I-hood," through the divine call to the individual self by personal name. Rosenzweig describes redemption as precisely the fusion of these unique qualities of world and self. Redemption infuses the network of living things in the world with the "I-hood" or "soul" awoken by God in the self through revelation. Thus Rosenzweig identifies redemption as the "ensouling of the growing life of the world" (266/257), and the redeemed world as a "wholly ramified life filled with soul" (269/259). "The Kingdom of God," Rosenzweig writes, "is indeed nothing other than the reciprocal unification of soul with the whole world" (260/251). The future redemption is thus conceived as a point at which all particular beings in the world both will be unique "I"s and will be united with all others in perfect community. As we shall see, this perfect community of "I"s is united, moreover, in the common recognition of the unity of God. Redemption thus amounts to the ultimate overcoming of the tension between self and world, because being a self and being part of the world would no longer stand in tension: every individual, in being a self, would at once take up her place in the community of all.

What makes the *Star*'s account of the reconciliation of self and world compelling is not simply that the book presents its readers with an image of redemption as the goal of a process in which self and world are unified. Rosenzweig's account also offers an explanation for *why* the self, insofar as it is a self, and the world, insofar as it is the world, "must" seek such reconciliation. Over the course of the second part of the *Star,* Rosenzweig suggests that the drive toward the reconciliation of creation and revelation lies implicitly within creation and revelation, respectively. Even as they stand opposed to each other, creation and revelation are pre-programmed, as it were, to press toward the same goal of mutual reconciliation.[42]

The governing idea here is the following. Neither creation nor revelation can be said to be "complete" until redemption. Odd as it may sound, the created world is not completely created, and the individual self, beloved of God, is not yet fully secure in her selfhood, until redemption. It is this character of not yet being what one is, in each case, that drives the created world and the self awakened in revelation into the kind of reciprocal interaction that yields their reconciliation in redemption. As a result, the opposition between self and world that Rosenzweig once took to be fundamental, he now presents as the *premature hypostatization of a moment that precedes self and world becoming in fact what they truly are.* Only so long as the world is not yet completely world, and only so long as the self is not yet fully self, are world and self experienced as mutually opposed. But the realization of self and world, respectively, will come through their mutual reconciliation in redemption.

Let's begin with the world. When Rosenzweig depicts creation as the relationship between God and world he makes special note of the fact that while creation may amount to a one-time past action on God's part, from the perspective of the world it nevertheless represents an ongoing process *that will only be completed in redemption.* Rosenzweig writes, "That which for God is past and immemorial, actually 'in the beginning,' can yet be thoroughly present for the world, even up to its end. The creation of the world needs find its end only in redemption" (132/130). How are we to understand creation as complete only in redemption? In *Franz Rosenzweig and the Systematic Task of Philosophy,* I suggest by way of answer to this question that the created world has an inherently unstable identity. Rosenzweig presents it as a vast collective of particular things, but the unity of that collective transcends the world (the created world's particulars are united together by the unity of their Creator), and the particular things themselves cannot be said to *be* as particulars, since they exist only as representatives of their species. From both the side of its unity and the side of its multiplicity, therefore, the world presses toward revelation and redemption: a course of relations that would ultimately unify the world and grant true particularity—selfhood—to its particulars. Indeed, it is here in the world's inherent *incompleteness* that we find the ground of the created world's role as "promise," as starting point of a course that leads through revelation and redemption.[43]

Rosenzweig explains the manner in which the world presses toward redemption in a further illuminating way when he discusses the redemptive Kingdom of God as the world's future. It is the unfinished character of the world, Rosenzweig suggests, that points to its need for redemption:

> The world is still not finished. There is still laughing and crying in it. The tear is still not washed away from every face. This condition of becoming, of unfinishedness, only lets itself be grasped now through a reversal of the objective relationships-of-time. . . . The future is to be grasped as what it is, namely as future, only through the means of anticipation. . . . The future is experienced only in expectation. . . . So it [the world] is at each inch something coming, no: it is a coming. It is that which should come. It is the kingdom. (244–45/235–36)

From the perspective of the unfinished world, the idea of its completion in redemption must be grasped through anticipation or expectation. What that means, according to Rosenzweig, is that the world is to be grasped not in its actual, unstable, and troubled present form, but rather as the becoming of what it "should" be. What the world is has not yet been realized. The world, in truth, *is* the "kingdom"; it *is* "that which should come." Even though the world is created in its primordial relation with God, Rosenzweig thus suggests, it does not yet become what it is—it does not become the world in truth—until redemption. The "should" of the world demands of its inhabitants, moreover, to realize the kingdom it is meant to be.

There is a striving for redemption from the side of the soul in revelation, as well. Here too, moreover, the individual soul strives out of a need for self-realization left unfulfilled in revelation itself. The individual soul was awakened to "I-hood" through revelation, we recall, and was thereby torn from out of the world into a sense of his unique selfhood and his concomitant intimate relation with the divine. Grasping his past life in the world as prediction fulfilled in his awakening to selfhood in revelation allowed the individual self to begin to reconcile his worldliness and his selfhood. But the soul's unique revelatory relation to the divine, and his I awakened through that relation, were as of yet still a matter that was entirely private. According to Rosenzweig, the realization of selfhood demands that this selfhood, and its attendant intimate relation to the divine, be recognized out in the world. Only through such public recognition, Rosenzweig claims, do the results of revelation become "eternal," and only thus do they become part of "actuality" and "truth." The recipient of revelation, according to Rosenzweig, "is anxious for an eternalization of love, as it could never sprout out of the all-timely presentness of feeling; an eternalization, namely, that no longer grows in the I and You, but rather longs to be grounded in the view of all the world" (228/219). The intimate context of revelation in which divine love awakens the "I" of the self, the relationship between I and You, is incomplete as such. That relationship, and the "I" emerging from it, seek permanence through its grounding "in the view of all the world."

Rosenzweig explains this point, in the context of his reading of the *Song of Songs*, as follows:

> Does life not need more than . . . calling-by-name? Does it not need actuality? And out of the blissful overflowing heart of the beloved a sob climbs and forms itself into words, words that, stammering, point to something unfulfilled, something incapable of being fulfilled in the immediate revelation of love: "Oh that you were like a brother to me." It is not enough that the beloved [i.e., God] calls his bride by the name of sister in the flickering half-light of allusion. The name must be truth, heard in the bright light of the street, not whispered in the beloved's ear in the dimness of intimate solitude of two, no, before the eyes of the masses fully counted—"who would grant" this! (227/218–19)

In this rhapsodic interpretation of the cry of the beloved from the *Song of Songs,* Rosenzweig suggests that the self who has been awakened to "I-hood" through divine love longs to have this relationship grounded in and recognized in the context of the world. He longs to have his relationship of love become a relationship of worldly fellowship—a relationship between siblings—and to have that relationship recognized "in the bright light of the street . . . before the eyes of the masses." As Rosenzweig proceeds to argue, the "I-hood" of the self awakened in divine love can only be recognized by others in the world who have likewise become "I"s and are likewise bound to one another through love. It is thus that the longing for a worldly recognition for the self's selfhood becomes the demand that the self take on the task of creating a redemptive community in which all participants are selves, connected through love:

> The kingdom of brotherliness for which the soul longs . . . this bond of a beyond-the-natural [*über-natürlichen*], wholly personally felt and yet wholly worldly existing community, can no longer be founded for her by the love of the lover. . . . Should this longing be fulfilled, the beloved soul would have to step beyond the magic circle of belovedness, forgetting the lover, and open her own mouth, no longer to answer, but rather to her own word. (228/219)

Fulfilling one's selfhood, Rosenzweig implies in this passage, paradoxically demands leaving that revelatory relationship in which one's selfhood was initially awoken and secured. The self must open her mouth now, "no longer to answer" the call of the divine, but rather to direct "her own word" of love to others in the world. The characteristics of the community the self seeks to form here are striking: the community must be a "beyond-the-natural [*über-natürlichen*], wholly personally felt and yet wholly worldly existing community." The redemptive kingdom the soul is to strive to realize must be a community that both is worldly and at once steps beyond the natural, that both is actually existent and at once "personally felt." For the self awakened through revelatory love, that is to say, fulfillment can only come through the realization of a redemptive community that fuses perfectly creation and revelation, world and self. As we shall see below, this redemptive community attains to such perfect unity in the moment when all particular beings in the world are joined together within it, as individual selves, in collective recognition of the divine.

The *Star*'s account of redemption thus amounts to a compelling response to self-world perplexity not only because it depicts redemption as reconciling self and world, but more importantly, because it suggests that self and world *must* each enter into redemptive reciprocal relations with the other precisely in order to be what it is respectively. The world must be redeemed; its "ramified life" must be "filled with soul" before creation is complete and before it can claim to be the world it "should" be. The self must create a redemptive "kingdom of brotherliness" out of the world, transforming it into a community of selves who recognize its selfhood and thereby grant it "truth" and "actuality." The resolution of the opposition between self and world thus only comes through the recognition that each requires merging with the other in order to realize what it truly is.

We have covered considerable ground in this section, tracing in broad strokes the entirety of the *Star*'s course from creation to redemption, and trying to show how that course serves as a response to the self–world perplexity with which the *Star* opens. The two parts of this section highlighted Rosenzweig's account of the promise–fulfillment relation between creation and revelation, on the one hand, and his account of redemption as the reconciliation of creation and revelation, on the other. It sought to show, along the way, how Rosenzweig's ideas and language are stamped by the intellectual and personal process he went through in the wake of the *Leipziger Nachtgespräch,* when he overcame his own inclination to Marcionism. Now that we have traced the *Star*'s elaboration of Rosenzweig's response to Marcionism in broad strokes, we will turn to examine a number of central themes within the *Star* that are uniquely illuminated by the insights we have gained regarding Rosenzweig's struggle with Marcionism.

HER OWN WORD: LOVE, COMMAND, AND FREEDOM BETWEEN REVELATION AND REDEMPTION

One of the ways Rosenzweig identified his early Marcionism, we've seen, is as an experience of the tension between one's relation to God and one's relation to others in the world. Thus, we recall, Rosenzweig shared in the view expressed in Rudolf Ehrenberg's *Halbhunderttag* that "too great love directed to [a] human being is the highest danger to love of God." He was likewise caricatured in Rudolf Ehrenberg's *Ebr. 10:25: ein Schicksal in Predigten* as a heretic who "took from faith and not from love," that is, who held onto his faith relation to God so single-mindedly that he refused to recognize that faith as a seed meant to grow into love for others in his community. Rosenstock, on the other hand, had not been inclined toward the radical opposition between the individual's relation to God and his relation to others in the world, because he believed from the start in "the Word." We took this designation to allude to Rosenstock's view that the speech through which human beings express love to each other is in fact rooted in divinity. Furthermore, we explored a plausible account of Rosenstock's role in the *Leipziger Nachtgespräch* according to which Rosenzweig's experience of redemptive love through Rosenstock's own word contributed to his conversion to the position that redemption demanded worldly engagement and not world denial.

This whole complex of themes central to Rosenzweig's 1913 crisis—the tension between loving God and loving others, and the role of the divine Word in both generating and mitigating that tension—feature prominently in Rosenzweig's account of the path to redemption in the *Star.* Divine love finds its purest expression, according to Rosenzweig, in the form of a verbal *command* to the individual soul to love God in return. This command to the individual soul to love God is the centerpiece of the revelatory experience that, as we've seen, pulls the individual out of the world. But as Rosenzweig claims, this command to love God is only truly fulfilled when the individual beloved of God breaks out of her relation to God and turns in love to others in the world.

This section will track the way the path from revelatory to redemptive love in the *Star* articulates the very crisis of love we found Rosenzweig underwent during the period of the *Leipziger Nachtgespräch.* As we shall see, although the *Star* makes clear that revelatory love of God *should* lead to redemptive love of neighbor, this transition from revelation to redemption is in no way assured. The figure of the "mystic" exemplifies the way the individual often strives to hold onto her private relation to God at the expense of the world—much as Rosenzweig himself apparently did—and thereby delay or derail the redemptive process. The *Star* depicts this moment, in which the human being decides between clinging to God and denying the world or turning to the world in love, as critical within the course of redemption. It is the moment in which redemption depends on human action, and thus the moment in which human freedom is most evident and of the greatest significance.

Let us begin our examination of the relations of love meant to span the course from revelation to redemption by returning to Rosenzweig's account of revelation. Recall that over the course of revelation, the individual self is awoken to "I-hood" and thereby torn out of his former position as a "thing among things" in the world. This awakening of the I occurs through a dialogue of love—an exchange of loving "words"—whose centerpiece is God's command to the soul: "love Me." Paradoxical as a command to love may sound, Rosenzweig claims, as an imperative spoken directly by the loving God, "the command of love is . . . nothing but the voice of love itself. The love of the lover has no other word at all to express itself than the command" (197/190–91).[44] Now, as "the only pure command," God's command to the individual soul to love Him stands at odds with the laws that have governed past life in the world and will govern worldly life in the future. Revelation "knows only of the moment" (197/191) of the command itself.[45] But Rosenzweig's discussion of the command of revelation already signals that this very command of love that tears the individual out of the world at once holds the potential to orient life in the world for the beloved soul. According to Rosenzweig, as "the only pure command," the command to love is also "the highest of all commands." Thus, he explains,

> where it stands at the top, there everything which otherwise and from the outside could well also be law, equally becomes command. Thus, because God's first word to the soul opening himself up to Him is the "Love Me," everything that he otherwise may have revealed still in the form of law becomes, without further ado, words that he commands them "today," becomes elaboration of the one and first command to love him. (197–98/191–92)

When a system of commands is grounded in God's call to the individual soul to love Him, Rosenzweig suggests here, all commands—even those which might otherwise be indistinguishable from the outside from the conventional laws of the world—become elaborations of this command to love. The purest expression of divine love to the individual soul thereby becomes the basis for a certain kind of life in the world.[46]

Moreover, as we saw in the previous section, Rosenzweig proceeds to show that the individual's revelatory loving relation with God *demands* confirmation in the world itself, and "longs to be grounded in the view of all the world." And such confirmation can only be attained if the individual soul leaves the intimacy of her relation to God and turns back toward the world, newly inspired now through the love that God has awoken in her. "Should this longing be fulfilled," Rosenzweig claims, "the beloved soul would have to step beyond the magic circle of belovedness, forget the lover and herself open her mouth, no longer to answer, but rather to her own word. Because in the world what counts is not being loved . . . but rather eternally—loving" (228/219–20)

The word that begins as the pure expression of God's love for the individual soul in revelation, and that thereby pulls that individual out of the created world, thus demands translation into the word with which the individual soul turns lovingly back toward the world.[47] For redemption to be realized, the soul who has received revelation must turn to the world and thereby turn away from her relation to the divine. In the language of commandments, Rosenzweig suggests, this means that obedience to the command to love God is only fulfilled through neighborly love in the world: "Love of God should express itself in the love of neighbor" (239/230). The command to "love your Other," Rosenzweig asserts, "stands written over the bridge that leads from . . . revelation to creation" (305/ 292) because it calls for those loving actions that will unite together the soul beloved of God and the created world in redemption.

The *Star*'s account of this key moment in the individual's experience of the turn from revelation toward redemption mirrors in important ways Rosenzweig's own struggle leading up to the *Leipziger Nachtgespräch* and the decisions he reached in its wake. What is noteworthy is the way his account of the move from revelation to redemption both takes seriously the opposition he felt at that time between self and world, and yet overcomes it through a development of the very notion of redemption unfolding in the world he had adopted after the *Leipziger Nachtgespräch*. Thus, as we have seen, God's revelatory word does indeed divorce the individual soul from the world he has inhabited, but the individual only fulfills the response to God's commanding word when he turns back to the world with his own word of love. Again, Rosenzweig clearly accepts that the laws according to which communities live in the world and the divine love through which the individual soul is awakened are categorically distinct. But Rosenzweig at once mediates this Marcionist opposition between law and love in the way that he posits divine *command* as the purest expression of love, one that holds the potential to ground a new kind of redemptive community in the world—a "beyond-the-natural, wholly personally felt and yet wholly worldly existing community" (228/219).

While Rosenzweig makes it clear in the *Star* that revelation *should* find its fulfillment through the individual soul's redemptive turn to the world, he in no way suggests that this turn from God back to the world is easy. Indeed, in depicting neighborly love as the extension of one's relation to the divine, Rosenzweig is arguing explicitly against a position we know he himself once took seriously, to wit, that "too great love directed to human being is the highest danger to the love of God." As the *Star* shows, it is not only the experience of createdness that stands in tension with one's experience of being a self beloved of God. The very redemptive call that issues out of revelation, according to Rosenzweig, once again places the human being at the crossroads of world denial. If revelation grants me a sense of selfhood and an intimate connection to God so sublime that it shades my previous worldly life in darkness, then why would I leave that intimate connection to God for the sake of reengagement in the world? Is redemptive action in the world truly worth abandoning one's intimate experience of the divine? Can one truly love others in the world without diminishing one's love of God? As we recall, these questions stood at the heart of Rudolf Ehrenberg's *Halbhunderttag,* and they likewise took center stage in the chapter from Ehrenberg's *Ebr. 10:25: ein Schicksal in Predigten* in which the depicted heretic was modeled on Rosenzweig himself. In his account of redemption in the *Star,* Rosenzweig describes the spiritual single-mindedness of the "mystic" in terms that loudly echo that position of world denial he once upheld personally. Such an individual who is "only loved-by-God is closed before the whole world and closes himself," Rosenzweig now writes:

> This is the uncanny thing . . . about mystics, and what also objectively brings such calamity: that it becomes such a magic hood to the mystic. His soul opens itself to God, but because it only opens itself to God, so it is invisible to the whole world and closed to it. The mystic turns the magic-ring on his finger with arrogant trust, and immediately he is alone with "his" God, and has nothing more to say for the world. This only becomes possible for him insofar as he wants to be nothing at all other than God's darling. In order to be so, thus in order to see only the one track upon which the connection from him to God and from God to him runs, he must deny the world. . . . It is no coincidence, but rather wholly essential for him, that he treat it, since now it is there, as if it doesn't truly "exist," has no existence [*Da-sein*]. . . . He must treat it as if it were not—created . . . , as if it were not God's creation, not set there by the same God whose love he claims for himself. . . . Rather, he must treat it just as if it

> were created by the devil. . . . This fundamentally unethical relationship of the pure mystic to the world is thus quintessentially necessary for him, if he otherwise wants to prove and preserve his pure mysticism. (231–32/223–24).

The mystic's celebration of the intimacy of his relation to God, Rosenzweig suggests here, comes at the expense of the world. The mystic must close himself off from the world, must in fact deny the world a right to exist, in order to preserve "his pure mysticism." Here Rosenzweig once again draws heavily on the thoughts that occupied him during and in the wake of his 1913 crisis. For what the mystic denies most basically, Rosenzweig makes clear is the discovery Rosenzweig claims to have made at the *Leipziger Nachtgespräch,* to wit, that "God created the world and is not just the God of revelation." The mystic's God is solely the God of revelation, such that the mystic treats the world "as if it were not God's creation," as if it were "not set there by the same God whose love he claims for himself," "as if it were created by the devil." The mystic embodies the very conflict Rosenzweig himself endured in 1913: How to preserve one's selfhood and unique relation to the divine while still existing in the world? The *Star* responds to this question by pressing for the view that creation and revelation, initiated by the same God, likewise find their fulfillment in the same redemptive end. But Rosenzweig's account of the mystic shows that he still takes this temptation to spiritual world denial with the utmost seriousness.[48]

Moreover, the position of the mystic vividly recreates the temptation to world denial that Rosenzweig introduced in the very first pages of the *Star.* The experience of divine love removes the mystic from the world, and tempts him to turn his back on the world completely, to court a form of the suicide to which Rosenzweig claimed all human beings are drawn at one point in their lives. But here too, in the turn from revelation to redemption, it may be said that "the earth claims him again." The fulfillment of the selfhood and the spiritual love roused in revelation, Rosenzweig has argued, demands the return of the self to the world. The divine may indeed tear the individual self out of the world; but viewed in the context of the whole course that leads from creation to redemption, this decisive removal of the self from the world is done *for the sake of the redemption of the world.* For only by being awakened to selfhood through the divine command, Rosenzweig suggests, does the self arm himself with the capacity to enter into those loving relations with others that can realize redemption.

The mystic's desire to preserve the purity of her relation to God is thus a threat to the advance of redemption. The mystic exhibits a one-sided response to the problem of self and world: she identifies wholly with the self in relation to God and denies the world, thereby hindering the process through which self and world are reconciled. It is noteworthy that Rosenzweig also warns against taking up the alternative one-sided position to that of the mystic. Contrary to the mystic, the pantheist views himself as completely at one with the world and as lacking that selfhood that would charge him with turning to the world in love. Rosenzweig thus urges the person called on to turn redemptively toward his neighbor in the world not to forget his *self* in the process:

> The human being should love his neighbor as himself. As himself. Your neighbor is "like you." The human being should not deny himself. His self just here in the command of the love of neighbor first becomes confirmed finally in his place [*an seiner Stätte be-stätigt*]. The world is not thrown like an infinite mixture before his eyes, and with finger pointing at this whole mixture it is not said to him: you are this. You are this—thus stop distinguishing yourself from it, enter into it, dissolve in it, lose yourself in it. No, rather quite differently: out of the infinite chaos of the world a neighbor, his neighbor is set before the soul, and of this and at first only of this one it is said: he is like you. "Like you," thus not "you." You remain you and should remain that way. But he should not remain a He for you, and thus merely an It for your You, but rather he is like You, like your You, a You like You, an I—soul. (267/257)

For the human being called on to act redemptively by turning in neighborly love to the other in the world, it is crucial that he not forget himself in the process. Just as the mystic's denial of the world to preserve his personal relation to God blocks the path toward redemptive reconciliation, so too does the pantheist's denial of his selfhood by way of dissolving into the world. Transforming the other in the world into an "I," a soul, and working thereby toward the formation of a redemptive community of "I"s, demands one hold onto one's own selfhood even as one opens up redemptively toward the world.[49]

The mystic and the pantheist are some of the figures Rosenzweig presents in the *Star* who remind us of the crucial importance of human freedom within his system. The human being has a critical role to play in the redemptive process. For she finds herself in the middle of the course of relations between God, world, and self; and as both part of the created world and as an individual self who has received revelation she experiences the call to forge the kind of community that advances redemption. At the same time, however, she is pulled by both spiritual and worldly forces away from her redemptive task: her desire to preserve the purity of her relation to God pulls her away from the world; her sense of oneness with the world tempts her into a pantheistic merging with the world that would allow her to dissolve her own selfhood in the world. These temptations to one-sidedness—to declare oneself either wholly world or wholly self—invite the human being to shirk her redemptive responsibilities, to avoid thereby the task she has been called on to play in the redemptive reconciliation of self and world.

How will the human being respond to such a summons to responsibility? This question highlights the fact that for Rosenzweig the problem of self and world is not merely a theoretical problem—however vexing—but rather a practical one as well. For how I understand my own being—as a soul imprisoned in a body, as one with the world, or as both self and world—will help determine how I respond to the call to act redemptively. It is no exaggeration to say that redemption depends on what the individual chooses to do in response to the command to love.

At the end of chapter 2, we examined the view of human freedom Rosenzweig developed in his reflections on Gnosticism and monotheism from 1916. We noted his conclusion there that contrary to what might be claimed on behalf of a dualistic account of freedom—*viz.* that it can give an account of freedom in its purity, unhindered by any relation to the laws of nature—precisely an account of human freedom as wrapped up with the purpose of creation best allows freedom to be conceived as realizable and meaningful. When creation and revelation are viewed as part of the same cosmic process of redemption, as originating in the same God, Rosenzweig writes there, freedom "is the meaning of the world from the beginning. The world is created for the sake of the *decision*." The biblical account of creation as the beginning of a redemptive process that demands human participation, Rosenzweig thereby suggested, grants human decision in every given moment gravity and significance—"the pathos of the moment!"—because it invests human freedom with the responsibility of making decisions upon which the advance of redemption in the world depends. But the scope of freedom is at once limited in this account. The human being doesn't choose between myriad possibilities, Rosenzweig suggests, but rather between a "Yes" and a "No," between actively affirming or denying the redemption of the world.

I want briefly to examine here how the view of human freedom Rosenzweig developed in his reflections on Gnosticism and monotheism in 1916 can help us understand a particular distinction he makes, in the *Star,* between Kant's view of freedom and his own. In his discussion of the love of neighbor, Rosenzweig argues that his account of the command to love others in the world does a better job explaining the significance of human freedom than does Kant's account of the categorical imperative:

> The love of God should express itself in the love of neighbor. For this reason, the love of the neighbor can be commanded and must be commanded. Only through the form of command does the assumption of the being-beloved-of-God become visible behind its origin . . . through which it distinguishes itself from all moral acts. Moral laws don't merely want to be rooted in freedom—the love of neighbor also wants this—but rather want to recognize no other assumption than freedom. This is the famous demand of "autonomy." The natural consequence of this demand is that the laws, which should determine this act, lose all content; because any content would exert a power through which autonomy would be disturbed. One cannot will "something" and despite that only will "in general"; and the demand of autonomy demands that man will only quintessentially, only in general. And because the law thus comes to no content, so as a consequence the individual act also comes to no assurance. In morality everything is uncertain, everything can ultimately be moral, but nothing is moral with certainty. In contrast to the necessarily purely formal and thus in terms of content not merely ambiguous but unlimitedly ambiguous moral law, the unambiguous command to love neighbor that is clear in terms of content, which springs out of the directed freedom of character, needs an assumption beyond freedom: *fac quod jubes et jube quod vis* [have done what you command and command what you will]. Since the content of the order here is to love, the divine "already having-done" what he orders must precede that God "order what he wills." Only the soul beloved-by-God can receive the command of the love of neighbor toward fulfilling it. God must have first turned Himself to the human being before the human being can turn himself over to God's will. (239–40/230–31)

In this passage, Rosenzweig contrasts Kant's moral law with the command of neighborly love.[50] One who wills in accordance with the moral law is free, according to Kant, insofar as his will is not determined by any object of desire, but rather he wills in accordance with the *form* of rational law-giving. As Rosenzweig explains, "any content would exert a power through which autonomy would be disturbed," and thus maxims that determine the will are moral only when they take the *form* of a universal law with no determined content. But Rosenzweig here suggests that the very lack of content that, according to Kant, leaves the human will able to determine action freely, likewise leaves entirely ambiguous what an individual *should* do to be moral. If "everything can ultimately be moral" as long as it can be adapted to fit the form of a universal law, Rosenzweig asserts, "nothing is moral with certainty."[51]

Rosenzweig argues that in contrast to Kant's moral law, which thereby remains "unlimited in its ambiguity with respect to content," the command to love one's neighbor is "clear and unambiguous." This is because, Rosenzweig suggests, when the individual attends to this command, her action is not only grounded in her own freedom—"to be . . . rooted in freedom, the love of neighbor also wants this"—but is likewise grounded in the love God has already directed toward her. That is to say, for Rosenzweig, the command to love others in the world has the power to give content and significance to human action not simply because it comes from God, but rather because the divine source of the command has already imparted to the recipient of the command the very love she is called on to impart to others.[52] Thus Rosenzweig interprets Augustine's plea that God grant him the strength to love only for God's sake, and not for the sake of worldly pleasures—"*fac quod jubes et jube quod vis* [have done what you command and command what you will]"[53]—as emphasizing that "the divine 'already having-done' what he orders"—that is, love His other—"must precede that God 'order what he wills.' . . . God must have first turned Himself to the human being before the human being can turn himself over to God's will."

Rosenzweig's distinguishing of the command to love others from Kant's moral law here recalls two notable aspects of the conception of human freedom he developed in his 1916 reflections on Gnosticism and monotheism. The first is Rosenzweig's limiting of the scope of that freedom, which I mentioned earlier. The human decision upon which the fate of the created world depends, recall, is not a decision made between myriad possible choices, but rather, is a binary choice between affirming or denying redemption in the world.[54] In his critique of the moral law, Rosenzweig suggests that the very unlimited scope of the maxims the moral law might in principle condone—again because what makes such maxims moral is solely their form—leaves the morality of the actions to which such maxims guide the individual "uncertain." The very limited scope of human freedom within the context of the course between creation and redemption in which the individual finds herself, we might suggest, is part of what grants the moments of human free decision their certain significance.

The second aspect of Rosenzweig's 1916 discussion of human freedom in the context of monotheism I wish to recall is Rosenzweig's realization that once one assumes a single all-powerful God—rather than two opposing divinities—human freedom must be conceived on the basis of the self-limitation of that God which opens up a space within which humans can act freely. Now, the metaphysical landscape of the *Star* is different from that of the "Paralipomena." The task of the first part of the *Star* is to show how God, world, and individual self each generates itself elementally out of its own respective nothing. As we shall discuss in the following section, this means among other things that God is not the unified whole of what is *from the beginning,* and thus human action cannot be said to require the same kind of divine act of *tsimtsum* as its presupposition. At the same time, God's turning to the individual soul in love, the centerpiece of the relations between God, world, and self that will yield redemption in the *Star,* does share important elements with Rosenzweig's earlier account of divine self-restriction. For reasons I have outlined in *Franz Rosenzweig and the Systematic Task of Philosophy,* and to which I will return below, God, world, and self break out of their inherently unstable elemental forms when they enter into the reciprocal relations of creation, revelation, and redemption, and they do so because they can only hope to attain ontological stability through these relations which ultimately produce "the All."[55] The divine turning into relation with individual selves (along with the divine entry into the relation of creation with the world) is predicated upon God splitting up out of God's elemental form.[56] In breaking out of His elemental unity and entering into a relation of love with the individual soul in revelation, moreover, God places His own fate, as it were, into the hands of individual human beings. Indeed, during the whole span from revelation to redemption, Rosenzweig suggests, God is dependent—odd as this sounds—on the decisions and actions of human beings. So, for example, once God turns out of Himself in love to the individual soul in revelation, God requires that the individual soul confirm His being by reciprocating God's love. In the reciprocated love of individual soul, the God of revelation

> finds that which It could not find in itself: affirmation and duration [*Dauer*]. . . . The faith of the soul bears witness in its faithfulness to the love of God and gives it enduring being. "If they bear witness to me, then I am God, and otherwise not,"—thus the master of the Kabbalah lets the God of love speak. The Lover, who gives Himself away in love, is created anew in the faithfulness of the Lover and now for always. (191/185)

In order to attain "affirmation and duration," we see here, God must "give Himself away in love." God is "created anew" through the individual soul's love of and faith in His being. The human response to the divine here is invested with exceptional importance: God will only realize His own divinity if the individual soul bears witness to God. And God can only attain the confirmation of His being if He risks the possibility that the human being will *not* bear witness to Him.[57]

Let me cite another example of the way human freedom is predicated on the divine self-restriction that comes with God's act of love. In the discussion of prayer in the introduction to the third part of the *Star,* Rosenzweig highlights the odd "views of faith" according to which God and human being have the power to "tempt" or to "try" [*versuchen*] each other on the path to redemption. God tries the human being by making it "difficult, indeed impossible for the human being to see" God's rule in the world, and he does so, Rosenzweig suggests, "so that he has the opportunity to believe and to trust in Him truly, thus in freedom." For "God manifestly wants only the free for His own" (296/284). But precisely in being free either to take up or to deny his redemptive task in the world, Rosenzweig explains, the human being is likewise in a position to tempt God. As Rosenzweig understands it, the core of this freedom lies in human prayer: it is the human being's "freedom to decide, [i.e.,] the prayer" (295/283) in which she engages when tasked with turning back toward the world in neighborly love. Rosenzweig writes that it is "actually only in the relation of the act of love to that changing life of the world, nowhere else before, [that] there stands the possibility to try God. And this relation is produced through prayer" (297/285). If the human being prays properly for the imminent arrival of the Kingdom of God, then his prayer opens up a redemptive horizon that enables him to love effectively—redemptively—in the world. But the human being can also decide to pray in improper fashion—for selfish or for tyrannical purposes—and thereby delay the redemption, causing the opportunity for neighborly love "to be blown into the void [*ins Leere verströmt sein*]" (302/288).[58]

Both the human being's power to confirm divine being in response to revelation and the human being's power through prayer to advance or delay redemption thus exemplify how human freedom in the *Star* is made possible through a form of divine self-limitation that recalls the conditions for human freedom that Rosenzweig formulated in his thinking about Gnosticism and monotheism in 1916. The individual soul who is commanded to love others in the world is empowered to do so through a concrete limitation of divine power that occurs in God's own act of loving the individual soul. Below, I will shed further light on this point, as we will find that the redemption that depends on human decision in the *Star* is the redemption of *God* even more essentially than it is the reciprocal redemption of selves and the world. Here I want only to emphasize how Rosenzweig's account of freedom in the *Star,* and the distinction there between Kant's moral law and his own account of the command to love, rests on the ideas he developed as the alternative to the Gnostic view of human action in the world. For Rosenzweig, human freedom is limited to deciding to enact or to deny redemptive love. But the certainty that actions based on that freedom will be redemptive rests on the fact that the command to love others in the world is grounded in God's own love of the individual soul in revelation, in which God limits Himself by placing the task of redemption—even the redemption of God Himself—in the hands of human beings.

Understanding the struggle Rosenzweig himself underwent in 1913 thus greatly illuminates the moment of human freedom in the *Star.* Having been awoken to selfhood through God's personal command to love Him, and being charged with fulfilling that command through turning *away* from God and toward the world, the individual soul oscillates between world denial, on the one hand, and a redemptive return to the world through neighborly love, on the other. This moment of freedom between the word of revelation and the word of redemption, is the "decision" for which, Rosenzweig has claimed, the world was created. And it is this very decision that Rosenzweig understood himself to have faced in the wake of the *Leipziger Nachtgespräch.*

"HE CANNOT DO WITHOUT EITHER": JUDAISM AND CHRISTIANITY IN THE *STAR*

On July 7, 1919—six years to the day after the *Leipziger Nachtgespräch*—Rosenzweig wrote to Hans Ehrenberg, responding to pressure he felt from the Ehrenbergs and from Eugen Rosenstock to publish the *Star* in a Christian publishing house. As part of his argument that doing so would undermine the *Star*'s "Jewishness," Rosenzweig points out what he appears to consider a decisive factor in making the *Star* a Jewish book: "above all, the whole concept of 'redemption,' which I posit as foundational [*wie ich ihn zugrundelege*], is un-Christian. . . . For the Christian, Christ (the one who has come) is indeed Redeemer and Revealer at once. The sharp holding-apart of the two concepts is Jewish."[59]

As evidence for the Jewishness of the *Star*, we find, Rosenzweig cites here a distinction between Judaism and Christianity to which he had first pointed when he recommitted himself to Judaism in the fall of 1913. Since Christians hold Christ to be both the redeemer and the one who has already come to reveal divinity in the world, Rosenzweig claims, Christians do not make the sharp differentiation between revelation and redemption that Jews do. Rosenzweig had suggested in 1913, recall, that this blurring of revelation and redemption always leaves Christianity at risk of celebrating the experience of faith in Christ and forgetting the "Christian world-activity" that is vital to the advance of redemption. The Jewish insistence on the futurity of redemption, the "sharp holding-apart of the two concepts" of revelation and redemption, reminds Christians that redemption does not come through revelation alone. Rather, since "God created the world and is not just the God of revelation," redemption is a task Christians must fulfill through love in the world. Judaism thereby prevents Christianity from falling into Marcionism.

As Rosenzweig's letter to Hans Ehrenberg suggests, the *Star*'s account of Judaism and Christianity is built upon the very views regarding the economy of redemption to which Rosenzweig committed himself in the wake of the *Leipziger Nachtgespräch*. Rosenzweig develops here his view that Jews and Christians have complementary redemptive tasks to carry out in the world. Through Church mission and political imperialism, Christians oversee the expansion of redemptive love across the globe. The Jewish people, on the other hand, anticipates the future redemptive community of all individuals before God, and by doing so, ever reminds Christians of the gap that still remains between the state of the world today and the goal of their redemptive activity. As we noted in our discussion of his 1913 account, the task Rosenzweig assigns to the Jewish people in preventing Christians from falling into a form of Marcionism brings Judaism itself remarkably close to the kind of world denial Rosenzweig identified with Marcionism. Rosenzweig would have the Jewish people remind Christians to attend to their redemptive task in the world only by seemingly stepping out of the world themselves in the anticipation of the world's ultimate redemption.

In this section, I aim to review the *Star*'s development of those views Rosenzweig arrived at in 1913 concerning the complementary roles Jews and Christians play in the economy of redemption. I will then examine the *Star*'s account of the "dangers" Christianity courts in taking up its task, and how this account both builds upon and deviates from Rosenzweig's 1913 view. As we shall see, Rosenzweig remains committed in the *Star* to the view that the continued existence of the Jewish people is the foremost defense Christians have against their own periodic tendency toward Gnosticism.

According to the *Star,* Christianity is tasked with the expansion of redemptive love through the world, and the Church is that Christian institution which directs and carries out this redemptive work. Indeed, Rosenzweig understands the very meaning of the term *church* (*ekklesia*) as indicating both the subject and the goal of Christian redemptive efforts:

> The Christian faith, the witness of the eternal way, is thus creative in the world. It unites those who bear witness into a union in the world. It unites them as individuals, because bearing witness is always a matter of the individual. Moreover the individual here should bear witness concerning his attitude to an individual, because the witnessing, after all, concerns Christ.... But those united as individuals, are now directed by the faith toward common action in the world.... And so faith establishes that union of individuals as individuals, for common work which is rightly called *ekklesia.* (380–81/363–64)

Rosenzweig suggests here that faith in Christ, and in the "Way" of Christianity itself, brings individual selves as such together in the world. The Christian "church" is indeed precisely a collective union of individual souls, based on faith and committed to redemptive work in the world. Moreover, the "common action in the world" this union of individuals is called upon to carry out is nothing but its own expansion. The church is to become an ever-larger and more expansive union of individual selves, and ever-larger and more expansive *ekklesia.*

Missionizing is the primary means through which Christians carry out their redemptive task. It is the means through which the Church includes all others it encounters in the world in its own community of love. "The bond that ties . . . the mother Church itself with the fate of the world, is love," Rosenzweig writes:

> In the love of the missionary to those who still sit in darkness, there occurs the moving-out of the outer borders, the widening of the outer, visible structure. In the visible sacrifice of pious work, in the visible offering of physical and spiritual good deed, it is also love within the church, which connects men with it and thereby with the whole. (311/297)

We see here how Christian missionary work expands the "borders" of Christianity in the world through the same love that unites individuals together within the Church itself. According to Rosenzweig, Christians also unite the individuals of the world through political means. The striving for global empire, Rosenzweig suggests, serves not merely the crass interests of political power, but rather the very redemptive goal of uniting disparate individuals living across the globe toward which the Church labors. And this imperial striving will continue, Rosenzweig writes, even in the face of the political fragmentation that has occurred in and in the wake of World War I:

> And if this will to empire has been pulverized reciprocally between the nations [*Völkern*], it will assume a new form. Because in its double anchoring, both in the divine world-creator, whose power it reflects, and in the world's longing for redemption, which it serves, it opens one necessary way of Christianity in the part of the All which is the world. (391/374)

The reciprocal political pulverization that has taken such violent form in World War I has brought about the splintering of formerly powerful European empires. But Rosenzweig asserts here that the quest for empire will endure as part of the Christian redemptive work in the world. Indeed, imperial politics "serves the world's longing for redemption."[60]

In the introduction to the third part of the *Star,* Rosenzweig charts the historical advance of the Church's redemptive activity in the world as a tripartite movement in which world and self fall under the sway of Christianity, first consecutively, and only subsequently in unison. It is the early Catholic Church, the Church of Peter as Rosenzweig designates it, that first works to unite and to convert the world: "The Petrine Church creates a visible body, first for itself and for the men who are its members . . . ; yet again, also for the world outside, which it gradually structures and rules-through in the unity of the empire [*Kaisertüm*] over the kingships of the nations" (311/297). This body of the Christian world then appears to dissolve with the rise of the Protestant Church, the Church of Paul, which according to Rosenzweig turns its attention to the "Christianization of the soul" (313/299). If love is that force which united the individuals of the world under the Catholic Church, Rosenzweig suggests, faith is the force of "the soul on itself, a self-conversion of man, which disregards the world in order thereby to attain the soul and the soul alone" (312/299). Only in the third, Johannine epoch of Christianity which Rosenzweig claims began with Goethe and endures into Rosenzweig's own time, are the world and self, the body and soul brought together under Christian auspices through the power of "hope."

Christianity thereby marches through the world and its history, uniting all individuals through its redemptive work into a larger and more expansive collective, reconciling world and self, creation and revelation, through its "world activity." The Jewish people has a very different role to play in the *Star*'s economy of redemption. Jews anticipate the redemptive unity toward which the world strives under Christian auspices, and thereby orient Christians toward that redemptive goal. The Jewish people "had sublated for itself the opposition between creation and revelation. It lives in its own redemption. It has anticipated eternity" (364/348). According to Rosenzweig, it is in the liturgical practices of its insular communal life that the Jewish people anticipates year after year the redemptive goals toward which Christians labor in the world. Over the course of the Jewish liturgical calendar, culminating in the High Holidays of Rosh Hashanah and Yom Kippur that anticipate redemption most directly, individual Jews are united into a collective before God that anticipates the natural-supernatural community of All that is the goal of redemption. On Yom Kippur, according to Rosenzweig, the Jew who wears his burial garment stands "in naked loneliness immediately before God's throne," and yet he does so as a "member of an assembled humanity" (363/346). "To such collective-solitary [*gemeinsam-einsam*] imploring of the one humanity in death-shrouds, of a humanity . . . of souls," Rosenzweig writes, "God inclines his face" (363–64/347).

It is the Jewish people's anticipatory experience of the ultimate redemptive unity of all in the world that frees Jews from the historical course along which the rest of the world strives for redemption. "What he [the Jew] possesses already in the all-yearly circuit as an event, the immediacy of all individuals to God in the complete community of All with God, this he needs no longer to acquire in the long course of a world-history," Rosenzweig writes. "The Jewish people is already for itself at the goal to which the peoples of the world only strive" (368/ 351).

In thus anticipating the goal of redemptive work in the world, the Jewish people orients the historical advance toward the redemption. But the Jewish people serves this essential role in redemption precisely insofar as its anticipation of redemption situates it *outside* the course of that historical advance. Rosenzweig writes that "the course of world history ever only reconciles creation in itself, so long as the kingdom of God is still coming, ever only the next moment to the previous. So long as redemption is still coming, it is only through the eternal people set outside of all world history that creation itself as a whole is held together with redemption in all time" (372/355). Without the orientation provided by the Jewish people, Rosenzweig suggests here, world history is entirely a matter of worldly temporality, one moment succeeding the next. But through the Jewish people's anticipation of redemption, the whole of the historical process is "held together with redemption," and advances toward it. And yet the Jewish people can only ensure that history advances toward redemption by anticipating redemption "outside of all world history."

We will return to this curiously world-transcending character of the Jewish people at the end of this section. Here I want to note that while Rosenzweig appears to view this task of anticipating the redemptive goal of Christian work in the world as spanning the whole of history, properly speaking, he likewise implies that Jews have the chance to be particularly effective in their task during Rosenzweig's own time. The "emancipation and the taking-up of Jews in the Christian world," Rosenzweig claims, is a "great event in [the] Church history" of the Johannine epoch of Christianity. By infusing the Christian world with hope for redemption, "that hope which love would prefer to forget and faith thinks it can do without," the Jews help Christians unite body and soul and "convert the pagan" within themselves (317/303).

In the third part of the *Star,* Rosenzweig thus develops that account of the complementary redemptive roles of Christianity and Judaism to which he had committed in the fall of 1913. "Christian world-activity" advances redemption in the world; but only because it is oriented by the Jewish anticipation of the goal of redemption. The Christian need for the Jewish people to continue to serve its anticipatory redemptive task emerges most clearly when Rosenzweig turns to speak of the "dangers" to which Christianity threatens to succumb in the midst of its redemptive work. It is in this context, moreover, that Rosenzweig once again raises the specter of Marcionism as a tendency toward which Christianity is drawn and against which the Jewish people helps Christians defend themselves.

Recall that in the fall of 1913, Rosenzweig came to view the early Church decision to bind itself to Judaism as essential to its conquest over "Gnostic heresy" in the midst of its "struggle for existence." The insistence that "'salvation' has come from the Jews," and that "the God who 'created Heaven and Earth,' the 'God of Abraham and the God of Isaac and the God of Jacob' . . . is the 'Father of Jesus Christ,'" Rosenzweig suggested, gave Christianity the grounding in creation that enabled it to take its redemptive work in the world seriously. Ever since, Rosenzweig suggested, it has been the task of the Jewish people to remind Christians that "God created the world and is not just the God of revelation," and hence to protect Christians from their own tendency to blur revelation and redemption, and to forget that the created world still requires their redemptive work. Rosenzweig would write that without the Jew there to orient them in their redemptive task in the world, "the world would never be finished." "Judaism," said Rosenzweig, "is the crude factuality through which Christianity is hindered from a dissolution of its eschatology into the pneumatic."[61]

The *Star*'s account of the Jewish people's role in helping Christianity turn away from its temptation to Gnosticism once again recalls the grounds for Rosenzweig's decision, in the fall of 1913, to return to Judaism. But Rosenzweig's description of the Christian tendency toward the pneumatic is broader in the *Star* than in those letters written in the wake of the *Leipziger Nachtgespräch*. The Gnostic denial of the created world is merely one symptom, according to the *Star*'s account, of a spiritualism into which Christian theology has a tendency to fall when it speculates regarding God, world, and the self. The "dangers . . . Christianity never gets beyond," according to the *Star*, are "spiritualization of God, apotheosis of man, pantheizing of the concept of the world" (447/424–25). "The outermost of Christianity is this complete getting-lost in individual feeling, this sinking into the divine Spirit, the divine man, the divine world" (459/436). As we shall see in the following section, in the culminating moment of their redemptive integration, according to Rosenzweig, self and world will indeed become identical with the divine. But Christianity's tendency is to collapse revelation and redemption *in the present*, and thereby to conceive of God, world, and self as if they were already redeemed, as if self and world were already God, and as if God was spirit alone. The dangers Christianity courts as it carries out its redemptive work, according to the *Star,* is thus not Gnostic dualism or world denial per se. But the spiritualism to which Christianity tends exhibits the same kind of denial of worldly redemptive activity that Rosenzweig identified earlier with Marcionism.

As he did in his deliberations from 1913, moreover, Rosenzweig asserts that it is the actual existence of the Jewish people that turns Christians away from their tendency to spiritualization and reminds them of the redemptive goal toward which they must work in the world. The "existence of the Jew forces upon Christianity at all times the notion that it is not at the goal, has not come to the truth, but rather always—remains on the way," Rosenzweig writes. "If the Christian did not have the Jew at his back, he would become lost wherever he was" (459, 460/436).

The very existence of the Jewish people, Rosenzweig asserts here, reminds Christians that their task of spreading redemptive love through the world has not yet been fulfilled. The Jewish people thereby orient the Christian advance toward redemption. They prevent Christians from getting lost in the feeling of redemption before they have actualized redemption in the world. Despite Rosenzweig's expansion of his view of the dangers of spiritualization to which Christianity is drawn in the *Star,* it is noteworthy that Rosenzweig nevertheless cites Gnosticism explicitly as exemplary of this tendency to spiritualization from which the very existence of the Jewish people protects Christians:

> This relationship, this necessity of the existence—nothing more than existence—of Judaism for its own becoming is also very much conscious for Christianity. It was always the disguised enemies of Christianity, from the Gnostics to the present day, who wanted to take from it its "Old Testament." A God who would only still be Spirit, no longer the Creator who gave the Jews His law; a Christ who would only still be Christ, no longer Jesus; and a world only still All, whose middle would no longer be the Holy Land—they would indeed no longer set up the least resistance to deification and divinization, but there would also no longer be anything in them that would call the soul out of the dream of this deification back into unredeemed life. They would not only get lost; no—they would remain lost. (460/437)

In this passage, the Marcionist's rejection of the Old Testament, the Creator God, and the bodily actuality of Jesus, are all understood as part and parcel of the Christian tendency toward "deification and divinization."

Without the very existence of the Jewish people arguing for the identity of the God of creation and revelation, and thereby for the actuality of individual embodied selves like Jesus and worldly places like the Holy Land, Rosenzweig suggests, nothing would call the Christian "soul out of the dream of this deification back into unredeemed life." Christians "would remain lost" in the realm of spirit, and would leave their redemptive task unfulfilled. And yet the temptation toward spiritualization is great, Rosenzweig proceeds to suggest, because it frees human beings from *responsibility*. One could so "easily and happily" believe in a spiritual God, while forgetting that God "'created the world in order to rule over it'" and rather consider it as if "from the devil," because this would "leave us the world at our free disposal." It would be so much easier to worship Christ "philosophically or nationally" as the symbol for an "'Idea,'" rather than to take seriously what the actual "historical Christ" who "really wanders in the market of life" demands that one *do* in the world. It would be so much easier to view the world as a spiritualized All in which one could simply dissolve oneself, rather than recognize oneself "as its responsible middle-point, around which all turns" (461/437).

The Jewish people help Christians overcome their temptation toward spiritualization, their temptation to shirk worldly responsibility, simply by virtue of the fact that Jews actually exist, and are not merely ideal or spiritual. Once again invoking Gnosticism to designate the drive to spiritualization that the existence of the Jewish people thwarts, Rosenzweig writes,

> As that always actual struggle of the Gnostic shows, it is the Old Testament, which makes possible for Christianity the resistance against this its own danger. And the Old Testament only because it is more than mere book. The mere book would easily be broken down through the arts of allegorical interpretation. Just as Christ denotes the idea of man, just so the Jews of the Old Testament, had they disappeared from the earth like Christ, would denote the idea of people, Zion the idea of world-midpoint. But the firm, not to be denied vitality of the Jewish people, testified to indeed in Jew-hatred, sets itself against such "idealization." Whether Christ is more than an idea—no Christian can know. But that Israel is more than an idea, that he knows, that he sees. Because we live. We are eternal, not as an idea may be eternal, but rather we are so, if we are so, in full actuality. And so we are the really indubitable thing for the Christian. The pastor argued conclusively, who, asked for the proof of Christianity, answered Friedrich the Great "Majesty, the Jews." The Christians cannot doubt us. Our existence guarantees them their truth. (461/437–38)

The Old Testament, Rosenzweig reminds us here, is in his view the basis for the Church's resistance to Marcionism. By grasping the revelation of Christ as the fulfillment of what was promised in the Old Testament—in God's creation of the world and God's relation with the Jewish people—Church fathers like Augustine and Tertullian, we recall, viewed Christ's message as more compelling and more certain than would be a "Christ unexpected." But here Rosenzweig insists that without the continued actual existence of the Jewish people to bear witness to the Old Testament, it too would fall prey to spiritualization: Jews would denote the "idea" of a people, Zion the "idea" of the midpoint of the world, and Christ merely the "idea" of man rather than as one come to fulfill the actual course of redemption begun in creation.[62] But as even Christian "Jew-hatred" shows, Rosenzweig suggests, the actuality of the Jewish people cannot be denied. As the "actually indubitable thing for the Christian," the Jewish people thus confirms for Christians the actuality of the course from creation to redemption staked out in the Testaments, and thereby reminds Christians of the point they actually occupy on that course, and of the actual task they themselves must not leave unfulfilled on that course. It is the actual, visible existence of the Jewish people in the world that orients Christians in their redemptive course through the world, the same "vitality" of the Jewish people that Rosenzweig identified in his letter to his mother of October 23, 1913 as the key to the Christian overcoming of its own Gnostic heresy.[63]

This emphasis on the actuality of the Jewish people in the world certainly appears odd, however, when we recall the peculiarly other-worldly form of Jewish communal life that permits the Jewish people to anticipate redemption and thereby orient "Christian world-activity" toward redemption. The position the Jewish people occupies "outside of all world history" begs the question: Would Rosenzweig have the Jewish people defend Christianity against its own tendencies toward Gnosticism precisely by exhibiting the Gnostic quality of world-denial he had turned away from in 1913? The following passage, which surveys the Jewish theological dangers that parallel the Christian dangers we examined earlier, certainly suggests this is so:

> If there [i.e., in Christianity] the dangers were spiritualization of God, humanization of God, worldification of God, so now here [in Judaism] they are world denial, world contempt, world mortification. It was world denial when the Jew in the nearness of his God anticipated for himself redemption in feeling and forgot that God

> was Creator and Revealer and that as Creator he sustains the whole world, and as Revealer ultimately yet turns his face to the human being quintessentially. It was world contempt when the Jew felt himself as remnant and so as the true human being originally created in the image of God and waiting in this original purity for the end, and drawing himself back from the human being, to whom—in his God-forsaken hardness—revelation of divine love happened, and who must now work out this love in the limitless work of redemption. Finally it was world mortification when the Jew in possession of the law revealed to him and having become in his spirit flesh and blood, now presumed to regulate the existence renewed at each moment and the silent growth of things, indeed presumed even to be able to judge them. (452–53/430)

Rosenzweig makes explicit here the tendency toward world denial that threatens Judaism as it anticipates the ultimate redemption toward which the world is advancing. If Christianity, as we've seen, runs the risk of spiritualizing God, world, and the self—described here, from the opposite direction, as the tendency to make God into spirit, world, and human self—Judaism risks "world denial, world contempt, world mortification." Anticipating redemption tempts the Jew to forget "that God was Creator and Revealer," and to forget that it is not only the Jews, but rather the whole world and all selves in it who have been granted divine grounding and will receive divine love. It leads the Jew to forget the work that has to occur in the world before redemption will be actual and not just a matter of anticipation.

Now, strange as it may appear for Rosenzweig to embrace a world-denying Judaism as part of his overcoming of a world-denying Marcionism, the resemblance of Rosenzweig's Judaism to Marcionism gains some clarity if we recall Rosenzweig's account of his decision to convert to Christianity in the wake of the *Leipziger Nachtgespräch.* In that summer of 1913, when Rosenzweig committed himself to a view of redemption that demanded action in the world rather than escape from it, Rosenzweig decided to convert to Christianity, we recall, because "Christian world-activity" promised a redemptive course that would reconcile self and world. "There appeared to be no place for Judaism" in Rosenzweig's newly acquired view of the Christian realization of the Kingdom of God, precisely because he already held Judaism to have exited the world and its history in the year 70. That is to say, *Jewish* world-denial was indeed one of the reasons Rosenzweig cites for his initial decision to convert to Christianity once he has turned away from Marcionism.

Rosenzweig's decision in October 1913 to recommit himself to Judaism, however, came with a slight but important change in his sense of the proximity between Judaism and Marcionism. Yes, Judaism denied the world in the here-and-now, but it did not deny worldliness per se as did Marcionism. From the perspective of a Judaism that Rosenzweig now viewed as anticipating redemption, the world and its history were incomplete, not unredeemable. Thus, even as it courts this world denial, Rosenzweig came to believe, the Jewish people, in its anticipation of redemption, can be understood as playing an essential role in advancing the actual course toward redemption in the world, indeed even as insisting on the *createdness* of the world that needs to be redeemed.

Rosenzweig points to this same distinction between Jewish and Marcionist world-denial in the *Star* itself. Why does Jewish other-worldliness or even world denial advance the course of redemption in the world while other forms of world denial identified in the *Star* thwart it? Rosenzweig's answer in the *Star* just seems to be that Jews actually do anticipate the goal toward which the world is striving. To the extent that Jews deny the world, they do so from the perspective of the world's future completion. They do not reject the world as such, but only its character as "not-yet" being the world it should be. Recall that when Rosenzweig describes the advance of the world toward redemption, he claimed that it is only in redemption that the world actually finishes becoming what it truly is. When the Jews deny the world in the present, they do so only on the grounds of their anticipation of the world's being complete. Note how Rosenzweig describes Jewish other-worldliness in the following passage:

> And so the people of eternity must forget the growth of the world, it may not think about it. The world, its world, must count for it as finished. . . . Its world is at the goal. The Jew finds in his people the most perfect entry into a world that is its own, and in order to find the entry, must give up not even a bit of his idiosyncrasy [*Eigenart*]. . . . for the Jewish people there is no tension between the own-most and the highest, for it self-love becomes immediately love of the neighbor. (365/348–49)

The Jew stands outside history, outside the growth of the world, according to this passage, not because he denies the world as such, but rather because the Jew anticipates the world *as finished*. In the Jew's integration of his selfhood into the Jewish community, he anticipates, according to Rosenzweig, the complete fusion of self and world that will be in redemption, and thus anticipates the moment in which the world itself will be completely actualized. The stumble in Rosenzweig's description here—"the world, its world, must count for it as finished"—highlights Rosenzweig's intention to present the anticipated redemptive "world" of the Jewish community as both the particular world of the Jews alone, and at once as the true anticipation of "the world" as it will be in redemption.

Despite the Jewish rejection of the world in the here-and-now, Rosenzweig thus suggests, the Jew does not deny the world the possibility of its being redeemed as does the Marcionist who would escape the world because the world is unredeemable. The Jew's contempt for the world in its present form is simply the other side of the coin of his anticipation of the redeemed world.[64]

The *Star* thus elaborates that view of the complementarity of Judaism and Christianity in the redemption of the world, which Rosenzweig adopted, in his turn away from Marcionism, in the fall of 1913. Near the end of the *Star*, Rosenzweig describes this working relationship between Jews and Christians as follows:

> So, before God the both, Jew and Christian, are workers in the same work. He cannot do without either. He has set animosity between both in all time and yet he has bound them in the narrowest mutuality to one another. To us he gave eternal life, in that he kindled the fire of the star of his truth in our hearts. Them he set on the eternal way, in that he made them run after the rays of that star of his truth in all time up to the eternal end. We thus see in our hearts the true image [*Gleichnis*] of truth, yet we turn ourselves away thereby from temporal life and the life of time turns itself from us. They on the contrary run after the current of time, but they have the truth only at their back. They are indeed led by it, because they follow its rays, but they don't see it with their eyes. The truth, the whole truth, thus belongs neither to them nor to us. (462/438)

God requires both Jew and Christian to fulfill their respective tasks, according to this passage, if redemption is to be actualized. God is equally dependent, one might suggest, on both Jew and Christian, despite the fact that neither Jew nor Christian possesses the truth completely. Jews see an image of the truth that will be fully actual in redemption, but this vision depends on their standing outside the "temporal life" of the world. Christians advance the work of redemption through history, oriented by the Jewish anticipation of redemption, but they cannot achieve the anticipatory experience of redemption that Jews live. The "whole truth thus belongs neither to" Christians nor to Jews, but rather to God alone. The following section will examine exactly what Rosenzweig means by this "whole truth," and how God's identity with truth is wrapped up in the unity that God only achieves in redemption.

DIVINE UNITY IN THE *STAR*

When Rosenzweig came to accept the view that "God created the world and [is] not just the God of revelation," he turned away from his former flirtation with world denial, and began to view the created world as the site for redemptive activity, and creation itself as the beginning of the redemptive process. We have seen how the *Star* develops Rosenzweig's insights from the summer of 1913 into a comprehensive account of actuality, according to which the tension we experience between our respective selfhood and worldliness amounts to a call to the kind of action that would reconcile the oppositions between creation and revelation and would realize redemption. But perhaps the most interesting and far-reaching consequences Rosenzweig draws in the *Star* from his 1913 conversions concern neither the self nor the world—at least not directly—but rather the divine Itself. This is how it should be. After all, although sensitivity to the tension within human existence between selfhood and worldliness may have been the spur that drove Rosenzweig toward Marcionism, Marcionist doctrine as Rosenzweig understood it is first and foremost a statement about the metaphysical: two Gods, not one. By describing himself as having been "on the best path to Marcionitism" in the period leading up to the *Leipziger Nachtgespräch,* Rosenzweig was attributing to himself a view about divinity, and not just about the ambivalent relationship to the divine in which the human being in the world stands.

The account of redemption that the *Star* offers culminates in the declaration of the Oneness of God. In the ultimate redemption, God will be the unity of "the All." God's redemptive Oneness is, however, only the ending of the story the *Star* tells. Just as the image of a redemptive reconciliation of self and world both highlighted the absence of that reconciliation in the present, and indicated the task of reconciliation to which individuals in the world must attend, so divine unity must likewise be *achieved* in redemption. And this redemptive unity again points to an actual division within the divine in the here and now, to a divine dualism that must be overcome. Such a division within the divine is in fact reflected in Rosenzweig's very depictions of creation and revelation in the second part of the *Star.* As creatures in the world, we have a relation to the "Creator"; as individual selves, we receive the love of the "Revealer." Can we be certain that these different manifestations of divinity are manifestations of one and the same deity? The path that leads to an affirmative answer, Rosenzweig suggests, is the path of redemptive action. The proof that they are one and the same—and the proof that they are manifestations of the same God who is the Redeemer, as well—is to emerge from the very realization of the Kingdom of God in which creation and revelation, and thus Creator and Revealer, are united into One. God *will* be One in redemption: it is a statement that like others Rosenzweig makes about redemption must be taken as both description and imperative.

Rosenzweig's account of divine redemptive unity shows once again how Rosenzweig develops in the *Star* an alternative to Marcionism that at once takes seriously the Marcionist position, explaining Marcionist dualism as a hypostasization of that opposition within the divine which is in fact a moment in the process of God's becoming One. The metaphysical dualism toward which Rosenzweig was drawn before 1913 is thus shown to have grounds for justification. It is just that the Marcionist perceives the opposition inherent to the path to unity as static, and not as a necessary moment in the course of unification.

This section will examine the account of divine unity Rosenzweig offers in the *Star*, and will show how it exhibits the metaphysical consequences of Rosenzweig's turn away from Marcionism in dramatic fashion. We will look at how he depicts the unity God attains in redemption, and will return to the path through Creation and Revelation to investigate the role human beings in the world play in enabling God to become One. We will also have to confront a question any thoughtful reader may come to ask Rosenzweig regarding his developmentally monistic alternative to Marcionism: *Why?* Why must God *become* One in the first place? Why does God need selves in the world to enter into loving relations with their others? How could God plausibly need to undergo a process in which He enters into relations with others?

These are arguably among the biggest questions the *Star* poses. For us, the magnitude of these questions rests on the fact that they carry the weight of nearly all the questions, ideas, and experiences in which we've seen Rosenzweig engaged from the period before his 1913 conversion through the *Star* itself. Why am I both a self and part of the world? Why do I sense this split within my experience? Marcionism may be said to answer these questions through its positing of a metaphysical dualism. But Rosenzweig cannot escape these questions simply by turning away from Marcionism toward the view that self and world will be reconciled in redemption. For if there is only One God, if "God created the world and is not just the God of revelation," then I surely have the right to ask why I must endure the oppositions I endure. Why must God engage me and all others in the world in a redemptive process? Can't God just be One without me?

We will have to address these questions as we proceed. I aim to show here Rosenzweig's preoccupation with these questions, and to sketch out the response he suggests for them as best I can. Doing so will indeed demand making some sense of the view that even God requires relations with others in order to realize Himself.

The great eleventh-century Jewish commentator Rashi offered a rather bold interpretation of the "Shema" that evidently caught Rosenzweig's eye in the period following the *Leipziger Nachtgespräch.* Regarding this biblical passage that has become the centerpiece of the Jewish prayer service, "Hear O Israel, YHWH Our God, YHWH [is] One," Rashi writes, "YHWH, who is 'Our God' now and not the God(s) of idolators, He will be 'YHWH [is] One,' in the future." Rashi cites as a prooftext for his interpretation, Zechariah 14:9: "On that day YHWH will be One and His name One." In a diary entry from October 9, 1914, just a year after his decision to return to Judaism, Rosenzweig writes approvingly of Rashi's interpretation: "Rashi's commentary to the שמע ["Shema," i.e., "Hear"] corresponds completely to my interpretation of אחד [One]; he too explains it out of 'ביום ההוא' ["On that day"], i.e., thoroughly futuristically."

This diary note marks one of the earliest explicit indications that Rosenzweig had adopted a "futuristic" view of divine unity in the wake of the *Leipziger Nachtgespräch.* Not only are self and world, revelation and creation only to unite together in the redemptive Kingdom of God, but divinity Itself is to become One only "on that day" of the future redemption.

In a number of passages in the *Star,* God is likewise claimed only to achieve unity in redemption, but here divine unity is of a peculiar sort: God will be in redemption the unity of "the All." As we proceed, we will have to explore exactly what kind of redemptive unity Rosenzweig is attributing to God, but we can note at the outset that God's unification in redemption is wrapped up—in some yet-to-be determined manner—with the unification of self and world in redemption that yields "the All," the comprehensive community of particulars that are both "I"s and equally parts of the world. I want to introduce three passages in the *Star* in which God's becoming One can hardly be distinguished from God's becoming "the All." These passages are difficult, and we will have to address how they relate to one another in what follows, but I will cite them here nevertheless from the outset. In the book on "Redemption" in the second part of the *Star,* Rosenzweig describes how God will become in redemption the unity of "the All" that all particular beings have come together through relations to actualize, but which philosophers have mistakenly asserted as already actual:

> In the redemption of the world through the human being and of the human being by the world, God redeems Himself. Human being and world disappear in redemption; God, however, completes Himself. God first becomes in redemption that which the recklessness of human thinking sought everywhere and claimed everywhere, and yet found nowhere, because it was just still nowhere to be found, because it was not yet: All and One. The All of the philosophers, which we had consciously broken into pieces, here, in the blinding midnight sun of the completed redemption is finally, yes truly final-ly, grown together into One. (266/256)

We will have to delay addressing a number of points in this passage—the disappearance of self and world in redemption, the exact relation between the "All and One" that the elements have united to form and God as the subject of that totality—until further on in this section. Here I simply want to highlight how God only "completes Himself" in redemption, and God does so by becoming the unity of "The All and One," that is, the unified totality of all beings that have united together through relations over the course toward redemption. Philosophers who have tried to grasp "the All" as the totality of *what is,* throughout the ages, have failed in their efforts because they have failed to understand that such a totality was "not yet" actual. All beings will be one only in the future redemption; and God will—again only "on that day"—become that unity of all beings.

Rosenzweig makes this same claim about God as the unity of all that is in redemption when he suggests this is the meaning of the statement "God is Truth." In his clearest explanation of this statement, Rosenzweig writes, "In the All and One, life completes itself, it is wholly living. Insofar as truth is one with this whole living actuality, it is its essence; insofar as it nevertheless can separate itself from it—without in the least sublating the connection—it is the essence of God" (429/408). Here Rosenzweig makes an important distinction that he does not make elsewhere between truth as the unity of the

All which is the All itself ("insofar as truth is one with this whole living actuality"), and truth as this same unity but now able to "separate itself from" that All (although without "sublating" its connection to that All). To say "God is truth" points to this latter unity—the unity of the All but viewed, we might say, as "One" and not as a totality. Such a view is echoed in a passage that appears to reject the separability of "truth" from the All, when Rosenzweig writes that "truth bears witness to itself, it is one with all that is actual, it does not separate in it" (427/406). Here, as we shall see, Rosenzweig depicts the truth that God will be in redemption as an act or a state of self-recognition, of divine self-witnessing. In this bearing witness to God's self, God is a unity, but God's unity here "is one with all that is actual." Whether and in what sense God's unity can be separated from that of "the All" will indeed concern us in what follows.

When Rosenzweig discusses God's name, finally, the sanctification of which he identifies with human action toward redemption, Rosenzweig notes how Jews do not articulate "the revealed name" even in the present. This silence, Rosenzweig suggests, is an anticipation of the redemptive moment in which even God's name will fall silent in the light of God's unity: "The name itself is silent in our mouths . . . as it will at one time be silent in the whole world, when He is All-one [*all-ein,* i.e., "alone" but also "All-one"]—One" (427/407).

Explaining the relation of the God who will be One in redemption and the All which all beings realize through the redemptive relations between selves in the world will demand that we make sense of the relations between the difficult passages I've cited here. But before we turn to this task, I want to return to what is perhaps a rather obvious consequence of the claim that God only attains unity at the end of the course stretching from Creation to Redemption. This is that God is, of course, "not yet" One for the span of that whole course from Creation to Redemption. We may take as confirmation of this conclusion the fact that Rosenzweig regularly names the manifestations of divinity active in relation to the world and to the self in creation and revelation, respectively, as "the Creator" and "the Revealer." Thus, "God the Creator is in the beginning"(124/123), "God the Creator is essentially powerful"(125/124), and "for the Creator, things offer themselves only in the universal context of the whole of existence"(135/133), while it is "the concept of the Revealer" (181/175) to which "the love of the lover" applies, the "Revealer [who] reveals Himself out of love" (182/176). Again, Rosenzweig writes that the "law of growth is just as much set into the world here by the Creator as the overflowing force of its love is set into it by the Revealer" (269/259); and he suggests that the human being "must live there where he is set because he is set there by the hand of the Creator. . . . He must go there where he is sent because he has received direction from the word of the Revealer" (437/415).

Rosenzweig in no way means to assert that "the Creator" and "the Revealer" are eternally distinct deities. As we have seen, "Creator" and "Revealer" will be united in the One God of redemption, and as we shall soon explain, "the Creator" and "the Revealer" are shown to have emerged out of the same elemental God. Nevertheless, one may suggest that were Rosenzweig intent on denying the insights of Marcionism completely, he would have used other designators available to him and could have avoided the regular naming of God as "Creator" and "Revealer" in creation and revelation, respectively. Indeed, even the formula Rosenzweig offered for his turn from Marcionism, "God created the world and is not just the God of revelation," implies the identity of the God who creates and reveals as an identity of two different manifestations of the divine. Here too we find evidence of the way in which Rosenzweig's alternative to Marcionism still takes seriously the insights of Marcionism.[65]

The God who will be One thus does manifest Itself in different, even opposed forms over the course from Creation to Redemption. It is perhaps not surprising to note that God the Creator and God the Revealer stand in a relationship to each other that mirrors the relationship we have seen holds between creation and revelation. Creation and revelation are opposed to each other, recall, but they at once share in the same course toward redemption. On this course, creation appears as the prophecy whose fulfillment begins in revelation; and redemption itself is to be seen as the unification and reconciliation of creation and revelation. The development divinity takes toward unification in redemption charts the same course. Here, for example, is one of Rosenzweig's descriptions of the relation between Creator and Revealer:

> God is more than just Creator. Were one to want to conclude from the world-picture, as we give it, and the demand for the Creator arrived at in it, to the Creator-hood of God—one would rightfully throw the question in the path of this conclusion, who

> then God is. The Creator itself must be proven, that is, pointed out in His wholeness, in order to answer this question. The Creator is also the Revealer. Creation is the prophecy, which is only confirmed in the miraculous sign of revelation. (149/146)

The attempt to grasp the world as it is may indeed lead one to posit a Creator for the world, Rosenzweig argues here, but by itself this conclusion cannot justify positing *God* as the Creator. One can only grasp God as the Creator, Rosenzweig suggests, when one has grasped God "in His wholeness," and this demands recognizing that "the Creator is also the Revealer." Just as one can only trust one's experience of revelation as "true" when it has been promised or prophesied through one's creaturely experience of the world, so Rosenzweig claims here that creation alone cannot "prove" God. Only the person who understands and experiences that "the Creator is also the Revealer," only the person whose grasp of creation finds fulfillment in an experience of "the voice of revelation," can claim to know God. While Rosenzweig thereby acknowledges that one encounters different manifestations of divinity in creation and revelation, respectively, he asserts that the one God who is both Creator and Revealer can only be known as the one God insofar as this God is known to be both.

This is as much as to say what we've already seen: God only becomes Himself, "completes Himself," at the end of the course along which creation and revelation—and hence His own roles as Creator and Revealer—have been played out. Let us then return to Rosenzweig's discussion of redemption and try to discern how God attains unity. To do so, we need to begin to make some sense of Rosenzweig's claim that the unity that God will attain in redemption is the unity of the "All" which all particular selves in the world will have joined together to form. Note the way in which God is claimed to be uniquely involved in redemption in the following passage from the *Star* II 3, part of which we have already encountered:

> Redemption thus has as its last result something that raises it beyond comparison with creation and revelation, namely God Himself. He is—we said it already—Redeemer in a weightier sense than he is Creator and Revealer; because He is not only the one who redeems, but also the one who is redeemed. In the redemption of the world through the human being and of the human being by the world, God redeems Himself. Human being and world disappear in redemption; God, however, completes Himself. God first becomes in redemption that which the recklessness of human thinking sought everywhere and claimed everywhere, and yet found nowhere, because it was still nowhere to be found, because it was not yet: All and One.

> The All of the philosophers, which we had consciously broken into pieces, here, in the blinding midnight sun of the completed redemption, it is finally, yes truly final-ly [*end-lich*], grown together into One. (266/256)

This passage—and several others like it in the *Star*—depict God as the unrivaled "star" of redemption. God completes Himself in redemption; God becomes the unity of the All in redemption that philosophers have long tried to grasp; God is "Redeemer in a weightier sense than he is Creator and Revealer." And yet, when we recall our earlier discussion of the *Star*'s account of redemption, this foregrounding of the divine appears quite surprising. For redemption, according to the descriptions we examined above, does not involve God directly at all. Rather, it is an event that occurs between the self and the world, in which the awakening of "I-hood" through neighborly love throughout the world forges "the All": a vast community of "I"s, each one a self, each one equally part of the world, collectively acknowledging God. Rosenzweig indeed at least acknowledges his former depiction of redemption as happening between self and world. It is "in the redemption of the world through the human being and of the human being by the world" that "God redeems Himself." Such a formulation certainly implies that God depends on the reciprocal loving relations between self and world. God depends—as we've seen—on the human decision to enter into redemptive loving relations with others in the world, in order for Him to attain His own redemption. For it is only when the self redeems the world and, conversely, the world redeems the self, that God finds redemption. But at the same time, Rosenzweig claims here that what is unique about God's centrality to redemption is that God is both the subject and the object of redemption. God is "not only the one who redeems, but also the one who is redeemed."

We need to understand, then, how it is the case that God is both redeemer and redeemed, both *subject* and *object* of redemption, when the immediate actors and recipients of redemptive love are evidently selves and the world. First I will address the question of how God can be grasped as the subject of redemption, and then I will address how God can be grasped as redemption's object. As we begin to make sense of God's relationship to the course toward redemption that involves selves and the world, we will also be in a position to ask *why* God must undergo the process Rosenzweig depicts in the *Star*, and what this teaches us about the human experience of self-world dualism.

We begin with God as the subject of redemption. Redemption, we've seen, involves the reconciliation of world and selves, of creation and revelation, through loving relations that realize a unified totality of selves in the world: the "All." God may be grasped as the Redeemer, despite the fact that human beings in the world are getting all the action, firstly, because it is God who begins the process of reciprocal relations between the elements that ultimately leads to redemption. World and self may engage with each other directly in the course toward redemption, but they do so only because God first turned toward the elemental world as Creator and grounded its existence, and because God first awoke the self to "I-hood" as Revealer through the personal call and command to love. Viewed from the perspective of the course of redemption as a whole, one might suggest, creating the world and revealing the self may both be seen as occurring in the service of the redeemer. Moreover, since God is eternal, Rosenzweig reminds us, what human beings in the world experience as temporal development, God may indeed be said to experience all at once. Thus Rosenzweig writes, "He Himself doesn't need time for Himself, but rather He needs time as Redeemer of world and human being, and not because He needs it, but rather because human being and world need it. Because for God the future is not anticipation. He is eternal and the only eternal, the quintessential eternal. 'I am' in His mouth is like 'I will be,' and finds its explanation only in it" (303/290).

If God first opened up into those relations with the world and selves that begin the process that ultimately ends in redemption, and if God may be viewed as experiencing this whole process not in time but in an eternal instant, then God may indeed be designated as the Redeemer, as the subject of redemption, even when His redemptive act occurs indirectly, "in the redemption of the world through the human being and of the human being by the world." But here we are again entitled to ask Rosenzweig: *Why?* Why does God initiate a process of engagement with others that produces a world and human beings in it, and requires those human beings to carry out certain kinds of actions in the world? Why does God engage with others in such a way that God *needs* those others to perform certain actions for God's own sake? Why does God make Himself *dependent* on a process determined, at least in part, by the temporal character and the needs and—let's face it—the sheer caprice that typifies human life in the world?

These are questions with which Rosenzweig had been preoccupied, it turns out, since the period after the *Leipziger Nachtgespräch*. In 1914, he wrote his groundbreaking article on the origins of German Idealism, entitled "The Oldest System-Program of German Idealism." The article claimed that Schelling had been the original author of a fragmentary text, written in Hegel's hand, which Rosenzweig had discovered in the Prussian State Library in 1913, and it reconstructed how Schelling came to formulate the task of systematic philosophy that later defined German Idealism. Schelling came to view a "finished, closed system" as the only form in which one could answer the "problem of all philosophy," namely, "how the Absolute can go out of itself and can set up a world over against itself."[66] This question, which Rosenzweig views as perplexing Schelling over the course of his whole philosophical career, may be said to ask why that which is absolute and self-grounded comes to manifest itself in, or gives rise to a multiplicity of particulars that form a world. Why does the "One" give rise to the "All"?

Rosenzweig addresses the same question in systematic form in the *Star* itself—but with important variations. If we are to take his account of the self-generation of the respective elements God, world, and self, in part one of the *Star*, as ontology and not merely epistemology, then the divine represents just one of the primordial elements whose interrelations through creation, revelation, and redemption unfold into "the All."[67] God does not stand as the Absolute Unity of all that will be in that primordial moment before creation. The question Schelling asks might thus be translated into the language of the *Star* as follows: How and why does the elemental God step out of itself and enter into relations with the world and human selves in it?

The *Star* suggests the following answer. Before God opens up out of His elemental state into relations with the world and selves, God, world, and self are all to be grasped as isolated elements, each of which has generated itself out of its own respective state of nothingness. What allows each element to hold itself out of its own nothing, Rosenzweig suggests, is the way that it unites together the quality of substantiality or being and the quality of activity. By uniting these qualities, Rosenzweig suggests, the elements become "facts" in the strict sense; for a fact—a *Tatsache*—is nothing other than the unity of substantiality [*Sache*] and activity [*Tat*]. In this primordial state, the elemental God generates itself out of its nothing as the fusion of unconditional being [*Sache*] and infinite power or freedom [*Tat*] (e.g., 33–34/38–39).[68]

As I have argued in *Franz Rosenzweig and the Systematic Task of Philosophy,* however, the factual state in which the elements hold themselves out of their respective nothings in the first part of the *Star* remains unstable or uncertain. The elements thus remain at risk to collapse back into the very nothings out of which they emerged. For all of God's unconditional being and infinite power, God is no less uncertain in His elemental state than are world and self. This uncertainty appears to stem, in God's case, from the fact that the very unconditional being and infinite power that make God what God is remain *unrealized* and hence incomplete when God is an isolated element. The realization of God's power and being, and consequently the securing of God's factuality, can only be attained, Rosenzweig shows, through God's turning into relations with world and self. God can only realize His infinite power by grounding the existence of a network of things in the world as its Creator. God can only realize His unconditional being by having that being recognized and confirmed by selves that God as the loving Revealer awakens to "I-hood."[69] The suggestion that God must somehow restrict Godself in order to make room for human beings to recognize God's own divinity was an insight Rosenzweig appears to have pondered in 1916, we've seen, while reading Tertullian and reflecting on monotheism and the conditions for human freedom. In the *Star,* this movement of self-restriction for the sake of recognition and security may be said to hold for all beings—God, world, and selves.[70] But as we'll see, Rosenzweig still appears to claim that it serves God's redemptive needs in particular.

Throughout the *Star,* Rosenzweig describes the need that leads the elements to open up into relations with one another as their striving for "factuality," that is, for a secure realization and unification of the substantiality and activity through which they generated themselves out of their nothing. Once God turns as Creator to the world and thereby forfeits the unstable factuality of His elemental condition, for example, Rosenzweig claims the course of revelation "strives for a grounded factuality [for God] . . . not in the elements, but rather in a course of the one actuality itself that would rise out over all 'Perhaps' into the height of quintessential security" (176/171). God can hope to overcome the uncertainty—the "Perhaps"—that plagued his elemental condition and attain the "security" of "grounded factuality," Rosenzweig implies here, by entering into that course of relations with world and selves that, we've seen, is directed toward redemption. Indeed, Rosenzweig suggests that it is only in redemption that God, world, and selves attain that secure factuality which they seek and thereby free themselves from the threat of falling back into their primordial nothingness.[71]

Despite the fact that God does not act directly in redemption, God is thus properly identified by Rosenzweig as the "Redeemer" because God initiates the process of relations with world and with selves that lead them to engage in those unifying acts of love that realize redemptive community in the world. God steps out of His elemental state and enters into relations with the world and selves in it, we can now say, because God *needs* such relations in order to realize who He is. God must place His fate into the hands of human beings in the world, as it were. He must subject Himself to the temporality and the finitude that characterize worldly and human life, because only by creating the whole world can God realize His infinite power, and only by awakening the individual soul in revelation can God have His own unconditional being recognized by others. Redemption is the culmination of this process in which God's needs are fulfilled, in which God realizes God's self. When selves enter into relations of neighborly love with others that span the world, we have seen, they build through their relations a community that is both a unified, ramified whole and a collection of individual selves. Redemption unites together the created world that issued from God's infinite power and the revelation of "I-hood" that issued from God's loving being. Moreover, the crowning moment of this unification of self and world, of the recipients of revelatory love and creative power, is the moment in which this redemptive community of selves unites in the common acknowledgment of God. The following passage speaks to the way in which it is the acknowledgment of the unity of God that completes the process of unification of self and world initiated through neighborly love:

> The voice of the soul redeemed to harmony with all the world, and the voice of the world redeemed to common sensibility and song with the soul: how can these double-voices sound-together into one? How could the separated find themselves, except in the unity of that before whom they sing, whom they praise, whom they thank? What binds the one voice of the summoning one with all the world? He is different from all the world, two kinds of subjects, two kinds of nominative. What he has and sees is also different from that which the whole world has and sees, two kinds of objects, two kinds of accusative. Only He, whom he thanks, who is no object for him and thus bound to him, but rather "beyond" both him and all that can become object for him, only this is the same, whom the whole world thanks. Standing over

> against the beyond-all dative, the voices of this-side find their separate hearts. The dative is that which binds, which grasps-together; . . . so He can be the point, where all givers can unite themselves. The dative as this truly binding-one, can be the true freeing [*lösende*] for all not-truly, not-essentially bound, the redeeming one [*das Er-lösende*]—thank God. (259–60/250)

In this difficult passage, Rosenzweig suggests that soul and world, different as they are, can attain to a harmonious unity in redemption precisely because the God to whom each owes thanks is one and the same. In the common acknowledgment of God's unity, the individual selves who experienced God's revelatory love and the world that experienced God's creative power "unite themselves."

This passage now permits us to explain how God "redeems *Himself* . . . in the redemption of the world through the human being and of the human being by the world" and then, finally, what it means for God to be the unity of the All in redemption. God is redeemer, we have said, insofar as God initiates the process of relations that lead self and world to unite in the redemptive community of "the All." That process, we now recognize, serves divine need. God realizes His infinite power through the creation of the world. God has His unconditional being recognized by selves awakened to "I-hood" in revelation. But in redemption, not only are self and world reconciled. Through their reconciliation, the unity of the God who had to split apart out of His primordial, unstable elemental state is collectively affirmed and thereby secured. All particular beings, united in redemptive love, acknowledge the God who created them and loved them, respectively, as One.

To say then that God is the *object* of redemption is to say that through the redemptive relations between self and world, God attains to that secure unity which God lacked as primordial, isolated element, and for the purpose of which God entered into relations with self and world in the first place. I now suggest that there are two aspects, or perhaps two stages to God's redeemed Oneness described in the *Star,* and that these two aspects correspond to two statements about truth we examined at the beginning of this section.

In the acknowledgment of thanks they give to God in unison, I have suggested, the redemptive community of selves in the world affirm God's unity. They reunite the infinite power and unconditional being that had forged an unstable unity in the elemental God, by acknowledging God from their different perspectives as recipients of divine creative power and divine revelatory love. As "I"s all particular beings are able to recognize and affirm God's being. As individual parts of a ramified world, they are able to do so as a unified collective. By acknowledging that "God created the world and is not just the God of revelation," we might suggest, the redemptive community of selves in the world affirms God's unity and thereby secures it for God Himself.

But in Rosenzweig's account there is a further step in the redeeming of God, and a further step in God realizing unity. In the moment that God is redeemed *through* the reciprocal relations between self and world, Rosenzweig suggests, God is also redeemed *from* all those relations into which God had to enter in order to secure His own being. God is the object of redemption insofar as God is thereby redeemed from the others, and the relations with others, upon which God has depended throughout the whole course from creation to redemption. Thus, immediately after he writes that it is precisely "in the redemption of the world through the human being and of the human being by the world [that] God redeems Himself," Rosenzweig asserts that "human being and world disappear in redemption. God, however, completes Himself." In the moment that self and world are reconciled completely in the redemptive community of individuals who are at once "I"s and parts of the ramified world, and hence the differences between self and world disappear, Rosenzweig suggests, self and world themselves disappear, or rather, *their existence consists wholly—in that moment—in their collective reflection of God's unity.*

Rosenzweig elaborates rather dramatically on both aspects of the unity God achieves in redemption in the following passage:

> Immediately, however, redemption happens only to God Himself. For Him Himself it is the eternal act, in which He frees Himself from that which stands over against Him, from that which is not He Himself. Redemption frees Him from the work in creation as from the loving need of the soul. Redemption is His day of rest, His great Sabbath, to which the Sabbath of creation only foreshadows, the day where He, redeemed from everything outside Him, . . . will be One and His name: One. Redemption redeems God, in that it frees [*löst*] Him from His revealed name. In the name and its revelation the delivery of revelation begun in creation completes itself. "In the name" there happens henceforth everything that happens. Sanctification and desecration of the name—since revelation there is no act, which

does not effect one or the other; the course of redemption in the world happens in the name and for the sake of the name. But the end is nameless, beyond all names. The sanctification of the name itself happens so that the name at one time may be muted. Beyond the word—and what is the name other than the whole collected word—beyond the word shines silence. Where no other name confronts the one name any longer, where the one name is all-one and all that is created knows and acknowledges him and only him, there the act of sanctification has come to rest. Because sanctification counts only so long as there is still something unsanctified. Where all is sanctified, there the Sanctified itself is no longer sanctified. It is simply there. Such simple existence of the highest, such unimpaired all-ruling and alone-ruling actuality beyond all need and delight of actualization: that is the truth. Because the truth does not, as the masters of the schools believe, become known through error. Truth bears witness to itself, it is one with all that is actual, it does not separate in it." (426–27/406)

Rosenzweig's account of divine redemption in this passage sheds considerable light on the unity to which God attains in redemption. For God, we find, redemption is not only the moment of being freed from the threat of falling back into nothingness. Redemption also frees God from those others with whom God entered into relation in the first place. Redemption is the process through which God "frees Himself from that which stands over against Him," from that which is not God Himself. It frees him from world and self, "from the work of creation as from the loving need of the soul." Such is the implication, Rosenzweig suggests, of the passage from Zechariah that Rashi too had quoted in order to explain the divine unity proclaimed in the "Shema," asserting that in redemption God "will be One and His name One." Rosenzweig appears to interpret the unity of God's name in the following illuminating way. God's name is that through which God achieves *recognition* in the world: it designates the revealed word of love that brings redemption through the world and thereby awakens all selves in the world collectively to acknowledge God. As we've seen, Rosenzweig suggests that human freedom amounts entirely to the decision whether or not to take up the task of neighborly love in the world; and indeed, Rosenzweig writes here, "Sanctification and desecration of the name—since revelation there is no act that does not effect one or the other." But now Rosenzweig asserts that this sanctification of God's name, the spreading of redemptive love through all particular selves in the world, only occurs so that God's name will at one point be completely sanctified in the collective recognition of God by all—and then will be silenced. At this moment, when redemptive love has awoken all to selfhood and united all within the redemptive community, when all are thereby "sanctified," and thus "when the one name is All-one [*all-ein*] and all that is created knows and acknowledges Him and only Him," Rosenzweig writes, "there the act of sanctification has come to rest." In this moment in which all recognize God and acknowledge Him in thanks, Rosenzweig suggests, all likewise disappear into the sheer mirroring of God's unity. God alone is "simply there. Such simple existence of the highest, such unimpaired all-ruling and All-one ruling reality beyond all misery and joy of realization, that is truth."[72]

I suggest that both aspects of divine unity, and indeed the whole course through relations with others that leads God to attain unity, are implicit in this claim about truth with which ends the long passage we've been examining. When Rosenzweig writes that truth—the truth that God is in redemption—"bears witness to itself, it is one with all that is actual, it does not separate in it," he alludes, first of all, to the way in which God attains to self-certainty in redemption through the mediation of relations with world and selves. God initiates the course of relations that lead to redemption. Over that course, God awakens all selves (either directly or indirectly) in love in a way that enables them to recognize God's own being. In redemption itself, God is recognized by all beings as a collective. When Rosenzweig says "God is truth," and when he says "truth bears witness to itself" while being "one with all that is actual," I suggest he means to say that God bears witness to Himself *through* all others, through the recognition all others give him. The unity of this whole process of recognition amounts to God's bearing witness to Himself while being at once "one" with all that is actual. God's unity in redemption is to this extent mediated through the unification of self and world into the All. God attains self-certainty through the affirmation He receives from all particular beings who unite in recognition of Him. But as we now know, this mediated unity is not the whole story of God's redemption. To say that God is the *object* of redemption, we've seen, is to indicate that God is freed in redemption from those very relations to self and to world into which God had to enter. To this extent, once all particular beings acknowledge God's Oneness collectively and in unison, they lose their distinctness as others of God and simply mirror divine unity itself. Although the *process* through which God comes to bear witness to Himself as truth thus demands relations with others, the redemptive moment of God's self-recognition is God's alone. I think this is why Rosenzweig, while stressing in this passage that the truth which bears witness to itself "is one with all that is actual, [and] does not separate in it," later will assert that "insofar as truth is one with this whole living actuality, it is its essence; insofar as it nevertheless can separate itself from it—without in the least sublating the connection—it is the essence of God." God's unity is both inseparable from the All and at once separable. God is dependent for His unity upon the whole course from creation to redemption that realizes the All, and—in the culminating moment of redemption—God stands alone, bearing witness to Himself.[73]

This examination of Rosenzweig's most far-reaching speculations regarding divinity in redemption has, I hope, brought some clarity to Rosenzweig's account of divine unity. We have seen how God does indeed become One in redemption, how the unity God becomes in redemption is nevertheless intertwined with—or rather dependent upon—the unification of self and world in redemption. But at the same time that God may be said thus to attain redemption only indirectly, through the reciprocal loving actions between self and world, we have also seen how redemption may be viewed as God's event more properly than it is the world's or the self's, how God may indeed be seen as both subject and object of redemption. We have even explored the answer Rosenzweig implies through the whole of the *Star* as to *why* God enters into the relations that lead from creation to redemption, why God makes Himself dependent on the temporal process that must unfold between selves in the world. It is only through this redemptive process, we have seen, that God can attain to a state in which God is fully realized, fully self-certain, and thereby securely One.

After devoting so much of this book's study of Rosenzweig's response to Marcionism to the problem of self and world, our focus in this section has been squarely on the question of God's unity or duality. But the striking account of God's becoming One through the course from creation to redemption has important implications for the very struggle between self and world which we have found at the forefront of both Rosenzweig's deliberations in the wake of the *Leipziger Nachtgespräch* and his philosophical concerns in the *Star* itself. The *Star* opens with the claim that the fear of death makes manifest to human beings the tension between their respective worldliness and selfhood, and that it calls on human beings to seek redemption from this tension through action in the world rather than escape from it. Our present discussion of God's attainment of unity in redemption suggests a metaphysical basis for the human experience of tension between selfhood and worldliness made manifest in the fear of death, and hence a metaphysical purpose for the call to overcome that tension. We may be said to experience the split we experience within ourselves between self and world because of *the split within the divine.* We become worldly creature and soul beloved of God because God has split out of His elemental state and has become Creator and Revealer. The imperative to "remain in the fear of the earthly" is a call to act in the world in order to *redeem God,* that is, in order to restore God to unity. Only as creatures dependent on the Creator for our existence do we offer God the opportunity to realize God's infinite power. Only as "I"s awoken through the Revealer's command to love do we confirm God's being. And only as a redemptive collective of "I"s in the world do we allow God to bear witness to Himself through us all. The entirety of the struggle for reconciliation human beings experience, and of the struggle we know Rosenzweig himself to have experienced personally circa 1913, Rosenzweig now grasps as rooted in and for the sake of God.[74]

But even this dramatic metaphysical background to the tension between self and world doesn't tell the whole story. For if we take the first part of the *Star* seriously, then it is not only God who must open up out of His elemental state and enter into relations in order to attain stability and self-certainty. The elemental self and the elemental world likewise generate themselves out of their nothings through the unstable fusing of substantiality and activity—of logos and phenomenal particularization in the case of the world and of character and will in the case of the self—and elemental self and elemental world likewise achieve "grounded factuality" through the relations into which they enter with God and with each other which culminate in redemption. Although we've seen that God is the last unity of difference standing in redemption, it is no less true of self and world than it is of God that they find completion in redemption.

When we view the tension of self and world that first led Rosenzweig to court Marcionism but then directed him to a developmental account of God's unity in the light of the whole structure of factual generation, fragmentation, and restoration in the *Star,* we might suggest, that tension of self and world appears as an example, accessible through experience, of how all beings come to realize themselves. All particular beings generate themselves, hold themselves out of their respective nothings, only through a process of uniting securely within themselves substantiality and activity, worldliness and selfhood.

"GOD CREATED": TRUTH AND CREATURELINESS AT THE END OF THE *STAR*

We have seen how the *Star* opens with a depiction of the human fear of death as that experience which alerts human beings to the split between selfhood and worldliness inherent to who they are. An awareness of this opposition between selfhood and worldliness might lead us to deny the world in an attempt to realize our selfhood more purely and through a more intimate and solitary relation to the divine. It might lead us, that is to say, toward Marcionism. But Rosenzweig suggests that the fear of death points to a different response to the tension between self and world, one that does not ask that we deny one part of ourselves in order to realize the other. We are called on, Rosenzweig suggests, to hold onto our earthliness, and to reconcile self and world through redemptive action in the world rather than through escape from it.

The different sections of this chapter have set out to show how the *Star* articulates the alternative to Marcionism that had crystallized for Rosenzweig in the wake of the *Leipziger Nachtgespräch.* We have surveyed Rosenzweig's account of the course from creation to redemption as the context within which human beings discover the internal tension between self and world in themselves and within which they are thereby called to redemptive action. We have explored how Rosenzweig understands the possibility of human freedom as grounded in divine love and self-limitation, and examined the kinds of individual and communal human action upon which God depends in order for redemption to be achieved. We have analyzed, finally, Rosenzweig's account of the culminating moment of redemption and the unity that it achieves both between selves and the world, and for the divine. The *Star* thus leads the reader from the fear of death and the self–world tension it makes manifest along the course of loving action in the world that will bring redemption, to the ultimate moment in which God will be One, and selves and world—their differences reconciled—will exist merely as the reflection of divine unity itself.

In the closing pages of the *Star,* Rosenzweig leads the reader from the heights of speculation over divine redemptive unity back down to human life in the world. He leads the reader back, in fact, to the very decision he has suggested we are called on to make, between acting redemptively in the world and fleeing the world, between world redemption and world denial. The *Star* thus concludes by confronting the reader with the same challenge of Marcionism with which it began, and with a final extrapolation of his 1913 insight that "God created the world and is not just the God of revelation." But having equipped the reader over the whole of the book with an understanding of the context, the significance, and the urgency of this decision, Rosenzweig can now free the reader to make her own decision between Yes and No, between life and death. I want to conclude this chapter by examining these last movements of the *Star,* from the divine unity of redemption back to the creaturely existence of human beings in the world.

Soon after he has described the intuitive grasp of redemptive truth that the human being can attain through communal prayer, Rosenzweig reminds the reader that the human being has an important role to play in the actualization of truth. "Our Truly, our Yes and Amen, with which we answered God's revelation—they disclose themselves at the goal as the beating heart of the eternal truth, too," he writes. "But we must have the courage to find ourselves present in the truth, the courage to say our Truly in the middle of the truth" (436/414–15).

Rosenzweig here designates the contribution the human being makes to redemption as the "Truly" the human being speaks in affirmation of—indeed as part of the actualization of—the truth. We have seen how Rosenzweig presents divine truth as the culmination of redemption, as the unifying completion of the course of relations God initiates with the world and selves. The decision to take part in that redemptive course, to respond to revelation with an affirmative "Truly," is a decision to take part in the cosmic process of making truth true. But such a decision, as Rosenzweig himself well knew, is not a simple one. Deciding to turn to the world in the kind of action that will advance the course of redemptive truth threatens to undermine the purity of the self and her intimate relation to the divine. It takes *courage,* as Rosenzweig notes here—courage to affirm the path to redemption by taking the world seriously, courage to trust that the place and the moment in which one lives is indeed part of that path to truth.

In the closing pages of "The Star or the Eternal Truth," the last book of the last part of the *Star,* Rosenzweig identifies the "Truly" which human beings contribute to the ultimate truth as the fullest expression of human *creatureliness.* Highlighting the partiality of the truth to which Jews and Christians have access, he writes:

> So we are both, they as we and we as they, creatures just for the reason that we do not see the whole truth. Just for this we remain in the limits of mortality. Just for this—we remain. And we want to remain. Indeed we want to live. God does for us what we want, for as long as we want it. So long as we hang on life, He gives us life. He gives us of the truth only as much as we as living creatures can carry, namely our part. Were He to give us more, were He to give us His part, the whole truth, so He would raise us up out of the limits of humanity. But just so long as He doesn't do so, for so long we also carry no desire for it. We hang onto [*an*] our creatureliness. We don't want to let it go. And our creatureliness is conditioned in that we only have part, only are part. Life celebrated the last triumph over death in the Truly, with which it confirmed its own received become-part truth as its part in the eternal [truth]. In this Truly, the creature connects itself to its part, which was imparted to him. In this Truly it is creature. This Truly goes as a mute secret through the whole chain of beings; in the human being it attains speech. And in the Star it glows into visible, self-enlightening existence. But it always remains in the limits of creatureliness. The truth itself still speaks Truly when it steps before God. But God Himself no longer speaks Truly. He is beyond all that may become part, He is still beyond the whole, that by Him is indeed only a part. Still beyond the whole, He is the One. (463/439)

There are a number of points I want to highlight in this crucial but difficult passage. Having traversed the whole course to divine redemptive unity, Rosenzweig here insists that the human being's very engagement in this redemptive course highlights her creaturely character. Indeed, Rosenzweig here suggests that the "Truly," the human being's affirmation of and contribution to the redemptive course to divine unity, is the epitome of the human being's creatureliness: "in this Truly, it is creature." Rosenzweig implies that the "Truly" is nothing less than the "secret" of creation, a secret passed mutely through "the whole chain of beings" until "in the human being it attains speech."

We have indeed seen how the human being's decision to affirm redemptive truth and to participate in its realization comes through speech. It was "the Word" that allowed Rosenstock to overcome the tension between loving God and loving others in the world; and it was this same articulation of love that mediated revelation and redemption for Rosenzweig. The individual self is awakened to "I-hood" through the divine loving command, and fulfills that "I-hood" by turning with her own "word" to others in the world.

But why does Rosenzweig identify the human being's spoken "Truly" as the secret epitome of his *creatureliness*?

The culmination of the redemptive process, according to the *Star,* is the moment in which all individual selves in the world are united in the collective acknowledgment of God. I have suggested that God needs this acknowledgment from His others, indeed that this acknowledgment is the goal of the course of relations into which God enters, securing divine factuality. Such a collective unity of selves reflecting divine unity can only be achieved, we have seen, in the world: only God's grounding of the existence of all particulars in the world allows God to actualize divine power; only the world can serve as a site in which selves can actualize their own "I-hood" in community with others; only the world is a ramified collective of particulars that holds together all "I's" in recognition of the divine. The moment in which the individual I affirms divine truth with his "Truly," one might suggest, is the moment in which he expresses the full potential of his creatureliness, to be other than the divine, and nevertheless to acknowledge, even to reflect divine unity. But it is only as finite, mortal creatures, that we remain God's others, and can acknowledge divinity through relation. God requires of us not that we deny our worldliness, not that we negate our worldly natures. God needs precisely mortal creatures to decide for truth, and so we must "remain" creatures. But the ability we have as creatures to take part in the redemptive course through our "Truly" is at once life's "triumph over death." The divine need for the creaturely affirmation of truth and the creaturely ability to affirm it: these amount to the "secret" of creatureliness that only attains articulation and fulfillment through human speech.

In this insistence on our fundamental creatureliness, Rosenzweig gives last expression to that rejection of spiritualistic or philosophical world-denial with which he began the *Star.* Jews and Christians are "creatures just for the reason that we do not see the whole truth" but only our own respective parts in that truth. As such, Rosenzweig writes, returning to the struggle with the fear of death with which he began the *Star,* "we remain. And we want to remain. Indeed, we want to live." The taste of redemption granted within the liturgical communities of Jews and Christians might lead community members to forget that what they've seen is not the whole truth, but rather is a part that demands active affirmation. And Rosenzweig depicts this temptation to flee the world through religious communal visions of truth as of a piece with the philosophical, religious, and aesthetic forms of world denial which he has rejected since the very first pages of the *Star.*

Moreover, Rosenzweig reiterates this call to turn back from the vision of God's redemptive truth toward the world in the very last paragraphs of the *Star.* Here he describes a mystical vision in which he is led into "the innermost sanctum of the divine truth," "at that border of life where vision is permitted [*verstattet*]. Because no human being who sees Him remains in life" (471/446). In this vision, Rosenzweig suggests he sees, in the form of a star-like image of the divine face, the unity of the All which God will be in redemption. Throughout the *Star,* we've seen, Rosenzweig has documented the temptation human beings feel to hold onto such mystical intimacy with God at the expense of the world. But at the end of the book, Rosenzweig suggests the human being does not complete herself in this supreme moment of vision. The vision of divine truth itself directs the human being back into the world. The "mystical being-alone with the 'silent God,'" to which Rosenzweig had been inclined in his early years, is once again in this last instance, overcome by belief in "the Word." What one sees in this vision of redemptive unity, he asserts, "is nothing other than . . . what the word of revelation already said [*hiess*] in the midst of life. And to walk in the light of the divine face is only for him who follows the words of the divine mouth" (471/446). In the ultimate redemptive unity of the divine, Rosenzweig intimates, one perceives in visual form the consequences of the whole course of spoken words—God's awakening command to love, the human being's own redemptive words to others that affirm the course to truth through the "Truly"—that actualize truth in the world. The redemptive truth one envisions will only be actualized if one "follows the words of the divine mouth," if one remains creature. Just as Faust had been drawn back from the precipice of suicide "into life" through the redemptive announcements of Easter morning, Rosenzweig thus leads his readers from out of the realm of redemptive vision back "INTO LIFE" (472/447). We are called on to remain in the fear of earthly, to overcome the temptation to world denial, to affirm divine truth through redemptive action in the world, Rosenzweig suggests, because and insofar as we are creatures.[75]

Only in the ultimate moment of redemption, when God is One, and has been redeemed from the whole course of relations into which He has entered, does the truth no longer need to be affirmed by God's others. In that moment, Rosenzweig writes, "God Himself no longer speaks the Truly." But until then, Rosenzweig asserts, creatureliness defines the redemptive course to truth. "This last truth," the truth which God is in redemption, "is itself only—created truth" (464/440). That is to say, truth's actualization depends on the whole course of relations God initiates with His others that unfold from creation to redemption. When Rosenzweig introduced his view of the relationship between creation, revelation, and redemption, we've seen, he claimed that "revelation too, redemption too are precisely creation in a certain, not yet to be argued-out way" (114/113). The end of the *Star* illuminates Rosenzweig's earlier claim. Not only is the creation of the world to be grasped as a promise that is fulfilled along the course to redemption. That whole course to redemption is itself to be understood as the actualization of creation. The path to redemption is the path along which we actualize our creatureliness.

Rosenzweig makes this point at the end of the *Star* in terms that hearken back powerfully to the *Leipziger Nachtgespräch.* He writes: "That God created, this premonitory first word of Scripture does not lose its force until all is fulfilled" (463/440).

We have long seen how Rosenzweig left the *Leipziger Nachtgespräch* convinced that "God created the world and is not just the God of revelation." Indeed, Rosenzweig tells us that what stopped him from fully embracing a metaphysical dualism of God and devil that night was none other than "the first sentence of the Bible." Here, at the end of the *Star,* Rosenzweig returns to the opening of the Bible and declares that the message of its first words hold true for all time. Until redemption has been completed, it will for all time remain the case that "God created," that God has initiated a process of relations with others who depend upon Him but upon whom He likewise depends. Until redemption has been completed, it will for all time remain the case that truth is "created truth," that it depends on human affirmation, on the human decision to participate in the actualization of redemption in the world. Until redemption has been completed, human beings will remain creatures, they will remain in the fear of death, and they will continue to experience that tension between selfhood and worldliness which invites them to decide between world denial and world redemption.

Conclusion

Life and Thought Revisited

THIS STUDY HAS FOCUSED on a single night in Franz Rosenzweig's life, indeed, on a single conversation in which Rosenzweig participated. Scholars have long recognized the *Leipziger Nachtgespräch* as a transformative event for Rosenzweig, and this book certainly confirms its importance. But I have claimed that the stakes of that night-conversation, and hence its significance for Rosenzweig's personal and intellectual development, were vastly different than has been supposed up until now. In contrast to the account that has dominated the scholarship for the last sixty years, I have argued that the Leipzig night-conversation did not begin a process of faith-awakening for Rosenzweig. It did not lead him to break from the relativism of academic philosophy and history, and to find in the experience of Christian faith—and then in the experience of prayer among faithful Jews—the answers to the existential questions that had long plagued him. I have argued, to the contrary, that what was at stake for Rosenzweig over the course of and in the wake of the *Leipziger Nachtgespräch* was the moral and spiritual status of the world. July 7, 1913 marked the end of a period in which Rosenzweig entertained a theology of radical world-denial that took dying for God seriously, a theology Rosenzweig later identified with Marcionism. During this period, we have seen, Rosenzweig could not reconcile the possibility of personal salvation with the conditions of the world. At the *Leipziger Nachtgespräch,* however, Eugen Rosenstock and Rudolf Ehrenberg "converted" Rosenzweig back to the world. Over the course of a discussion that took its starting point from Selma Lagerlöf's *Antikrists mirakler,* the "first sentence of the Bible" forced Rosenzweig out of his dualism, and he became committed to the view that "God created the world and [is] not just the God of revelation." He came to take seriously the redemptive potential of Christian "world-activity" to realize the Kingdom of God in the world, perhaps as a result of an experience of redemptive love at the hands of Rosenstock and, to a lesser extent, of Ehrenberg. This radical shift in Rosenzweig's worldview led him toward a tremendously fruitful rethinking of the relations between the self, the world, and the divine, on the one hand, and between Christianity and Judaism, on the other. Thinking creation and redemption together led Rosenzweig to view the realization of the Kingdom of God in historical terms. Reflections on the possibility of human freedom under the conditions of monotheism led him to view the human free decision to act redemptively in the world as made possible through an act of divine self-limitation necessary—for reasons Rosenzweig would only spell out in the *Star*—for God Himself. Consideration of the dangers he came to see as inherent to the Christian redemptive vocation led him to the conclusion, finally, that the Jewish people too has a vital and unique role to play in the redemptive process, one which demands that Jews—Franz Rosenzweig among them—*remain* Jews.

In the introduction to this study, I argued that the reigning account of the *Leipziger Nachtgespräch* as a story about Rosenzweig's conversion from academic philosophy and scholarship to faith not only does not match the evidence at our disposal. More problematically, I suggested, this story of Rosenzweig's development has posed an obstacle to understanding his mature thought. The question that has plagued Rosenzweig scholarship under the paradigm of a 1913 conversion to faith, I suggested, is the following: if Rosenzweig had indeed discovered that faith experience, and not the dry scholasticism of contemporary philosophy, held the key to meaningful life, why did he proceed to write a book as dry and as scholastic as *The Star of Redemption*?

The account I have offered of Rosenzweig's series of conversions or near-conversions in 1913 tries to do justice to what Rosenzweig had to say, in myriad contexts, about this event that so transformed his life and his thought, and it tries to evaluate and take seriously a number of other sources for understanding what occurred. But I have also tried to make the case along the way that this depiction of Rosenzweig's turn from Marcionism to a developmental account of redemption in the world is *coherent*. The moment Rosenzweig abandons his "dualism of revelation and world," one can already catch a glimpse of the whole course Rosenzweig's thinking will take in the years to follow, culminating in his writing of *The Star of Redemption*. As the fourth chapter of this study shows, moreover, the problem of Marcionism and the task of overcoming it through a developmental account of redemption in the world remained of paramount concern to Rosenzweig as he wrote his magnum opus.

I have thus argued that the *Leipziger Nachtgespräch* played a considerable role in shaping Rosenzweig's life and thought. At the same time, I have in no way attempted here to produce a comprehensive intellectual biography of Rosenzweig. There is still quite a lot of important scholarly work to be done before we arrive at a sufficiently comprehensive and nuanced picture of Rosenzweig's intellectual and spiritual development. Such a picture would, of course, have to take into account other key moments and encounters, many of which have only been touched on here in passing: Rosenzweig's intense and complicated friendships with his cousins Hans and Rudolf Ehrenberg; his intimate affair with Margrit Rosenstock-Hüssy; his 1916 correspondence with Eugen Rosenstock and his ongoing fraught relationship with him; his discipleship under Hermann Cohen; his productive relationship with Martin Buber and the Lehrhaus circle; his marriage to Edith Hahn, and his family life.

But while this study has in no way aspired to be biographically comprehensive, its account of the importance of the *Leipziger Nachtgespräch* for Rosenzweig's later thinking does invite us to ask the question implicit in the title of Nahum Glatzer's *Franz Rosenzweig: Life and Thought*. How are we to understand the relationship between the life and the thought of a philosopher or religious thinker like Rosenzweig? Rosenzweig himself once claimed that since Nietzsche, "the philosopher ceased to be a *quantité négligeable* for his philosophy."[1] And yet, Steven Schwarzschild was right to question the "exaggeratedly biographical treatment which he [Rosenzweig] continues to receive from his real as well as self-declared disciples who . . . constantly distort his thought into a pale shadow of his life."[2] I must confess that when I embarked on this project I was skeptical about whether one could write intellectual biography without *reducing philosophy to the philosopher*, without, that is, striving to explain matters of ethics and metaphysics on psychological and physiological grounds. This inquiry into the stakes and details of the *Leipziger Nachtgespräch* has shown, I hope, that a proper understanding of a key moment in a philosopher's life can indeed illuminate his philosophy. But in Rosenzweig's case this is so largely because Rosenzweig himself appears to have lived and experienced the key events in his life *in metaphysical terms.* He viewed his personal decisions—including those about metaphysics!—on a metaphysical background and as entailing metaphysical consequences. The metaphysical position Rosenzweig developed in systematic form in *The Star of Redemption* can thus indeed be said to be rooted in the events of Rosenzweig's life, but only insofar as Rosenzweig experienced and reflected upon those very events metaphysically in real time.

The harmony between Rosenzweig's life and his thought is compelling. By this I mean that it permits us to tell a coherent story, to present the events of the summer of 1913 as a kind of biographical introduction to Rosenzweig's mature philosophical thought. The sort of harmony we find between Rosenzweig's life and his thought, I would hazard to say, makes for good thinking.

Does it make for good life?

NOTES

INTRODUCTION

1. On the location of the night-conversation, see Rosenzweig to Eugen Rosenstock, August 13, 1917, in *Die "Gritli-Briefe": Briefe an Margrit Rosenstock-Huessy,* edited by I. Rühle and R. Mayer (Tübingen: Bilam Verlag, 2002), 21 [Henceforth, *Gritli-Briefe*]. Rudolf Ehrenberg was Rosenzweig's cousin.

2. Two accounts that diverge from this dominant version of the story of Rosenzweig's *Leipziger Nachtgespräch* are Irene Kajon's chapter on Rosenzweig in her *Contemporary Jewish Philosophy: An Introduction* (New York: Routledge, 2006), 32–57, and Wolfgang Ullmann's little-known "Die Entdeckung des neuen Denkens: Das Leipziger Religionsgespräch und der Briefwechsel über Judentum und Christentum zwischen Eugen Rosenstock und Franz Rosenzweig," *Stimmstein: Jahrbuch der Eugen Rosenstock-Huessy Gesellschaft* 2 (1988): 147–78. I will note the virtues of these studies at various points in the chapters that follow.

3. Paul R. Mendes-Flohr and Jehuda Reinharz, "From Relativism to Religious Faith: The Testimony of Franz Rosenzweig's Unpublished Diaries," *Leo Baeck Institute Yearbook* 22 (1977): 161.

4. Cf. Eliezer Schweid, "Rosenzweig's Contribution to the Curriculum of Jewish Thought," in *Paradigms in Jewish Philosophy,* edited by R. Jospe (Cranberry, N.J.: Associated University Presses, 1997), 167: "Rosenzweig's personal impact as the main cause for his preferred position in the history of modern Jewish thought was a result not only of his direct relationships, through conversations and letters, with a wide and variegated circle of loving friends and enchanted admirers. It was also due to the indirect literary radiation created by his written testimony and his friends' personal depositions that conveyed the impact of his life story almost like that of a saint." Peter Gordon likewise notes that "in the postwar English-speaking world ... Rosenzweig was celebrated as much for his exemplary *personality* as for his actual ideas," "Rosenzweig Redux: The Reception of German-Jewish Thought," *Jewish Social Studies* 8, no. 1 (2001): 17.

5. See, for example, Rivka Horwitz, "From Hegelianism to a Revolutionary Understanding of Judaism: Franz Rosenzweig's Attitude toward Kabbala and Myth," *Modern Judaism* 26, no. 1 (2006): 48: "there was no specific Yom Kippur experience. This day was important for him; he had also fasted the year before; and he describes this day in extraordinary colors in *The Star.* Yet, as far as we can see, Yom Kippur played no specific role in 1913. Rosenzweig's return was a gradual process that took a number of months." Horwitz's early essays on Rosen-

zweig invoke the Yom Kippur experience as central to Rosenzweig's decision to remain a Jew, although they deny that this event occurred at a small Eastern European Orthodox shul. See her "Franz Rosenzweig's Unpublished Writings," *Journal of Jewish Studies* (1969): 57–80, and her "Judaism Despite Christianity," *Judaism* 24, no. 3 (1975): 306–318. By 1986, Horwitz had already begun to question the basis of the Yom Kippur story in its entirety. See her "Warum liess Rosenzweig sich nicht taufen?" *Der Philosoph Franz Rosenzweig (1886–1929) I,* edited by W. Schmied-Kowarzik (Freiburg/Munich: Alber, 1988), e.g., p. 88: "For us it is important that Rosenzweig provides as the decisive date for his decision to remain a Jew, the day of his arrival in Berlin. He must have found the solution before Yom Kippur, which is not mentioned in the letter to Rudolf Ehrenberg. Rosenzweig recognized this solution alone before this High Holiday and spent it with his faith-companions."

6. Glatzer published an earlier account of Rosenzweig's life and thought in Yiddish in 1945, "Franz Rosenzweig: His Life and His Ideas," in a special printing of the *YIVO Bleter, shrift fun yidishn wisenshaftlekhen institut* 2, xxv (1945): 3–39.

7. Eugene Sheppard notes that Glatzer attributed to the life stories of earlier Jewish figures like Leopold Zunz and even Hillel the Elder a structure parallel to that which he found in Rosenzweig's story: "In Glatzer's scholarly corpus, we detect the following template of a great Jewish figure: the hero emerges in a period of Jewish decay that leads him to disillusionment; he undergoes a deep-seated spiritual and intellectual crisis and is on the point of converting, but in the end he returns to Judaism and renews it for his generation," "'I am a Memory Come Alive': Nahum Glatzer and the Legacy of German-Jewish Thought in America," *Jewish Quarterly Review* 94, no. 1 (2004): 141.

8. Nahum Glatzer, "Introduction," *Franz Rosenzweig: Life and Thought* (New York: Schocken, 1953), xv.

9. Ibid., xix, xx, 25. Note as well Glatzer's attempt to link Rosenzweig's alleged religious experience to what was perhaps the most influential study of religious experience of its time, Rudolf Otto's *Das Heilige.* Glatzer writes, "A parallel experience is reported by the great Protestant interpreter of faith, Rudolf Otto, author of *The Idea of the Holy,* who conceived his notion of *tremendum* as a central factor in religion after participating in a Day of Atonement service in a North African synagogue," *Franz Rosenzweig: Life and Thought,* xviii.

10. Will Herberg, "Rosenzweig's 'Judaism of Personal Existence': A Third Way between Orthodoxy and Modernism," *Commentary* 10, no. 6 (1950): 541. Relying on drafts of Glatzer's work, Herberg published this assessment even before Glatzer's own essay was published in English.

11. Shmuel Hugo Bergman, "Franz Rosenzweig and His Path to Judaism," *Anashim u-derachim* [Hebrew: *People and Paths*] (Jerusalem: Mosad Bialik, 1967), 280–81.

12. Arthur A. Cohen, "Franz Rosenzweig's *The Star of Redemption:* An Inquiry into Its Psychological Origins," *Midstream* 18, no. 2 (February 1972); cited from *An Arthur A. Cohen Reader,* edited by D. Stern and P. Mendes-Flohr (Detroit: Wayne State University Press, 1988), 147–48.

13. Stéphane Mosès, *System and Revelation: The Philosophy of Franz Rosenzweig,* translated by C. Tihanyi (Detroit: Wayne State University Press, 1992), 34–35.

14. Emil Fackenheim, *To Mend the World: Foundations of Post-Holocaust Jewish Thought* (New York: Schocken, 1982), 60.

15. Paul Mendes-Flohr, "Introduction: Franz Rosenzweig and the German Philosophical Tradition," *The Philosophy of Franz Rosenzweig,* edited by P. Mendes-Flohr (Hanover/London: University Press of New England for Brandeis University Press, 1988), 5–6.

16. Richard Cohen, "Rosenzweig's Rebbe HaLevi: From the Academy to the Yeshiva," *Judaism* 44, no. 4 (1995): 449–52.

17. Michael Oppenheim, "Foreword" to Franz Rosenzweig, *The Star of Redemption,* translated by Barbara E. Galli (Madison: University of Wisconsin Press, 2005), xi.

18. Indeed, Glatzer takes Rosenzweig's silence about the experience as evidence of its great personal import: "He guarded it as the secret ground of his new life," *Franz Rosenzweig: Life and Thought,* xviii.

19. Rosenzweig to Rudolf Ehrenberg, August 25, 1919, "My whole experience at that time was not [of] Christ (an experience of faith), but rather [of] Christians (an experience of love)," *BT II,* 642–43.

20. See, for example, Ronald Miller, *Dialogue and Disagreement: Franz Rosenzweig's Relevance to Contemporary Jewish-Christian Understanding* (Lanham, Md.: University Press of America, 1989), 181: "[Rosenzweig] is a Jewish thinker who is able to write about Christianity with a real feel for it from within. . . . He really went far, not in just studying Christianity intellectually, but feeling it from within. . . . Reading what he writes about Christianity, one knows that he is writing not only with the knowledge he had, but with a feeling for that knowledge. That is most unusual in religious dialogue, and most difficult to attain."

21. On the rise of "faith experience" as a category of religious thought, see, e.g., Wayne Proudfoot, *Religious Experience* (Berkeley: University of California Press, 1985), 1–40.

22. In his "Rosenzweig Redux: The Reception of German-Jewish Thought," Peter Gordon notes that "the great difficulty with mixing hagiography into scholarship is that this kind of worship erects a powerful taboo against serious thought." He proceeds to add the following insightful reflection: "The assumption that reverence for personal belief forbids textual criticism is a recurrent obstacle in the scholarly study of religious thought. There is, of course, some warrant for this assumption. The core 'experience' that often first prompts the written work cannot—and probably should not—be interrogated. Biographers now generally assume that Rosenzweig's great awakening to the vitality of Judaism can be traced to a 1913 Yom Kippur service in Berlin, and this epiphany became the core inspiration for the *Star.* But it would be odd to *judge* that experience. . . . The difficulty . . . is that our justifiable reluctance to judge the private experience also has a way of looming over our public efforts to discuss the written work. So what began as a feeling of justifiable restraint when faced with personal piety may in the end nourish an overly pious attitude in scholarship as well" (11). Gordon's attention to the dangers which reverence for personal experience may impose upon scholarship is instructive. Since I intend to question the assumption that Rosenzweig's personal transformation rests on an experience that cannot be thought through or explained, however, I will question further whether our "reluctance to judge the private experience" in this case is truly "justifiable."

23. Nahum Glatzer, "Introduction," *Franz Rosenzweig: Life and Thought,* xviii.

24. Already in 1953, Steven Schwarzschild cautioned against "the exaggeratedly biographical treatment which he [i.e., Rosenzweig] continues to receive from his real as well as self-declared disciples who . . . constantly distort his thought into a pale shadow of his life. This life, to be sure, was an extraordinary and inspiring life, and it is also true that this life was more intimately and consciously interwoven with the thought which it produced than is usual with academic philosophers. . . . His epigones tend to draw the fallacious and misleading conclusion . . . that Rosenzweig was no more than an ideologue, albeit a marvelous one, who conceptualized his personal, idiosyncratic experiences into a personal philosophy and that they themselves are, therefore, entitled to do the same thing," "Franz Rosenzweig and Existentialism," *Yearbook of the CCAR* 62 (1953): 418.

25. Eliezer Schweid, "Rosenzweig's Contribution to the Curriculum of Jewish Thought," in *Paradigms in Jewish Philosophy,* edited by R. Jospe (Cranberry, N.J.: Associated University Presses, 1997), 175–76.

26. See Rosenzweig to Eugen Rosenstock, August 13, 1917, *Gritli-Briefe,* 21, and Eugen Rosenstock, "Prologue/Epilogue to the Letters—Fifty Years Later," *Judaism Despite Christianity: The "Letters on Christianity and Judaism" between Eugen Rosenstock-Huessy and Franz Rosenzweig,* edited by Eugen Rosenstock-Huessy (New York: Schocken, 1971), 73. Lagerlöf's novel appeared in 1897, twelve years before she became the first woman to receive the Nobel Prize for Literature.

1. REVELATION AND WORLD SKEPTICISM

1. Selma Lagerlöf, *The Miracles of Antichrist,* translated by Pauline B. Flach (Boston: Little, Brown, and Co., 1910), 1–13.

2. Ibid., 13–18.

3. Ibid., 18–23.

4. Eugen Rosenstock, "Einleitung" to "Franz Rosenzweig und Eugen Rosenstock: Judentum und Christentum," in Franz Rosenzweig, *Briefe,* edited by Edith Rosenzweig with collaboration from Ernst Simon (Berlin: Schocken, 1935), 639.

5. See chapter 2, section titled "Rosenstock as Facilitator" for my account of Rosenstock's role in the night-conversation, but also for a justification for my selective use of Rosenstock's "recollections" from that night.

6. Paul Mendes-Flohr and Jehuda Reinharz, "From Relativism to Religious Faith: The Testimony of Franz Rosenzweig's Unpublished Diaries," *Leo Baeck Institute Year Book* 22 (1977): 161; Nahum N. Glatzer, "Introduction" to *Franz Rosenzweig: His Life and Thought* (New York: Schocken, 1953), xv.

7. Contemporary scholars are far more skeptical than those of Rosenzweig's time regarding the legitimacy and appropriateness of using such an umbrella term as *Gnosticism* to cover the wide range of communal faiths and practices from the ancient Near East which it is often employed to cover. See Michael A. Williams's excellent *Rethinking "Gnosticism": An Argument for Dismantling a Dubious Category* (Princeton, N.J.: Princeton University Press, 1996).

8. Adolf von Harnack, *Lehrbuch der Dogmengeschichte,* Vol. I (Freiburg: Mohr-Siebeck, 1886), 212. Rosenzweig's letters and diary entries indicate he read this influential work. See, e.g., Rosenzweig to Margrit Rosenstock, February 20, 1921, in *Die "Gritli"-Briefe. Briefe an Margrit Rosenstock-Huessy,* edited by I. Rühle and R. Mayer (Tübingen: Bilam Verlag, 2002) [henceforth, *Gritli-Briefe*], 736, and online, http://www.argobooks.org/gritli/1921.html.

9. von Harnack, *Dogmengeschichte,* Vol. I, p. 203; see also Michael Allen Williams, *Rethinking "Gnosticism": An Argument for Dismantling a Dubious Category* (Princeton, N.J.: Princeton University Press, 1996), 26.

10. Wolfram Kinzig shows how Harnack makes explicit the trajectory he sees leading from Marcion to Luther and on to Schleiermacher as early as his *Preisschrift* of 1870: "He [Harnack] would like to know whether there arose with the subjectivism of a Marcion . . . a historical 'process' that leads over 'the reformatory strivings of the Middle Ages' to the 'Theses of 1517,' and concludes 'with a form of religion' that believes to be able to do without all historical content, and believes to have achieved the true essence of religion with the consciousness of a subjective feeling of dependence on God, and is to be judged as 'the process of the dissolution of the positive Christian religion.' Clearly there shines through in the talk of 'religious' vis-à-

vis 'pious feeling' the religious terminology of Schleiermacher. The object of investigation is set in the philosophy-of-religion categories of interpretation of the nineteenth century," *Harnack, Marcion und das Judentum* (Leipzig: Evangelische Verlagsanstalt, 2004), 45–46.

11. To the best of my knowledge, only two scholars have noticed evidence for Rosenzweig's early so-called Gnostic theology in the published works. In 1988—and without the benefit of numerous revealing texts that have been published since—Wolfgang Ullmann published a masterful but virtually unknown essay, "Die Entdeckung des neuen Denkens: Das Leipziger Religionsgespräch und der Briefwechsel über Judentum und Christentum zwischen Eugen Rosenstock und Franz Rosenzweig," *Stimmstein: Jahrbuch der Eugen Rosenstock-Huessy Gesellschaft* 2 (1988): 147–78, which notes the implicit Gnostic dualism in Rosenzweig's declaration, in his October 31, 1913 letter to Rudolf Ehrenberg, that had he "been able to bolster my dualism of revelation and world with the metaphysical dualism of God and the devil, I would have been unassailable" to Rosenstock's attacks. Irene Kajon also notes that during the *Leipziger Nachtgespräch,* Rosenzweig was "confronted with the inconsistency of his position, which on one side looks to a Gnostic God placed beyond the absurdity of the world, and on the other to a God who reveals Himself, as held by Judaism and Christianity," *Contemporary Jewish Philosophy: An Introduction* (New York: Routledge, 2006), 36.

12. Franz Rosenzweig, "Paralipomena," *Zweistromland. Kleinere Schriften zu Glauben und Denken. Franz Rosenzweig. Der Mensch und sein Werk Gesammelte Schriften III,* edited by Reinhold and Annemarie Mayer (Dordrecht: Martinus Nijhoff, 1984) [Henceforth, *Zweistromland*], 99.

13. Franz Rosenzweig to Margrit Rosenstock-Huessy, February 20, 1921, *Gritli-Briefe,* 736, and online, http://www.argobooks.org/gritli/1921.html. Harnack's monograph on Marcion appeared in the same year as did Rosenzweig's *Star.* For an account of its influence on interwar German theology, see Benjamin Lazier, *God Interrupted: Heresy and the European Imagination between the World Wars* (Princeton, N.J.: Princeton University Press, 2008), 29–33.

14. Rosenzweig, "Paralipomena," 93.

15. Rosenzweig draws a link between the theologies of Marcion and of Barth in his comments on Yehudah HaLevi's poem, "יה אנה אמצאך". The thought "that the distant God is none other than the near, the unknown none other than the revealed, the Creator none other than the Redeemer," is a thought, according to Rosenzweig, that is "forgotten ever anew . . . from Paul and Marcion up to Harnack and Barth," *Der Mensch und sein Werk. Gesammelte Schriften 4. Sprachdenken im Übersetzen: Hymnen und Gedichte des Jehuda Halevi* (Hague, Martinus Nijhoff, 1983), 70. On Barth's response to claims of his Marcionism, see Lazier, *God Interrupted,* 31–32.

16. Rosenzweig to Martin Buber, February 14, 1923, *BT II,* 893. In a letter to Margrit Rosenstock of October 13, 1920, Rosenzweig appears to include the controversial Kierkegaardian theologian Christoph Schrempf among those whose accounts of faith he turned away from after the *Leipziger Nachtgespräch:* "Do you know that I also once had a Schrempf period? He is a good test case. But at a certain point, one then stops and wants never again to be tested. Because he does not *nurture,*" *Gritli Briefe,* 672. For an example of Schrempf's tendency toward a religious view that isolates the individual's relation to God from her worldly situation, see his *Drei Religiöse Reden* (Stuttgart: Frommanns Verlag, 1893), 24: "In religion, we have to do with God, not with orders of the Church, not with the rights of the communities and universities, not with confessions, not with holy Scriptures, not with human authorities, but rather unconditionally and directly with God."

17. Cf. Hans Blumenberg, *The Legitimacy of the Modern Age,* translated by R. Wallace (Cambridge, Mass.: MIT Press, 1983), 129: "The fundamental thought that underlies Mar-

cion's Gnostic dogmatics is, I think, this: A theology that declares its God to be the omnipotent creator of the world and bases its trust in this God on the omnipotence thus exhibited cannot at the same time make the destruction of this world and the salvation of men from the world into the central activity of this God."

18. Rosenzweig to Rudolf Ehrenberg, October 31, 1913, *BT I*, 137.

19. For an introduction to the intellectual exchange between Rosenzweig and Rudolf Ehrenberg, generally, and between *The Star of Redemption* and Ehrenberg's *Schicksal in Predigten* in particular, see Heinz-Jürgen Görtz, "Der Stern der Erlösung als Kommentar: Rudolf Ehrenberg und Franz Rosenzweig," *Rosenzweig als Leser. Kontextuelle Kommentare zum "Stern der Erlösung,"* edited by M. Brasser (Tübingen: Niemeyer, 2004), 119–71.

20. Rudolf Ehrenberg, *Ebr.10, 25. Ein Schicksal in Predigten* (Würzburg: Patmos Verlag, 1920), 114–117.

21. Ibid., 115.

22. Ibid., 117–120.

23. Rosenzweig claims Goethe oscillates between the Protagorean "man is the measure of all things" and the "Nature—surrounded by her" of his own "Natur Fragment." See diary entry of January 11, 1906 in *BT I*, 18.

24. Ibid. According to Mendes-Flohr and Reinharz, the "mild cynicism" articulated in this suggestion that something as fleeting as "mood" could make it possible for the modern individual to occupy such opposing standpoints, "points to a mounting intellectual and spiritual uneasiness," "From Relativism to Religious Faith: The Testimony of Franz Rosenzweig's Unpublished Diaries," *Leo Baeck Institute Year Book* 22 (1977): 162.

25. *BT I*, 56.

26. Diary entry of December 15, 1907, *BT I*, 74.

27. Rosenzweig's diaries of 29.IX.06–4.III.08, Franz Rosenzweig Collection, AR 3001 (typescript of diaries in Series II, Subseries I, Box 1, Folder 21), Leo Baeck Institute, New York, 12. Paul Mendes-Flohr and Jehuda Reinharz offer a helpful introduction to Rosenzweig's early skepticism in "From Relativism to Religious Faith: The Testimony of Franz Rosenzweig's Unpublished Diaries," 162–69.

28. Rosenzweig's diaries of 29.IX.06–4.III.08, Franz Rosenzweig Collection, AR 3001, p. 12.

29. Rosenzweig's diaries of 29.IX.06–4.III.08, Franz Rosenzweig Collection, AR 3001, p. 13.

30. Cf., Sextus Empiricus, *Outlines of Scepticism [Pyrrhonism]*, translated by J. Annas and J. Barnes (Cambridge: Cambridge University Press, 2000), I: 169, p. 41: "The reciprocal mode occurs when what ought to be confirmatory of the object under investigation needs to be made convincing by the object under investigation; then, being unable to take either in order to establish the other, we suspend judgment about both."

31. Rosenzweig's diaries of 29.IX.06–4.III.08, Franz Rosenzweig Collection, AR 3001, p. 14.

32. *BT I*, 74–75.

33. "Die Leitsätze des Baden-Badener Kreises," edited by Wolfgang D. Herzfeld in "Die Leitsätze des Baden-Badener Kreises und das Referat von Franz Rosenzweig auf der Tagung vom 9. Januar 1910 mit dem Titel 'Das 18. Jahrhundert in seinem Verhältnis zum 19ten und zum 20ten,'" *Rosenzweig Jahrbuch 3: Die Idee Europa*, 243.

34. See the collection of letters Rosenzweig wrote leading up to the symposium, in *BT I*, 97–101.

35. Rosenzweig to Franz/Erich Frank, undated, *BT I*, 101.

36. "Die Leitsätze des Baden-Badener Kreises und das Referat von Franz Rosenzweig auf der Tagung vom 9. Januar 1910 mit dem Titel 'Das 18. Jahrhundert in seinem Verhältnis

zum 19ten und zum 20ten,'" edited by Wolfgang D. Herzfeld, *Rosenzweig Jahrbuch 3: Die Idee Europa*, 251–52.

37. Rosenzweig to Hans Ehrenberg, December 28, 1910, *BT I*, 115–16.

38. Ibid., 116.

39. *BT I*, 112.

40. In his "Die Entdeckung des neuen Denkens: Das Leipziger Religionsgespräch und der Briefwechsel über Judentum und Christentum zwischen Eugen Rosenstock und Franz Rosenzweig," *Stimmstein: Jahrbuch der Eugen Rosenstock-Huessy Gesellschaft* 2 (1988): 152, Wolfgang Ullmann notes the Gnostic dualism implicit in the ideas of this diary entry.

41. *BT I*, 420–21.

42. "Der Selbstmord Europas," *Hochland: Monatsschrift für alle Gebiete des Wissens, der Literatur und Kunst* 16, no. 2 (1919): 553, reprinted in *Die Sprache des Menschengeschlechts II* (Heidelberg: Lambert Schneider, 1964), 83.

43. *Gritli-Briefe*, 326, and online, http://www.argobooks.org/gritli/1919.html. The letter continues: "The theme of the Rilkean *Book of the Hours*. The theme of Max Brod (in *Tycho Brahe*, etc. . . .). The theme of the whole Buber circle. The theme of the coffee houses." The texts and trends Rosenzweig lists here may likewise be said to share a concern for the relationship between, or the tension between, God and the world. Explaining how each makes manifest the same theme would exhaust too much space at this juncture. For a study of Buber's and Rosenzweig's thought on the background of the German expressionist aesthetics of their time, see Zachary Braiterman, *The Shape of Revelation: Aesthetics and Modern Jewish Thought* (Stanford, Calif.: Stanford University Press, 2007).

44. Rosenzweig's letter to Rudolf Ehrenberg of July 9, 1917, implies that an unpublished text written by Hans Ehrenberg, which he refers to as "Mephisto," may likewise share in the theme of these three texts. I have been unable to find extant manuscripts of this text.

45. I owe a great debt of gratitude to Dr. Maria Ehrenberg, professor emerita of botany at the University of Würzburg, and daughter of Rudolf Ehrenberg, for entrusting me with what appears to be the penultimate typescript draft of this play.

46. The farcical situation created by each individual's quest for his or her own divinity and collective quests to fuse some of these divinities appear directed to mock the experience the Ehrenbergs and Rosenzweig had at Baden-Baden.

47. Rudolf Ehrenberg, *Halbhunderttag*, unpublished transcribed manuscript, Act II {Act III in the version Rosenzweig read}, 125.

48. Ibid., 131.

49. Ibid., 133.

50. Ibid., Act IV {Act V in the version Rosenzweig read}, 191.

51. Ibid., 215–216.

52. Ibid., Act III {Act IV in the version Rosenzweig read}, 172.

53. Ibid., Act II {Act III in the version Rosenzweig read}, 139–42.

54. Hermann's and Hedwig's decision not to consummate their love physically, but to devote it to the service of the divine is reminiscent of other modern literary adaptations of Gnostic themes. In *The Modern Revival of Gnosticism and Thomas Mann's* Doktor Faustus (Rochester, N.Y.: Camden House, 2002), Kirsten Grimstad cites the influence of Villiers de l'Isle-Adam's *Axel* (1890), in which lovers Axel and Sara renounce the possibility of erotic union, and instead unite in a suicidal negation of the worldly, thereby reenacting a Valentinian rite meant to reunite Sophia with the divine Father. See *Modern Revivial of Gnosticism*, 103–107.

55. Franz Rosenzweig Nachlass, University of Kassel Library (Box G 2, 2).

56. Rudolf Ehrenberg, *Halbhunderttag,* Act III {Act IV in the version Rosenzweig read}, 178.

57. Rudolf Ehrenberg, *Halbhunderttag,* Act IV {Act V in the version Rosenzweig read}, 207–208.

58. The different approaches Hermann and the Religious Leader take in aiming for the same goal may well rest on their respective views of the masses. Cf. Rosenzweig's comment on the two characters, in Rosenzweig to Rudolf Ehrenberg, July 21, 1911: "The greatness of the Cult-leader is that he *understands* the Volk (so that he is indeed one with them, even if he hasn't grown out of them). So he stands on an even-plane over against Hermann, because his *understanding* of the Volk is just as deep as Hermann's *misunderstanding,*" Franz Rosenzweig Nachlass, University of Kassel Library (Box 2, 3).

59. Rudolf Ehrenberg, *Halbhunderttag,* Act IV {Act V in the version Rosenzweig read}, 194.

60. Ibid., 215.

61. In Rosenzweig's comments to Ehrenberg of July 21, 1911, he identifies Hermann's desire for a solitary relation to the divine, with egoism. At the same time, Hermann's desire to love God for now earthly motives provokes Rosenzweig to compare him to the Baal Shem-Tov: "everyone must now notice the main thing that gives him so much pleasure to die. The Baal-Shem legends would express the moral of [Act] 5 [of *Halbhunderttag*] thus: . . . a voice from heaven came to him and announced to him that his part in the "future world" (this, the Jewish expression for eternal blessedness) was taken from him; thereupon, full of joy, [the Baal Shem-Tov said]: I can finally love God aright." Rosenzweig to R. Ehrenberg, July 21, 1911, Franz Rosenzweig Nachlass, (Box G, 2, 3).

62. Rudolf Ehrenberg, *Halbhunderttag,* Act IV {Act V in the version Rosenzweig read}, 221.

63. The extant letters written by Rosenzweig to Rudolf Ehrenberg, from July 12–26, 1911, housed at the Rosenzweig Nachlass at the University of Kassel Library, include both Rosenzweig's comments on *Halbhunderttag* and what appear to be copies of drafts of parts of "The Shechina." But there is little resemblance (besides the characters) between these drafts and the final product.

64. Two copies of "Die Schechina," both written in Rosenzweig's hand, one with the neatness and clarity suggestive of a final draft, are housed in the Nahum Glatzer Collection at Vanderbilt University (Franz Rosenzweig Papers, I. H; Box 2, folder 44). The folder holding the sonnet cycle also holds copies of a handful of letters Hans Ehrenberg wrote to Rosenzweig commenting on the poem and its connections with Rudolf Ehrenberg's *Halbhunderttag.* The file also contains what appear to be the outline for, and the first few pages of a set of Baal-Shem Tov stories that Rosenzweig is apparently poised to compose. I've seen no mention of such stories in any of Rosenzweig's letters.

65. Rosenzweig, "Die Schechina," First Sonnet, lns. 9, 13–14.

66. Ibid., Second Sonnet, lns. 1, 10–12.

67. Ibid., Third Sonnet, lns. 5 ff.

68. Ibid., Fourth Sonnet, lns. 3–4.

69. Ibid., lns. 12–14.

70. Ibid., Fifth Sonnet, lns. 1, 4, 9–14.

71. Ibid., Sixth Sonnet, lns. 2–4, 8–11.

72. Ibid., lns. 12–14 (italics mine—BP).

73. Hans Ehrenberg's comments on Rosenzweig's sonnet-cycle from his letter of September 9, 1911 (held with the poem in the Glatzer Collection Rosenzweig Papers [Box 2, folder 44])

include an attempt to link up particular sonnets with particular acts and scenes from Rudolf Ehrenberg's *Halbhunderttag.*

74. The collection in Kassel is primarily composed of the papers of Franz Rosenzweig kept by his son, Rafael Rosenzweig, until his death, and includes many of the original letters from which the published *Briefe und Tagebücher* was assembled. The collection also contains a significant number of letters written between Rosenzweig and Rudolf Ehrenberg, housed until recently by the Estate of Rudolf Ehrenberg.

75. For a more thorough analysis of this letter, see Benjamin Pollock, "'Within Earshot of the Young Hegel': Rosenzweig's Letter to Rudolf Ehrenberg of September 1910," in *German-Jewish Thought between Religion and Politics: Festschrift in Honor of Paul Mendes-Flohr on the Occasion of His Seventieth Birthday,* edited by Christian Wiese and Martina Urban (Berlin: Walter de Gruyter, 2012), 185–207.

76. Undated letter to Rudolf Ehrenberg, Franz Rosenzweig Nachlass, University of Kassel Library (B 45), 1d–2a (original letter uses folded sheets to create four sides for each page, and numbers each page. I will cite the letter page number with a numeral and the side number with letters a–d).

77. Undated letter to Rudolf Ehrenberg, 5b.

78. Ibid., 7d. Cf. Rosenzweig's letter to Hans Ehrenberg, September 26, 1910: "We today emphasize the practical, the Fall, history, this last not as does Schleiermacher, i.e., as Being set apart in time for the viewing [*Anschauung*] of the spectator, but rather *as act of the actor.* Thus we also refuse to see 'God in history,' because we want to see history (in religious relation) not as image, not as Being; rather, we *deny* God in *it,* in order *to restore* Him in the process through which it *becomes,*" *BT I,* 112.

79. Undated letter to Rudolf Ehrenberg, 7a.

80. Ibid., 7b.

81. Ibid., 8b.

82. Ibid., 9b.

83. Ibid.

84. Rosenzweig's diary entries from September 1910, show he was reading Rilke's *Geschichten vom lieben Gott* at the time, a collection of stories in which divinity does indeed appear in myriad, often surprising guises. See, for example, the diary entry of September 20, 1910, in which Rosenzweig copies down the beginning of "von einem, der die Steine belauscht," and apparently sees fit to compare "Wie der Fingerhut dazu kam, der liebe Gott zu sein" to Buber's *Legends of the Baal Shem-Tov,* in Rosenzweig's diaries of July 31, 1910 to September 21, 1910, Franz Rosenzweig Collection, AR 3001 (typescript of diaries in Series II, Subseries I, Box 1, Folder 22), Leo Baeck Institute, New York, 25–26. On the interest in individuated objects which the early Buber shared with Rilke and other neoromantics, see Zachary Braiterman, *The Shape of Revelation,* 8–9, 72–74.

85. Undated letter to Rudolf Ehrenberg, 11d–12b.

86. Ibid., 12b–12c.

87. Two studies that explore the relationship between love of God and martyrdom are Daniel Boyarin, *Dying for God: Martyrdom and the Making of Christianity and Judaism* (Stanford, Calif.: Stanford University Press, 1999), and Michael Fishbane, *The Kiss of God: Spiritual and Mystical Death in Judaism* (Seattle: University of Washington Press, 1996).

88. Nahum Glatzer, "Introduction," *Franz Rosenzweig: His Life and Thought* (New York: Schocken, 1953), xiv.

89. Rosenzweig to Rudolf Ehrenberg, October 31, 1913, *BT I,* 133.

90. Paul Mendes-Flohr and Jehuda Reinharz, "From Relativism to Religious Faith: The Testimony of Franz Rosenzweig's Unpublished Diaries," *Leo Baeck Institute Year Book* 22 (1977): 161.

91. Stéphane Mosès, *System and Revelation: The Philosophy of Franz Rosenzweig*, translated by Catherine Tihanyi (Detroit: Wayne State University Press, 1992), 34.

92. Eugen Rosenstock, "Prologue/Epilogue to the Letters—Fifty Years Later," in *Judaism Despite Christianity: The "Letters on Christianity and Judaism" between Eugen Rosenstock-Huessy and Franz Rosenzweig*, edited by Eugen Rosenstock-Huessy (New York: Schocken, 1971), 73.

93. *BT I*, 133. We will examine this statement in detail in the following chapter.

94. As I indicated earlier, I view the historical relativism of Rosenzweig's Baden-Baden phase as an attempt to unify self and world within the historical moment. But if one wanted to continue to hold that the relativism Rosenzweig identifies in his October 31, 1913 letter is historical relativism, this seems plausible so long as one takes historical relativism as grounded in (or as a sub-case of) subjectivism.

95. Franz Rosenzweig, *Der Stern der Erlösung* (Frankfurt am Main: Suhrkamp, 1996), 117.

2. CHRISTIAN "WORLD-ACTIVITY" AND THE HISTORICAL RECONCILIATION OF SOUL AND WORLD

1. *BT I*, 346.

2. Franz Rosenzweig, *Hegel und der Staat I: Lebensstationen* (Munich/Berlin: Oldenbourg, 1920), 75. Rosenzweig's portrait of the young Hegel is likely influenced by Wilhelm Dilthey's *Die Jungendgeschichte Hegels*. See, for example, the sub-chapter "Das Schicksal Jesu und die Religion seiner Gemeinde" in the edition published in Dilthey's *Gesammelte Schriften* IV (Stuttgart: B.G. Teubner, 1959), 107–117.

3. In Hegel's day, the diagnosis of "hypochondria" described not the anxiety over possible or imagined illness, but rather a general melancholy or anxiety, often seen as the male counterpart to female hysteria. See Esther Fischer-Homberger, "Hypochondriasis of the Eighteenth Century—Neurosis of the Present Century," *Bulletin of the History of Medicine* 46, no. 4 (July–August 1972), 391–401.

4. Franz Rosenzweig, *Hegel und der Staat I*, 101. Rosenzweig here cites a manuscript, likely written by Hegel between 1822 and 1825, that was later published as "Fragment zur Philosophie des Geistes." See G. W .F. Hegel, *Werke 11: Berliner Schriften 1818–1831* (Frankfurt/Main: Suhrkamp, 1970), 537.

5. Franz Rosenzweig, *Hegel und der Staat I*, 102. For the source Rosenzweig cites, see Hegel to Windischmann, May 27, 1810, *Briefe von und an Hegel. Band 1: 1785–1812*, edited by J. Hoffmeister (Hamburg: Felix Meiner, 1952), 314.

6. Rosenzweig, *Hegel und der Staat I*, 70.

7. Ibid., 85. Rosenzweig cites manuscript drafts of Hegel's "Spirit of Christianity and Its Fate," but compare, G. W. F. Hegel, "Der Geist des Christentums und sein Schicksal," *Werke 1. Frühe Schriften* (Frankfurt am Main: Suhrkamp, 1971), 402–403.

8. G. W. F. Hegel, "Der Geist des Christentums und sein Schicksal," 400–401, cited in part by Rosenzweig, *Hegel und der Staat I*, 87.

9. Rosenzweig to Gertrud Oppenheim, September 28, *BT I*, 120. The comment suggests that Rosenzweig was in fact waiting expectantly for an experience like that of the Leipzig night-conversation to happen to him!

10. Cf. Pierre Bouretz, *Witnesses for the Future,* translated by M. Smith (Baltimore: Johns Hopkins University Press, 2010), 109: "To choose to use one's strength against the world, or to fall in line with it in one's time: for Rosenzweig, this was the issue whose resolution organized the entire Hegelian approach."

11. Rosenzweig, *Hegel und der Staat I,* 98, 97.

12. Franz Rosenzweig, *Hegel und der Staat II: Weltepochen* (Munich/Berlin: Oldenbourg, 1920), 79.

13. By the end of 1913, Rosenzweig is describing "world-history" not as a process immanent to the world, but rather as a process of interaction between God and human beings that extends from out of an absolute beginning in creation toward an absolute end in redemption. See his letter to Hans Ehrenberg, December 6, 1913: "In that one constructs *World-history* . . . one sets absolute beginning and absolute end—but (in complete contrast to biography) a beginning or rather an end, before or rather after which it is impossible for a *Nothing* to be thought; because it is just *absolute* beginning and *absolute* end, i.e., climbing out of and entering into the Absolute. Thereby the absolute powers themselves become co-starring personae in world-history. Objectivity, which otherwise can become biographied-forth, is here not to be eliminated, and a 'history of man' forbids itself. I mean thus: you set there [in Hans Ehrenberg's *History of Man of Our Times*] the struggle between the reason and the faith of man, and I believe one must and can only present the struggle between man and God, thus—excuse the hard expression—Church-history," *BT I,* 144–45.

14. Ibid., 133.

15. Paul Mendes-Flohr's "Rosenzweig and Kant: Two Views of Ritual and Religion," *Divided Passions: Jewish Intellectuals and the Experience of Modernity* (Detroit: Wayne State University Press, 1991), 283–309, offers a brief account of Rosenzweig's crisis which, while still depicting Rosenzweig's conversion as a turn toward faith, is at once sensitive to Rosenzweig's dualistic leanings: "Had Rosenzweig's relativism indeed been, as suggested, a Kantian critical relativism, then we may assume that the dualism between God and the devil refers to a radical separation between God and the world *qua* the sovereign realm of evil. Rosenzweig was, however, ultimately prevented from endorsing such a dualism 'because,' as he says, 'of the first sentence of the Bible.' God created the world and beheld it was good. An abiding, naïve faith did not permit him to deny the possibility of God's relationship to creation. In the conversation of July 1913 Rosenstock-Huessy apparently convinced Rosenzweig that God may speak to man, that 'faith based on revelation' was a tenable position for a man of critical awareness" (292). Wolfgang Ullmann suggests some interesting parallels to Rosenzweig's own Marcionism when he discusses Rosenzweig's ultimate decision to turn away from it on the basis of the first sentence of the Bible: "We know how it looked when it was decided differently than as by Rosenzweig. Then one must explain friend and foe as the ground-categories of politics with Carl Schmitt; and one must set as the order of the day the meaninglessness of the Old Testament for the Church with neo-Protestantism, and the criminalization of the Russian October revolution with liberal historiography," "Die Entdeckung des neuen Denkens: Das Leipziger Religionsgespräch und der Briefwechsel über Judentum und Christentum zwischen E. Rosenstock und F. Rosenzweig," *Stimmstein: Jahrbuch der Eugen Rosenstock-Huessy Gesellschaft* 2 (1988): 154.

16. Franz Rosenzweig, "Paralipomena," *Zweistromland. Kleinere Schriften zu Glauben und Denken. Franz Rosenzweig. Der Mensch und sein Werk Gesammelte Schriften III,* edited by Reinhold and Annemarie Mayer (Dordrecht: Martinus Nijhoff, 1984), 99.

17. *BT II,* 680.

18. Rosenzweig to Margrit Rosenstock-Huessy, June 30, 1919, *Gritli-Briefe,* 356.

19. *BT I,* 133.

20. Rosenzweig to Margrit Rosenstock-Huessy, March 16, 1918, *Gritli-Briefe,* 61.

21. *BT I,* 134.

22. See Franz Rosenzweig to Eugen Rosenstock, August 13, 1917, *Gritli-Briefe,* 20–22.

23. *BT I,* 420–21.

24. See for example, "Vierte Rede in der Ritterschaft vom heiligen Georg am 18 Januar dem Gründungstage des Deutschen Reichs," 6, in "Die Sankt Georgs Reden," on *The Collected Works of Eugen Rosenstock-Huessy on DVD.* The "Sermons of St. George" were a series of imagined sermons to a tight-knit religious brotherhood that Rosenstock composed in 1915–1916, while serving on the Western war front.

25. Eugen Rosenstock, "Angewandte Seelenkunde," *Die Sprache des Menschengeschlechts: eine Leibhaftige Grammatik in vier Teilen* (Heidelberg: Lambert Schneider, 1963), Vol. 1, 781–82.

26. Franz Rosenzweig, "'Urzelle' des Stern der Erlösung," *Zweistromland,* 125–26; translated into English in Franz Rosenzweig, *Philosophical and Theological Writings,* translated by Paul W. Franks and Michael L. Morgan (Indianapolis: Hackett, 2000), 49–50.

27. See Eugen Rosenstock, *Soziologie I: Die Kräfte der Gemeinschaft* (Berlin/Leipzig: Walter de Gruyter, 1925), e.g., 125, 128.

28. Cf., Eugen Rosenstock, *Ja und Nein: Autobiographische Fragmente* (Heidelberg: Lambert Schneider, 1968), 15: "There is history only in the time reckoning for which Jesus is the standard of measure." See likewise Eugen Rosenstock, *Die Hochzeit des Kriegs und der Revolution* (Würzburg: Patmos, 1920), 290: With the "beginning of our reckoning of time" in "the sacrifice of Christ, . . . world history begins—the return of the world under God's rule. Christ strides through time and fulfills it, in that he forces the natural chaos into form through the force of the Cross." See likewise Eugen Rosenstock, *Soziologie* I, 209: "Thus the carriers of Christianity, supported by Judaism, become the carriers of world-history, as far as this is not eternal death and murder, but rather world-transformation."

29. Rosenstock, *Ja und Nein,* 21.

30. Rudolf Ehrenberg, *Ebr.10, 25. Ein Schicksal in Predigten* (Würzburg: Patmos Verlag, 1920), 115.

31. *BT II,* 642–43.

32. *Gritli-Briefe,* 111.

33. The German term *Umkehr* (literally "turn-around"), which I translate above as "reversal," is closely related to one of the German terms for conversion, *Bekehrung,* and the Grimm *Deutsches Wörterbuch* suggests *Umkehr* derives from the Middle High German word *Umbkehr,* linking the word even closer to conversion. I treat the philosophical role of *Umkehr* in Rosenzweig's *Star* in chapter 4 of my *Franz Rosenzweig and the Systematic Task of Philosophy,* but I do not address there the relation of the term to conversion.

34. Rosenzweig, *The Star of Redemption,* 267/257.

35. For thoughtful comparisons of the mature grammatical philosophies of Rosenstock and Rosenzweig, see Robert Gibbs, *Correlations in Rosenzweig and Levinas* (Princeton, N.J.: Princeton University Press, 1992), 62–79, and Martin Brasser, "Rosenstock und Rosenzweig über Sprache: Die *Angewandte Seelenkunde* im *Stern der Erlösung,*" in *Rosenzweig als Leser, Kontextuelle Kommentare zum "Stern der Erlösung"* (Tübingen: Niemeyer Verlag, 2004), 173–207.

36. See Rosenstock, *Ja und Nein,* 67.

37. Franz Rosenzweig to Eugen Rosenstock, August 13, 1917, *"Gritli-Briefe,"* 21–22.

38. Eugen Rosenstock, "Prologue/Epilogue to the Letters—Fifty Years Later," *Judaism Despite Christianity: The "Letters on Christianity and Judaism" between Eugen Rosenstock-Huessy and Franz Rosenzweig,* edited by Eugen Rosenstock-Huessy (New York: Schocken, 1971), 74.

39. *BT I,* 133–34.

40. Nahum N. Glatzer, "Introduction," *Franz Rosenzweig: Life and Thought* (New York: Schocken, 1953), xv.

41. Eugen Rosenstock, "Biblionomica," *Ja und Nein,* 155.

42. Compare Rosenstock's recollection of the impression he made upon Rosenzweig in *Ja und Nein,* 70: "If there were even only one German University-instructor, who saw prayer as just as immediate, no for much more immediate and more true than the little cathedral-thinking, who ascribed more force and meaning to a command [*Geheiss*] than to a concept, then there was thus in fact a victory over Greekdom with the coming of Christ. Then there was thus not only Christianity as struggle against Judaism, but rather also against the academic-platonic world of mere thinking. Then however there must have been for him, the Jew Rosenzweig, and me, the Christian, a common language and where possible, a common history."

43. Rosenzweig to Eugen Rosenstock, August 13, 1917, *Gritli-Briefe,* 21.

44. *BT I,* 133.

45. Glatzer's account of the night-conversation does imply that Rosenstock communicates his own "simple faith" to Rosenzweig through a kind of revelation of a secret. He writes that, over the course of the night-conversation, "Rosenzweig asked: what would you do when all answers fail? Rosenstock replied, with the simplicity of faith: I would go to the next church, kneel and try to pray. These simple words did more than all the previous discussions . . . to convince Rosenzweig that Christianity was a living power in the world," in Nahum N. Glatzer, "Introduction," *Franz Rosenzweig: Life and Thought,* xv.

46. Franz Rosenzweig to Eugen Rosenstock, September 4, 1917, in *Gritli-Briefe,* 28–29.

47. On Rosenzweig's post–7.7.13 sense that he had previously been using his views on religion as some form of "alibi," see also the comment in his "Paralipomena," 93: "The destruction of my praescriptio alibi on 7.7.13 was really my de-Schleiermachization." Rosenzweig may be using Schleiermacher here to designate a kind of passive religiosity of *feeling,* away from which he turned in 1913 when he began to take Christian "action" seriously. But since *Schleiermacher* also means "veil-maker," Rosenzweig is likely punning here: a religiosity of feeling was a way for Rosenzweig to fool himself, to "veil" from himself whatever it was he was permitting himself for so long as he believed that action in the world had no value.

48. Eugen Rosenstock, "Prologue/Epilogue to the Letters—Fifty Years Later," *Judaism Despite Christianity,* 73.

49. Compare W. Ullmann, "Die Entdeckung des neuen Denkens. Das Leipziger Religionsgespräch und der Briefwechsel über Judentum und Christentum zwischen Eugen Rosenstock und Franz Rosenzweig," *Stimmstein* 2 (1988): 155: "Rosenzweig also tells us that it was not Rosenstock's position, but rather he [Rosenstock] himself who forced him to leave the path of historicism."

50. Rosenstock's organized the sermons of "Die Sankt Georgs Reden" according to the yearly calendar, taking up a theme in each sermon that related to the natural, historical, personal, and spiritual significance of that date in the course of the year. About one-third of the planned speeches can be found on the *Eugen Rosenstock-Huessy Collected Works DVD.* An outline for these speeches can be found in Eugen Rosenstock to Franz Rosenzweig, November 26, 1916, *BT I,* 311–312. In his 1916 reports to Rosenzweig about such philosophizing "in calendar-form," Rosenstock claims that this fourfold perspective on each date of the calendar

depicts how "one finds oneself in every month in the *Crux,*" that "this 'Four of Actuality,' this *crux cogitanda* can, should, and must be thought at every moment." Eugen Rosenstock to Franz Rosenzweig, November 26, 1916, *BT I,* 311–312.

51. Eugen Rosenstock, "Volkstaat und Reich Gottes," *Europa und die Christenheit* (Kempten/Munich, 1919), 26–27.

52. Eugen Rosenstock, "Zur Ausbildung des mittelalterlichen Festkalenders," *Archiv für Kulturgeschichte* 10 (1912): 272.

53. Ibid., 280–81.

54. Eugen Rosenstock to Franz Rosenzweig, May 29, 1916, *BT I,* 191.

55. Franz Rosenzweig to Eugen Rosenstock, June 8, 1916, *BT I,* 193.

56. Franz Rosenzweig to Margrit Rosenstock, June 13, 1919, *Gritli-Briefe,* 326.

57. Cf. Rosenzweig to Eugen Rosenstock, June 21, 1919, *Gritli-Briefe,* 338: "And just because you earlier (say, in Halbhunderttag—please take for yourself the exemplar that Hans has; it's there in the book-cabinet in the hall), thus, because you had rejected it so sharply earlier, for this reason it was now so striking."

58. Rosenzweig to Eugen Rosenstock, August 13, 1917, *Gritli-Briefe,* 21–22.

59. *Gritli-Briefe,* 626–27; *BT II,* 675. In *Judaism Despite Christianity,* the English-language publication of the 1916 correspondence between Rosenzweig and Rosenstock which Rosenstock edited and published first in 1969, this letter to Margrit Rosenstock is quoted at the end of Rosenstock's "Prologue to the Letters," and it includes the sentence I've placed here within curly brackets (citing "an unpublished letter," *Judaism Despite Christianity,* 76). This sentence does not appear, however, in any of the German-language publications of Rosenzweig's letters. I suspect this sentence was not part of the original, but I have not inspected the original handwritten letter to verify.

60. See, for example, Rivka Horwitz, "Warum liess Rosenzweig sich nicht taufen?" *Der Philosoph Franz Rosenzweig (1886–1929),* edited by Wolfdietrich Schmied-Kowarzik (Freiburg: Alber, 1988), 87: "In the course of this night [i.e., July 7, 1913], he communicated to his friends that he was ready to convert. His promise led to a crisis. . . ."

61. Relying in part on the research of Edwin Starbuck, William James famously spoke of a "crisis of self-surrender" as central to religious conversion. See his *The Varieties of Religious Experience: A Study in Human Nature* (New York: Penguin, 1982), 205–216.

62. Franz Rosenzweig, "Paralipomena," Franz Rosenzweig Collection, AR 3001 (Manuscript in Series II, Subseries III:D, Box 2, Folders 39–40), Leo Baeck Institute, Center for Jewish History, New York, p. 18a. The published version in *Zweistromland,* 98, is missing the reference to "Fridugisus [d.] 834."

63. Harnack had identified as basic to Gnostic doctrine the belief in matter as an independent and eternal ground of evil that was opposed to divine, real being. See Adolf von Harnack, *Lehrbuch der Dogmengeschichte,* Vol. I (Freiburg: Mohr-Siebeck, 1886), 168, 190–91.

64. Franz Rosenzweig, "Paralipomena," Franz Rosenzweig Collection, AR 3001 (Manuscript in Series II, Subseries III: D, Box 2, Folders 39–40), Leo Baeck Institute, Center for Jewish History, New York, 21a.

65. Tertullian, *Adversus Marcionem,* edited and translated by E. Evans (London: Oxford University Press, 1972), II.5, 101.

66. Ibid., II.6, 100, 101.

67. Ibid., 101.

68. Ibid., 105.

69. Rosenzweig, "Paralipomena," *Zweistromland,* 63.

70. See note 63, above, regarding Harnack's claim that the belief in matter as an independent metaphysical ground was central to Gnostic doctrine.

71. Rosenzweig, "Paralipomena," *Zweistromland,* 81–82.

72. Rosenzweig may be drawing here on a Bratslaver idea introduced by Martin Buber in his *Die Geschichten des Rabbi Nachman,* first published in 1906. See, for example, the saying entitled "Purpose of the World": "The world was only created for the sake of the choice and the one who chooses. The human being, the master of the choice, should say: the whole world was only created for my sake. Thus every human being should take care and see to it that he redeem the world and fill its lacks at every time and at every place," *Die Geschichten des Rabbi Nachman* (Frankfurt am Main: Ruetten u. Loening, 1920), 36.

73. Ibid., 82.

74. Elsewhere, Rosenzweig reiterates the monumental character of human decision in equally striking terms. Thus, in a November 1916 note in the "Paralipomena," Rosenzweig suggests God has "set the man in the bottleneck [*Engpass*] of this one but absolute decision," i.e., that "between 'life' and 'death,'" *Zweistromland,* 104. And in an August 2, 1917 letter to Gertrud Oppenheim, Rosenzweig asserts, "He who has not yet come to this crossroads of *Yes* and *No,* is just in the real sense not yet a man, he is still 'speechless' like nature," *BT I,* 427.

75. Rosenstock, *Ja und Nein,* 21.

76. Hans Blumenberg's account of Augustine's response to the problem of evil—one which Blumenberg views as part and parcel of Augustine's turning away from Gnosticism—makes for an instructive parallel and precursor to Rosenzweig's account of human freedom under the conditions of monotheism (just as it of course shares much in common with Tertullian's response to Marcion cited earlier in this section): "In the aftermath of Gnosticism, the problem of the justification of God has become overwhelming, and that justification is accomplished at the expense of man, to whom a new concept of freedom is ascribed expressly in order to let the whole of an enormous responsibility and guilt be imputed to it. . . . The premise of human freedom allows Augustine to interpret the deficiencies of the world not as an original failure of the construction of the world for man's benefit but rather as the result of God's subsequent intervention in His work in order to put nature in the service of justice with respect to man," *The Legitimacy of the Modern Age* (Cambridge, Mass: MIT Press, 1983) 133. Blumenberg suggests, however, that Augustine's transferring of responsibility for the world's lack of order from God to the human being left a legacy of resignation rather than action: "The price of this preservation of the cosmos was not only the guilt that man was supposed to assign himself for the condition in which he found the world but also the resignation that his responsibility for that condition imposed upon him: renunciation of any attempt to change for his benefit, through action, a reality for the adversity of which he had himself to blame. The senselessness of self-assertion was the heritage of the Gnosticism which was not overcome but only 'translated'" (136).

77. Rosenzweig to Rudolf Ehrenberg, January 27, 1917, *BT I,* 341.

78. Rosenzweig to Rudolf Ehrenberg, February 23, 1917, *BT I,* 351–52.

79. Ricarda Huch, *Luthers Glaube: Briefe an einen Freund,* in *Gesammelte Werke* Bd. 7: *Schriften zur Religion und Weltanschauung,* edited by W. Emrich (Köln/Berlin: Kiepenheuer & Witsch, 1968), 127.

80. Ibid.

81. Ibid., 131.

82. Ibid., 257: "As he [Luther] very often told, he experienced the greatest temptation, that of Lucifer, through the spirit, terrible in itself, which drives man to equate himself with God.

It is characteristic that the outbreak of his melancholy began with his entry into the cloister, a separation. He appeared to feel that he must come purely in loneliness with his self."

83. Ibid., 257–58.

3. *"ICH BLEIBE ALSO JUDE"*

1. Stéphane Mosès, *System and Revelation: The Philosophy of Franz Rosenzweig,* translated by Catherine Tihanyi (Detroit: Wayne State University Press, 1992), 35.

2. Paul Mendes-Flohr, "Franz Rosenzweig and the German Philosophical Tradition," in *The Philosophy of Franz Rosenzweig* (Hanover/London: University Press of New England for Brandeis University Press, 1988), 6.

3. Eugen Rosenstock, "Prologue/Epilogue to the Letters—Fifty Years Later," in *Judaism Despite Christianity: The "Letters on Christianity and Judaism" between Eugen Rosenstock-Huessy and Franz Rosenzweig,* edited by Eugen Rosenstock-Huessy (New York: Schocken, 1971), 74.

4. Nahum N. Glatzer, "Franz Rosenzweig: The Story of a Conversion," *Judaism* I, no. 1 (1952). 69–79.

5. Glatzer published an early account of Rosenzweig's life and thought in Yiddish in 1945, "Franz Rosenzweig: His Life and His Ideas," in a special printing of the *YIVO Bleter, shrift fun yidishn wisenshaftlekhen institut,* 2, xxv (1945): 3–39.

6. Nahum N. Glatzer, *Franz Rosenzweig: His Life and Thought* (New York: Schocken, 1953), xvii, 25.

7. Ibid., xviii.

8. Ibid. In a footnote in his Yiddish article of 1945, Glatzer writes that he "has the information directly from Adele Rosenzweig, Franz Rosenzweig's mother" (7), although he does not make clear which aspects of his reconstruction he may have taken from Rosenzweig's mother and which not. In his "Introduction" to *Franz Rosenzweig: Life and Thought,* Glatzer writes, "His alert mother realized immediately the connection between her son's attendance at the Day of Atonement service and his new attitude, and later confided this conclusion of hers to the present writer. But the mother's contention could only be convincing if confirmed by some internal evidence" (xviii). I have been unable to find reference to the events of 1913 in the letters Adele Rosenzweig wrote to Glatzer in the late 1920s and 1930s, housed at the Glatzer library at Vanderbilt University.

9. Franz Rosenzweig, *Der Stern der Erlösung* (Frankfurt am Main: Suhrkamp, 1996), 363–64.

10. Glatzer, *Franz Rosenzweig: His Life and Thought,* xvii, xix.

11. Deviating slightly from Glatzer's master account is Rivka Horwitz's "Warum liess Rosenzweig sich nicht taufen?" *Der Philosoph Franz Rosenzweig (1886–1929) I* (Freiburg/Munich: Alber, 1988). Although she claims to have been informed by Bruno Strauss that Rosenzweig indeed attended the "Potsdam Bridge" synagogue in Berlin for the Day of Atonement, 1913, she concludes—based on a careful reading of Rosenzweig's letter to Rudolf Ehrenberg of August 25, 1919—that Rosenzweig had already decided not to go through with his conversion several days before the Day of Atonement that year. Horwitz nevertheless suggests that "Rosenzweig was probably very impressed and strengthened by this experience" (88), even if it did not precipitate his *volte face.* In 1979, in a letter to the editor of *Jewish Spectator* (44), p. 60, Jakob Petuchowski criticizes the standard story of Rosenzweig's return to Judaism, retold in the prior issue of the journal, based on the information from B. Strauss that Horwitz transmitted. Chiding the journal for repeating "the much retold, but completely unproved,

story that Franz Rosenzweig's decision not to convert to Christianity, and to devote his life to Jewish learning-and-living 'was made under the impact of the Yom Kippur *davenning* he witnessed in a small Beth Medrash of Ostjuden in Berlin,'" Petuchowski notes that his grandfather Marcus Petuchowski had in fact been the rabbi of the "Potsdam Bridge" synagogue in which Rosenzweig had, according to Strauss, prayed on Yom Kippur of 1913. But this synagogue, J. Petuchowski points out, quoting Max Sinasohn's *Die Berliner Privatsynagogen und ihre Rabbiner 1671–1971* (Jerusalem, 1971, 87), "'was, at the time, considered to be a millionaires' synagogue,'" and not a small *shtiebel* for Orthodox East European Jews. "Nothing would be lost," Petuchowski concludes, "if we were to 'occidentalize' our retelling of the well-known story." By 2006, Horwitz no longer considered a Yom Kippur experience to have played any role in Rosenzweig's return. She writes, "there was no specific Yom Kippur experience. This day was important for him; he had also fasted the year before; and he describes this day in extraordinary colors in *The Star*. Yet, as far as we can see, Yom Kippur played no specific role in 1913. Rosenzweig's return was a gradual process that took a number of months," "From Hegelianism to a Revolutionary Understanding of Judaism: Franz Rosenzweig's Attitude towards Kabbalah and Myth," *Modern Judaism* 26, no. 1 (2006): 48.

12. Compare, e.g., Nahum Glatzer's foreword to the Hallo English translation of *The Star of Redemption* (Notre Dame: University of Notre Dame Press, 1971), x: "it is essential to realize that this turning point [i.e., 1913] was determined not by objective, theoretical speculation but by a personal need." See Peter Eli Gordon's "Rosenzweig Redux: The Reception of German-Jewish Thought," *Jewish Social Studies* 8, no. 1 (2001): 1–57, for a sensitive reflection on Glatzer's tendency to overemphasize "life" over "thought" in his account of Rosenzweig. Steven Schwarzschild and Moshe Schwarz are noteworthy for having resisted this tendency. See Schwarzschild's "Franz Rosenzweig and Existentialism," *Yearbook of the CCAR* 62 (1953), noted in the Introduction above. See also Moshe Schwarz's *From Myth to Revelation* (Tel Aviv: Bar-Ilan University and HaKibutz HaMeuchad, 1978), 203: "Rosenzweig was about to convert to Christianity in 1913, but as becomes clear from his letters, avoided taking this fateful step, not only, as is often thought, because of a deep Jewish religious-experience which he had on the eve of his baptism to Christianity on Yom Kippur in an ultra-Orthodox synagogue of Polish Jews, but rather even because of a spiritual-philosophical transformation that occurred to him in that same time."

13. *BT I*, 132. As early as 1970, Dan Clawson—then an undergraduate student studying with Steven Schwarzschild—pointed out how Rosenzweig's insistence on having arrived at his decision through reflection contradicted Glatzer's claim that Rosenzweig's decision "betrays a certainty that does not come to a man through thinking; it points to a profound, instantaneous event." Clawson responds as follows: "But what then of the prolonged and thorough self-explanation Rosenzweig mentions above? And what then of the three months of struggle?" "Rosenzweig on Judaism and Christianity," *Judaism* (Winter 1970): 94. I'd like to thank Dr. Clawson for sharing his recollections with me regarding Schwarzschild's attitude toward trends in the American reception of Rosenzweig.

14. *BT II*, 963.

15. Rosenzweig to Martin Buber, July 16, 1924, *BT II*, 979. See note 33 in chapter 2 above regarding the German term *Umkehr*.

16. See the discussion in chapter 1 above of Rosenzweig's account of his early theology in terms of Barthianism and Marcionism. Given Rosenzweig's aligning of Barth with Marcion, Barth's own impression of the Patmos group to which Rosenzweig belonged is quite humorous. See Samuel Moyn, *Origins of the Other: Emmanuel Levinas between Revelation and Ethics*

(Ithaca, N.Y.: Cornell University Press, 2005), 130: "Karl Barth, when he recalled his own flirtation with this so-called Patmos group of young thinkers, noted that he avoided full affiliation because the circle 'wanted to overwhelm me and choke me with its Gnosticism.' Relentlessly attacked himself in the Weimar period for his 'Gnostic' overestimation of God's transcendence of the world, Barth found in the Patmos circle a group, including Rosenzweig, that was even more monomaniacal than he was in their insistence on the centrality of revelation to theology."

17. Although there is no record of Rosenzweig writing about a 1913 Yom Kippur experience, he does discuss a Yom Kippur experience he had in the Hidesheimer synagogue in 1914, in a letter to his parents dated September 22, 1917. "I really had to smile about my great piety in the Hildesheimer Temple. I was there in 1914 over the High Holidays (when I was in the Virchow-hospital), because it is by far the most beautiful prayer service in Berlin, even an Almemor [a central *Bima*] in the synagogue—an exception in Berlin. I remained in Kol Nidre because I wanted to see once whether here there were really some who stayed the whole night: some stayed, then the lamps were shut out, and finally there was still a small group reading enormous tomes by the great wax candle—a pittoresque picture, which I observed to the end. But then about an hour or an hour and a half after the end of the prayer service they also left; I don't believe this 'act' will contribute to my active-account in Heaven" (*BT I*, 446–47). It is noteworthy that there is no mention of the "Yom Kippur experience" in Rosenstock's 1935 introduction to the 1916 correspondence. Only in 1969 does Rosenstock write that "As he was to learn later, his outburst in the Lagerlöf debate had shaken Franz' agnosticism to the extent that in the months from June to September, 1913 Franz was resolved to become a Christian, and to confess as radically as Eugen had to a faith in the revealed, living God. But in September, 1913 Franz attended services of the highest Jewish holidays, and his participation in this act of divine worship convinced him, much to his own surprise, that he could remain, that he would *have to remain*, a Jew—but on a different basis than before. He was, in effect, converted to Judaism as the guiding force in his life. But Eugen, and the point is worth repeating, knew nothing of the intense resolve to which his confession of faith in the Leipzig conversation had given rise, nor of its later modification by Franz' visit to the Jewish place of worship" (*Judaism Despite Christianity*, 74). In the absence of any earlier mention of it, one is tempted to conclude that Rosenstock adopted Glatzer's own account of the Yom Kippur experience here (perhaps unconsciously) and integrated it into his own.

18. *BT I*, 133–34.

19. See the discussion in chapter 2, above. Cf. Rosenzweig to Margrit Rosenstock-Huessy, March 16, 1918, *Gritli-Briefe*, 61: "Up until that Leipzig night . . . I let Christianity count only as 'persecuted Church' [*ecclesia pressa*]; . . . and the year 313, when it became a state-religion, counted as a fall. So I gave the true Church the look of the synagogue."

20. *BT I*, 107.

21. Paul Mendes-Flohr, "Franz Rosenzweig and the German Philosophical Tradition," 6.

22. Wolfdietrich Schmied-Kowarzik, "Einführendes zu Leben und Werk von Franz Rosenzweig," *Rosenzweig im Gespräch mit Ehrenberg, Cohen, und Buber* (Munich: Alber, 2006), 17–18.

23. Glatzer, *Franz Rosenzweig: His Life and Thought*, xiv.

24. *BT I*, 132–33.

25. Ibid., 34.

26. Ibid., 134.

27. Ibid., 131.

28. *Gritli-Briefe*, 528.

29. *BT I*, 129.

30. Rosenzweig's account of the formation of Catholic doctrine out of a struggle with Marcionism finds its precedent—along with the theological views he regularly assigns to Marcion and Gnostics—in Harnack, and in Harnack's *Dogmengeschichte* in particular. But see Harnack's summary statement in *Wesen des Christentums* (Leipzig: JC Hinrichs, 1902), 129: "If one designates by 'Catholic' the church of doctrine and of law, then it came into being, at that time, in the struggle with Gnosticism." Cf. Hans Blumenberg, *The Legitimacy of the Modern Age*, translated by R. Wallace (Cambridge, Mass.: MIT Press, 1983), 130: "Harnack had advanced the thesis that 'Catholicism was constructed in opposition to Marcion.' Taken more broadly, this corresponds to the thesis that the formation of the Middle Ages can only be understood as an attempt at the definitive exclusion of the Gnostic syndrome."

31. Cf. Franz Rosenzweig to Rudolf Ehrenberg, October 1916: "One can get to know Gnosis out of Tertullian, which is amazingly interesting, in each and every relation. This one struggle teaches about how the Church's sticking to the connection with the Old Testament is constitutive for it up to the present day," *BT I*, 240.

32. Wolfgang Ullmann has recognized the role of Marcionism in Rosenzweig's decision to remain a Jew, just as he recognized Rosenzweig's preoccupation with Marcionism in the period leading up to the *Leipziger Nachtgespräch:* "Rosenzweig reports how in view of the reading of the writings of Tertullian's *Against Marcion* it occurred to him that it was not the Council dogmas of the fourth–eighth centuries but rather the anti-Gnostic confession of the first and second centuries that established the substantial content of the Christian dogma, that in Christ the son of the Creator is invoked as Lord. And he dares from here out to outline the breathtaking perspective of a concordance of Christian and Jewish history of dogma," "Die Entdeckung des neuen Denkens: Das Leipziger Religionsgespräch und der Briefwechsel über Judentum und Christentum zwischen Eugen Rosenstock und Franz Rosenzweig," *Stimmstein: Jahrbuch der Eugen Rosenstock-Huessy Gesellschaft* 2 (1988): 163.

33. *BT I*, 131.

34. Ibid., 136.

35. Franz Rosenzweig, "Paralipomena," *Zweistromland*, 106.

36. *BT I*, 401–402.

37. Compare Rosenzweig's later insistence on the Jewish character of *The Star of Redemption*, when he writes to Hans Ehrenberg, on July 6, 1919: "Above all, the whole concept of 'redemption,' which I posit as foundational [*wie ich ihn zugrundelege*], is un-Christian. . . . For the Christian, Christ (the one who has come) is indeed Redeemer and Revealer at once. The sharp holding-apart of the two concepts is Jewish. But my whole structure is actually based on this distinction," *BT I*, 637–38. I discuss this letter in some detail in chapter 4.

38. *BT I*, 412.

39. See my discussions in chapter 4, below of Augustine, *City of God*, VII: 32 and Tertullian, *Adversus Marcionem* III.2. A note Rosenzweig writes while reading Tertullian suggests he views the promise–fulfillment relationship Church fathers like Irenaeus and Tertullian assign to the Old and New Testament as drawing on the legacy of Paul: "Tertullian I,21, very nice how he here demonstrates just out of the *struggle* of Paul against the law the continuity of the revealed concept of God by him. Indeed, the whole predicament of Marcion actually stands in the appeal to Paul. Because in Paul's repudiation of the Old Testament there stands at once just its preservation (*tollere = conservare* [to abolish = to conserve])," "Paralipomena," *Zweistromland*, 99.

40. Cf., Adolf von Harnack, *Lehrbuch der Dogmengeschichte* (Freiburg: Mohr/Siebeck, 1886), 489: "Now, the struggle with the Gnostics and with Marcion and the creation of a New Testament had to have a double consequence. On the one hand, the thesis: 'the Father of Jesus Christ is the Creator of the world and the God of the Old Testament' demanded the strictest carrying-through of the idea of the unity of the two Testaments. The traditional apologetic view of the Old Testament had to experience accordingly the strictest elaboration. On the other hand, in the moment when the New Testament was created, the insight was unavoidable that this Testament was superior to the Older—the view of the newness of Christian life which the Gnostics and Marcion had carried through was thus in some way to be presented and grounded. We now also see the Early Church fathers in the process of the solution to this double task, and the way they have fulfilled it, has remained the prevailing way in all churches up to the present day, insofar as the contradictions remain—they show themselves in ecclesiastical and dogmatic praxis—that the Old Testament is to be treated as a Christian book in the strict sense, and yet the New Testament is superior to it; the ceremonial law is to be interpreted through types, and yet a covenant of the Jewish people with God is to be acknowledged."

41. Cf. Paula Fredriksen, *Augustine and the Jews: A Christian Defense of Jews and Judaism* (New Haven, Conn.: Yale University Press, 2008), 68: "Paul's Jewish enemies, Marcion concluded, had corrupted Paul's letters by introducing these and other similar assertions into later copies of them. Marcion purged these statements, which he regarded as interpolations. Elegantly, decisively, he thereby produced both a de-Judaized apostle and the de-Judaized Christian canon, a 'new' testament."

42. Cf. the note Rosenzweig wrote while reading Tertullian's *Adversus Marcionem*, III: 12–21, under the Novemer 19, 1916 date in his "Paralipomena," *Zweistromland*, 100: "Marcion as critic of the relation of Isaiah to the Christ of the New Testament.—In that Gnosis here *splits Messianism*, it shows how the Church here carried out the struggle also for *us*, in that it has salvaged for the messianism of the prophets its universal sense, which Gnosis (already!) denied it."

43. Friedrich Schleiermacher, *Aus Schleiermachers Leben in Briefen*, vol. 4, edited by L. Jonas and W. Dilthey (Berlin: Reimer, 1863), 394, cited in Paul Capetz, "Friedrich Schleiermacher on the Old Testament," *Harvard Theological Review* 102, no. 3 (2009): 300.

44. Adolf von Harnack, *Marcion: Das Evangelium von fremden Gott. Eine Monographie zur Geschichte der Grundlegung der katholischen Kirche* (Leipzig: J.C. Henrichs, 1924), X, 217. Eugen Rosenstock was to provoke Rosenzweig with a similar claim about the Old Testament's obsolete canonical status during their 1916 correspondence. See Eugen Rosenstock to Rosenzweig, November 19, 1916: "Today Christianity has a new Old Testament instead of your old one: namely today its living Old Testament is—Church History, the *Passional* of the holy ones, the festival calendar. . . . Today the Western world, Europe (through 1789 and 1914) has come so far that it may forget the Old Testament, Greeks, Romans, Jews, and Persians, because there are the English, the popes, the Germans, etc. . . . And what is worse, my poor *ben Yehuda*, it *will* forget its Old Testament," cited in *BT I*, 298. Rosenzweig retorts on November 30: "The Old Testament is something that will disappear. You say it.—and I say it.—But why do you not say: it *has* disappeared??? I answer: because it *has* not disappeared, but rather '*will*' disappear, so long as this Johannine epoch of Christianity begun in 1789 will endure," *BT I*, 303.

45. Rosenzweig, *The Star of Redemption*, 460/437.

46. It is relevant to note here that contemporary critics of Harnack's call to decanonize the Old Testament likewise viewed the Old Testament as Christianity's link to the world. Wolfram Kinzig cites a critique of Harnack from 1921 by Old Testament scholar Otto Eissfeldt,

arguing that "the Old Testament has 'laid the bridge from the New Testament to the world' for Christianity, and this service 'it will ever have to achieve': 'A Christianity without the Old Testament must either—so by Marcion—lead to the most decisive asceticism, and that means quintessentially to the negation of life; or it lets world and life on the one side, and religion on the other split from each other as two completely different areas. And in both cases the dangers of insincerity and hypocrisy lie near," *Harnack, Marcion, und das Judentum,* 130.

47. *BT I,* 135.

48. Cf. Dana Hollander's account of the view of Jewish chosenness Rosenzweig developed in the wake of the Leipzig Night-Conversation: "Here the idea of chosenness converges with a messianic view of history: the Jews are chosen in the sense of having a unique role to fulfill in world history. Their existence testifies to a messianic history, because unlike the Christians, whose path to redemption leads through history, the Jews are always 'already with God'; their relationship with redemption is an immediate one. As Rosenzweig will argue in *The Star of Redemption,* the Jewish people is in this sense 'outside history,'" *Exemplarity and Chosenness: Rosenzweig and Derrida on the Nation of Philosophy* (Stanford, Calif.: Stanford University Press, 2008), 176.

49. *BT I,* 137.

50. Ibid., 142. Cf., Franz Rosenzweig to Eugen Rosenstock, September 4, 1917: "Only the Jew, the actual Jew-within . . . is the exception" to the shared sinfulness of individuals in the world, while "for the borderline Jew . . . there is a *becoming*-Jew (a becoming indeed, that is not a rebirth, but rather a return home)," *Gritli Briefe,* 28.

51. *BT II,* 642–43.

52. Rivka Horwitz, "Warum liess Rosenzweig sich nicht taufen?," 88. By 2006, Horwitz no longer considered a Yom Kippur experience to have been part of Rosenzweig's return. See her "From Hegelianism to a Revolutionary Understanding of Judaism: Franz Rosenzweig's Attitudes towards Kabbalah and Myth," *Modern Judaism* 26, no. 1 (2006): 148.

53. Rosenzweig to Eugen Rosenstock, January 15, 1920, *Gritli-Briefe,* 528.

54. Rosenzweig, "Paralipomena," *Zweistromland,* 62.

55. Ibid., 108.

56. *BT I,* 132.

57. *Gritli-Briefe,* 528.

58. Rosenzweig, "Paralipomena," *Zweistromland,* 99.

59. *BT I,* 133.

60. Ibid., 135.

61. Rosenzweig, "Paralipomena," *Zweistromland,* 81–82.

62. *BT I,* 135.

63. Franz Rosenzweig, *Hegel und der Staat II:Weltepochen* (Munich/Berlin: Oldenbourg, 1920), 203–204.

64. Selma Lagerlöf, *The Miracles of Antichrist,* translated by Pauline B. Flach (Boston: Little, Brown, and Co., 1910), 366, 368.

65. Ibid., 373.

66. Ibid., 376–77.

4. WORLD DENIAL AND WORLD REDEMPTION IN *THE STAR OF REDEMPTION*

1. Franz Rosenzweig, *Der Stern der Erlösung* (Frankfurt am Main: Suhrkamp, 1996, 1988), 3; *The Star of Redemption,* translated by Barbara E. Galli. (Madison: University of Wisconsin

Press, 2005), 9. Translations are my own, but I will cite the Galli English translation page alongside the original for convenience. Henceforth, page numbers will be cited from both versions, the German followed by the Galli English translation, in the text itself in parentheses following each quotation, e.g., (3/9).

2. Cf. Heinz-Jürgen Görtz, *Tod und Erfahrung: Rosenzweigs "erfahrende Philosophie" und Hegels "Wissenschaft der Erfahrung des Bewusstseins"* (Düsseldorf: Patmos, 1984), 395: "It is *death,* which distinguishes the 'being of man' from the 'being of the world'; in view of death, man steps 'out of everything natural,' he distinguishes himself in his "freedom," a freedom though which itself only first means the 'poverty, loneliness and torn-ness' of the individual."

3. This is already promised in the programmatic sentence with which the *Star* begins: "From death, from the fear of death begins all knowledge of the All." See Benjamin Pollock, *Franz Rosenzweig and the Systematic Task of Philosophy* (Cambridge/New York: Cambridge University Press, 2009) [henceforth, *FRSTP*], 127–31.

4. In *Platonic Piety: Philosophy and Ritual in Fourth-Century Athens* (New Haven, Conn.: Yale University Press, 1990), Michael L. Morgan notes that "unlike the traditional, Delphic theology, the central separations in the *Phaedo* are not along a line between the divine and the human but rather along a line between the physical or worldly, on the one hand, and the divine and psychic, on the other" (58–59).

5. Plato, *Phaedo,* 63e–64a, translated by G.M.A. Grube in Plato, *Complete Works,* edited by J. Cooper (Indianapolis: Hackett, 1997), 55.

6. Ibid., 67d, 58.

7. Ibid., 64e, 56.

8. Ibid., 65e–66a, 57. Morgan suggests that for Plato, "there is nothing wrong with sensation by itself," rather "what is wrong with sensation are its objects which are ontologically unsuitable as objects of knowledge." It is for this reason, Morgan explains, that the "rational inquiry and knowledge" through which the soul fulfills its divine potential "involves turning away from the senses to reason and thereby rejecting the physical world in favor of a different domain of objects altogether," *Platonic Piety,* 60, 64–65.

9. Ibid., 66b, 57.

10. Ibid., 66e, 58.

11. Ibid., 67d, 58.

12. Ibid., 67e, 59.

13. Michael Fishbane's *Garments of Torah: Essays in Biblical Hermeneutics* (Bloomington: Indiana University Press, 1989), 143–44, and Benjamin Sax's "Language and Jewish Renewal: Franz Rosenzweig's Hermeneutics of Citation" (Ph.D. dissertation, University of Chicago, 2008), 113–118, both note Rosenzweig's reference to Paul's First Letter to the Corinthians, and to the sources from the Hebrew Bible, Isaiah 25:8 and Hosea 13:14, which Paul himself draws on in the passages Rosenzweig cites. Fishbane suggests that Paul's text is the "base text" Rosenzweig is working from here, and that this "is further proved by the fact that his allusion to these prophetic passages follows Paul's Greek version (and not that of the received Hebrew or Septuagint version)" (143). I take Fishbane to be correct that Rosenzweig's "base text" is Paul's, but it does seem that he had a few other books proverbially open before him while composing. His reference to the pestilential breath of "Hades," rather than "She'ol," for example, appears to point to the Septuagint version of Hosea 13:14. Rosenzweig's claim that philosophy seeks "dem Tod seinem *Gift*stachel, dem Hades seinen *Pest*hauch zu nehmen" also may suggest the influence of Luther's translation of Hosea 13:14: "Tod, ich will dir ein *Gift* sein; Hölle ich will dir eine *Pestilenz* sein."

14. Hans Conzelmann and Martinus De Boer have championed this view. De Boer, for example, claims that "Paul's argument for the resurrection and its bodily character in I Corinthians 15 appears to be directed against this gnostic anthropological dualism. The deniers of the resurrection of the dead thus implicitly affirmed that bodily death meant the liberation of their inner, pneumatic nature," *The Defeat of Death: Apocalyptic Eschatology in I Corinthians 15 and Romans 5* (Sheffield, England: JSOT Press, 1988), 103. But see also Dale B. Martin, who claims in his *The Corinthian Body* (New Haven, Conn.: Yale University Press, 1995) that "most scholars now reject this older view" (71) and suggests that the exchange between Paul and the Corinthians shouldn't be reduced to a "matter/nonmatter dichotomy" (106).

15. Cf. De Boer, *The Defeat of Death,* 123: "In denying the resurrection of the dead, the Corinthian gnostics could sacramentally and pneumatically claim Christ's exaltation as their own. But once the reality of death is looked in the face, as Paul did everyday (v. 30–31), and regarded in view of Christ's resurrection from the dead, the soteriological application of Christ's exaltation over the powers can only be construed in terms of promise."

16. Tertullian, *Adversus Marcionem,* edited and translated by E. Evans (London: Oxford University Press, 1972), V.10, 575.

17. Ibid., 577.

18. Peter Gordon discusses Rosenzweig's citation of "Das Ideal und das Leben" and suggests "the entire opening passage of *The Star of Redemption*" may be read "as an ironic commentary on idealism as it is embodied in Schiller's poem." "What Schiller's poem illustrates," Gordon suggests, "is nothing less than the idea of redemption as proffered by all of Western philosophy since the pre-Socratics. And it is this idea—that idealism promises a quasi-religious deliverance from life—that is the crucial target in Rosenzweig's introduction," *Rosenzweig and Heidegger,* 147, but see 144–50 throughout.

19. Friedrich Schiller, "Das Ideal und das Leben," lns. 7–8, cited from F. Schiller, *Das Ideal und das Leben,* edited by E. Grosse (Berlin: Weidmannsche Buchhandlung, 1908), 5.

20. Ibid., lns. 21–22, 6.

21. E.g., lns. 24, 36, and 152.

22. "Das Ideal und das Leben," lns. 31–40 (emphasis mine—BP).

23. On Schiller's debt to the Platonic tradition, and on the Platonism of "Das Ideal und das Leben" in particular, see David Pugh, *Dialectic of Love: Platonism in Schiller's Aesthetics* (Montreal: McGill-Queen's University Press, 1997), especially 3–20, 39–57.

24. Rosenzweig may be alluding here to the famous story, retold by Cicero and Augustine among others, about a certain Cleombrotus of Ambracia who committed suicide after reading Plato's *Phaedo.* See James Warren, "Socratic Suicide," *Journal of Hellenic Studies* 121 (2001): 91–106, and G. D. Williams, "Cleombrotus of Ambracia: Interpretations of a Suicide from Callimachus to Agathias," *Classical Quarterly* 45, no. 1 (1995): 154–69.

25. Rosenzweig's allusions to this scene from *Faust* have been noted by a number of scholars. See, e.g., Heinz-Jürgen Görtz, *Tod und Erfahrung,* 391. William Hallo went so far as to insert the words "Like Faust" into his translation of the relevant passages of the *Star.* See Rosenzweig, *The Star of Redemption,* 4.

26. Rosenzweig plays off of Faust's language in this scene throughout his account of suicide. Thus, compare "Ich grüße dich, du einzige Phiole! / Die ich mit Andacht nun herunterhole" (*Faust,* Part I, lns. 690–91), to "er muss einmal die kostbare Phiole voll Andacht herunterholen" (*Stern,* 4); "Hier ist ein Saft, der eilig trunken macht. / Mit brauner Flut erfüllt er deine Höhle" (*Faust,* Part I, lns. 732–33) to Rosenzweig's "braunen Saft" (*Stern,* 4); and "die Erde hat mich wieder!" (*Faust,* Part I, ln. 784) to "die Erde verlangt ihn wieder" (*Stern,* 4).

27. Goethe, *Faust,* Part I, lns. 703–706.

28. Ibid., lns. 708–713, 718–719.

29. Ibid., lns. 735, 770, and 784.

30. Franz Rosenzweig, *Zweistromland,* 104.

31. Rosenzweig to Eugen Rosenstock, August 13, 1917, *Gritli-Briefe,* 21–22. In a letter to Rosenstock written on September 1, 1919, Rosenzweig is in fact explicit about the connection between his standing "face-to-face with the nothing" in the wake of the *Leipziger Nachtgespräch* and his allusion to Faust in the opening of the *Star:* "At that time, I actually did not dismiss prayer. Remember I reminded you just in the following evening, that in the previous night had begun the *seventh year* since the night where I was set, through you, for the last (and wholly seriously also for the first) time in my life face-to-face with the nothing, i.e., vis-à-vis the devoutly downed vial, which night I began with complete [no longer interrupted] consciousness, but for you only began with the later consciousness of the Kierkegaard run-in," *Gritli-Briefe,* 420.

32. Inken Rühle also notes how the account of the temptations of suicide in the first pages of the *Star* draws on both *Faust* and Rosenzweig's own personal experience of standing *vis-à-vis du rien* after the *Leipziger Nachtgespräch*. See her "Leben im Angesicht des Todes: Zum Verständnis des Todes im *Stern der Erlösung,*" *Rosenzweig als Leser: Kontextuelle Kommentare zum "Stern der Erlösung,"* edited by Martin Brasser (Tübingen: M. Niemeyer, 2004), 374–76.

33. The reading of the *Star* I will suggest in this chapter, rooted in our new understanding of the *Leipziger Nachtgespräch,* is thus in basic agreement with Peter Gordon's claim that "*Rosenzweig's chief aim is to expound a new concept of redemption that accords with the post-metaphysical human desire to remain in the world* [italics in original]," *Rosenzweig and Heidegger,* 149. Gordon's explanation of this point is helpful, e.g.: "The idea of remaining indicates that we do not and cannot give over what is constitutive of our human being, as if we could trade one nature for another and somehow profit by the exchange" (149).

34. Rosenzweig, "Paralipomena," *Zweistromland,* 99.

35. According to Rosenzweig, the contemporary emphasis on faith as a present experience of the divine directing the individual towards future redemption has its roots in Pietism, but it found its "classical representative" in Friedrich Schleiermacher (*Stern/Star* 110–12/109–11).

36. So, for example, it is the task of the first part of the *Star* to construct the elements of our experience—God, world, and self—through thought, elements that then serve as philosophical "predictions" or prophecies of what we experience as the relations between these elements, creation, revelation, and redemption, described in the book's second part. Elsewhere I have argued for the philosophical cogency of Rosenzweig's "miraculous" method of promise and fulfillment, and tried to situate that method within Kantian and post-Kantian contexts. See my *Franz Rosenzweig and the Systematic Task of Philosophy,* 244–48, and my "What Makes a Good Witness? Rosenzweig's Transcendental Argument *per miraculum,*" forthcoming in special volume of *Revue Internationale de Philosophie,* Paul W. Franks, editor.

37. *BT I,* 129.

38. See chapter 3, above.

39. In his notes and diaries, Rosenzweig regularly builds on the ideas and writings of Tertullian and Augustine as he works out his own account of the relation between Judaism and Christianity. See "Paralipomena," throughout, but especially 61–66, 99–102.

40. Augustine, *City of God,* VII: 32, translated by H. Bettenson (London: Penguin Books, 2003), 293.

41. Tertullian, *Adversus Marcionem* III.2, 173.

42. See Pollock, *FRSTP*, 216–225.

43. Ibid., 191–92.

44. Cf. Immanuel Kant, *Critique of Practical Reason*, in *Akademie Textausgabe* V: 83, translated by M. Gregor (Cambridge: Cambridge University Press, 1997), 71: "To love God means, in this sense, to do what He commands *gladly;* to love one's neighbor means to practice all duties toward him *gladly*. But the command that makes this a rule cannot command us to *have* this disposition in dutiful actions but only to *strive* for it. For a command that one should do something gladly is in itself contradictory because if we already know of ourselves what it is incumbent upon us to do and, moreover, were conscious of liking to do it, a command about it would be quite unnecessary; and if we did it without liking to do it but only from respect for the law, a command that makes this respect the incentive of our maxim would directly counteract the disposition commanded. That law of all laws, therefore, like all the moral precepts of the Gospel, present the moral disposition in its complete perfection, in such a way that as an ideal of holiness it is not attainable by any creature but is yet the archetype which we should strive to approach and resemble in an uninterrupted but endless progress." Rosenzweig no doubt also has Hegel's early barb at Kant in mind when he articulates his views here on the command to love. See "The Spirit of Christianity and Its Fate," in *Werke I. Frühe Schriften* (Frankfurt: Suhrkamp, 1999), 362–63: "Love can indeed not be commanded, indeed it is pathological, an inclination—but therewith nothing is taken from its greatness, it is therewith not at all diminished in that its essence is not domination over something foreign to it. . . . For love, it is a sort of dishonor if it is commanded, that it, something living, a spirit, is named with names. Its name, reflected over it, and expression of the same, is not spirit, not its essence, but rather set over against it, and only as names, as word can it command. It can only be said: you should love. Love itself expresses no 'should.' It is no universal set over against a particularity, not a unity of concept, but rather oneness [*Einigkeit*] of spirit, divinity. To love God is to feel oneself in the All of life limitless in the infinite. . . ."

45. Robert Gibbs's account of Rosenzweig's distinction between command and law is illuminating in this context: "Here is one of Rosenzweig's greatest insights, for he distinguishes the lawful aspect of an imperative from [the] obligatory aspect of the urgency of hearing and responding. . . . To be able to distinguish the binding and heeding of an imperative from the normative force of law is a staggering insight. And only the command to love can force us to see this distinction—because no other command cannot wander into the form of a law," "*Gesetz* in *The Star of Redemption*," *Rosenzweig als Leser: Kontextuelle Kommentare zum "Stern der Erlösung"* (Tübingen: Max Niemeyer, 2004), 398.

46. In a number of important works, Robert Gibbs has both insisted on the "urgent now" quality of the command to love—and how it thus interrupts the temporality of worldly laws—and has investigated the path that leads from command to law in Rosenzweig's thought and in modern Jewish philosophy broadly speaking. See, for example, his "Law and Ethics," *Revista Portuguesa de Filosofia* 62, no. 2 (2006): 395–407, and his "*Gesetz* in *The Star of Redemption*," *Rosenzweig als Leser*, 395–410.

47. Bernhard Casper notes this way in which the command to turn back to the world is already part of the very experience of divine love: "Redemption, then, is the future that unveils itself at the very moment of the occurrence of the divine love. But this means that man, as the beloved one awakened from his metaethical imprisonment, is referred through the command of love to the whole reality that is other than him, that is, to the reality of all other human beings and of the whole world. The command of love is expressed in the biblical commandment 'As he loves you, so shall you love,'" "Responsibility Rescued," in *The Philosophy of Franz*

Rosenzweig, edited by P. Mendes-Flohr (Hanover, N.H.: University Press of New England, 1988), 100.

48. Rosenzweig suggests the mystic shares this denial of the world with the "sinner" who prays that ill befall others so that he can hold onto his "own." See *Star* 304–05/291–92.

49. See chapter 2, above, in which I discuss Rosenzweig's interpretation of this same passage as a comment on what he learned from Eugen Rosenstock at the *Leipziger Nachtgespräch*; i.e., that redemptive love serves to actualize the personhood of both lover and beloved.

50. Cf. Paul Mendes-Flohr, "Rosenzweig and Kant: Two Views of Ritual and Religion," in *Divided Passions: Jewish Intellectuals and the Experience of Modernity* (Detroit: Wayne State University Press, 1991), 283–309.

51. Rosenzweig's critique of Kantian ethical formalism has important precedents. See G. W .F. Hegel, *Werke* 7. *Grundlinien der Philosophie des Rechts*, para. 135–37, 252–56. See also Christoph Schrempf, *Die christliche Weltanschauung und Kants sittlicher Glaube* (Göttingen: Vandenhoeck & Ruprecht, 1891).

52. Rosenzweig clearly draws on Schrempf's concept of "theonomy" in his suggestion that divine command, properly understood, grounds moral action and grants it certain content without amounting to heteronomy. See, for example, C. Schrempf, *Die christliche Weltanschauung und Kants sittlicher Glaube*, 36: "Kant's fundamental law of practical reason only determines namely a demand which maxims must satisfy in order for a rational being to be able to think of them as practical universal laws. It is thus evidently only critical, not constitutive principle for the determination of universal practical laws. But he who wants to give his life actually unconditional ethical necessary content, requires a law, which prescribes actions for him positively, which doesn't give only instruction towards the critique of possible ways of acting and for this reason also only determine what can be a duty. Such a positive law, an actual categorical imperative (Kant's categorical imperative is only categorical in the sense in which a hypothetical judgment contains a categorical statement) is offered by the theonomous morality of Christ. This same also satisfies completely Kant's demand for an ethical law, without indeed being able to derive one. Thus Kant cannot indeed drive one directly to Christ; but he who sharply holds to Kant's demands for an ethical law, cannot remain by Kant and will only find what he seeks by Christ: a law that requires him and makes it possible for him to give his whole life and all individual parts of it ethically necessary content." However, the account of divine love as divine self-limitation, which I attribute to Rosenzweig below, does not have its roots in Schrempf, so far as I can tell. I thank Paul Franks for encouraging me to investigate Rosenzweig's link to Schrempf.

53. Augustine, *Confessions* X: 29.

54. See chapter 2, above.

55. Cf. Pollock, *FRSTP*, 169–77, 181–94.

56. If there is a Kabbalistic precedent for such a divine move, it is surely *shvirat hakelim* and not *tsimtsum*. Gershom Scholem points in this direction in his "Franz Rosenzweig and His Book *The Star of Redemption*," in *The Philosophy of Franz Rosenzweig*, edited by Paul Mendes-Flohr (Hanover/London: University Press of New England for Brandeis University Press, 1988), 34–37.

57. See Elliot Wolfson, "Effacing the Effaced: Mystical Eschatology and the Idealistic Orientation in the Thought of Franz Rosenzweig," *Zeitschrift für Neure Theologiegeschichte* 4 (1997): 77: "The particular point that Rosenzweig makes here is that just as the lover who sacrifices himself in love is created anew by the trust of the beloved, so God's existence is dependent on the affirmation of the soul."

58. Rosenzweig gives as examples of such fruitless prayers those of sinners, who pray selfishly for goods in exclusion of all others, and of religious fanatics [*Schwärmer*] who seek to bring the Kingdom of God before its time. See *Star*, 302–06/289–93.

59. *BT I*, 637–38.

60. On the relation of Rosenzweig's account of Christian imperial politics in the *Star* to his wartime political writings, see Benjamin Pollock, "Rosenzweig's Redemptive Imperialism," *Jewish Studies Quarterly* 11 (2004): 332–53.

61. Rosenzweig, "Paralipomena," 106.

62. Leora Batnitzky interprets these passages compellingly as evidence for her claim that it is the task of the Jewish people to help cure Christianity of its particular form of idolatry. See *Idolatry and Representation* (Princeton, N.J.: Princeton University Press, 2000), 162–68.

63. As I've noted, Augustine's views about the relation between Judaism and Christianity are critical for Rosenzweig's development. Amos Funkenstein offers the interesting suggestion that Rosenzweig's account of the Jews as a community that anticipates the future redemption may be based on Augustine's notion of the "City of God." See his "An Escape from History: Rosenzweig on the Destiny of Judaism," *History and Memory* 2, no. 2 (1990): 117–35. On Rosenzweig as a reader of Augustine, see Francesco Paolo Ciglia, "*Confessiones* und *De civitate Dei* als Quellen des *Stern der Erlösung*," *Rosenzweig als Leser*, 223–44.

64. Cf. Batnitzky, *Idolatry and Representation*, 93: "Rosenzweig . . . argues that Jews are always being wrenched away from the world by God's revelation (are made *unheimlich*) *for the sake of the world*."

65. Cf. Moshe Schwarcz's account of the methodological importance of Rosenzweig's presentation of the divine as both far and near, in his *From Myth to Revelation* [Hebrew] (Tel Aviv: HaKibbutz HaMeuchad, 1978).

66. Franz Rosenzweig, "Das älteste Systemprogramm des deutschen Idealismus," *Zweistromland*, 37, 12. I have addressed the centrality of this question for Rosenzweig's interpretation of Schelling, and for his own conception of systematicity in *FRSTP*, 14–65. See also, Benjamin Pollock, "Rosenzweig's 'Oldest System-Program,'" *New German Critique* 37.3 111 (2010): 59–95.

67. See my argument for the ontological reading, in *FRSTP*, 155–69.

68. Cf. Pollock, *FRSTP*, 159–65.

69. Cf. Pollock, *FRSTP*, 167–69, 190–91, and 230–32.

70. Compare Rosenzweig's suggestion, in a diary note dated June 30, 1922, that the *Star* shows "how the kabbalistic problem is not specifically theological (rather likewise enters as אין סוף [*En Sof*] for M[an] and W[orld])," *BT II*, 800.

71. See my discussion of "factuality" in *FRSTP*, especially 230–32.

72. Cf. Wolfson, "Facing the Effaced," 69: "For Rosenzweig, redemption is not only the redemption of humanity and cosmos but, and perhaps most significantly, also that of God, an idea that resonates deeply with one of the most important themes in the kabbalistic tradition, especially prevalent in the sixteenth-century theosophy developed by Isaac Luria and his disciples." Wolfson sees Rosenzweig's emphasis on God's self-redemption at the end of the *Star* as evidence that Rosenzweig maintains "an essentially pessimistic—one might even say gnostic—assessment of the physical world as inherently unredeemable" even in the *Star* itself. See Wolfson's forthcoming "Apophatic Vision and Overcoming the Dialogical," *Giving Beyond the Gift: Apophasis and Overcoming Theomania* (Fordham University Press).

73. For an alternative account of Rosenzweig's conception of truth, see Kenneth Hart Green, "The Notion of Truth in Franz Rosenzweig's *The Star of Redemption:* A Philosophical Enquiry," *Modern Judaism* 7, no. 3 (1987): 297–323.

74. I take this "for the sake of God" to be what Martin Kavka has in mind when he writes, "Rosenzweig's model of religious action sets itself up for a critique that the neighbor is no more than a stepping stone to God. . . . The words 'I,' 'neighbor,' and 'world' are seen in the light of redemption to be synonymous in their nature of being possessed by God," *Jewish Messianism and the History of Philosophy* (New York: Cambridge University Press, 2004), 151–52.

75. In his "Facing the Effaced," Elliot Wolfson foregrounds the mystical step "beyond life" in the closing sequence of the *Star,* and presents it as a kind of celebration of spiritual death: "The dialogical love of revelation overcomes the physical death imposed by creation, but that love itself is overcome by the spiritual death experienced in redemption, which results in the reintegration of the self in the oneness of God. . . . The way to exit from the mystical death of the self and to enter back into life is through acts of piety summarized by the prophetic injunction to walk humbly with God. There can be no doubt that Rosenzweig felt the tug pulling him back into the life of community and dialogue. It is nevertheless clear that he embraced a mystical understanding of the religious life that demands the renunciation of this world and the restoration of the Godhead" (80–81). Wolfson's reading is an important one, and it highlights the way in which not only the moments of mystical intimacy with the divine throughout the *Star* recall Rosenzweig's former courting of Marcionism, but also the way redemption itself in the *Star* ultimately is portrayed as dissolving self and world into the divine. As I have argued throughout, I understand the call away from mysticism and back into the world to serve the ultimate purpose of divine redemption. But I have suggested that denying the world *today* for the sake of union with God and working in the world redemptively to bring about divine unity remain distinct, and even opposed, positions. For a recent nuanced formulation of this position, and for his response to my position, see Wolfson's forthcoming "Apophatic Vision and Overcoming the Dialogical." Zachary Braiterman has likewise suggested that Rosenzweig celebrates the step "beyond life" more than scholars have recognized: "Just because these are the last words of the *Star* does not mean that 'life' represents the highest good in Rosenzweig's system. . . . In our view, 'into life' represents a diminuendo! In the same way that the gray realia symbolized by Sukkot follow the spiritual apex of Yom Kippur, 'into life' follows the climactic vision of God's face like a decrescendo. According to our reading, death, light, silence, and a spectacular vision of the truth represent the highpoint and highest good in Rosenzweig's thought," "'Into Life'??! Franz Rosenzweig and the Figure of Death," *AJS Review* 23, no. 2 (1998): 212. Braiterman's emphasis on Rosenzweig's "morbidity" certainly finds support in the account of Rosenzweig's flirtation with dying for God we've uncovered here. But I would again suggest there is an important difference between the morbidity of one who views death as the task of the hour, and that of one who sees death as the positive ending of a fully lived life.

CONCLUSION

1. Franz Rosenzweig, *Stern/Star,* 10/16. Cf., Franz Rosenzweig to Rudolf Ehrenberg, December 1, 1917, in *BT I,* 485–86.

2. "Franz Rosenzweig and Existentialism," *Yearbook of the CCAR* 62 (1953): 418.

BIBLIOGRAPHY

WORKS BY FRANZ ROSENZWEIG

Die "Gritli"-Briefe. Briefe an Margrit Rosenstock-Huessy. Edited by Inken Rühle and Reinhold Mayer, with a preface by Rafael Rosenzweig. Tübingen: Bilam Verlag, 2002. [Endnotes use the abbreviation *Gritli-Briefe.*]

Briefe und Tagebücher. 1. Band 1900–1918. 2. Band 1919–1929. Edited by Rachel Rosenzweig and Edith Rosenzweig-Scheinmann with the cooperation of Bernhard Casper. Hague: Martinus Nijhoff, 1979. [Endnotes use the following abbreviations: *BT I* and *BT II*].

Franz Rosenzweig, Der Mensch und sein Werk. Gesammelte Schriften I–IV. Hague: Martinus Nijhoff, 1976–1984.

Franz Rosenzweig Nachlass, University of Kassel Library.

Hegel und der Staat. Munich and Berlin: R. Oldenbourg, 1920, reprint Aalen: Scientia, 1962.

"Die Leitsätze des Baden-Badener Kreises und das Referat von Franz Rosenzweig auf der Tagung vom 9. Januar 1910 mit dem Titel 'Das 18. Jahrhundert in seinem Verhältnis zum 19ten und zum 20ten,'" edited by Wolfgang D. Herzfeld, 240–52. *Rosenzweig Jahrbuch 3: Die Idee Europa,* 2008.

"Paralipomena." Franz Rosenzweig Collection, AR 3001. Manuscript in Series II, Subseries III:D, Box 2, Folders 39–40. Leo Baeck Institute, Center for Jewish History, New York.

Rosenzweig to Rudolf Ehrenberg, Undated ("Young Hegel Letter"), Franz Rosenzweig Nachlass, University of Kassel Library (B 45).

Rosenzweig's Unpublished Diaries, Franz Rosenzweig Collection, AR 3001. Diaries in Series II, Subseries I. Leo Baeck Institute, New York.

"Die Schechina." Nahum Glatzer Collection at Vanderbilt University. Franz Rosenzweig Papers, I. H; Box 2, folder 44.

Sprachdenken im Übersetzen. 1. Band: *Hymnen und Gedichte des Jehuda Halevi.* Edited by Rafael N. Rosenzweig. Hague: Martinus Nijhoff, 1983. 2. Band: *Arbeitspapiere zur Verdeutschung der Schrift.* Edited by Rachel Bat Adam. Dordrecht: Martinus Nijhoff, 1984.

Der Stern der Erlösung. Frankfurt am Main: Suhrkamp, 1996, 1988. [Endnotes use the abbreviation *Stern.*]

Zweistromland. Kleinere Schriften zu Glauben und Denken. Edited by Reinhold and Annemarie Mayer. Dordrecht: Martinus Nijhoff, 1984. [Endnotes use the abbreviation *Zweistromland*].

ENGLISH TRANSLATIONS OF ROSENZWEIG'S WRITINGS CONSULTED

Franz Rosenzweig: His Life and Thought. Presented by Nahum Glatzer, with a new foreword by Paul Mendes-Flohr. Indianapolis: Hackett, 1998.

God, Man, and the World: Lectures and Essays. Edited and translated by Barbara E. Galli. Syracuse, N.Y.: Syracuse University Press, 1998.

Judaism Despite Christianity: The "Letters on Christianity and Judaism" between Eugen Rosenstock-Huessy and Franz Rosenzweig. Edited by Eugen Rosenstock-Huessy and translated by Dorothy Emmet. New York: Schocken Books, 1971.

Philosophical and Theological Writings. Translated and edited, with notes and commentary, by Paul W. Franks and Michael L. Morgan. Indianapolis: Hackett, 2000.

The Star of Redemption. Translated by Barbara E. Galli. Madison: University of Wisconsin Press, 2005. [Endnotes use abbreviation *Star* for pages from this translation.]

The Star of Redemption. Translated by William W. Hallo. New York: Holt, Rinehart, and Winston, 1971.

PRIMARY SOURCES

Augustine. *City of God*. Translated by H. Bettenson. London: Penguin Books, 2003.

———. *Confessions*. Translated by R. S. Pine-Coffin. London: Penguin Books, 1961.

Buber, Martin. *Die Geschichten des Rabbi Nachman*. Frankfurt: Rütten u. Loening,1906.

———. *Die Legende des Baal-Schem*. Frankfurt: Rütten u. Loening, 1908.

Ehrenberg, Rudolf. *Ebr.10, 25. Ein Schicksal in Predigten*. Würzburg: Patmos Verlag, 1920.

———. *Halbhunderttag*, unpublished transcribed manuscript.

Goethe, Johann Wolfgang. *Faust. Eine Tragödie*. Deutscher Taschenbuch Verlag Ausgabe 9. Munich: Deutscher Taschenbuch Verlag, 1962.

von Harnack, Adolf. *Lehrbuch der Dogmengeschichte*, Vol. I. Freiburg: Mohr-Siebeck, 1886.

———. *Marcion: Das Evangelium von fremden Gott. Eine Monographie zur Geschichte der Grundlegung der katholischen Kirche*. Leipzig: J. C. Henrichs, 1924.

———. *Wesen des Christentums*. Leipzig: J.C. Henrichs, 1902.

Hegel, Georg Wilhelm Friedrich. *Werke im zwanzig Bänden*. Edited by Eva Moldenhauer and Karl Markus Michel. Frankfurt am Main: Suhrkamp, 1970. [Endnotes cite volume and page number.]

Huch, Ricarda. *Luthers Glaube: Briefe an einen Freund*, in *Gesammelte Werke* Band 7: *Schriften zur Religion und Weltanschauung*. Edited by W. Emrich, 119–335. Cologne/Berlin: Kiepenheuer & Witsch, 1968.

Kant, Immanuel. *Critique of Practical Reason*. Translated by Mary Gregor. Cambridge: Cambridge University Press, 1997.

———. *Kants Werke. Akademie Textausgabe*. Berlin: Walter de Gruyter & Co., 1900–. [Endnotes cite volume and page number.]

Lagerlöf, Selma. *The Miracles of Antichrist*. Translated by Pauline B. Flach. Boston: Little, Brown, and Co., 1910.

Plato. *Phaedo*. Translated by G.M.A Grube in *Complete Works*, edited by John M. Cooper, 49–100. Indianapolis/Cambridge: Hackett, 1997.

Rilke, Rainer M. *Geschichten vom lieben Gott*. Leipzig: Insel Verlag, 1922.

Rosenstock-Huessy, Eugen. *Angewandte Seelenkunde*. In *Die Sprache des Menschengeschlechts* II, 739–819. Heidelberg: Lambert Schneider Verlag, 1963–1964.

———. "Zur Ausbildung des mittelalterlichen Festkalenders." *Archiv für Kulturgeschichte* 10 (1912): 272–82.

———. *Europa und die Christenheit*. Kempten/Munich, 1919.

———. *Die Hochzeit des Kriegs und der Revolution*. Würzburg: Patmos, 1920.

———. *Ja und Nein: Autobiographische Fragmente*. Heidelberg: Lambert Schneider, 1968.

———. "Die Sankt Georgs Reden," on *The Collected Works of Eugen Rosenstock-Huessy on DVD*.

———. "Der Selbstmord Europas." *Hochland: Monatsschrift für alle Gebiete des Wissens, der Literatur und Kunst* 16, no. 2 (1919): 529–53, reprinted in *Die Sprache des Menschengeschlechts II*, 45–84. Heidelberg: Lambert Schneider, 1964.

———. *Soziologie I: Die Kräfte der Gemeinschaft*. Berlin/Leipzig: Walter de Gruyter, 1925.

Schiller, Friedrich. *Das Ideal und das Leben*. Edited by E. Grosse. Berlin: Weidmannsche Buchhandlung, 1908.

Schrempf, Christoph. *Die christliche Weltanschauung und Kants sittlicher Glaube*. Göttingen: Vandenhoeck & Ruprecht, 1891.

———. *Drei Religiöse Reden*. Stuttgart: Frommanns Verlag, 1893.

Sextus Empiricus. *Outlines of Scepticism [Pyrrhonism]*. Translated by J. Annas and J. Barnes. Cambridge: Cambridge University Press, 2000.

Tertullian. *Adversus Marcionem*. Edited and translated by E. Evans. London: Oxford University Press, 1972.

SECONDARY SOURCES

Altmann, Alexander. "Franz Rosenzweig on History." In *The Philosophy of Franz Rosenzweig*, edited by Paul Mendes-Flohr, 124–37. Hanover, N.H.: University Press of New England for Brandeis University Press, 1988.

Amir, Yehoyada. דעת מאמינה: עיונים במשנתו של פרנץ רוזנצוויג. [*Believing Knowledge: Studies in the Philosophy of Franz Rosenzweig*]. Jerusalem: Am Oved, 2004.

Batnitzky, Leora. *Idolatry and Representation: The Philosophy of Franz Rosenzweig Reconsidered*. Princeton, N.J.: Princeton University Press, 2000.

Bergman, Shmuel Hugo. *Dialogical Philosophy from Kierkegaard to Buber*. Translated by Arnold A. Gerstein. Albany, N.Y.: SUNY Press, 1991.

———. אנשים ודרכים [Hebrew: *People and Paths*]. Jerusalem: Mosad Bialik: 1967.

Bieberich, Ulrich. *Wenn die Geschichte göttlich wäre: Rosenzweigs Auseinandersetzung mit Hegel*. St. Ottilien: EOS Verlag, 1990.

Bienenstock, Myriam. "Rosenzweig's Hegel." *Owl of Minerva* 23, no. 2 (Spring 1992): 177–82.

———. "Auf Schellings Spuren im *Stern der Erlösung*." In *Rosenzweig als Leser: Kontextuelle Kommentare zum "Stern der Erlösung,"* edited by Martin Brasser, 273–90. Tübingen: M. Niemeyer, 2004.

Bloth, Hugo G. "Was geschah im "Leipziger Nachtgespräch" am 7. 7. 1913 zwischen den Freunden Eugen Rosenstock, Franz Rosenzweig und Rudolf Ehrenberg?" *Mitteilungsblatt der Eugen Rosenstock-Huessy-Gesellschaft* 31 (1981): 2–13.

Blumenberg, Hans. *The Legitimacy of the Modern Age*. Translated by R. Wallace. Cambridge, Mass.: MIT Press, 1983.

Bouretz, Pierre. *Witnesses for the Future*. Translated by M. Smith. Baltimore: Johns Hopkins University Press, 2010.

Boyarin, Daniel. *Dying for God: Martyrdom and the Making of Christianity and Judaism*. Stanford, Calif.: Stanford University Press, 1999.

Braiterman, Zachary. "Cyclical Motions and the Force of Repetition in the Thought of Franz Rosenzweig." In *Beginning/Again: Toward a Hermeneutics of Jewish Texts,* edited by Aryeh Cohen and Shaul Magid, 215–38. New York: Seven Bridges Press, 2002.

———. "'Into life'??! Franz Rosenzweig and the Figure of Death." *AJS Review* 23, no. 2 (1998): 203–221.

———. *The Shape of Revelation: Aesthetics and Modern Jewish Thought.* Stanford, Calif.: Stanford University Press, 2007.

Brakelmann, Günther. *Hans Ehrenberg: Ein jüdenchristliches Schicksal in Deutschland. Band 1: Leben, Denken, und Wirken 1883–1932.* Waltrop: Spenner, 1997.

Brakke, David. *The Gnostics: Myth, Ritual, and Diversity in Early Christianity.* Cambridge, MA: Harvard University Press, 2011.

Brasser, Martin. "Rosenstock und Rosenzweig über Sprache: Die *Angewandte Seelenkunde* im *Stern der Erlösung.*" In *Rosenzweig als Leser: Kontextuelle Kommentare zum "Stern der Erlösung,"* 173–207. Tübingen: Niemeyer Verlag, 2004.

———, ed. *Rosenzweig als Leser: Kontextuelle Kommentare zum "Stern der Erlösung."* Tübingen: Niemeyer Verlag, 2004.

Capetz, Paul. "Friedrich Schleiermacher on the Old Testament." *Harvard Theological Review* 102, no. 3 (2009): 297–326.

Casper, Bernhard. *Das Dialogische Denken: Eine Untersuchung der religionsphilosophischen Bedeutung Franz Rosenzweigs, Ferdinand Ebners und Martin Buber.* Freiburg: Herder, 1967.

———. *Religion der Erfahrung: Einführungen in das Denken Franz Rosenzweigs.* Paderborn: Schöningh, 2004.

———. "Responsibility Rescued." In *The Philosophy of Franz Rosenzweig,* edited by Paul Mendes-Flohr, 89–106. Hanover, N.H.: University Press of New England for Brandeis University Press, 1988.

Ciglia, Francesco Paolo. "*Confessiones* und *De civitate Dei* als Quellen des *Stern der Erlösung.*" In *Rosenzweig als Leser: Kontextuelle Kommentare zum "Stern der Erlösung,"* edited by Martin Brasser, 223–44. Tübingen: Niemeyer Verlag, 2004.

Clawson, Dan. "Rosenzweig on Judaism and Christianity." *Judaism* (Winter 1970): 90–98.

Cohen, Arthur A. "Franz Rosenzweig's *The Star of Redemption:* An Inquiry into its Psychological Origins." *Midstream* 18, no. 2 (February 1972): 13–33; reprinted in *An Arthur A. Cohen Reader,* edited by D. Stern and P. Mendes-Flohr. Detroit: Wayne State University Press, 1988), 146–72.

Cohen, Richard A. "Rosenzweig's Rebbe HaLevi: From the Academy to the Yeshiva." *Judaism* 44, no. 4 (1995): 448–66.

Conzelmann, Hans. *1 Corinthians: A Commentary on the First Epistle to the Corinthians.* Philadelphia: Fortress, 1975.

Cristaudo, Wayne. *Religion, Redemption, and Revolution: The New Speech Thinking of Franz Rosenzweig and Eugen Rosenstock-Huessy.* Toronto: University of Toronto Press, 2012.

Dagan, Hagai. "Franz Rosenzweig—Biography and Personal Standpoint." *Journal of Jewish Thought and Philosophy* 10, no. 2 (2001): 289–312.

———. "Philosophizing in the Face of Death—Schopenhauer and Rosenzweig." *Jewish Studies Quarterly* 8, no. 1 (2001): 66–79.

De Boer, Martinus. *The Defeat of Death: Apocalyptic Eschatology in I Corinthians 15 and Romans 5.* Sheffield, England: JSOT Press, 1988.

Dilthey, Wilhelm. "Das Schicksal Jesu und die Religion seiner Gemeinde." In *Die Jugendgeschichte Hegels* in *Gesammelte Schriften* IV, 107–117. Stuttgart: B.G. Teubner, 1959.

Dober, Hans Martin. *Die Zeit ernst nehmen: Studien zur Franz Rosenzweigs "Der Stern der Erlösung."* Würzburg: Königshaus und Neumann, 1990.

Fackenheim, Emil. *To Mend the World: Foundations of Future Jewish Thought*. New York: Schocken, 1982.

Fishbane, Michael. *Garments of Torah: Essays in Biblical Hermeneutics*. Bloomington: Indiana University Press, 1989.

———. *The Kiss of God: Spiritual and Mystical Death in Judaism*. Seattle: University of Washington Press, 1996.

Franks, Paul W. "Everyday Speech and Revelatory Speech in Rosenzweig and Wittgenstein," *Philosophy Today* (Spring 2006), 24–39.

Franks, Paul W., and Michael L. Morgan. "From 1914 to 1917." In *Franz Rosenzweig, Philosophical and Theological Writings,* edited by Paul W. Franks and Michael L. Morgan, 25–47. Indianapolis: Hackett, 2000.

Fredriksen, Paula. *Augustine and the Jews: A Christian Defense of Jews and Judaism*. New Haven, Conn.: Yale University Press, 2010.

———. "Paul and Augustine: Conversion Narratives, Orthodox Traditions, and the Retrospective Self." *Journal of Theological Studies* 37 (1986): 3–34.

Freund, Else-Rahel. *Franz Rosenzweig's Philosophy of Existence: An Analysis of the* Star of Redemption. Translated by S. L. Weinstein and Robert Israel. The Hague: Martinus Nijhoff, 1979.

Funkenstein, Amos. "An Escape from History: Rosenzweig on the Destiny of Judaism." *History and Memory* 2, no. 2 (1990): 117–35.

Gibbs, Robert. *Correlations in Rosenzweig and Levinas*. Princeton, N.J.: Princeton University Press, 1992.

———. "*Gesetz* in *The Star of Redemption*." In *Rosenzweig als Leser: Kontextuelle Kommentare zum "Stern der Erlösung,"* edited by Martin Brasser, 395–410. Tübingen: Niemeyer Verlag, 2004.

———. "Law and Ethics." *Revista Portuguesa de Filosofia* 62, no. 2 (2006): 395–407.

———. "Lines, Circles, Points: Messianic Epistemology in Cohen, Rosenzweig, and Benjamin." In *Toward the Millennium: Messianic Expectations from the Bible to Waco,* edited by Peter Schäfer and Mark Cohen. Leiden/Boston: Brill, 1998, 363–82.

———. *Why Ethics? Signs of Responsibilities*. Princeton, N.J.: Princeton University Press, 2000.

Glatzer, Nahum N. "Franz Rosenzweig: His Life and His Ideas" [Yiddish]. *YIVO Bleter, shrift fun yidishn wisenshaftlekhen institut* 2, no. xxv (1945): 3–39.

———. "Franz Rosenzweig: The Story of a Conversion." *Judaism* 1, no. 1 (1952): 69–79. Reprinted as part of "Introduction," *Franz Rosenzweig: Life and Thought,* presented by Nahum N. Glatzer, ix–xxxviii. New York: Schocken, 1953.

Görtz, Heinz-Jürgen. "Der Stern der Erlösung als Kommentar: Rudolf Ehrenberg und Franz Rosenzweig." In *Rosenzweig als Leser. Kontextuelle Kommentare zum 'Stern der Erlösung,'"* edited by Martin Brasser, 119–171. Tübingen: Niemeyer Verlag, 2004.

———. *Tod und Erfahrung: Rosenzweigs "erfahrende Philosophie" und Hegels "Wissenschaft der Erfahrung des Bewusstseins*. Duesseldorf: Patmos Verlag, 1984.

Gordon, Peter Eli. *Rosenzweig and Heidegger: Between Judaism and German Philosophy*. Berkeley: University of California Press, 2003.

———. "Rosenzweig Redux: The Reception of German-Jewish Thought." *Jewish Social Studies* 8, no. 1 (2001): 1–57.

Green, Kenneth Hart. "The Notion of Truth in Franz Rosenzweig's *The Star of Redemption:* A Philosophical Enquiry." *Modern Judaism* 7 (October 1987): 297–323.

Grimstad, Kirsten. *The Modern Revival of Gnosticism and Thomas Mann's* Doktor Faustus. Rochester, N.Y.: Camden House, 2002.

Herberg, Will. "Rosenzweig's 'Judaism of Personal Existence': A Third Way between Orthodoxy and Modernism." *Commentary* 10, no. 6 (1950): 541–49.

Hollander, Dana. *Exemplarity and Chosenness: Rosenzweig and Derrida on the Nation of Philosophy.* Stanford, Calif.: Stanford University Press, 2008.

Horwitz, Rivka. "Franz Rosenzweig's Unpublished Writings." *Journal of Jewish Studies* 20 (1969): 57–80.

———. "From Hegelianism to a Revolutionary Understanding of Judaism: Franz Rosenzweig's Attitude toward Kabbala and Myth." *Modern Judaism* 26, no. 1(2006): 31–54.

———. "Judaism Despite Christianity." *Judaism* 24, no. 3 (1975): 306–318.

———. "Warum liess Rosenzweig sich nicht taufen?" In *Der Philosoph Franz Rosenzweig (1886–1929), I,* edited by Wolfdietrich Schmied-Kowarzik, 79–96. Freiburg: Alber, 1988.

Idel, Moshe. "Franz Rosenzweig and the Kabbalah." *The Philosophy of Franz Rosenzweig,* edited by Paul Mendes-Flohr, 162–71. Hanover, N.H.: University Press of New England for Brandeis University Press, 1988.

James, William. *The Varieties of Religious Experience: A Study in Human Nature.* New York: Penguin Books, 1982.

Jonas, Hans. *The Gnostic Religion: The Message of the Alien God and the Beginnings of Christianity.* Boston: Beacon Press, 1991.

Kajon, Irene. *Contemporary Jewish Philosophy: An Introduction.* New York: Routledge, 2006.

Kaplan, Marion A., editor. *Jewish Daily Life in Germany, 1618–1945.* Oxford/New York: Oxford University Press, 2005.

Kartheininger, Markus. *Heterogenität: Politische Philosophie im Frühwerk von Leo Strauss.* Munich: Wilhelm Fink Verlag, 2006.

Kavka, Martin. *Jewish Messianism and the History of Philosophy.* Cambridge: Cambridge University Press, 2004.

Kinzig, Wolfram. *Harnack, Marcion und das Judentum.* Leipzig: Evangelische Verlagsanstalt, 2004.

Lazier, Benjamin. *God Interrupted: Heresy and the European Imagination between the World Wars.* Princeton, N.J.: Princeton University Press, 2008.

Martin, Dale. *The Corinthian Body.* New Haven, Conn.: Yale University Press, 1995.

Meir, Ephraim. "The Unpublished Correspondence Between Franz Rosenzweig and Gritli Rosenstock-Huessy on the 'Star of Redemption.'" *Jewish Studies Quarterly* 9, no. 1 (2002): 21–70.

Mendes-Flohr, Paul. "Franz Rosenzweig and the Crisis of Historicism." In *The Philosophy of Franz Rosenzweig,* edited by Paul Mendes-Flohr, 138–61. Hanover, N.H.: University Press of New England for Brandeis University Press, 1988.

———. "Franz Rosenzweig and the German Philosophical Tradition." In *The Philosophy of Franz Rosenzweig,* edited by Paul Mendes-Flohr, 1–19. Hanover, N.H.: University Press of New England for Brandeis University Press, 1988.

———. "Franz Rosenzweig's Concept of Philosophical Faith." *Leo Baeck Institute Year Book* 34 (1989): 357–69.

———. *German Jews: A Dual Identity.* New Haven, Conn.: Yale University Press, 1999.

———. "Rosenzweig and Kant: Two Views of Ritual and Religion." In *Divided Passions: Jewish Intellectuals and the Experience of Modernity*, 283–310. Detroit: Wayne State University Press, 1991.

———. "Rosenzweig's Concept of Miracle." In *Jüdisches Denken in einer Welt ohne Gott: Festschrift für Stephane Moses*, edited by Jens Mattern, Gabriel Motzkin, and Shimon Sandbank, 53–66. Berlin: Vorwerk 8, 2000.

Mendes-Flohr, Paul, and Jehuda Reinharz. "From Relativism to Religious Faith—The Testimony of Franz Rosenzweig's Unpublished Diaries." *Leo Baeck Institute Year Book* 22 (1977): 161–74.

Meyer, Michael A., editor. *German-Jewish History in Modern Times. Volume 3: Integration in Dispute 1871–1918*. New York: Columbia University Press, 1997.

Miller, Ronald. *Dialogue and Disagreement: Franz Rosenzweig's Relevance to Contemporary Jewish–Christian Understanding*. Lanham, Md.: University Press of America, 1989.

Morgan, Michael L. *Dilemmas in Modern Jewish Thought: The Dialectics of Revelation and History*. Bloomington: Indiana University Press, 1992.

———. "Franz Rosenzweig: Objective Truth and the Personal Standpoint." *Judaism* 40 (Fall 1991): 521–30.

———. *Platonic Piety: Philosophy and Ritual in Fourth-Century Athens*. New Haven, Conn.: Yale University Press, 1990.

Mosès, Stéphane. *System and Revelation: The Philosophy of Franz Rosenzweig*. Translated by Catherine Tihanyi. Detroit: Wayne State University Press, 1992.

Moyn, Samuel. *Origins of the Other: Emmanuel Levinas between Revelation and Ethics*. Ithaca, N.Y.: Cornell University Press, 2005.

Oppenheim, Michael. "Death and Man's Fear of Death in Franz Rosenzweig's *Star of Redemption*." *Judaism* 27, no. 4 (1978): 458–67.

———. "Foreword" to Franz Rosenzweig, *The Star of Redemption*. Translated by Barbara E. Galli, xi–xv. Madison: University of Wisconsin Press, 2005.

O'Regan, Cyril. *Gnostic Return in Modernity*. Albany, N.Y.: State University of New York Press, 2001.

Pollock, Benjamin. "'Erst die Tatsache ist sicher vor dem Rückfall ins Nichts': Rosenzweig's Concept of Factuality." In *Franz Rosezweigs "neues Denken,"* edited by Wolfdietrich Schmied-Kowarzik, 359–70. Freiburg: Alber, 2006.

———. *Franz Rosenzweig and the Systematic Task of Philosophy*. Cambridge/New York: Cambridge University Press, 2009. [Abbreviated as *FRSTP*]

———. "From Nation State to World Empire: Franz Rosenzweig's Redemptive Imperialism." *Jewish Studies Quarterly* 11, no. 4 (2004): 332–53.

———. "Rosenzweig's 'Oldest System-Program,'" *New German Critique* 37, no. 3 (2010): 59–95.

———. "What Makes a Good Witness? Rosenzweig's Transcendental Argument *per miraculum*." *Revue Internationale de Philosophie* (forthcoming).

———. "'Within Earshot of the Young Hegel': Rosenzweig's Letter to Rudolf Ehrenberg of September 1910." In *German-Jewish Thought between Religion and Politics: Festschrift in Honor of Paul Mendes-Flohr on the Occasion of His Seventieth Birthday*, edited by Christian Wiese and Martina Urban, 185–207. Berlin: Walter de Gruyter, 2012.

Proudfoot, Wayne. *Religious Experience*. Berkeley: University of California Press, 1985.

Pugh, David. *Dialectic of Love: Platonism in Schiller's Aesthetics*. Montreal: McGill-Queen's University Press, 1997.

Rambo, Lewis R. *Understanding Religious Conversion*. New Haven, Conn.: Yale University Press, 1993.

Rosenstock-Huessy, Eugen. "Einleitung" for "Franz Rosenzweig und Eugen Rosenstock: Judentum und Christentum." In Franz Rosenzweig, *Briefe*, edited by Edith Rosenzweig with collaboration from Ernst Simon, 637–39. Berlin: Schocken, 1935.

———. "Prologue/Epilogue to the Letters—Fifty Years Later." *Judaism Despite Christianity: The "Letters on Christianity and Judaism" between Eugen Rosenstock-Huessy and Franz Rosenzweig*, edited by Eugen Rosenstock-Huessy, 71–76. New York: Schocken, 1971.

Rubinstein, Ernest. *An Episode of Jewish Romanticism: Franz Rosenzweig's* Star of Redemption. Albany, N.Y.: SUNY Press, 1999.

Rühle, Inken. "Leben im Angesicht des Todes: Zum Verständnis des Todes im *Stern der Erlösung*." In *Rosenzweig als Leser, Kontextuelle Kommentare zum "Stern der Erlösung,"* edited by Martin Brasser, 369–93. Tübingen: Niemeyer Verlag, 2004.

Santner, Eric L. *The Psychotheology of Everyday Life: Reflections on Freud and Rosenzweig*. Chicago: University of Chicago Press, 2001.

Sax, Benjamin. *Language and Jewish Renewal: Franz Rosenzweig's Hermeneutics of Citation*. Ph.D. diss., University of Chicago, 2008.

Schmied-Kowarzik, Wolfdietrich. *Existentielles Denken und gelebte Bewährung*. Freiburg: Alber, 1991.

———, editor. *Franz Rosenzweigs "neues Denken."* Freiburg: Alber, 2006.

———, editor. *Der Philosoph Franz Rosenzweig (1886–1929)*. Freiburg: Alber, 1988.

———. *Rosenzweig im Gespräch mit Ehrenberg, Cohen, und Buber*. Munich: Karl Alber, 2006.

Scholem, Gershom. "Franz Rosenzweig and his book *The Star of Redemption*." In *The Philosophy of Franz Rosenzweig*, edited by Paul Mendes-Flohr, 20–41. Hanover/London: University Press of New England for Brandeis University Press, 1988.

———. *The Messianic Idea in Judaism and Other Essays on Jewish Spirituality*. New York: Schocken Books, 1971.

Schwarz, Moshe. ממיתוס להתגלות [*From Myth to Revelation*]. Tel Aviv: Bar-Ilan University and HaKibutz HaMeuchad, 1978.

Schwarzschild, Steven. "Franz Rosenzweig and Existentialism." *Yearbook of the CCAR* 62 (1953): 410–429.

———. "Rosenzweig on Judaism and Christianity." *Conservative Judaism* 10, no. 2 (1956): 41–48.

Schweid, Eliezer. "Rosenzweig's Contribution to the Curriculum of Jewish Thought." In *Paradigms in Jewish Philosophy*, edited by R. Jospe, 166–81. Cranbury, N.J.: Associated University Presses, 1997.

Segal, Alan F. *Paul the Convert: The Apostolate and Apostasy of Saul the Pharisee*. New Haven, Conn.: Yale University Press, 1990.

Sheppard, Eugene. "'I Am a Memory Come Alive': Nahum Glatzer and the Legacy of German-Jewish Thought in America." *Jewish Quarterly Review* 94, no. 1 (2004): 123–48.

Ullmann, Wolfgang. "Die Entdeckung des neuen Denkens: Das Leipziger Religionsgespräch und der Briefwechsel über Judentum und Christentum zwischen Eugen Rosenstock und Franz Rosenzweig." *Stimmstein: Jahrbuch der Eugen Rosenstock-Huessy Gesellschaft* 2 (1988): 147–78.

Urban, Martina. *Aesthetics of Renewal: Martin Buber's Early Representation of Hasidism as Kulturkritik*. Chicago: University of Chicago Press, 2008.

Welch, Claude. *Protestant Thought in the Nineteenth Century. Volume 2, 1870–1914*. New Haven, Conn.: Yale University Press, 1985.

Wiese, Christian. *Challenging Colonial Discourse: Jewish Studies and Protestant Theology in Wilhelmine Germany.* Translated by Barbara Harshav and Christian Wiese. Leiden/Boston: Brill, 2005.

Williams, Michael A. *Rethinking "Gnosticism": An Argument for Dismantling a Dubious Category.* Princeton, N.J.: Princeton University Press, 1996.

Wolfson, Elliot R. "Apophatic Vision and Overcoming the Dialogical." In *Giving Beyond the Gift: Apophasis and Overcoming Theomania.* New York: Fordham University Press, (forthcoming).

———. "Facing the Effaced: Mystical Eschatology and the Idealistic Orientation in the Thought of Franz Rosenzweig." *Zeitschrift für neuere Theologiegeschichte* 4 (1997): 39–81.

———. "Light Does Not Talk but Shines: Apophasis and Vision in Rosenzweig's Theopoetic Temporality." In *New Directions in Jewish Philosophy,* edited by A. Hughes and E. R. Wolfson, 87–148. Bloomington: Indiana University Press, 2010.

———. *Through a Speculum that Shines: Vision and Imagination in Medieval Jewish Mysticism.* Princeton, N.J.: Princeton University Press, 1994.

Zank, Michael. "The Rosenzweig–Rosenstock triangle, or, What Can We Learn from 'Letters to Gritli'? A Review Essay." *Modern Judaism* 23, no. 1 (2003): 74–98.

INDEX

BENJAMIN POLLOCK is Associate Professor of Religious Studies at Michigan State University. He is the author of *Franz Rosenzweig and the Systematic Task of Philosophy* (2009).

www.ingramcontent.com/pod-product-compliance
Lightning Source LLC
LaVergne TN
LVHW041110090826
844660LV00056B/140

* 9 7 8 0 2 5 3 0 1 3 1 2 5 *